(AN)ARCHIVE

(An)Archive

Childhood, Memory, and the Cold War

Edited by Mnemo ZIN

https://www.openbookpublishers.com

©2024 Zsuzsa Millei, Nelli Piattoeva, and Iveta Silova (Mnemo ZIN) (eds). Copyright of individual chapters is maintained by the chapters' authors.

This work is licensed under an Attribution-NonCommercial 4.0 International (CC BY-NC 4.0). This license allows you to share, copy, distribute and transmit the text; to adapt the text for non-commercial purposes of the text providing attribution is made to the author (but not in any way that suggests that they endorse you or your use of the work). Attribution should include the following information:

Mnemo ZIN (eds), *(An)Archive: Childhood, Memory, and Cold War*. Cambridge, UK: Open Book Publishers, 2024, https://doi.org/10.11647/OBP.0383

In order to access detailed and updated information on the license, please visit https://www.openbookpublishers.com/product/0383#copyright

Further details about CC BY-NC licenses are available at https://creativecommons.org/licenses/by-nc/4.0/

Copyright and permissions for the reuse of many of the images included in this publication may differ from the above. This information is provided in the captions and in the list of illustrations.

All external links were active at the time of publication unless otherwise stated and have been archived via the Internet Archive Wayback Machine at https://archive.org/web

Updated digital material and resources associated with this volume are available at https://www.openbookpublishers.com/product/0383#resources

Every effort has been made to identify and contact copyright holders and any omission or error will be corrected if notification is made to the publisher.

ISBN Paperback: 978–1–80511–185–6
ISBN Hardback: 978–1–80511–186–3
ISBN Digital (PDF): 978–1–80511–187–0
ISBN Digital eBook (EPUB): 978–1–80511–188–7
ISBN HTML: 978–1–80511–190–0

DOI: 10.11647/OBP.0383

Cover image by Hanna Trampert, all rights reserved
Cover design: Jeevanjot Kaur Nagpa

Contents

Acknowledgments	1
Introduction. The Anarchive of Memories: Restor(y)ing Cold-War Childhoods *Mnemo ZIN*	5
1. Who Do I Remember For? Memory as Genre and Dark Pleasures of Trauma Witnessing *Petar Odak*	27
Diasporic Knowledges in Central Asia: (Re)membering in *Jeong* *Olga Mun*	48
2. 'I Wanted to See the Man with that Mark on his Forehead': A Historian, Her Childhood Experiences, and the Power of Memory *Pia Koivunen*	51
Rua Liga Dos Comunistas *José Cossa*	77
3. Passing Bye *Hanna Trampert*	79
Breakfast Across Borders *Stefanie Weiss*	91
4. The Other Side of the Curtain? Troubling Western Memories of (Post)socialism *Erica Burman*	93
Smearing the Portrait *Lucian Țion*	116

5. You Can't Go Home Again…
    Especially if You Have Never Had One 119
    Madina Tlostanova

Smuggling Jewelry 135
    Tatyana Kleyn

Sleepy Smuggles 138
    Sarah Fichtner

6. The Power of Other Worlds:
    Civilisational Frames and Child-Adult Intimacies in Socialist
    Childhoods 139
    Jennifer Patico

The Door 156
    Khanum Gevorgyan

7. Growing up in Cold-War Argentina:
    Working through the (An)archives of Childhood Memories 167
    Inés Dussel

Searching for Childhood Gummi Bears 191
    Nadine Bernhard

8. The Secrets:
    Connections Across Divides 193
    *Irena Kašparová, Beatrice Scutaru, Zsuzsa Millei,
    Josefine Raasch, and Katarzyna Gawlicz*

Open Coffin 212
    Irena Kašparová

9. Mysterious Cotton Pieces:
    Childhood Memories of Menstruation 213
    Katarzyna Gawlicz and Zsuzsa Millei

Soviet Feminism? 235
    Nadia Tsulukidze

10. Lift Up Your Arms!
    Elite Athletes and Cold-War Childhoods 237
    Susanne Gannon and Stefanie Weiss

Losing Balance *Tatyana Kleyn*	255
Adult Hospital Ward *Irena Kašparová*	257
11. Children on their Own: Cold-War Childhood Memories of Unsupervised Times *Nadine Bernhard and Kathleen Falkenberg*	259
Nokia *Nelli Piattoeva*	281
Blackberry Picking *Rahim Rahimov*	283
12. Transcending the Border: Memory, Objects, and Alternative Memorialisation in Cold-War Childhoods *Ivana Polić*	285
Snowflake *Iveta Silova*	303
New Year's Frog *Nelli Piattoeva*	305
13. Anarchive and Arts-Based Research: Upcycling Rediscovered Memories and Materials *Raisa Foster*	307
The Tailor *Thoma Sukhashvili*	326
14. Anarchive, Oral Histories, and Teaching Comparative Cold-War Childhoods across Geographies and Generations *Elena Jackson Albarrán*	329
Pink Flamingo *Iveta Silova*	349
15. Connecting Across Divides: A Case Study in Public History of the (E-)Motion Comic 'Ghost Train—Memories of Ghost Trains and Ghost Stations in Former East and West-Berlin' *Sarah Fichtner and Anja Werner*	351

Traveling Stones 370
   Oshie Nishimura-Sahi

16. Re-membering Ceremonies:
    Childhood Memories of Our Relationships with Plants 371
    *Jieyu Jiang, Esther Pretti, Keti Tsotniashvili,
    Dilraba Anayatova, Ann Nielsen, and Iveta Silova*

List of Figures and Other Illustrations 395

About the Contributors 399

Index 413

Acknowledgments

This book is a result of an extraordinary journey, which brought together academics and artists from multiple generations and geopolitical contexts to remember their childhood experiences during and after the Cold War. Their memory stories have become the threads that weave together the rich tapestry of memories throughout this book and beyond, reminding us of the shared humanity that binds us together.

First and foremost, we are deeply grateful to all of the book contributors who have shared their memory stories and personal reflections, academic insights and artworks, photographs and artefacts, tears and laughs in ways that are most insightful, intimate, and imaginative. Your memory stories, imprinted with the complexities of being a child during the Cold-War era, have breathed life into the fading memories of the past, allowing a glimpse into the nuanced realities that lie beneath the surface of official records preserved in historical archives.

This book would not be possible without the collective contributions of all the participants of the Reconnect/Recollect project who joined the memory workshops in Berlin, Helsinki, Mexico City, Riga, and online in 2019–2020, as well as all those who have contributed to the various project initiatives throughout the last five years: Tamás Ördög, Aleksandra Đorđević, Anel Kulakhmetova, Anikó Varga Nagy, Anja Werner, Anne Harju, Anne Wihstutz, Astra Zoldnere, Beatrice Scutaru, Camila da Rosa Ribeiro, Cristina Popescu, Donald Lupo, Elena Albarrán, Eleonora Teszenyi, Elisha Salivon, Emese Ivan, Emilia Henkel, Ewa Pająk-Ważna, Ewa Sidorenko, Gordana Jovanovic, Gulzhamal Sheripkanova-Macleod, Hanna Sjöberg, Hanna Trampert, Ioana Luca, Irena Kašparová, Ivana Polic, Jelena Vićentić, Jennifer Patico, Joanna Omylińska-Thurston, José Cossa, Josefine Raasch, Katarzyna Gawlicz, Kathleen Falkenberg, Keti Chachkhiani, Keti Tsotniashvili, Lasha Tsertsvadze, Lucian Țion, Magda Karjalainen, Maria Tapola-Haapala, Mariia Vitrukh, Matej Blazek,

Mihaela Enache, Nadine Bernhard, Nikolai Jeffs, Nina Miholjcic, Olga Mun, Paola Diaz, Petar Odak, Pia Koivunen, Rahim Rahimov, Raluca Țurcanașu, Sarah Fichtner, Şeyma Akin, Silvana Rapeanu, Simona Szakács-Behling, Stefanie Weiss Santos, Tanya Bogacheva, Tatyana Kleyn, Teona Goderdzishvili, Thoma Sukhashvili, Trey Donovan Drake, and Victoria Pogosian. It is your curiosity, engagement, and willingness to explore childhood memories together that animated the memory anarchive, spilling into theatre performances, visual artworks, museum exhibitions, films and animations, scientific publications, academic courses, a major satellite conference with five hubs spinning the sticky web of childhood memories further, and many other creative expressions that we could have neither predicted nor imagined at the outset!

Our research assistants helped during some of the most intensive periods of the research process. We are grateful to Ioana Țîștea (Tampere University) for helping with organising logistics for workshops and meetings in multiple locations, as well as for gathering, editing, and publishing memories online. We are grateful to Esther Pretti (Arizona State University) for keeping the book production on track through her meticulous assistance in preparing this manuscript for publication—from editing memories and chapters, to tracking missing references, to compiling and organising the table of contents, index, biographical notes, as well as attending to other important manuscript details.

This book would not have been possible without the generous financial support of the Kone Foundation, Finland that enabled us to bring to fruition this research through the Reconnect/Recollect grant, as well as generous support for the open publication of this book.

We would also like to express our gratitude to the dedicated publishing team who has worked tirelessly behind the scenes. From editors to designers, your expertise and attention to detail have transformed our words and vision into a beautifully crafted book. Your commitment to open access and excellence, and your passion for bringing meaningful stories to life, have made this book project a reality.

Huge thanks to our families—including our human and more-than-human companions across generations—who supported us along the way. As we shared our childhood memories together, we understood each other a little bit better. Thanks for remembering with us.

And to Mnenomsyne, the daughter of Gaia and the mother of Nine Muses, thanks for inspiring us to explore the power of memory across time and space. It is through these shared experiences of remembering that we have emerged as Mnemo ZIN, not only to acknowledge our collective endeavour, but also as a way to shapeshift our fractured academic selves into more interdependent and creative expressions.

Lastly, we extend our gratitude to the readers of this book. We hope that delving into the pages of this book will not only spark curiosity but also nurture understanding, empathy, and dialogue across generational, cultural, and geopolitical divides.

Thank you from the bottom of our hearts.

Introduction
The Anarchive of Memories:
Restor(y)ing Cold-War Childhoods

Mnemo ZIN

How can we curate a collection of childhood memories to highlight multiple and multilayered stories beyond the fixed thematic organisation of a traditional archive? How can we archive memories in ways that offer audiences an opportunity to make their own interpretations and create new connections across memory stories, while inviting them to share memories in return? How can an archive be reflexive of its own creation, growth, and transformation, continuously arranging and rearranging, adding and affirming, disrupting and challenging the memories kept there? These questions guided the creation of this book, challenging not only ways of archiving 'data' but also the idea of memory as witness to history and complicating interpretations of childhoods lived during the Cold War. This chapter introduces readers to the anarchive, an evolving assemblage of childhood memories, artworks, scholarly articles, pedagogical frameworks, and methodological interventions that came out of our project 'Reconnect/Recollect: Crossing the Divides through Memories of Cold War Childhoods'. It explains connections between memory work, collective biography, childhood studies, and the Cold War, and it offers some suggestions for engaging with the anarchive, including multiple thematic, artistic, and affective threads that we have found interesting, insightful, or surprising. This chapter is an invitation to enter and explore the memory anarchive.

Even in a world where data of all kinds are constantly collected, sorted, exhibited, and archived, there is still a lot of 'missing' data. Mimi Onuoha's multimedia installation 'The Library of Missing Datasets' (2016) draws attention to these blank spots in the otherwise data-saturated world. By calling these datasets 'missing', she points to the ways in which the colonial matrix of domination is reflected in and relies on particular approaches to data collection and knowledge production. She explains on the project's website, 'That which we ignore reveals more than what we give our attention to. [...] Spots that we've left blank reveal our hidden social biases and indifferences'. Indeed, when libraries and archives draw upon predefined categories to institute a particular imaginary of society, cultural memory, and global (dis)connections, they leave parts of the population—women, children, or minoritised 'others'—unable to shape the archived content even when this content relates to and impacts their immediate lives and possible futures (Mbembe 2002; Vierke 2015).

Our book assembles some of these 'missing' data by restor(y)ing childhood memories from both sides of the Cold-War divide and sharing these memories (and their interpretations) in academic and artistic forms. It gathers those memory stories that were either erased or forgotten, delegitimised or essentialised, or, at best, reinterpreted nostalgically within continuing and rearticulated Cold-War power hierarchies, as well as public and scientific frameworks. It talks about silences that hid family secrets before 1989 as well as struggles and opportunities that accompanied geopolitical changes after 1989—from the economic turmoil and disintegration of the societal fabric to the new freedoms and expectations that unlocked promising possibilities for some people and hollowed out possible futures for many others. Our book brings into focus the colonial matrix of power that continues to shape people's lives after the Cold War by replacing the socialist version of modernity with the western capitalist one, that is, by merely reproducing the historical and existing divides. It offers a glimpse into what it felt like to wake up to the erased past and face 'a new reality of multiple dependencies and increased mental, if not economic and social, un-freedom, invisibility to the wider world and the continued forms of silencing and trivialisation by the dominant discourses of neoliberal modernity' (Tlostanova 2017, p. 2).

This book approaches the Cold War as a period in time characterised by intensified political and military conflicts between two alleged superpowers—the US and the USSR—which resonated in children's lives directly or indirectly across the globe. Often it unequivocally shaped their political points of views or offered civilisational frameworks, shaped adult-child relations, disciplined embodiment, mounted secrets and concerns for children, and materialised in their everyday life circumstances. At other times, the omnipresence of the Cold War faded, such as in children's free time or in their engagements with/in nature. Although the legacies of the Cold War continue to shape life trajectories in post-socialist contexts, many memories associated with this historical period either remain muted or become highly politicised. When memories of everyday childhood experiences are exhibited in museums—often alongside toys and other paraphernalia—they may attract tourists, but they can further alienate or add to the anxiety, disillusionment, and frustration felt by many people who struggle to find answers to their pasts and uncertain futures in spaces that continue to live with the enduring legacies of Cold-War divides. Art resurfaces to question and (re)form and (re)frame identities and relations in intergenerational spaces. Among many examples are Dasha Fursey's paintings of pioneer girls that challenge assumptions about the devotion of youth-organisation's members to communist heroes and ideologies (see Yurchak 2008).

By (re)connecting people with their pasts, presents, and futures through collective memory work, our book is an attempt to (re)collect and restor(y)e childhood memories shared by those who have been historically denied subjecthood—all those so-called 'others' who live/d in socialist and post-socialist societies. It foregrounds varied and contextually diverse children's experiences of everyday life which by nature perhaps are less structured by state institutions and ideological discourses, and have many similarities with children's experiences in the capitalist countries. Collectively, these memories multiply histories and complicate interpretations of childhoods lived during the Cold War.

We explore children's lives 'through memories' (Millei, Silova, and Gannon 2019) in which children exhibit agency, making sense of and purposefully acting in the world, following their own interests, and skillfully reading and negotiating intergenerational power relations. We understand memories as stories that tell about the past in the situated present with a view of the future and in which the past events are reconstructed from memory fragments with the help of imagination (Keightley and Pickering

2012). Therefore, we do not claim that they are true representations of historical events; rather, they are created in situations in which the memory sharers are being affected by prompts or events occurring in their lifetime.

Some of the memory stories assembled in this book come from memory workshops, while others spring from memory books, diaries, old photographs, and dusty boxes containing family archives. Unlike methodically organised records kept in traditional archives, the memory stories assembled here take you on a journey that is at once infinite and intricate, constantly shifting, branching, entangling, and perhaps even disorienting—a spider web of sorts. These memories spin 'data threads' that resist ordering, weave stories that question and complicate official historical narratives, and carry emotions that exceed any archival categories. Becoming a spider, its prey, or a part of the thread, you are about to join this journey, too.

Welcome to the Anarchive

An anarchive may be best defined by what it is not. First and foremost, it is not a physical and static archive in the traditional sense; it does not function to control and shape knowledge through the selective storage and classification of material, nor to regulate access to data. Neither is it 'a site of knowledge retrieval' that relies on data 'mining' without paying attention to their particular placement and form (Stoler 2002, p. 90). Refusing to separate (or extract) the archived information and documents from their authors and contexts—a process described by Achille Mbembe (2002) as 'dispossession' and 'despoilment'—the anarchive binds together seemingly disparate fragments of 'missing' data (for example, texts, material objects, bodies, memories, movements, performances, emotions, and lived histories), engendering reciprocity, building relations, and opening new possibilities of seeing the world. In our book, the anarchive restores but also restories the conventional narratives and official histories of the Cold War, a bygone era that is mostly memorialised in political terms and interpreted with construed binaries of East-West.

Second, the anarchive actively defies the control of the archivists (or historians) who use their authority to control, regulate, and govern the archived knowledge and materials. Archives exercise 'hermeneutic privilege' (Derrida and Prenowitz 1995) by classifying their material and thus already ascribing the stored data with a pre-set meaning. By selecting some materials (over others) for preservation, they define how and whose biographies will be accessible (Jakobsen and Beer 2021). While many archives today are open for citizens to retrieve information or to add their collected materials, the anarchive intentionally emerges from community-based, collective, and collaborative processes, 'opening up dynamic possibilities that push archival impulses in new and urgent directions' (Springgay, Truman, and McLean 2020, p. 205). In our work, the anarchive sprung from collective-biography workshops, which brought together academics and artists from both state post/socialist and capitalist societies to remember their childhood and schooling experiences during and after the Cold War. The aim was not necessarily to give witness to an era but, rather, to explore together the textures of everyday life through sharing childhood memories. It was about paying attention to the ways in which historical events are narrated, interpreted, and restor(i)ed through sharing and interrogating of one's own experiences. Collective biography collapses the binary that separates the knowledge-generating expert from the memory-recalling layperson and, ultimately, from the archivist recording and cataloguing it. Within the intersubjective sharing spaces, the intensity and affective flows of memories make them collective as listeners feel themselves within the tellers' stories (Davies and Gannon 2012; Foster et al. 2023) and sense the emerging connections across times and places.

Third, anarchives are not static and can never be complete as their organising idea and logic escape the urge for control and ordering. Thus, we work with 'an an-archic energy' that eclipses regulation and engages with and against the archive's own failures and utopian urges for mastery (Ring 2014, p. 388, with reference to Foucault and Derrida). This energy keeps the stories and the anarchive on the move—merging, mixing, connecting, but also juxtaposing personal experiences, public memory, political rhetoric, places, times, themes, and artifacts. In addition to memories, the anarchive spills into theater performances, artworks, museum exhibitions, films, academic courses, and more.[1] These are all anarchival forms that contain and prompt collaborative interactions that then go on to produce new anarchival forms and encounters. In this

---

[1] As we discuss further in this chapter, our project led to multiple types of scholarly and artistic works; it also inspired new memories. All of these compose the anarchive. See https://coldwarchildhoods.org

sense, the anarchive is a practice that 'catches experience in the making' and that 'catches us in our own becoming' (Manning 2020, p. 84). What may have once appeared as discrete, isolated, and immobile pieces of archival data come to vibrant life in the anarchive, 'making it other than it is just now, and already more than what it was just then' (Massumi 2015, p. 94) as collective memories carry all involved beyond their own selves.

Finally, the anarchive does not act to preserve the past, a function generally performed by traditional archives. Rather, it acts to re-configure the present and re-story possible futures. By refusing the linear flow of time, the anarchive works 'to germinate seeds for new processes', thus carrying the potential to unmoor the shape of the events and the contours of future possibilities as they reveal themselves today (Manning 2020, p. 94). In our work, we too endeavoured to move beyond storing undocumented experiences and childhood memories that problematise the representation of the past. Our purpose became to reimagine the future by actively 'undoing and unlearning' dominant categories and cartographies by restor(y)ing childhoods (Springgay et al. 2020; see also Tlostanova and Mignolo 2012). In this process, we were inspired by Foucault's (2002) idea that the 'archive is not something which belongs to the past but something which actively shapes us' in the present and future (cited in Agostinho, Dirckinck-Holmfeld, Grova Søilen 2019, p. 5). Building on the notion of anarchiving as a 'feed-forward mechanism' in a continuously changing creative process (Massumi 2016, cited in Springgay et al. 2020, p. 897), we were curious to explore what our anarchive could do in the present-future through disrupting narratives, or how it could depart from established archival techniques and procedures in restor(y)ing pasts, presents, and futures.

Thinking with decolonial, feminist, and post-structural theories of the anarchive, we asked ourselves: What datasets are missing from research and artistic work on everyday childhoods lived during the Cold War? What exclusions have a bearing on its aftermath? How do missing datasets—such as untold memories of personal experiences (forgotten or repressed), hidden objects, or dusty photo albums—disqualify, marginalise, and erase knowledge and ways of knowing and being otherwise? What remains unknown and unimaginable as a result? Moreover, as we reflect on our knowledge production, how can we practice a continuous critique of our own knowledge creation with the anarchive in ways that remain inclusive, while generating affective relations, new connections, and meaningful dialogues?

***

The memory stories which compose this growing anarchive originate from the 'Reconnect/Recollect' research project, which brought together more than seventy scholars and artists from thirty-six countries (across six continents) to share their childhood experiences during the Cold War. We gathered in places marked by old borders and newly erected walls: in Berlin (a city divided into East/West during the Cold War), Riga and Helsinki (two cities serving as Baltic Sea ports and marking the borders of Europe), and Mexico City (in close proximity to the most recently built wall at the Mexico–U.S. border), with additional workshops being held online for those unable to travel. We approached memory work via collective biography, foregrounding the shared generation and analysis of memories through processes of telling, acting, sensing, listening, reflecting, writing, rewriting, sharing, and collectively exploring and interrogating our memory stories (see, for example, Haug et al. 1987; Davies and Gannon 2006; Gonick and Gannon 2014; Hawkins et al. 2016; Silova, Piattoeva, and Millei 2018). From this perspective, childhood memories extend beyond the individual, connecting private and public remembering and collective interpretations in multifaceted and reciprocal ways (Millei, Silova, and Gannon 2022). Each telling of a memory story calls forth more stories—you hear one, you tell one—mobilising resonances and highlighting nuances of difference and detail between stories.

All of the memory stories produced during our collective-biography workshops and collected through exhibitions or our website make up a diverse, multivocal, and uneven collection. This digital, online, and open-access archive of over 250 childhood memories in 13 languages (https://coldwarchildhoods.org/memories/) invites further explorations of lived childhoods as we continue to remember and share memories. Personal memories are a key element in understanding the 'forces that sustain continuities in the social world' and humans' relations with the world (Fox and Alldred 2019, p. 31). Memories are, thus, 'territorializing forces moving bodies and initiating repetition' (ibid., p. 24); they uphold, shape, and reconfigure social processes and relations, recreating pasts, presents, and futures. As the scope and scale of the collection expands, so does the ever-growing internal web of inter-references, producing new meanings and connections across memories. In this sense, the digital collection of childhood memories is only 'a passing point' (3ecologies 2023), a springboard for the anarchive to expand into artworks, films, fictional stories, and more:

> [Such expansions are] activated in the relays: between media, between verbal and material expressions, between digital and off-line archivings, and most of all between all of the various archival forms it may take and the live, collaborative interactions that reactivate the anarchival traces, and in turn create new ones [...] organising and orienting live, collaborative *encounters*. (Manning 2020, p. 93, italics in the original)

As one of its readers, you become a part of the collaborative encounters, intentions, and creative processes that brought this book into being. No matter where or how you begin to engage with the stories presented in these pages, you may ponder these questions: What do childhood memories tell us about the Cold War and its aftermath? How can we archive or anarchive childhood? What bodies of knowledge, emotions, vibrancies are kept in our personal anarchives of memories? What do we archive in our own bodies? How can we explore the affective flows within events and experiences where collective memories may be invoked or mobilised alongside personal memories? How can memories extend history into the future? And what do memories of the Cold War tell us about the Anthropocene?

In short, there is no one way to read this book. You may start by picking an entry, a memory story, or an artwork, as you would open a traditional library catalogue, and pick out cards with the book titles that may not link thematically but follow an alphabetical order and connect with your own memories or interests (Figures I.1, I.2, I.3). You might explore the book from an academic perspective or dive into the pages where memory meets imagination in ways that you may find surprising and refreshing. Your own memories, imagination, and insights might start to roam, creating new connections. The book might move you to write your own memories and add them to the anarchive, filing away new entries for the next reader. Or, you may want to simply follow your intuition, only opening some chapters as drawers of the library catalogue, and leaving others shut. Below, we would like to introduce some thematic threads that emerged as we ourselves engaged with ideas across the anarchive. You can follow these sticky threads of childhood memories—or spin your spidery own—as we begin to (re)story childhood memories.

Fig. I.1 Sára Gink, *BETŰVÁSÁR—ISBN 963 18 1254 5*. Mixed media, 160×190 cm. Photo by Zsuzsa Millei of installation at the 'Whale of a Bad Time' exhibition, Budapest 2020.

Fig. I.2 Sára Gink, *BETŰVÁSÁR—ISBN 963 18 1254 5*. Mixed media, 160×190 cm. Photo by Zsuzsa Millei of installation at the 'Whale of a Bad Time' exhibition, Budapest 2020.

Fig. I.3 Sára Gink, *BETŰVÁSÁR—ISBN 963 18 1254 5*. Mixed media, 160×190 cm. Photo by Zsuzsa Millei of installation at the 'Whale of a Bad Time' exhibition, Budapest 2020.

An/archives as Bodies, Bodies as An/archives

While exploring the potential of the anarchive, our interest has extended beyond memory stories, artifacts, and objects to also include the idea of the body, thus interrogating the relationship between 'bodies' of archives and 'archival bodies' (Battaglia, Clarke, and Siegenthaler 2020, p. 9). On one hand, our anarchive of childhood memories is clearly composed of different bodies (or collective bodies), including bodies of knowledge, documents, photographs, objects, and memory stories—all of which seem to shift in contents and contexts as each reader browses through and engages with them. These bodies of anarchive offer new spaces and forms of collective work, bringing into conversation seemingly unrelated memory stories and objects. For example, a memory of travelling on the train in East Berlin unexpectedly triggers a memory of hearing an underground train pass by towards the other side of the Berlin Wall (see Chapter 15 by Sarah Fichter and Anja Werner), while stirring a broader conversation among listeners and readers about their experiences of border-crossing during the Cold War. Suddenly, we see traces of the train tracks criss-crossing the canvas in Hanna Trampert's paintings (Chapter 3) inspired by these memory stories. And in this process of anarchiving, the collective bodies of knowledge, experience, and art trouble the existing divides, while highlighting connections.

On the other hand, bodies also act as archives of knowledge, sensations, and feelings of the world. As Battaglia et al. (2020) note, 'archives are not only bodies of documents and knowledge, but also something fundamental to the body; the body *is* an archive, bodies are *in* the archive, and researchers intervene in either the material bodies of objects, files, or images that make up the archive' (p. 9, italics in the original). In memory workshops we did not only brainstorm but also body-stormed our personal memory archives, asking the participants to remember from the body: 'how did it feel, how did it look, what were the embodied details of this remembered event?' (Davies and Gannon 2006, p. 10). The writing of memories, too, focuses on the moments in which the body resists the effects of narrative structures that might impose linearity, causality, or closure. Writing, therefore, must be initiated 'from the body, not telling the story how it should be told, but as it is lodged in the body' (ibid.).

From this perspective, the traditional ontology of the archive is seriously challenged. Memories are, as Hart (2015) suggests, archived 'into/onto' the body and also move bodies as stories take shape and build new connections. The body is, thus, both a container of archival material and a powerful medium. In this process, the multisensorial, relational, affective, and embodied knowledge becomes animated and the body begins to 'speak'. In the words of the author and psychoanalyst Clarissa Pinkola Estés (1989),

> [the body] speaks through its colour and its temperature, the flush of recognition, the glow of love, the ash of pain, the heat of arousal, the coldness of non-conviction. It speaks through its constant tiny dance, sometimes swaying, sometimes a jitter, sometimes trembling. It speaks through the leaping of the heart, the falling of the spirit, the pit at the centre, and rising hope. The body remembers, the bones remember, the joints remember, even the little finger remembers. Memory is lodged in pictures and feelings in the cells themselves. Like a sponge filled with water, anywhere the flesh is pressed, wrung, even touched lightly, a memory may flow out in a stream. (p. 198)

In our book, 'bodies' of archives and 'archival bodies' are constantly entangled with each other. Bodies appear as historical symbols of the ideal future and instruments of soft power. Bodies are put on display in sports, parades, and performances (see Chapter 10, by Stefanie Weiss and Susanne Gannon, on children in elite sports or Chapter 2, by Pia Koivunen, on children's participation in parades during Gorbachev's visit to Finland). We come across carnal bodies—flesh, blood, strength, dexterity, agility—which are trained, capacitated, and skilled, while at the same time storing the memory and emotionality of these exercises. Bodies are also inseparable from their material and sociopolitical contexts as they are subjected to discourses, practices, affect, and ideals (see Chapter 9 by Katarzyna Gawlicz and Zsuzsa Millei on menstruation). There are dead bodies—both human and more-than-human—which are archived in children's memories, revealing how, even in their inert form, bodies can move children and continue to move them as the now-adults narrate their stories (see Chapter 8 about secrets by Irena Kašparová, Beatrice Scutaru, Zsuzsa Millei, Josefine Raasch, and Katarzyna Gawlicz or Chapter 13 by Raisa Foster on upcycling artworks). Bodies of all kinds are figuring in memories, photographs, and paintings, extending the archive into, onto, and across bodies, expanding the archive in embodied ways (see the artworks by Raisa Foster and Hanna Trampert). As you dive deeper into this anarchive of childhood memories, listen to how your own body archive is moved by the stories and what might arise in response.

Memory as Affect

Memories are created and take shape through affective pulls, relations between and across beings, times, spaces, places, feelings, historical events, and more (Reading 2022). Approaching memories as affect that has the capacity to move things, create realities, cut across many divides—the personal/collective, real/imagined, human/more-than-human, true/subjective—highlights 'how memories materially affect the world (just as they are themselves affected by events)' (Fox and Aldred 2019, p. 21). For example, social expectations shape the process of remembering and, in turn, the event remembered affects the identity and subjectivity of the memory-story teller. As Petar Odak explains in Chapter 1, in a memory workshop exploring the Cold War, the expectation is often to share memories with a particular political charge and to avoid describing mundane events that might be perceived as unsuitable or uninteresting. The context, thus, affects the choice; this, in turn, negates subjectivities and, in this case, the importance of one's being a 'regular' child. The choice of remembering and forgetting thus exposes the micropolitics of memory work.

Memory as affect also moves artwork. While painting inspired by her memory, Hanna Trampert remembers how something begins to crystallise and come to light, something that she feels must be dealt with. Trampert explains, 'actually, my art is about becoming conscious and, of course, about an aesthetic experience' (personal communication, 2022). She recalls how her memories of childhood lay dormant until our memory-workshop invitation made her work with them, inspiring a whole new series of paintings in which she explores the metaphysics of memory. Others in the workshops also recounted how childhood memories moved and energised them to explore their childhoods that also brought into their adult life's forgotten subjectivities. Memories and art as affect also move participants and authors closer. The various memories and artwork introduced and discussed in this book are more 'concerned with advancing collaborative ways of knowing and representation than with individual expertise and recognition, with advancing a more serious invitation for those with visceral experience of oppression to collaborate with the learned and cultured in the creation of knowledge that heals' (Moreira and Diversi 2014, p. 298).

The 'ethical and affective spaces of inquiry' (Gannon et al. 2019, p. 50) open real alternatives to the contemporary academy and its dominant culture of individualism, extractivism, competitiveness, and narrow specialisation. This process of reclaiming science, not as an academic institution but rather as a collective space of concerns for the world, entails the need to recuperate and heal ourselves as scientists as well. As Isabelle Stengers (2018) explains, we are 'sick' from being locked in a form of knowledge production that is bound by capitalist production and competition. This book is an attempt to recuperate from this sickness and to

> becom[e] capable of learning again, becoming acquainted with things again, reweaving the bounds of interdependency. It means thinking and imagining, and in the process creating relationships with others that are not those of capture. It means, therefore, creating among us and with others the kind of relation that works for sick people, people who need each other in order to learn—with others, from others, thanks to others—what a life worth living demands, and the knowledges that are worth being cultivated. (Stengers 2018, pp. 81–82)

For us, the affective (and emotional) force of this 'collaborative praxis' (Tlostanova et al. 2016, p. 2) and friendships are at the very core of surviving and meaningfully co-existing in academia—and the world more broadly—today.

Memory-work as Worldmaking

The Cold War provided collective-biography-workshop participants and some of the chapter authors a frame in which to raise questions about who counts as a 'real' contemporary with an 'authentic' first-hand experience of the historical period. Some of those who were brought up in non-socialist societies felt they could not personally add to the explorations. For example, see reflections shared by Pia Koivunen (Chapter 2), Elena Albarrán (Chapter 14), Inés Dussel (Chapter 7), and Erica Burman (Chapter 4). Others looked to such listeners for the criteria to decide which memories to recall, seeking reasons to judge a memory as 'worth' sharing in a group and to judge other memories as too generic or mundane to share. Thus, the Cold War operated as an active force in participants' decisions about how to evaluate their own experience and participation or how to invoke the desired response from their listeners (see Chapter 1). By highlighting the objects and materialities, such as colours, smells, textures of everyday life, stereotypically represented as symbols of the Cold War, some childhood memories inadvertently recreated divides or gave witness to the conjured myths about the 'Other' (see Jennifer Patico's chapter, Chapter 6, on mythical objects and Ivana Polić's argument in Chapter 12 about the connections made by objects). Rare time-spaces encountered in the memories of Cold-War childhoods, such as the Berlin ghost metro stations (Chapter 15 by Sarah Fichtner and Anja Werner), or occupied by children during unsupervised times (Chapter 11 by Nadine Bernhard and Kathleen Falkenberg) offer glimpses into how infrastructures and gendered work were interpreted in memories to create the textures of real or imagined Cold-War divides and existence.

How memories are judged as research data or the ways in which memory work is considered as methodological practice also hinge on onto-epistemological and disciplinary assumptions. These decisions in turn make up scientific worlds and construct the routes that researchers must take to arrive at a fruitful and rigorous memory work (see Pia Koivunen's journey highlighting her concerns about the use of memory in historical research in Chapter 2). Working with memories thus does not only connect to the past worlds but also constructs the world present in the memory works and disciplinary fields of analysis.

Secret/ive Memories of Children's Worlds

Reading across the chapters, we can see how ideology and divisions motivated children to ignore official lines and to disguise their resistance to norms and prohibitions. The politics of the public space folded onto the home space, creating secrets. The intricate practices of childhood secret-keeping mirrored the binary of official- and private-life secrets in the public culture of Czechoslovakia portrayed in the ethnodrama by Irena Kašparová and her colleagues (Chapter 8). Some were open secrets—ones transparent and known to everyone, but their status as secrets was, nevertheless, preserved. Those could not be uttered out loud, only whispered. The ethnodrama shows how children eagerly learned to keep secrets but sometimes slipped, even intentionally, imitating the norms that regulated the open existence of secrets. In another example of secretive practices explored by Katarzyna Gawlicz and Zsuzsa Millei in Chapter 9, young girls inherited the culture of menstruation as a taboo despite the official gender equality proclaimed by socialist parties and the inclusion of sexual education in schools. Girls hid the onset of the menarche and handled the blood in secret—one their mothers often knew but pretended not to know. Susanne Gannon and Stefanie Weiss show in Chapter 10 how the soft power of the Cold War manifested in elite-athlete training. The practice hid the unwanted individual sacrifices imposed on children in the name of building socialist nations, demonstrating the superiority of one political ideology over the other. Children also kept secret their pain, boredom, resistance, or the suffering caused by their parents, perhaps trying to avoid problems or seeing the expression of their feelings as futile. In unsupervised times, away from observation by school or family, children generated shared experiences of freedom and contentment; they also experienced loneliness that was not always known by parents (see Chapter 11 by Nadine Bernhard and Kathleen Falkenberg).

Although the keeping or revealing of secrets was mostly harmless, it sometimes carried life-or-death consequences for children or their families. Inés Dussel, a child of a leftist-activist couple growing up in Argentina during the military dictatorship of the 1970s and 1980s, tells in Chapter 7 how she was entrusted with keeping the family safe by keeping its secrets while moving discreetly between temporary homes and school. Keeping secret the family's location and political views punctuated the child's everyday life. The adult narrator remembers this childhood experience as the leading of a double life, knowing exactly which details to share and which to keep secret. Such double consciousness characterised everyday socialist lives.

All in all, secrets reveal important aspects of children's everyday life connecting these experiences across times and spaces. They also trouble the taken-for-granted notions of childhood in societies, such as the innocence or ignorance of children, their lack of competencies compared to adults, childhood's apolitical nature or the narrow view of children as victims of political agendas. At the same time, we can see how these notions and tropes help narrators to make sense of and (re)story their memories. Secrets help to create alternative spaces, however transient and hidden those might be. These spaces might even emerge in parallel to the creation of alternative worlds by their parents who experienced conflicts due to being estranged from and by the socialist regime (see Madina Tlostanova's fictional memory story in this book; Burman and Millei 2021).

Memory as Pedagogy

Children's learning in the socialist societies has been habitually portrayed as top-down and dominated by formal education or public pedagogies relaying official state ideologies. However, a different picture emerges when we examine the learning experiences portrayed in the memories presented in this book. In these, children keenly observe and partake in their everyday environments, in or beyond formal schooling. They collect, engage with, and puzzle together over many things—adults' minor gestures, gossip, smells, colours, textures, snippets of news in the media, and the presence or absence of consumer products—to create their own understandings of life. Memories particularly attune us to learning that is fluid and emerges relationally with everyday objects or affective atmospheres, and they foreground a type of learning beyond the notion of conscious sense-making. For instance, girls learned about the controversial status of women in their respective societies through their experience of a scarcity of feminine-hygiene products. Moreover, by handling self-made menstruation pads or by observing and connecting other objects and conditions—from stains on clothes to female pets in heat—they developed an understanding about menstruation amidst the silence of adults. They invented their own intimate and intricate practices to regain agency over controversial feelings and bleeding body (see Katarzyna Gawlicz's and Zsuzsa Millei's exploration of menstruation in Chapter 9).

Sometimes objects instigate children to misbehave and learn about 'the other' beyond the official narratives, such as in the case of a child pressing the forbidden buttons on a TV-set in East Germany (see Chapter 12 by Ivana Polić). Learning with objects is induced by and induces different affective states, including pleasure, curiosity, and desire that are less frequently referenced in research or media depicting everyday life and consumption in socialist societies. The affective and sensory experiences of the 'other side'—mediated by clothing catalogues, photographs, TV-programmes, or make-up—serve as a means of getting to know the West and the world at large but also of engaging in relationships at home. Experiencing the West often entwines with children's own maturation, developing perceptions of themselves, and their intergenerational relations (see also Chapter 6 by Jennifer Patico). Curiosity about 'the other' flourished on the Western side of the Iron Curtain, too, with children questioning the official narratives and developing their own interpretations of 'the other' through literature or music (see more in Ivana Polić's Chapter 12).

The anarchived memories operate as pedagogical devices in academic teaching and learning with the more-than-human world that both socialist and capitalist modernities perceive as a passive object of learning for perpetual extraction and progress. Elena Jackson Albarrán, in Chapter 14, describes how the course in comparative Cold-War childhoods she created for the post-socialist generation born in the 2000s intimates the diversity of Cold-War experiences and helps to understand the role of individuals as historical actors navigating historical forces then and now. Memories shared by family members and recorded and analysed by students make a distant history matter in the present in ways that a detached description of historical events and actors cannot achieve: the nuances and inconsistencies of history, the subjectivity of human actors, and the permeabilities of the Iron Curtain come into sharp focus (see also Chapter 2 by Pia Koivunen). By engaging students with the stories and the popular culture of the Cold-War period, learning with memories is a pedagogical device that reaches beyond historical knowledge to cultivate intergenerational empathy. Memories help us to re-member and re-learn from and with our plant-kin, where both memories and plants act as teachers in the process (Jiang et al. 2023). Here, the learning is bodily, emotional, and spiritual, building on 'the arts of noticing' (Tsing 2015, p. 37) the multispecies common worlds we inhabit in our research and practice. Recollecting and learning through 'eco-memories' cultivates curiosity, reciprocity, care, and gratitude to plants and other more-than-human companions. In this re-learning, intergenerational and interspecies relationships and mutual vulnerability nourish each other to reinstate the forgotten ways of being in and with the animate world (see Chapter 16 by Jieyu Jiang, Esther Pretti, Keti Tsotniashvili, Dilraba Anayatova, Ann Nielsen, and Iveta Silova).

Restor(y)ing Memory for the Anthropocene

Reading through the chapters in this book, parallels emerge between the two major events in the late history of modernity: the breakdown of the state-socialist systems in Southeast/Central Europe and the former Soviet Union and the 'patchy' unravelling of the Anthropocene on a global scale (Tsing 2015). Memories extend history into the present and trouble the feeling of discontinuity between generations and at the same time highlight the multiplicity of futures. State-socialist systems seemed immutable, steadily progressing towards the infinite and bright future of communism (Yurchak 1997). Disestablishment of the so-called Second World was abrupt but unsurprising—sort of expected—by the majority of its people. With its disappearance, the future it had created became unrealised and was discarded. 'Unrealised' or 'unrealisable' futures destabilise the straightforward assumption that 'pasts and presents have futures, that things just keep on going, that time and history keep unfolding' (Wenzel 2017, p. 502). Today, youth and children question the very existence of a future for them. This unrealisable future's past is what we are living now; it reminds us that we are, in fact, authoring the im/possibility of its very futures now.

Cold-War childhood memories richly animate the triumph of modern technological progress in stories of the infinite growth and the development promised by fossil fuels (see Foster et al. 2022; ZIN and da Rosa Ribeiro 2023). Memories also reveal other ways of relating to the world and other ways of engaging in collective remembering with the inclusion of more-than-human companions. As we listen to the memory stories about the children touching a dead bird, about children listening to the orchestra of bees, or about children engaging with farm animals and plants (see Chapter 16 by Jiang et al.), we recall the moments of our multisensory awareness, recognising our bodily belonging in a more-than-human world. In turn, we might start to remember the relations with Earth and cosmos, while re-animating our capacity for wonder and empathy. Anarchiving incites practices of restor(y)ing, challenging fascination with originality understood narrowly as newness. By doing so, the anarchive confronts the modern desire for progress as a never-ending production of new—the dominant logic that has also extended to artistic work (see Chapter 13 by Raisa Foster). There is an inspiring parallel between upcycling existing materials, ideas, and artworks to create sustainable practices and continuity in the arts and museum practices, and the restor(y)ing of memories for envisioning a future that connects and sustains all planetary companions. Starting with memories that recount our world-making relations, we can story futures that connect generations past, present, and future and that make kin and place without imposing human domination or nature/culture divisions. This is a future that sustains care, reciprocity, and humility for life.

These are just a few threads that we have begun to weave together while reading the book, and we invite you to spin your own threads as you dive deep into the anarchive of memories.

References

3ecologies (2023). 'Anarchive—Concise Definition', https://3ecologies.org/immediations/anarchiving/anarchive-concise-definition/

Agostinho, D.; Dirckinck-Holmfeld, K.; and Grova Søilen, K. L. (2019). 'Archives that Matter: Infrastructures for Sharing Unshared Histories. An Introduction'.

Nordisk Tidsskrift for Informationsvidenskab Og Kulturformidling, 8(2), 1–18, https://doi.org/10.7146/ntik.v7i2.118472

Burman, E. and Millei, Z. (2022). 'Post-socialist Geopolitical Uncertainties: Researching Memories of Childhood with "Child as Method"'. *Children and Society*, 36(5), 993–1009, https://doi.org/10.1111/chso.12551

Craps, S.; Crownshaw, R.; Wenzel, J.; Kennedy, R.; Colebrook, C.; and Nardizzi, V. (2018). 'Memory Studies and the Anthropocene: A Roundtable'. *Memory Studies*, 11(4), 498–515, https://doi.org/10.1177/1750698017731068

Davies, B. and Gannon, S. (eds). (2006). *Doing Collective Biography*. Berkshire, UK: Open University Press

Davies, B. and Gannon, S. (2012). 'Collective Biography and the Entangled Enlivening of Being'. *International Review of Qualitative Research*, 5(4), 357–76, https://doi.org/10.1525/irqr.2012.5.4.357

Derrida, J. and Prenowitz, E. (1995). 'Archive Fever: A Freudian Impression'. *Diacritics*, 25(2), 9–63, https://doi.org/10.2307/465144

Foster, R.; Zin, M.; Keto, S.; and Pulkki, J. (2022). 'Recognising Ecosocialization in Childhood Memories'. *Educational Studies*, 58(4), 560–74, https://doi.org/10.1080/00131946.2022.2051031

Foster, R.; Törmä, T.; Hokkanen, L.; and Zin, M. (2022). '63 Windows: Generating Relationality through Poetic and Metaphorical Engagement'. *Research in Arts and Education*, 2), 56–67, https://doi.org/10.54916/rae.122974

Fox, N. J. and Alldred, P. (2019). 'The Materiality of Memory: Affects, Remembering and Food Decisions'. *Cultural Sociology*, 13(1), 20–36, https://doi.org/10.1177/1749975518764864

Gonick, M. and Gannon, S. (2014). *Becoming Girl: Collective Biography and the Production of Girlhood*. Toronto: The Women's Press

Hart, T. (2015). 'How do You Archive the Sky?'. *Archive Journal*, https://www.archivejournal.net/essays/how-do-you-archive-the-sky/

Haug, F. et al. (1987). *Female Sexualization. The Collective Work of Memory*. London: Verso

Hawkins, R.; Falconer Al-Hindi, K.; Moss, P.; and Kern, L. (2016) 'Practicing Collective Biography'. *Geography Compass*, 10(4), 165–78, https://doi.org/10.1111/gec3.12262

Jacobsen B. N. and Beer D. (2021). *Social Media and the Automatic Production of Memory: Classification, Ranking and the Sorting of the Past*. Bristol University Press

Keightley, E. and Pickering, M. (2012). *The Mnemonic Imagination: Remembering as Creative Practice*. New York: Palgrave Macmillan

Massumi, B. (2016). 'Working Principles', in *The Go-To How To Book of Anarchiving*, ed. by A. Murphie. SenseLab, pp. 6–8), http://senselab.ca/wp2/wp-content/

uploads/2016/12/Go-To-How-To-Book-of-Anarchiving-landscape-Digital-Distribution.pdf

Mbembe, A. (2002). 'The Power of the Archive and its Limits', in *Refiguring the Archive*, ed. by C. Hamilton and others. Dordrecht: Springer, https://doi.org/10.1007/978-94-010-0570-8_2

Millei, Z.; Silova, I.; and Gannon, S. (2019). 'Thinking Through and Coming to Know with Memories of Childhood in (Post)Socialist Spaces'. *Children's Geographies*, 20(3), 324–37, https://doi.org/10.1080/14733285.2019.1648759

Moreira, C. and Diversi, M. (2014). 'The Coin will Continue to Fly: Dismantling the Myth of the Lone Expert'. *Cultural Studies ↔ Critical Methodologies*, 14 (4), 298–302, https://doi.org/10.1177/1532708614530300

Onuoha, M. (2016). *The Library of Missing Datasets*. mixed-media installation, https://mimionuoha.com/the-library-of-missing-datasets

Reading, A. (2022). 'Rewilding Memory'. *Memory, Mind and Media*, 1, E9, https://doi.org/10.1017/mem.2022.2

Ring, A. (2014). 'The (W)hole in the Archive'. *Paragraph*, 37(3), 387–402, https://www.jstor.org/stable/26418642

Silova, I.; Piattoeva, N.; Millei, Z. (eds). (2018). *Childhood and Schooling in (Post) Socialist Societies: Memories of Everyday Life*. New York: Palgrave Macmillan, https://doi.org/10.1007/978-3-319-62791-5

Springgay, S.; Truman, A.; and MacLean, S. (2020). 'Socially Engaged Art, Experimental Pedagogies, and Anarchiving as Research-Creation'. *Qualitative Inquiry*, 26(7), 897–907, https://doi.org/10.1177/1077800419884964

Stengers, I. (2018). *Another Science is Possible: A Manifesto for Slow Science*. Polity Press.

Stoler, A. L. (2002). 'Colonial Archives and the Arts of Governance'. *Archival Science*, 2, 87–109, https://doi.org/10.1007/BF02435632

Tlostanova, M. (2017). *Postcolonialism and Postsocialism in Fiction and Art: Resistance and Re-existence*. Cham: Palgrave Macmillan, https://doi.org/10.1007/978-3-319-48445-7

Tlostanova, M. and Mignolo, W. (2012). *Learning to Unlearn: Decolonial Reflections from Eurasia and the Americas*. Columbus: Ohio State University Press

Tlostanova, M.; Koobak, R.; and Thapar-Bjorkert, S. (2016). 'Border Thinking and Disidentification: Postcolonial and Post-socialist Feminist Dialogues'. *Feminist Theory* 17(2), 211–28

Tsing, A. L. (2015). *The Mushroom at the End of the World*. Princeton University Press, https://doi.org/10.1515/9781400873548

Vierke, U. (2015). 'Archive, Art, and Anarchy: Challenging the Praxis of Collecting and Archiving: From the Topological Archive to the Anarchic Archive'. *African Arts*, 48(2), 12–25

'Whale of a Bad Time' (2020). [museum exhibition]. KUBAPARIS, Budapest, https://kubaparis.com/archive/a-whale-of-a-bad-time

Wenzel, J. (2010). *Bulletproof: Afterlives of Anticolonial Prophecy in South Africa and Beyond*. University of Chicago Press, https://doi.org/10.7208/chicago/9780226893495.001.0001

Yurchak, A. (2008). *Dasha Fursey: Utopia at The Roof of the World*. Catalogueue for Art Exhibition 'At the Top of the World'. New York

—— (1997). 'The Cynical Reason of Late Socialism: Power, Pretense, and the Anekdot'. *Public Culture* 9(2), 161–88

Zin, M. and da Rosa Ribeiro, C. (2023). 'Timescapes in Childhood Memories of Everyday Life During the Cold War'. *Journal of Childhood Studies*, 48(1), 99–110, https://doi.org/10.18357/jcs202320547

1. Who Do I Remember For?
Memory as Genre and Dark Pleasures of Trauma Witnessing

Petar Odak

> There is a lot written on trauma-witnessing and childhood memories, very often in tandem. I am entering this discussion by engaging with two questions that have not been addressed extensively within the field of memory/trauma studies: (1) In which ways and from what places are memories being structured even before they come to be 'our' memories? In other words, can we talk of memory as a genre?; and (2) What kinds of dark pleasures are derived from trauma-witnessing—both from the side of the witness-teller and from the side of the listener? Finally: How are these two questions connected, and what does their intersection tell us about the possibilities and limits of memory-writing? This chapter is very personal; for, in it, I try to grapple with my own uneasiness when faced with these questions in the context of a memory-writing workshop. It is also a chapter that tries to contextualise its conclusions within the wider frame of memory-writing processes of different kinds.

Although I did not really know what to expect from something called a 'memory-writing workshop', I was surely intrigued by the concept. The event happened in September 2019 in Riga and brought together participants from different cultural/geographical and professional backgrounds. Our shared context was the Cold War or, rather, our common denominator was the fact that the Cold War and/or the post-Cold-War world had impacted our childhoods, in all the ways a historical period of that kind of varied political intensity and of that temporal and spatial span can exercise over everyday lives of children and young adults. To this, we should also add that, as a historical marker, the Cold War is fundamentally heterogeneous and somewhat evasive; in other words, any attempt to delineate its political, geographical, and temporal contours (including its afterlives) and, following that, to detect its influence over one's life, is inevitably fundamentally relative. It is necessary to take these remarks into account to fully understand the memory-writing that happened in a hotel in Riga. To summarise the process: during this three-day workshop, we were each invited to write and share three memories. No limitations were specified as to the content or the style of the written memories. The only request was that we write them in the third person.

It was certainly an enriching experience. The memory-writing made me both look into myself to seek for significant memories and, immediately afterwards, or maybe even simultaneously with the processes of memory-seeking and memory-writing, to reflect on the memories chosen and on my reasons for choosing them. Is my first encounter with a huge, shiny, and colourful supermarket really one of my most intense experiences? Or is it just an experience I am expected to have, taking into account that I grew up in the late-socialist and post-socialist timespace? (And here I am assuming, just for a moment, that there is a way to distinguish between these two: my own 'authentic' process of remembering and those seemingly imposed social expectations that surround and shape my process of remembering; I will get to this in more detail later on.) Continuing with this line: Am I really so strongly affected by that one particular traumatic memory of the Yugoslav war, which I shared with other participants? Or was I just catering to what I assumed were other people's expectations as to what should constitute my most important memories? If yes, why did I assume that in the first place? More broadly, why do we tend to assume that traumatic memories are the ones that marked us the most—in this case in relation to the Yugoslav Wars, or the Cold War more generally— and why are we so eager to hear other people's traumatic memories? Let me put it this way: should my most intense memories necessarily be tied to the Yugoslav war, post-socialist transition, the rise of right-wing nationalism, and other traumatic events and/or events widely considered to be 'historical'?

Because, maybe, my most intense memories are more or less the same as the most intense memories of people who grew up in seemingly peaceful Western democracies—of a toy, a Walkman, a desired piece of clothing, a birthday party. However, maybe identifying memories that are (at least to some extent) trans-cultural comes with a price, possibly causing me to lose some of my identity or even some of my subjectivity. Also, to what extent is this my choice at all? Finally: What is the relationship between personal history and social history here? By dealing with all of these mutually implicated questions, I will try to unpack the very process of memory-writing. It is always, simultaneously, a process of writing our own personal histories and of retrospectively projecting a teleology through which we explain/understand ourselves today. I also want to account for the gains and the pleasures derived on both sides of this process: by me, the witness-teller, and by the others, my fleeting audience, who listened to my memories, especially the dark and the traumatic ones. Another very important remark: although my audience was, indeed, of a fleeting kind, it stood there in the name of a wider, abstract, nameless, but unquestionably omnipresent audience—one towards which I feel a certain kind of obligation—surely more by necessity than choice.

Therefore, this chapter will be arranged around two questions that imposed themselves on me during the memory-writing process in the Riga workshop: (1) What constitutes a 'significant' memory? and (2) What attracts us to each other's traumatic memories? Although these two questions might seem somewhat far from each other, they are deeply connected, as they both try to ask something very fundamental about the nature of memory and the process of remembering.

I will structure this text through a series of my three memories—it is somewhere during this process that the idea for the essay-turned-chapter emerged, as is clearly visible from the third written memory (or, more accurately, the self-reflective take on the previous two written memories) I shared during the workshop. On a more subtle level, which I will recount and explicate below, it is possible to trace a trajectory from my first memory through the second one, and on to the last one—a trajectory that registers my own affective shifts during the workshop process.

First Memory: Ice Cream in Trieste/Palmanova/Graz

The first memory I shared was entitled 'Ice-Cream in Trieste/Palmanova/Graz', n.d.:[1]

Shopping abroad was usually done in packs of extended family. This time it was Petar, his father, his cousin, and his aunt. They left Zagreb early in the morning, before 6 AM, as this is how trips were done in this family. He hated waking up early, but this time the excitement for the trip abroad kicked in the second he opened his eyes. He doesn't remember the trip itself that much. Probably he was asleep most of the time. He did not notice crossing the border at all. After coming to Trieste/Palmanova/Graz, he first felt some sort of disappointment. Rows of stalls and stands selling cheap clothes and cheap toys reminded him of the open market of his Dalmatian small town, Šibenik. Was this all there was? Shouldn't this foreign country be more beautiful, more modern, more exciting—simply completely different? He was really not interested in buying clothes in the dirty open market. His attitude changed and the excitement reemerged when they approached a huge yellow building with the capital letters saying: B I L L A. White, yellow, red—it just seemed so colourful. This has to be something special, as his father and aunt were talking about Billa for a while—this was, it seems, their ultimate goal. They never mentioned that there was anything special about this store, but he could easily sense the excitement, which emanated from them while preparing for the trip. And now he was there, and he was happy, and this place was a complete shock to him: there were no stores of this size in his hometown. And the lights! It was so bright inside. Also, it looked so clean, as if he entered a pharmacy, rather than a huge busy marketplace. Among the sea of colourful products, what stayed with him the longest was an ice-cream. His father took him to the ice-cream freezer and told him to choose one, suggesting

---

1   The title was, of course, supposed to communicate the fact that, in my memory, these different places (Trieste, Palmanova, and Graz) are interchangeable, or, even, that they merge into a singular, fuzzy, and abstract place. This is because this particular memory is centred around the practice of shopping rather than the place where this shopping occurs. However, because I am fully aware that the name of the supermarket was Billa—which is an Austrian chain—the destination was most likely Graz.

the biggest one they had. Apparently, it was famous, and his father's favorite. They left the store, he unpacked the ice-cream and started eating it. 'Do you like it?', his father asked. He wasn't sure though. Excitement for the huge-sized sized ice-cream in a foreign country was way stronger than enjoyment in the taste of the ice-cream. Taste-wise, it was just another ice-cream, nothing more or less. But the size! However, pretty soon, it was exactly the size that became problematic. The boy simply could not finish this huge ice-cream. He felt bad, as he wanted to finish it, because it was obviously a special ice-cream, probably some big brand he just never heard of because you could not buy it in Croatia. He also did not want to make his father mad, as throwing food in his family was usually avoided at all cost. So he was walking down the streets of Trieste/Palmanova/Graz, with this huge ice-cream melting in his hand. His father noticed it, laughed, and just said 'Throw it away, it's too big for a kid, I should have known.' So he threw the ice-cream in a bin and continued shopping with his family.[2]

This is quite a commonplace, indeed, a very widespread motive when it comes to the subgenre of oral or textual accounts (including memoirs and autobiographies) of socialist childhoods: the first contact between a naïve post/socialist subject and the flashy world of consumer capitalism. It is, therefore, a very predictable memory—this realisation generates a certain uneasiness in me, maybe even some kind of embarrassment: my personal narrative is reducible to a set of memory tropes; these tropes govern my process of memory, they shape my self-reflective accounts, rather than the other way around (or at least, rather than my own act of memory-making simply emerging in the moment of reminiscence, in a completely ungoverned, spontaneous fashion).

In any case, this is my memory, for sure; something like this most definitely happened, even though some of the details, undoubtedly, were added later, fabricated in order to fill the memory gaps and give it a certain flavour, as the story always must be complete. Did my aunt and my father really mention Billa several times in the days before the trip?

---

2   Since I will rely on psychoanalysis further on in this essay, a certain, indeed, very stereotypical Oedipal moment (of which I became aware only now, while analysing this memory with more scrutiny, rather than during the workshop itself), which screams from this memory, simply cannot and should not be left unacknowledged. However, because it goes outside of the scope of this chapter-essay, this aspect will remain limited to this footnote.

Maybe, but most likely not. Were they 'emanating' excitement while talking about Billa? Most certainly not—this is above all, I have to admit, a retrospective performance of a poor post/socialist Eastern European.

I have no doubts that this memory is strongly framed by implied expectations that the very setup of the workshop posited; the name of the workshop, Reconnect/Recollect, urges the making of connections based on recollection. Therefore, unsurprisingly, my memory story resonated with most of the other participants in the workshop: they all could relate to it, they all knew what I was talking about. Moreover, within the scope of this project, mine was surely not the only memory that included or was centered around this moment of post/socialist consumer-object cathexis. Let me share here just two examples of others' memories:[3]

During the 80s or early 90s teenagers in Poland dreamed of walkmans. It was an object of divisions also. Visible ones. If someone was lucky enough to have a relative 'in the West', then could owe his/her walkman and every friend would know it. I still remember one boy, who wanted to make an impression on others, and was wearing only headphones, his hands hidden in the pockets. He had no walkman inside the pockets but wanted others to think he had been listening to music on his own walkman. ('Material Culture' n.d.)

She had the boots on her feet that she longed for so long. It was made of plastic, smelling a bit like that, but it felt good, looked fashionable, an out of ordinary piece on her feet. She felt that everyone would know she is different when she appeared in school. They might think that it came from foreign relatives from the West. She dreamed about having those relatives and receiving presents from them. Light gray boots, laced up to cover her ankles and a zipper under the lace. So unique, she thought. The boots felt tight a bit on her feet when she tried them on, but there was no larger size and the pain felt bearable then. For a short while

---

3   I am quoting these from the Cold War Childhoods' Memory Archive (https://coldwarchildhoods.org/memories/). Anonymous memories collected there come from the workshop in Riga in which I participated, but also from other memory-writing workshops that were held in Berlin, Helsinki, and Mexico City. I want to emphasise that English was not the mother tongue of most participants, nor is it the language they use on an everyday basis. I decided to respect the authors of these memories and restrain from any editing in regard to grammar or syntax. After all, the fact that this memory-writing workshop took place in the context of the language that was foreign for most of us necessarily adds another layer in our assessment of the whole process.

then it was, but now as she was sitting in the back seat of their Lada car with a car boot full of food, an LP of Queens, shampoos of flowery smell, it felt hurting. But she felt she is exceptional since she has the boots, from her shopping trip to Yugoslavia, the West. ('Gray Zipper Boots' n.d.)

My memory resonated with the rest of the group because we do, indeed, have some similar memories. But it also resonated with others because our memories (moreover, our very significant memories!) are inevitably entering and being shaped by a frame that preceded them. As one of the participants wrote later, reflecting on the workshop: 'I was very, very inspired. I loved to see how the memories speak to other memories and things suddenly get a wider meaning and context' (quoted in Millei et al. 2019). Another workshop participant went even further, claiming that 'many of the features that we thought of as distinct to our respective contexts (cultures, countries, socioeconomic background, etc.) were in fact perhaps more universal to the human condition across a generation' (ibid.). For sure, to talk about universal categories and to invoke universalising notions such as the 'human condition' in this day and age (and in the context of contemporary feminist, decolonial, critical-race, posthumanist etc. theory) is in itself problematic. But we do not even have to get that political to recognise that, even within the context of white subjects of the global West, this kind of universalism that can be recognised in the way our memories relate to each other is at least partly conditioned by the very expectation that these memories should relate to each other. In other words, the notion of the 'universal human condition' is not a conclusion that spontaneously and logically emerges once we let our memories speak to each other and we notice their similarities. It is actually the other way round: the 'universal human condition' is a pre-existing notion, a frame that precedes our very process of remembering and that shapes the course of our memory-selection and our memory-writing, and which is, in its final effect, exactly that force which makes our memories 'speak to each other'.

The Genre of Memory

This all leads to the conclusion that, when it comes to memory, we are dealing with something akin to a genre. Indeed, it seems that there are certain (genre) motives and (genre) codes that are iterable across different people's memories. How to approach this idea of memory as a genre? The most obvious scholarly path we can follow when trying to address this question is literary studies, more specifically the work on the genre of autobiography and memoir. I would like to briefly examine this path in order to offer some preliminary conclusions relevant to our object of inquiry here: memory as a genre.

In his book on the literary genre of memoir, Couser (2012) recognises that, on a very fundamental level, there is no clear set of criteria according to which certain texts are assigned to a certain genre category: sometimes this is done based on the form (e.g., sonnet), sometimes regarding both the content and the form (e.g., an elevated style and a serious tone of the epic), and sometimes primarily in relation to the subject matter of a given text. He places the genre of memoir in the last category, as we read certain texts as memoirs not because of their style or content per se but, rather, because of the very fact that we know, even before we start reading, that these texts are supposed to communicate someone's personal narrative of the event(s) that really happened. In other words, what determines if a piece of writing is a memoir, transcends the text itself. This is something in line with what Genette (1997) calls paratexts, or those elements that 'enable a text to become a book and to be offered as such to its readers and, more generally, to the public' (p. 1). The elements he focuses on are book covers with all the information they include, such as authors' names, publisher's notes etc., but we can easily, via analogy, take paratext to stand for everything that surrounds a given text (especially if the 'text' is something as evasive as personal memory) and frames it in a certain way in front of the public.

Memories shared within the memory-writing workshop I took part in clearly come to us as part of a genre that is, above all, determined by a certain paratextual framing, which was, in this case, simply the context of me and the others claiming that what we shared were our own memories. It was, of course, very possible that, in writing and sharing my memory, I lied or, even more likely, that I misremembered the event I narrated to the group (as I have already admitted). Nonetheless, the implied agreement was that what I shared was true, or at least that my report was as truthful as it could be, considering that the event I described happened almost thirty years ago. This was the common framework all of us in the workshop accepted and counted on: what we share really happened. Therefore, what makes memory a genre in itself and, effectively, what gives it its tone and colour, as well as its affective impact, is this context that frames it as a personal true story.

However, the question of what delineates the potential genre of memory is not the most crucial here, or at least it is not the question that brought forth the initial set of dilemmas that animate this essay. In addition, and more importantly, it does seem that, indeed, there are certain genre motives that repeat themselves across memories shared by different individuals; that is, the paratext is not all there is. Therefore, it might be useful, at this point, to look into different types of memoirs, both in regard to their content and their style.

Couser (2012) detects several subgenres of memoir writing; the two relevant for our discussion here are conversion and testimony. Conversion brings 'the story of a radical (and usually sudden) reversal in the narrator's perspective' (p. 38), this traditionally being applied to religious narratives of faith conversion, most often to Christianity; however, as Couser himself asserts, the term is applicable to ideological shifts as well. It is clear that we cannot easily equate the moment of a post/socialist subject's first encounter with the world of consumer capitalism with the ideological or political conversion, especially if the subject is a child, with limited cognitive capacities and, more importantly, with limited awareness of the socio-historical context. But there was certainly in my memory something like a 'reversal in the narrator's perspective', some kind of a marking moment, which both encapsulates wider ideological shifts and announces further ideological shifts, at the same time personal and collective. It is for this reason that both I and many other workshop participants, when choosing which significant memories to share, opted for those moments of encountering consumer capitalism for the first time—because we feel this encounter says something important about the historical moment or the historical period of post/socialist transition and, by extension and by necessity, something important about our lives as well.

The second subgenre of memory relevant for our discussion here is testimony, a narrative that is distinguished 'by the relation between the I and the world' (Couser, p. 41), and where the narrator, above all, serves as a witness. My memory clearly functions as a witnessing one, because it, again, not only represents one individual encounter with the alien and mythical West but it also resonates with the wider socio-political context, or even operates on the level of allegory. Once again, this is why we so often go for the motive and the narrative I detected here: this event encapsulates something larger than us, something that transcends our own lives, something that we are maybe even obliged to remember and share.

In her book on global iconic events, Sonnevend (2016) describes a historical event as some kind of aberration from history, a history that is usually taken to be a fundamentally repetitive and slow process. Historical events are 'split off from the regular rhythms of daily life and stand out in memory as unique, marked as uplifting or traumatic (p. 1). Among several criteria that qualify a certain event as a historical one, Sonnevend lists condensation, which is 'the event's encapsulation in a "brand" of a simple phrase, a short narrative, and a recognisable visual scene' (p. 25). Although her focus is on one-off events of limited duration, rather than political contexts of longer period—the book's exemplary case study is the fall of the Berlin Wall—this condensation perfectly describes the memory story I offered above. My first encounter with shiny objects in an enormous superstore is both a short narrative and a very recognisable visual scene. This is what makes this memory so powerful: it comes as a shortcut that captures a historical moment and that cuts through both personal and political. In other words, it is a repeatable genre motive.[4]

Before moving on to the second memory and the question of pleasure in witnessing trauma, I would like to emphasise that my aim here is not to suggest that the memory stories I recounted above, because they can be coded as having an iterable genre motive, are nothing but derivative

---

4 I do not want to overburden this essay with too many examples (in addition to my memory and the two others I chose as exemplary). However, I would like to briefly mention two other cases to further support my claim of this being an iterable genre motive. When conducting fieldwork in Germany, I interviewed a Berliner who grew up in former East Berlin. One of the most intense memories he decided to share with me included an intricate plan his family came up with, in order to procure him a very-desired Kinder Surprise chocolate egg from an Intershop, without anyone noticing (as it was politically frowned upon to shop in this store, which was aimed at foreigners and only accepted foreign currency). Another example comes from a German TV show *Deutschland 83*—a very powerful scene of a young GDR spy entering, for the first time in his life, a huge, shiny and loud supermarket in West Berlin. He gets so overwhelmed that he experiences what seems to be a panic attack.

or, even worse, inauthentic; in other words, it is not my intention here to question the validity of other people's memory (or my own, for that matter). If anything, my claim is that validity, truthfulness, authenticity, etc. are not adequate criteria when approaching the question of memory, precisely because memories and memory-making processes exist outside parameters that could be verified through these categories.

Moreover, as Bakhtin (1984), in one of the pivotal studies on genre, puts it in regard to the context of fiction writers: 'What interests us is precisely the influence of the *generic tradition itself* which was transmitted through the particular authors,' because exactly 'throughout this process the tradition is reborn and renewed in each of them in its own way, that is, in a unique and unrepeatable way' (p. 159, emphasis in original). If this is true of the classical fiction writers Bakhtin analyses, it is certainly true of all of us recounting our own memories. And finally, the claim from my side is not that we opt for these stories only in a compliant and passive manner. Inasmuch as these codes come to us as unavoidable and impose themselves on us, we also go for them and seek them, as they offer us a language through which we can both articulate ourselves and understand others.

Second Memory: Her Shoes

All of the above is but my current analysis, developed as I am re-thinking my memory choices, and as I am writing this chapter-essay; that is to say, I did not assume the same kind of reasoning and the same level of self-reflection back then, during the memory workshop (at least until the very last memory I shared there). I did, however, feel certain things. For example, I felt that the emotional impact of my first shared memory was very limited, that there was no affective punch to it. I had to do better. That is why, the same night in my hotel room, I sat down to write the following memory, titled by the memory-archive editors as 'Her Shoes' (n.d.). The next day I shared it in the workshop:

It was a beautiful day—warm and sunny. His mom picked him up from the kindergarten. They first had to go to the market to buy some groceries and then go home, where his sister was waiting for them, as she had already come back from school. However, the second they left the grocery store they heard sirens— the ones that indicated they were under air attack. They ran to the closest shelter, as that was the usual drill in situations like this one. The shelter was basically a fire station—huge, but dark and quite stuffy, because of all the people that were crammed inside. It was his first time in this shelter—usually, they used the one next to their house—and he did not like it at all. Yes, he appreciated some grownups' attempts to calm him down by offering cookies, but all he really wanted was to leave this terrible place. His mom wanted the same, as they had another reason: his sister was home alone. He was listening as she was consulting with other grownups about what to do now. Some people advised her to stay here with the boy, because here they were safe and the daughter probably already went to the shelter next to their house. This did not satisfy her. She turned to him and asked: 'Do you mind staying here while I go home to check on your sister? And one of these ladies from our neighborhood will bring you home after the attack is over?' This he refused immediately, with unhinged fear and panic that left no space for negotiation. At that moment his mom leaned over, put her arms on his shoulders, looked him in the eyes and said: 'In that case, we run.' And then she did something that, for him, marked the seriousness of the situation: she took off her heeled shoes. This strange act confused him deeply. 'This way I will run faster.' Yes, it made sense, but in his mind this whole thing was just wrong. His mom taking off her shoes in public? Running away barefoot? On a dirty road? He has never seen her doing something similar. 'Ready?' she asked. He nodded. They started running. All he could see were the beige heeled shoes in his mom's hand. All he could hear was the sound of her bare feet hitting the asphalt.

First of all, we should recognise that this memory also perfectly fits into the argument of memory as a genre which I outlined in the previous section. For one, it is, again, 'a short narrative, and a recognisable visual scene' (Sonnevend 2016, p. 25) that condenses a broader historical moment. It is also most certainly a witnessing memory, even more so than the previous one, especially if we follow the criteria of what is conventionally considered to be historical witnessing in the scholarly field of memory studies; that is to say, it is, fundamentally, a traumatic memory. This is the aspect I want to focus on in this section.

As I finished reading my memory, I put the paper down and looked up and around the room at other participants. There was complete silence. Several people made a sound of consternation, some kind of a long gasp that traversed the room. I heard one or two 'Oh my god!' and 'This is terrible'. On some level, I got what I wanted: I shared a story that produced a solid affective punch. On another level (or maybe this is the same level after all), other participants got what they wanted as well: an intense story and the pleasure derived from it. To be clear, what was very palpable in the room was a feeling of discomfort; but this discomfort was most definitely accompanied by a certain feeling of pleasure, a pleasure that pushes us towards sharing and hearing personal traumatic narratives in the first place. How to account for this? What is the place of this pleasure?

It goes without saying that, inasmuch as traumatic memories are personal, they are also, on a very basic level, always collective and social—that is, political. In other words, they are very much invested in the production and maintenance of a certain collective identity. In this case, the memory of the Yugoslav Wars and the suffering on the Croatian side were and still are one of the pillars of the nationalistic discourse that generates a lot of its affective political power exactly from these self-victimising narratives. The fact that I am not ideologically aligned with this discourse does not mean that my processes of remembering were not shaped by it. In this context, an (unintended) political work of my memory can be understood through Landsberg's (2004) concept of 'prosthetic memory', which stands for any kind of media that allows us to experience events that are far gone, in the form of a 'privately felt public memories that develop after an encounter with a mass cultural representation of the past, when new images and ideas come into contact with a person's own archive of experience' (p. 19). The fact that Landsberg is above all focused on (visual) mass-media representations should not bother us here. As I showed in the previous section, the affective power of our shared memories lies exactly in the fact that they fluctuate as iterable genre motives that transcend different registers of articulation, including different media. In the case of this memory workshop, I shared a memory that activated a certain affective aspect already present in the personal emotional baggage carried in by the other participants.

Although not unaware of its pitfalls, Landsberg is predominantly interested in the politically progressive potential of prosthetic-memory practices. Sodaro (2017), in her take on the matter, twists the idea and offers us a concept of 'prosthetic trauma', which is, above all, invested in generating a 'simplistic, divisive dualism between right and wrong, good and evil in a way that has important and dangerous political implications' (p. 2). No matter how uneasy it is to face this, I have to accept that my chosen memory, at least to some extent, did participate in the reproduction of the self-victimising Croatian nationalistic identity. None of this, of course, calls into question the legitimacy of me sticking with this traumatic memory, nor the decision to share it in the workshop; in other words, the fact that this memory fits the mainstream Croatian memory narrative, does not take away of its affective importance for me. This is also why we need to go further in the examination of the reasons for participating, in one way or another, in the processes of traumatic memories and go back to the question: What is the place of this pleasure, the pleasure of hearing other people's traumatic experiences?

A very straightforward take on this issue would focus on the fact that people in the room were faced with a terrible story and simply reacted with instinctual empathy. Although this would not be an incorrect summary of what went on, it is important to analyse this moment more carefully and in more detail, instead of taking both the act and the concept of empathy for granted. I believe there are at least three different types of possible pleasures extracted from these kinds of experiences—ones in which we are faced with political violence and the suffering of others—and they are all centered around processes of identification.

For sure, we should start by recognising the pleasure of identifying with the victim, which goes two ways. First, we identify with victims-narrators of a certain historical violence—that is, we temporarily assume the position of the victim ourselves—and we extract a certain pleasure out of it. This might as well be related to the complex of repetition compulsion, as it is conceptualised in psychoanalysis. In his famous essay 'Beyond the Pleasure Principle' (1955), Freud assumes several different takes on the repetition compulsion, in one of them focusing on an individual's unconscious tendency to re-enact the traumatic event or traumatic experience in order to deal with it again, or to feel that he or she has mastered it, gained control over it. In the famous and oft-quoted analysis of the *fort-da* game enacted by his grandson, Freud describes the boy's act of throwing away a reel tied to a piece of string while saying 'gone', and then retrieving it back by pulling and happily exclaiming 'there!'.⁵ According to Freud, this was a re-enactment of the boy's mother leaving the room, that is, leaving the boy, and then coming back to him. According to Freud, although 'at the outset he was in a *passive* situation—he was overpowered by the experience', exactly through the process of repeating this experience, 'unpleasurable as it was, as a game, he took on an active part' (p. 16, emphasis in the original).⁶ Finally, Freud concludes, we should explain the boy's efforts as an 'instinct for mastery that was acting independently of whether the memory was in itself pleasurable or not' (Ibid).

Although Freud is dealing with an individual case here, meaning that his grandkid's repetition compulsion is invested in and arranged around the act of repeating the boy's own unpleasant experience, trauma studies very often invoke this concept of repetition compulsion in order to explain collective (political) trauma.⁷ Following this, we can claim that the pleasure of identifying with the witnessing victim is derived, at least partly, from the illusion of mastery that accompanies our processes of identification, after the witness's account affectively activated our

---

5   A more extensive description of the *fort-da* game: 'This good little boy, however, had an occasional disturbing habit of taking any small objects he could get hold of and throwing them away from him into a corner, under the bed, and so on, so that hunting for his toys and picking them up was often quite a business. As he did this he gave vent to a loud, long-drawn-out "o-o-o-o", accompanied by an expression of interest and satisfaction. His mother and the writer of the present account agreed in thinking that this was not a mere interjection but represented the German word "fort" [gone]. I eventually realised that it was a game and that the only use he made of any of his toys was to play "gone" with them. One day I made an observation which confirmed my view. The child had a wooden reel with a piece of string tied round it. It never occurred to him to pull it along the floor behind him, for instance, and play at its being a carriage. What he did was to hold the reel by the string and very skilfully throw it over the edge of his curtained cot, so that it disappeared into it, at the same time uttering his expressive "o-o-o-o". He then pulled the reel out of the cot again by the string and hailed its reappearance with a joyful "da" [there]. This, then, was the complete game—disappearance and return. As a rule one only witnessed its first act, which was repeated untiringly as a game in itself, though there is no doubt that the greater pleasure was attached to the second act' (Freud, 1955, pp. 14–15).

6   Freud asserts something very similar in his paper 'Inhibitions, Symptoms and Anxiety' (1959), wherein he writes that 'Anxiety is the original reaction to helplessness in the trauma and is reproduced later on in the danger-situation as a signal for help. The ego, which experienced the trauma passively, now repeats it actively in a weakened version, in the hope of being able itself to direct its course' (pp. 166–67).

7   See, for example, Caruth (1996), Felman and Laub (1992), Leys (2000).

own past traumas. Yes, we put ourselves in the shoes of victims while listening to their stories, but we are constantly in charge of the situation; we are in proximity of violence, while at the same time keeping our distance and our illusion of control.

Unlike the first course of identification with the victim, where the main process is one of temporarily assuming the victim's position (albeit from a distance), the second one can be understood as a more straightforward process of identification through empathy: we gain pleasure by empathising with the other. However, even this process of empathic identification is at least double-layered, as the identification with the other necessarily comes together with the dissociation from the other. In other words, if we empathise with the other as the other, we are not putting ourselves in the position of the other but, rather, in a position next to the other. Therefore, it would be more precise to talk of empathic identification/dissociation. We get pleasure exactly by knowing that the victim is someone else, not us.

There is a very popular German expression, *Schadenfreude*, which already found its way into the English language, exactly because it does not have a satisfying equivalent therein, but can be translated as 'malicious joy'.[8] More specifically, *Schadenfreude* stands for the pleasure or joy in witnessing others' pain, and it ranges from the very widespread comic trope of a person falling (over a banana peel, for example) to the more sinister pleasure in someone else's intense agony. In her famous essay on war photography, Susan Sontag (2004) recognises something akin to *Schadenfreude* in the moments of witnessing other people's suffering: a comfort we find in the fact that we are not the ones suffering. She looks into philosophical accounts of this phenomenon, going all the way back to Edmund Burke's 1757 claim that all of us 'have a degree of delight, and that no small one, in the real misfortunes and pains of others'. Further on, he asks rhetorically: 'Do we not read the authentic histories of scenes of this nature with as much pleasure as romances and poems, where the incidents are fictitious?' (Burke 2017, p. 45). This is another type of pleasure that I recognise as being derived while listening to personal accounts of suffering: we are happy we are not the ones in pain, while simultaneously feeling good about ourselves as we

---

8   Equivalents do exist in some other languages, for example in Serbo-Croatian: *zluradost*.

still do care about the other's pain. Not only do we care, but we show we care very clearly. As the reaction to my traumatic memory showed—we gasp and exclaim ('Oh my god!') in utter shock because we are faced with inexpressibly violent acts.

Finally, the third pleasure that we obtain when listening to others' traumatic memories is derived from us identifying with the perpetrator. This one is the most controversial, and without a doubt the one most people would not be ready to admit, or at least would not be comfortable with recognising in themselves. In addition to identifying (in different ways) with victims, we also identify with perpetrators of violence because this grants us a pleasurable feeling of power. Indeed, these two are inseparable: the feeling of pleasure in assuming the position of the perpetrator is only increased as it parallels the feeling we get while identifying with the victim. This is what Radstone calls the 'gray zone', 'a site of fantasised identifications with victims and perpetrators that symbolise the prospects of omnipotence and coherent control that are lacking on a psychosocial level and must be disavowed on a moral one' (quoted in Ball 2003, p. 33).

Although I describe the pleasure derived from listening to the witness's account of political violence as a tripartite structure for the sake of analysis and clarity, it is more sensible to think of it as a singular affect of pleasure. This affect constantly shifts between the three aspects of pleasure or, to be more precise, does not allow for any delineation between them: it is a constant co-presence of these three pleasures. Finally, it is from this affective mixture that these kinds of memories draw their strength and exercise a strong grip over us.

At this point, I want to make one thing clear: I do not exclude myself from the affective operation described above. This includes both sides of the process. Most certainly, the same mixture of discomfort, empathy, and pleasure is what I myself feel in situations in which I am made to, or I decide to, listen to someone else's traumatic witnessing. Also, and more importantly in the context of the workshop I am describing here, I cannot negate my own pleasure in narrating my own personal traumatic experience. This is the pleasure of assuming the role of the victim, with all the symbolic capital this position carries. After all, to negate this pleasure would also mean to eliminate my own agency from the equation, which would, as its final consequence, have a de-subjectifying effect of just another kind.

Third Memory: A Conclusion

Towards the end of the workshop, I began to feel strange. At first, I could not really put it into words. However, as I started to think intensely about the two memories I shared in the workshop, I realised that the last one could not be yet another memory but that it had to be a self-reflective account of my process of remembering; it had to articulate the certain discomfort I myself felt when I looked back at the memories I chose. I would like to offer this meta-memory here, as part of the conclusion to this chapter, in conjuncture with the similar feelings and thoughts that Jana Hensel (2004) shares in her piercing memoir on living in the German Democratic Republic and in what came after. First, the final piece of writing I shared in the workshop:

It is really hard for me to invoke one particular memory that would be significant as either specific (in a one-of-a-kind, aberrant way) or representative of my childhood in a broader sense. The reason is: when I try to think of something that might be interesting to other people who do not share my background, my mind instinctively goes towards memories that involve Yugoslav wars and might be termed 'traumatic' (both of my grandparents had to flee their houses that were burnt to ground, my uncle was imprisoned and tortured, I was separated from my parents for a couple of years, etc.). However, although these memories come in abundance, I do not feel they represent my childhood or the memory of my childhood (if the two can ever be distinguished) in a fair way. That is to say, I remember my childhood through more positive, colourful tones: friends, games, school, cartoons, books, candies... (my favorite popular example here is Anne Frank's diary which, in the midst of the terribly violent events that stand as its background, notes as the most important things such as first love, games with cousins, the collection of cards of famous actors, etc.). This leads to another problem that emerges here—the relationship between private and collective/ political. For example, one of my most intense childhood memories (the one that regularly and frequently comes back to me) is my father buying me a fluffy toy. It was a blue bear. The reason I remember it is because that was one of the rare moments he expressed his affection towards me. (The toy was the only one I kept for years, it was falling apart, and my mom had to sew it back several times). However, this memory has to do primarily with my relationship with my father, which is both private (i.e. awkward or even unpleasant to share) and probably not that interesting to people who do not know me. In other words, my most vivid childhood memory has nothing to do with the Cold War, socialism, postsocialism, transition, Yugoslav wars, the rise of nationalism, etc. At the same time, this memory is extremely political, as it touches upon the conditions of (the lack of) paternal male bonding in a patriarchal society, which is greatly represented by Croatia in the 1990s. So, in brief, these are the reasons why, instead of offering one concrete memory, I made this reflection on the process my remembering went through in the context of this project. ('My Process of Remembering' n.d.)

This account brings me back to the very beginning of this essay and the rhetorical question I posed: What if my most intense memories are more or less the same as the most intense memories of people who grew up in seemingly peaceful Western democracies—of a toy, a walkman, a desired piece of clothing, a birthday party?

Writing about Western visitors coming to the former GDR for touristic sightseeing, Hensel (2004) tells us that

> as long as you took them to the Secret Police Museum, and showed them St. Nicholas Church, where all the Monday night demonstrations had taken place in 1989, carefully pointing out where the surveillance cameras had been placed to monitor those demonstrations, they were happy (p. 24).

The others expect something, and we give it to them. However, was the fact that 'we lost touch with our true experiences, and one memory after another slipped away', as Hensel (ibid.) is lamenting, a result of the wish of the other or, on the contrary, a precondition of the wish of the other? She continues: 'We repressed our actual experiences and replaced them with a series of strange, larger-than-life anecdotes that didn't really have anything to do with what our lives had been like' (ibid., p. 25). To this, I relate completely, as I tried to show in this chapter-essay. It certainly feels that I myself reduced my past to a cluster of larger-than-life stories, including, or especially, the traumatic ones. Truth be told, Hensel loses me when she concludes that 'we had forgotten how to tell our own life stories in our own way, instead adopting an alien tone and perspective' (ibid.). As I explicated above, I do not think there is an authentic memory that should be salvaged from others who are seemingly trying to coerce us into remembering what was not even remotely relevant to us. Our memories might be modulated from places that are not our own, but we are not innocent, as we still participate in this memory production, and we gain some pleasures from it. Nonetheless, Hensel's feeling that the pressure is there and that something is being lost needs to be accounted for. It is, finally, the feeling I myself undoubtedly share.

References

Bakhtin, M. (1984). *Problems of Dostoevsky's Poetics*. Minneapolis: University of Minnesota Press

Ball, K. (2003). 'Unspeakable Differences, Obscene Pleasures: The Holocaust as an Object of Desire'. *Women in German Yearbook: Feminist Studies in German Literature and Culture*, 19(1), 20–49

Burke, E. (2017). *A Philosophical Enquiry Into the Origin of Our Ideas of the Sublime and Beautiful* (reis. From 1757). University of Notre Dame Press

Caruth, C. (1996). *Unclaimed Experience: Trauma, Narrative, and History*. Cleveland: John Hopkins University Press, https://doi.org/10.56021/9781421421650

Couser, G. (2012). *Memoir*. Oxford University Press, https://doi.org/10.1093/acprof:osobl/9780199826902.001.0001

Felman, S. and Laub, D. (1992). *Testimony: Crises of Witnessing in Literature, Psychoanalysis and History*. New York: Routledge, https://doi.org/10.4324/9780203700327

Freud, S. (1955). 'Beyond the Pleasure Principle' (1920), in *The Standard Edition of the Complete Psychological Works of Sigmund Freud*, 24 vols., ed. by J. Strachey. Vol. XVIII (1920–22), pp. 7–64, London: The Hogarth Press

Freud, S. (1959). 'Inhibitions, Symptoms and Anxiety' (1926) in *The Standard Edition of the Complete Psychological Works of Sigmund Freud*, 24 vols., ed. by J. Strachey. Vol. XX (1925–26), pp. 75–175, London: The Hogarth Press

Genette, G. (1997). *Paratexts*. Cambridge University Press, https://doi.org/10.1017/CBO9780511549373

'Gray Zipper Boots' (n.d.). Memory story. *Cold War Childhoods*, https://coldwarchildhoods.org/portfolio/gray-zipper-boots/

Hensel, J. (2004). *After the Wall. Confessions from an East German Childhood and the Life that Came Next*, trans. by J. Chase (original published 2002). [n.p.]: Public Affairs

'Her Shoes' (n.d.). Memory story. *Cold War Childhoods*, https://coldwarchildhoods.org/portfolio/her-shoes/

'Ice-Cream in Trieste/Palmanova/Graz' (n.d.). *Cold War Childhoods*, https://coldwarchildhoods.org/portfolio/ice-cream-in-trieste-palmanova-graz/

Landsberg, A. (2004). *Prosthetic memory. The transformation of American remembrance in the age of mass culture*. Columbia University Press

Leys, R. (2000). *Trauma: A Genealogy*. The University of Chicago Press

'Material Culture' (n.d.). *Cold War Childhoods*, https://coldwarchildhoods.org/portfolio/material-culture/

Millei, Z., Silova, I., Piattova, N., and Țîștea, I. (2019). 'Remembering Childhoods Across Time and Space: Reflections from Collective Memory Workshops (part 1)'. Blogpost. *Cold War Childhoods*, https://coldwarchildhoods.org/blog/remembering-childhoods-across-time-and-space-reflections-from-collective-memory-workshops-part-1/

'My Process of Remembering' (n.d.). *Cold War Childhoods*, https://coldwarchildhoods.org/portfolio/my-process-of-remembering/

'Re-connect/re-collect: Memories of Everyday Childhoods: De-colonial and De-Cold War Dialogues in Childhood and Schooling', *Cold War Childhoods*, https://coldwarchildhoods.org/re-connect-re-collect/

Sodaro, A. (2017). 'Prosthetic Trauma and Politics in the National September 11 Memorial Museum'. *Memory Studies*, 12(2), 1–13, https://doi.org/10.1177/1750698017720257

Sontag, S. (2004). *Regarding the Pain of Others*. New York: Picador

Sonnevend, J. (2016). *Stories Without Borders: The Berlin Wall and the Making of a Global Iconic Event*. Oxford University Press, https://doi.org/10.1093/acprof:oso/9780190604301.001.0001

Diasporic Knowledges in Central Asia: (Re)membering in *Jeong*[1]

Olga Mun

I wrote this poem based on my impressions and participation in the Reconnect/Recollect project as it has inspired me to conduct more considerate research. From the project's inception, all research participants were involved in designing research focus and methods, which ensured the project design to be inclusive. The principal investigators, though formally having a leadership status, very attentively considered the intertwined personal and professional circumstances and contexts of the participants. For instance, at the time of the workshop in Helsinki, I required a Schengen visa to visit Finland. Such bordering practices frequently prevent me from participating in international conferences as visas increase the cost of attending academic events. In this project, however, visa costs were covered at the initiative of the organising team, welcoming my participation.

Furthermore, the project has invited the participants to rethink how we engage with our childhood memories. It has profoundly impacted me to reevaluate and take my own childhood experiences seriously and highlight my own diasporic memories and Korean culture, which in Central Asia is sometimes referred to as Koryo-saram traditions, as valuable. Hence, the name of the poem is *Jeong*, referring to a Korean philosophy of relatedness and kindness to human and non-human objects, such as nature. In our earlier work, we have theorised *jeong* in

---

1 This is a childhood memory produced as part of the Reconnect/Recollect project discussed in the introduction to this book.

the context of South Korean higher education, but I argue that *jeong* can be helpful in rethinking many more social processes to make our research designs inclusive to both human and non-human actors in many geographical contexts (Mun and Min, 2022). Since in the current workshop we were inspired to actively consider the environmental impact of our research through this project, we were encouraged to travel by train to minimise the harmful impact of air travel, for instance, I decided that *jeong* would be the most meaningful lens to reflect on my experience.

Memory Workshops in *Jeong*

In the age of equity nationalism in higher education
and borders within borders,
liberatory meetings
provide a space for contemplation
and tranquillity.
Walking together on a cold day in Helsinki,
thinking about memories
and experiences
opened windows to rethink the future.
At the workshop
the aesthetics of formalism and status hierarchies
blurred over-time
creating space
for participants to remember
they are more than academics and artists divided by borders
within borders.
Borders
between nature and humans.
Borders
between the past and the future.
Borders
Between disciplines,
vocations,
age,
and geographical belonging.
Jeong is a Korean philosophy of kindness.
To me, the workshop was
a workshop in *jeong*,
a workshop in kindness, humility and humanity.

As a doctoral researcher, I was grateful to participate in the research project where it was highlighted that the knowledge-production process is complex, contested, and socially constructed. In an age of climate change and post-Brexit Britain, I found the project liberatory in a sense that participants have had the freedom to define their own topics, choose collaboration groups, and participate in collective writing regardless of career-stage hierarchies and professional positionalities. Finally, underrepresented scholars, regardless of their nationalities, were given all necessary support without adding the emotional labour and material burden on academics and artists of colour themselves, which sets an example for future decolonial and feminist research as a practical guideline for conducting inclusive research.

Reference

Mun, O. and Min, Y. (2022). 'Global Public Good in Korea as Jeong.' In S. Marginson and X. Xu (eds). *Changing Higher Education in East Asia* (pp. 33–50). London: Bloomsbury Academic.

2. 'I Wanted to See the Man with that Mark on his Forehead':

A Historian, Her Childhood Experiences, and the Power of Memory

Pia Koivunen

This chapter discusses the use of one's own memory as a source in historical research. As a historian who has employed interviews, memoirs, travelogues, and diaries in my research, I now put my own memory to a test and examine how using my own memories differs from studying the memories of others. The chapter explores my memories of Mikhail Gorbachev's visit to Finland in 1989 and compares them with other sources, such as interviews with classmates, contemporary print media, photographs, and film material of the event. In a dual role of researcher and the researched, I demonstrate how lived experiences are supported by narrative elements and, in the end, how powerful memory can be.

On an autumn afternoon in October 1989, a nine-year-old girl left school and headed toward the downtown. Accompanied by her classmates, she soon reached the square in front of the town hall and started to wait for the world-famous guest who was going to visit her home town that day. This guest was Mikhail Gorbachev, the leader of the Soviet Union, who had traveled to Finland for a state visit. The girl and her friends eventually witnessed the Soviet leader arriving at the town hall, surrounded by thousands of enthusiastic spectators. The actual event was quickly over and she left home.

***

As a historian of the Soviet Union and the Cold War, I have often contemplated my own relationship with the Cold-War world. Born in 1980, I was six years old at the time of the Chernobyl nuclear accident, nine years old when the Berlin Wall was torn down, and eleven when the USSR collapsed. Since the beginning of my research career, I have heard 'real' Cold-War contemporaries, such as former diplomats, emphasising their insider knowledge of the period and half seriously questioning the ability of those who had not lived through that period to understand its spirit and peculiarities. These comments have made me think about my position with regard to the Cold-War era. I lived during the years that were historically defined as the Cold-War period, but did I experience and understand the Cold War in those years? Was I a contemporary in the most serious sense or an outsider, someone to whom that period was 'a foreign country'?

Over the years, I have worked on Cold-War history but also on memory and experiences. I have tried to understand how other people lived back then. How did they think about and experience bipolar antagonism; did they even come across it in their daily lives? I have been exploring diaries, travelogues, and memoirs to ascertain how people related to the battle between the two societal systems and the dividedness of the world but also to shared values that bypassed ideological, political, and other boundaries. All this thinking has been reflected upon and filtered through my own perceptions, experiences, feelings and family history, even if I have not written it into my works. In my childhood, for example, I faced and experienced numerous aspects and consequences of the Cold-War world without realising at the time what they were or where they came from. One such issue was the clear-cut division between socialist and non-socialist sports organisations.[1] Moreover, I came up with a topic for my doctoral dissertation—Soviet cultural diplomacy and the World Youth Festivals—while browsing through my grandfather's

---

[1] The division between socialist and non-socialist (or working-class and bourgeois) sports and other hobby associations goes back to the late nineteenth century and is, thus, older than the Cold-War era. However, this division became an instrument of Cold-War world politics in Finland and elsewhere; therefore, I also consider it to be a feature of the Cold War.

photographs from a youth festival held in Bucharest, Romania in 1953. All of these questions and pondering led me to think about the role of insider knowledge/contemporary knowledge/participatory knowledge of the past and to search for a Cold-War memory of my own. And then, at the right moment and in the right context, I found it. I was that nine-year-old girl who went to see Gorbachev in 1989.

This chapter is an extraordinary and very unusual personal experiment, which seeks to combine my scholarly interest in studying memory and my own memories of Gorbachev's visit to Finland in the late 1980s. I seek to examine how personal memory influences research and how it is different to study one's own memory than that of others. How does personal memory interact with one's choice of research topics? What does it feel like to interrogate one's own memory? And, what are the mechanisms through which we create stories from unorganised glimpses, feelings, smells, and bodily sensations to recall the past? I use my memories of Gorbachev's visit as the primary data and analyse them together with other sources, such as interviews with other witnesses to the event, contemporary media sources, documentary film material, and photographs. In conducting this exploration, I seek to examine the power of using one's own memory, its potential and its limits, as well as to observe the process of remembering. Let the exploration begin.

Background

Historians in their scholarly publications rarely draw explicitly on their own memories or experiences. This is partly due to the fact that historians were relative latecomers to the research practice of reflecting on one's own position and background. Until the 1960s, an ideal historian was a detached, objective observer, one who attempted to reconstruct the past by drawing on written materials, preferably documents held in official archives. This 'traditional' history-writing by 'traditional' historians considered oral history and memory to be unreliable sources: people might lie, exaggerate, misremember, or be selective in what they recount. In the search for information on actual happenings; usually wars, diplomacy, and power struggles; stories based on oral narration were thought to be of secondary significance or even of no use at all (Abrams 2010; Kalela 2012).

Since the linguistic turn and the interest in everyday life, women's history, and the history of minorities from the 1960s onwards, the methodology in historical research and the hierarchy of sources have changed a great deal. It is nowadays widely acknowledged that strict objectivity is unfeasible, that a researcher's own subjectivity influences the way of doing research in many respects. Explicating one's position and background as a researcher has become part of the research process. Instead of focusing on the history of great men, historians today are increasingly interested in how ordinary people in the past felt, experienced, and lived their lives. (Abrams 2010). Moreover, subjectivity, once considered the weakness of sources based on memory, is now regarded as their key element. As oral historian Alessandro Portelli (1998) has pointed out, subjective narratives do not necessarily add much factual information about past events, but they do reveal what meanings people attach to the past, what emotions they associate with it, and what kind of psychological effects it has left on them.

Even though historians today are more likely to examine their own positions and to deem memory valid material for research, it is not a common practice to turn to one's own memory. On the contrary, some historians may still consider the use of their own memory or experiences to be odd, unscientific, and, however interesting, risky. This became very clear in 2017, when, for the first time, I discussed the topic of Gorbachev's state visit at a history conference in Finland. I had included my classmates' and my own experiences in the presentation. At that moment, the idea of employing my memories as sources had not crossed my mind. However, I thought it would be transparent to reveal my relation to the topic because this particular memory was the reason for my initial interest in the subject. While the response was largely positive, one comment from an elderly historian cut the air. After hearing my presentation, she declared that she was not at all interested in the experiences of myself and my classmates and that she was worried about how I could raise any scientific interest in my case.

This senior colleague seemed to be implying that our own memories are not an appropriate starting point for research, not to mention scientific material to be examined. Reading between the lines, her commentary also seemed to suggest that we historians should not be too close to our subjects; we should instead keep separate ourselves and the topic we study. It is often thought that a certain temporal distance is essential for historians to be able to see the past with a clear perspective; one's own past, following this rationale, would be far too close. The notion of distance may also describe the relationship between the recent practice of historians positioning themselves in their work and to the still-unconsciously-prevailing idea of the historian as an objective researcher who avoids subjectivity. Despite criticisms of purely objective research and its abandonment in many fields of research, this once noble ideal seems to be sitting surprisingly persistently on our shoulders and whispering in our ears.

While remaining open to exploring new ways of doing research, even searching my own memory, I nevertheless share that senior colleague's concern about generalisation—a point also raised in autoethnographic research. For example, Anderson (2006) has pointed out that, while delving into one's own memories can bring fruitful insights, the risk remains that self-analysis fails to elevate these memories above personal, individual descriptions. Without the necessary context and broader cultural, social, and political framework, individual memory remains merely individual memory and does not make a broader contribution to the study of cultural and social memory. Any kind of memory narrative, whether it is another's or one's own, must be analysed deeply and set in a broader context.

Memory

Memory is studied in a number of fields, and much has been written about how to theorise memory. There are different types of memories (individual, collective, social, political, cultural memory) and ways to approach it (Arnold-de Simine and Radstone 2013). Using one's own memory as research material raises multiple questions with regard to epistemology, research ethics, and research practices. Here I mention a few aspects that I find important when examining our own memories.

First, remembering is a communicative practice. Regardless of the form of remembering (interview, questionnaire, memoir, collective biography, individual/collective memory), narration of the past is always communicated to an audience. Moreover, remembering is connected to the cultural and social world of the narrator and is born out of the needs and interests of the present (Abrams 2010). In examining other people's memories, the researcher is dealing with oral or written narratives and is positioned as an outside observer of the narrator and the events being narrated. This stance changes when one starts to analyse one's own memories. The distance narrows down as the researcher becomes both the observer and observed and contributes an insider's narrative of the events under scrutiny (Anderson 2006). But what happens in such cases to the communicative nature of memory? Is there still a dialogue between the observer and the observed, and how can one be sure if the reflections on the research subject are produced by the self who is remembering or by the self who is conducting the analyses? To summarise, from a methodological perspective, is it different to examine one's own memories?

Susanne Gannon (2017) has argued that the reduced distance between researcher and researched is a positive factor, considering it to help in the comprehension of the underlying meanings of the memory narrative and of the changes in the power relations between the knowing subject and the subject to know about. Silova et al. (2018), in their study of socialist childhoods, suggest that using one's own memories can work as a strategy to challenge earlier modes of knowledge production by raising aspects that otherwise would not be studied. However, they also acknowledge the possible risk that, when shifting from the child in the past to the researcher in the present, one may suppress some parts of the experience to construct a coherent story from the fragments of memory.

A second difference between examining one's own memories and those of others concerns the wider access available with the self. While we usually work with oral or written accounts produced by others, in examining our own memories we can revisit them more thoroughly. In order to explain this difference further, I approach memory from a specific angle. Some scholars make a distinction between memory as a neurophysiological capacity to recall the past and as a process of narrating (writing or telling) that past. For example, Miettunen (2014) distinguishes between memory (what a person can cognitively remember) and remembering as a process by which a person produces a narrative of the past based on memory and other elements (see also Arnold-de Simine and Radstone 2013).

This way of dividing memory comes close to what the German philosopher Wilhelm Dilthey (who is much quoted in studies in the history of experience) has argued about experience. In his theory, experience is divided into two types: *Erlebnis* and *Erfahrung*, both of which can be rendered as 'experience' in English. Dilthey understands *Erlebnis* to represent non-verbal, non-interpreted experience and uses *Erfahrung* to name the verbal, processed, and interpreted form of the experience (see, for example, Eiranen 2015). He distinguishes, that is, between lived and reflective experience.

A similar distinction could also be applied to memory. One type of memory exists in the mind/body and another type assumes different shapes when reflected upon for the purpose of recounting to others. When we examine others' memories and experiences, we can only access the narrated, verbal forms of their memories, while the non-verbal form of memory is beyond our reach. In examining one's own recollections, however, a researcher can also access the non-verbal, non-narrated layers of memory and can compare these with the narrated forms of memory. Therefore, theorising memory in this way can be fruitful.

There is, nevertheless, an ethical concern that requires particular honesty on the part of the researcher. No one else can access the non-verbal memory 'living' in the mind/body, so the researcher should be honest and open in the research process (see Anderson 2006; Winkler 2018). Honesty and openness are naturally required in any field of research, but special consideration needs to be given in this kind of self-analysis. Unlike other people's written or oral memory narratives, which, at least in theory, are available to other researchers, one's own memory (in its complete, dual form) is a source that the self-researcher alone can access. The question could be raised whether the study of one's own memory requires it to be narrated prior to analysis. Even so, verbal articulation of the memory does not deprive the individual of the option to consult and revisit the 'behind-the-scenes' part of the memory at any time, adding new information, meanings, and interpretations to the story already told. This is something a researcher cannot do when working with the memories of others.

From Experience to Research

How did I end up studying my own memory? After completing my doctorate on Soviet cultural diplomacy and the World Youth Festivals, I began to search for new research topics. While attending a seminar in 2014 about the end of the Cold War, the memory of the visit by Gorbachev to Finland activated in my mind. I gradually became interested in state visits in general and the various ways they were used as a form of cultural diplomacy.

Without knowing what I would eventually do with the topic, I decided to start collecting materials on Gorbachev's (and other Soviet leaders') visits to Finland. One of my first actions was to write down my memories of Gorbachev's visit. Initially, I had no plans to use my memory as a source itself, but, knowing how vulnerable memories can be to external factors, I thought I should write mine down before consulting any other materials and without learning things from other sources. There is no right or wrong remembering since the lived life flows through us, leaving signs in our minds and our recollections. However, I wanted to document my memory narrative of my experiences of Gorbachev's visit before collecting other materials and embarking on research which might influence my memory or my narrative. I, therefore, sat down and wrote about the visit as I remembered it in June 2016—27 years after the event had taken place.

I later recalled that this was not my first revisitation of this memory. In 2010, I attended a conference of the International Council for Central and East European Studies in Stockholm, Sweden. Gorbachev was invited there as the guest speaker, but, in the end, he could not travel due to health issues. His name activated my memory, and I remember mentioning his visit to my hometown to a few colleagues at the conference but cannot recall what exactly I told them then. At that time, I only remembered the event but was not interested in it in terms of research.

Between 2016 and 2022, I gathered a variety of sources alongside my other research projects. I read official protocols of the visit in the National Archive of Finland, browsed through the documents of the Ministry of Foreign Affairs and the materials stored in the city archive of Oulu. I visited the Gorbachev Foundation during a research trip to Moscow and consulted the collections of newspaper and magazine articles compiled on the event as well as memoirs of politicians and diplomats. I also established a Facebook group to locate possible interviewees. In 2019, on the thirtieth anniversary of the visit, I organised a small exhibition entitled 'Gorby is coming—are you ready?' in cooperation with the Northern Ostrobothnia Museum in Oulu in October–November 2019 (Koivunen 2019a). The local newspaper *Kaleva* (Kaitasuo 2019) published an article prior to the exhibition to encourage people to recall the visit. Over thirty people sent me their written memories and/or an agreement to be interviewed. I even sent a letter to Mr. Gorbachev himself telling him how the memory of his visit had caused me to mount a small exhibition to commemorate the event. He did not reply.

Based on the aforementioned materials and their analysis, I wrote two peer-reviewed articles about memory and the popular reception of Gorbachev's visit to Finland, excluding my own memories. I found it too difficult to incorporate them because it would have required a different kind of methodological discussion, one that positioned myself both as a researcher (outside observer) and as a participant (observed) in the study. Including my own memories would also have complicated the anonymisation of my research data. I had decided to anonymise the interviewees and faced the choice of either also anonymising myself, which would have been dishonest, or including my own name, which, as the only one, would also have seemed an odd choice (Koivunen 2019b; Koivunen 2022). While I have not published anything based on my own memories until now, I have discussed the use of one's own memories in three conference papers (the annual convention of the Association for Slavonic, East European and Eurasian Studies 2017, the conference of the International Oral History Organisation 2018, and the 'Childhood Memories' conference organised as part of the Reconnect/Recollect project in 2021).

This chapter or, rather, this methodological experiment, is based on a long and, at times, slow process of gathering materials, understanding the possibility of employing one's own memories, and daring to work with them. The main impetus to employ my own memories came from a workshop organised by Zsuzsa Millei, Nelli Piattoeva, and Iveta Silova. They had published an edited volume on the use of collective biography, autobiography, and autoethnography in the study of socialist and post-socialist childhoods (Silova et al. 2018; see also Millei et al. 2022). Fascinated by their book, I wanted to try this method myself and signed up for the workshop that they held in Helsinki in 2019. In that workshop, we experimented with various scholarly and artistic methods for exploring our childhood memories, attempting to reconnect with the child self and childhood agency. This was done by (re)telling memory stories and discussing them in small groups. Inspired by Silova et al. (2018), I began to deconstruct and explore the layers of my memory. As part of this process, I systematically compared the fragments of my memory, my classmates' interviews, the film material from the USSR, contemporary print media, and photographs taken during Gorbachev's visit to Oulu in 1989.

Background to the Visit

Before delving into my personal memories, I briefly present some background explaining the context of my remembered experiences. During the Cold-War period, Finland was not a socialist society but was tied to the USSR through a formal policy defined in the Agreement on Friendship, Cooperation, and Mutual Understanding, signed in 1948. Because the Soviet Union had such an enormous impact on Finland, its leader's visit to the country was a long-awaited event. Gorbachev had come to power in 1985 and, since then, the Finnish President Mauno Koivisto had invited him several times for a state visit in order to discuss Finland's position in the new era of *Perestroika* and *Glasnost*. When the visit finally took place on 25–27 October 1989, it was the first time in fifteen years that a Soviet head of state officially visited an adjacent capitalist country.

For the Finnish political establishment, the most important outcome of the visit was that Gorbachev, in his speech at the celebration organised as part of the official protocol in Helsinki, finally acknowledged Finland as a neutral Nordic country and, thus, became the first Soviet leader to do so. Neutrality had been one of the key foreign-policy formulations that, for years, Finnish politicians had been unsuccessfully trying to include in the renewed Agreements on Friendship, Cooperation, and Mutual Assistance. Neutrality was both a pragmatic tool to allow Finland room to maneuver with the East and the West and a way of asserting Finland's national identity in the Cold-War world (Aunesluoma and Rainio-Niemi 2016; Ritvanen 2021).

In addition to political talks, Gorbachev's visit also included negotiations on new business contracts, a visit to the Finnish parliament, and a famous phone call to Moscow with one of the first Nokia mobile phones Mobira Cityman 900 (later known as Gorba—the Finnish nickname for the general secretary) (Ritvanen 2021). Gorbachev's visit provided a wonderful showcase for Finnish technology but, most importantly, it demonstrated that the USSR was changing politically. It also signalled a new, more open, and freer era for Finland. For, despite its independence, Finland had been politically under the influence of its giant Eastern neighbour since the end of WWII, for example, without hope of joining Western military and economic alliances such as NATO and the EEC (Aunesluoma and Rainio-Niemi 2016).

While the state visit to Helsinki and the negotiations that would take place there required lengthy and meticulous preparations, Gorbachev's brief visit to Oulu, a city in Northern Finland, was organised at very short notice. Information about the extra visit was announced less than a week before Gorbachev flew to Helsinki. According to the Finnish press, the Soviet leader himself had asked for a trip to Oulu because he wanted to see the 'Technology Village', a high-tech centre located there, and to network with local companies. Finnish newspapers speculated that Gorbachev was planning to use the high-tech complex as a model for building something similar back home. His choice of Oulu came as a surprise, especially to bigger cities in Southern Finland that were keen to host Gorbachev after the official tour in Helsinki.

In Oulu, Gorbachev was welcomed by crowds of smiling and cheering Finns. Newspapers wrote about the 'Gorbachev fever' that had taken over the small city and its residents (*'Sinitakit tuskailivat kun Oulu hullaantui'* 1989). Thousands of locals gathered at different locations in the centre and at the university, where the honoured guests were expected to make an appearance. Among the cheering crowds, there were also a lot of schoolchildren, who, according to a local newspaper, had come there 'with or without permission from school' (*'Mihail ja Matti Oulussa'* 1989).

During the less than two hours that Gorbachev and his wife were able to spend in Oulu, they had time to shake hands and talk with ordinary people, see a music performance in the city hall, take a short tour around the 'Technology Village', and talk to university staff and students. Gorbachev, at the time, was one of the most popular (if not the most popular) heads of state in the world, especially outside his own country; he gave exactly what people expected of him, demonstrating that he was the man who would change the Soviet Union, who would truly foster peace, and who would reunite the world that had been divided into two blocs.

My Memory Stories

My experiences relate to the last part of Gorbachev's visit in the Northern town of Oulu. Shortened and translated from Finnish, the first written version of my memory goes like this:

It was autumn, the snow had not yet come. The classmates and I knew that Gorbachev was coming and our teacher had let us see the visit, if we wanted. Those who stayed in the school would have a chance to leave early some other day. A few girls from my class and I left school to go downtown after the morning classes and lunch (don't remember who they were). We positioned ourselves in front of the city hall, where there was already a rather big crowd waiting. The area was marked with ropes. There were a lot of media present. We spoke with a Russian journalist and a cameraman, probably from Soviet Karelia because they spoke Finnish. They asked us something, I cannot remember what exactly, but I do remember that we shouted 'Karelia back' (Karjala takas). I left with the impression that the cameraman filmed us and we were excitedly frightened that we might end up on television. Probably not. Perhaps it was shown on Soviet television.

Eventually Gorbachevs' car arrived, and we saw a glimpse of them and the Finnish presidential couple. We were not interested in (the Finnish) President Koivisto, instead we tried to see the birthmark on Gorbachev's forehead. That was the thing to see. The situation was over very quickly compared to the time we had waited for it (Koivunen 2016).

The second and the latest of my written memories is from a conference paper which I wrote for the ASEEES 2017 convention.

It was October 1989. I was nine years old and had just started the third class in elementary school. One day our teacher told us there would be an important visitor to our little town Oulu: the leader of the neighbouring country, Mikhail Gorbachev. The teacher said we could choose either to go down to the centre to see Gorbachev coming to the city hall, or to stay at the school and get one day off later. A few classmates and I decided to go and see what was going to happen around the city hall. I cannot remember too many details, for example, with whom I went there, but I do remember the feeling that something big was happening and the enormous crowd that started to gather behind the ropes dividing the area between the audience and the main scene on the square right in front of the city hall. I had not seen so many people at one place before.

It took some time before the show began. While we were waiting for Gorbachev to arrive on the scene, a couple of Soviet journalists and a cameraman—possibly from Soviet Karelia because they knew Finnish—started to talk with us. I cannot recall exactly what they asked us. I only have a bit of an uncertain memory of us, schoolgirls proclaiming in front of the camera: 'we want Karelia back!', referring to the area Finland had lost to the Soviet Union after the Second World War. I do not remember having been afraid to talk with the representatives of the Soviet media back then, nor do I remember any kind of fear or negative feelings while they supposedly filmed us. I only later realised how risky saying anything like that would have been just a couple of years earlier, before Perestroika began. Finally, big black cars started to flow to the restricted area and we saw the man we had been waiting for. The guy with that thing on his forehead (Koivunen 2017).

The first of these reminiscences was originally in Finnish and meant for my own personal use only. The second one was integrated into a conference paper, talking more generally about the popular perception of Gorbachev's visit.

In these two memory stories, I recall the same event and we can already see variations in how the narrative is constructed and what contextualising elements I have used in the different versions. While in the first version, I had tried to remember as much as I could and as accurately as I could, the second version contains more elements seeking to explain and contextualise the memory for an international audience. For example, I felt that I needed to explain the shout 'We want Karelia back' (or, more precisely, 'Karelia back') within the reminiscence to make its meaning more understandable. Also, I explained why I was not afraid to talk to the Soviet film crew, having later acquired an adult understanding that there were some topics that, perhaps, should not be talked about with Soviet journalists. Moreover, I sought to make the second telling more of a story by adding bridges and comments not included in the collection of fragments and visual glimpses that comprise what I remember of the event.

These additions and contextualising elements aptly demonstrate what many scholars have already pointed out: memory narratives may vary depending on the language, audience, and time; in other words, each telling of a memory can be different (Keightley 2010). The main difference between studying other people's memories and my own is that, when examining my own memory, I can more easily see what is added for the sake of the story and what things, emotions, reflections, and senses I actually recall.

Deconstructing the Memory

When I started to revisit my personal memories of Gorbachev's visit for the purposes of research, the first thing that came to my mind was, why on earth did we go there? Did we really understand what turbulent times we were living in at that time? Did we know how important a figure Gorbachev was, and, if so, what constituted our understanding of his importance? Besides these politically oriented, analytical questions produced by an adult and a researcher, I could not stop wondering with whom I had shared the moment in front of the city hall. Being unable to answer this simple question gave me an unpleasant sense of the limitations and difficulties of consulting my own memory. Was this project worthwhile at all?

While reading and looking at the rich collection of sources I had compiled, I started noticing interesting contradictions. Some small details did not quite match with the flashes I had in my mind. I also received joyful surprises when I found something I had not been able to remember. One of those happy moments of discovery was a film that a friend of mine found through a Russian colleague and sent to me in June 2017. It is a two-part documentary, archived on the website of a Russian film company, about Gorbachev's visit to Finland in 1989. The first part covers his activities in Helsinki, and the second shows his stop in Oulu. In the second part of the film, there is a fleeting moment that, though it lasts no more than one second, contains crucial information. That short clip offers a glimpse of four girls within a huge crowd of people, standing in the front row behind a rope waiting for the Gorbachevs to arrive (Net Film 1990). There we were, three classmates and I, watching the event, unable to imagine that one day this frame of film would end up on something called a website and be accessible to the whole world.

This brief moment in the film gave me a lot of material to compare with my memory and allowed me to expand the story. It resolved the puzzle of which classmates had accompanied me on the day: the short clip revealed their identities by showing their faces. I recognised the other students and was then able to contact them in order to learn more about our shared experience and whether, like me, they considered it something of an adventure.

The film was significant for me in other ways. Until then, I had been remembering and visualising the event from my own perspective. Suddenly, I was able to see it through other eyes, those of the Soviet film crew. The child in my mind who remembered the event instantly acquired a kind of objective existence when she appeared on the film. I was better able to distinguish the child-me from the adult-me, and, in this moment, I allowed myself to become a subject of my research.

Comparing my memory and the short clip enabled me to see, concretely, how memory captures some parts of lived life and ignores others. I assume that the second of the film in which we appear depicts a moment in time that is later than the one that survives in my memory. What I can still visualise happened earlier, the square was not so crowded and it was long before the Gorbachevs arrived on the scene. One can only guess why my memory retained the earlier moment and not the one shown in the film. It may be that unusual and unexpected things are more easily retained in memory than ordinary and predictable moments. Our chat with a Soviet film crew was something spontaneous and singular, whereas waiting for a long time amidst a large crowd of people at such an event was foreseeable and made up of a series of indistinguishable (non)happenings. Consequently, the former is part of my memory, while the latter is not.

The short clip also gave me a feeling of certainty, a small proof that I had indeed been there to see Gorbachev's visit and also confirmed my assumption of our having been filmed by the Soviet crew. It was not merely a child's fantasy or imagination. This proof was not important for me as a researcher, but it was for me as the one remembering and narrating the past. While I was sure I had been there, I still felt relieved that there was another source showing that I was not wrong. Doubts about the authenticity of one's recollections is not uncommon. Almost everyone with whom I talked about their childhood experiences of Gorbachev's visit at some point in the interview mentioned uncertainty about their memories. Some started by saying that they remembered hardly anything, and some even refused to be interviewed because they thought they had nothing to tell (Koivunen 2019b). As an interviewer, I have tried to convince people to tell their stories even if they claim to remember only very little or are not sure if they remember the past correctly. As an interviewee, however, I was suspicious about the authenticity of my own memory. I was not able to avoid this feeling, despite having a scholarly awareness of the limitations of memory and not being interested in authenticity so much as in ways of remembering the past.

One small detail I firmly recalled and was later able to authenticate was that Gorbachev's visit happened on a Friday. This was one of the first details I checked when I started this journey. It was important for me to confirm the day of the week even though, dismissing it as trivial, I never included it in my written memories. The reason why I remembered it as happening on a Friday was that it was the end of the school week, and I connected the event with the feeling of free time and not having to go to school the next day. This timing may also explain why I have no recollection of talking about the visit with my classmates: by the time we next convened in school on Monday, we probably had other things that happened at the weekend to talk about.

In one of the conference papers I gave on this topic, I wrote that seeing the film would probably ruin my memory, that, ever afterwards, I probably could not help imagining the four of us being there together. But actually, the film did not affect me like that. Seeing it neither supplemented nor changed the fragments of memory in my mind. I now know with whom I attended the event and can add this knowledge to my memory narrative, but I still do not remember the classmates in the memory stored in my mind.

Memories in a Dialogue

After discovering who my 'partners in crime' had been, I contacted them and managed to arrange (separate) interviews with two of those three classmates.[2] Interviewing people who had been in the same class, heard the same instructions from the teacher, participated in the same events, and shared the same atmosphere was especially enlightening. Finding the classmates made the project closer to a collective endeavour rather than a lonely journey. I did not engage them in the analysis or writing but dialogues with them widened the possibilities for interpretation and collective remembering.

---

2 The following analysis is based on two interviews that I conducted with the two classmates who were with me in the short clip filmed by the Soviet film crew in October 1989. The interviews were conducted in August 2017, and I deliberately withhold their names to allow them some anonymity, even if this is not entirely possible.

So, what did I find out by interviewing two old classmates? Of course, all three of us told quite different stories with some elements in common. From a memory-studies perspective, this is nothing new or revealing. What was unexpected about studying my classmates' memories in dialogue with my own was that it involved an emotional aspect. As a historian who has worked with memories and experiences before, I knew that people may remember the same moments and lived experiences differently. Still, on an emotional level, I hoped my classmates' stories would confirm my remembered experience. I was especially curious to find out whether they also recalled us shouting 'Karelia back'. As the person remembering, I had a strong emotional attachment to the story, and I wanted this detail, in particular, to be validated as true.

Discussing Gorbachev's visit with different people who were there provided new perspectives and new ideas on what kind of an event it was and could have been. Both the classmates with whom I talked wondered how much deliberate guidance there had been from above to get as many school children as possible to the town centre. According to their memories, our teacher had been clearly in favour of our going and experiencing this momentous event. One of my classmates thought that our teacher underlined the historic significance of the visit and created an atmosphere that made participation seem appealing. I do not remember it like that.

It never occurred to me that we might have been pushed or encouraged to go and see Gorbachev. As I recall, our teacher said we could go or stay at school and those who did not go could get some hours off later. In my second memory from 2017, I wrote that the teacher said there would be an important visitor in our town, but when I (re)visit my memory, there was no such a thing. It is also missing from the first memory narrative, wherein I only refer to the two options offered by the teacher.

Something else that I do not remember but my two classmates do is making little paper flags of Finland and Soviet Union. At first, this appeared to me a minor detail about which I had nothing to say. But as I started to study my own thinking, I found myself doubting whether my classmates were telling the truth (as if 'the truth' even mattered here). I have no memories whatsoever of making those flags, but, then again, I do not remember most of what happened in the past. Still, I feel that I am not entirely convinced of this and am inclined to believe my own memory rather than those of two other people.

Although this is only a minor observation, it gives me a slightly uneasy feeling about how I as a historian evaluate my sources in general and how my relation to the objects and topics studied influences the ways in which I assess the information coming from different sources. I have seen photographs of Gorbachev's visit to Oulu, where schoolchildren and even kindergarten children are waving Soviet and Finnish flags on the streets, so it is possible that we, too, had flags. In the short clip in the Soviet documentary film, however, we do not have flags in our hands. It is common in remembering to combine elements from different times and events that were not actually related. Making flags was so common in elementary schools that it is highly likely that my classmates' memories of making and waving flags are actually related to some other event.

One element of our experiences and memory stories that is partly shared is the presence of the Soviet film crew. Neither of the other two recalled us saying 'Karelia back'. That was, to be honest, a little disappointing for me, since the 'adult I' had hoped to find support for this recollection because it seems such a surprising and somehow incongruous part of the story. It feels disconcerting that I do not remember more profound thoughts or feelings related to saying 'Karelia back' to the journalists, although I am very confident that I did say it. In fact, I believe that the unexpected and 'out of the blue' nature of this glimpse of memory is the very reason why I remember it. It seems implausible, yet something I could not have invented afterwards because it does not make my memory story any more coherent or understandable—quite the contrary.

Moreover, before interviewing the classmates who attended the event with me, I was led by own memory to imagine us as politically conscious students. We could have been aware of the broader context of Gorbachev's visit, especially about the talks about returning those parts of Karelia that Finland ceded to the Soviet Union after World War II. But this was not the case. The interviews with my classmates suggested that we had no recollection of discussions about Karelia, or any other political debate of that time, not to mention the broader framework of the Cold War. Yet, the return of the ceded territory in Karelia was a big issue. Regularly featured in the Finnish media in the late 1980s and early 1990s, it was a topic that a child could easily pick up and relate to the leader of the Eastern neighbour. During my interviews with my classmates, it became clear that each of us only remembered a single political event from early childhood, if anything. For example, one recalled the murder of the Swedish Prime Minister Olof Palme in 1986, an event she had been very curious about. I recalled the execution of Romania's head of state, Nikolae Ceaușescu, and his wife Elena in 1989, because a couple of friends and I included the topic in a recording of 'our own news' program on a cassette. The lost status of Karelia was, thus, not among the topics we were interested in, and it remains a mystery how I happened to recall it in my memory. My classmates, however, remembered the presence of a film crew and the feeling of being filmed. One of them said that she was sure we would end up on the evening news on Finnish television, and the other one said she might have told the people at home that we had been filmed. These mentions confirmed my own memories of the presence of the film crew.

Instead of remembering us as politically alert children, my classmates raised ethical concerns over the political purposes of the event. They asked why children had been encouraged to take part in such a political celebration and pondered whether we had been used as propaganda tools. Neither interviewee recalled having had any negative thoughts about the Soviet Union or even understood the political situation in the world at that time. With the wisdom of hindsight, they thought they had been living in a comfortable bubble, without much knowledge about the world surrounding us. In comparison to myself, my two classmates reflected much more on the historical significance of Gorbachev's visit. They recalled having understood back then how momentous the event had been, one of them mentioning that our teacher had highlighted the event's importance in an attempt to persuade us to go and witness the visit.

What was certainly less historically significant but of sufficient interest to the three of us that we all commented upon it was the best-known visual characteristic of the Soviet leader. We all knew who

Gorbachev was and we could recognise him by the birthmark on his forehead, or the 'spot on his head', as one of my classmates put it. The other one recalled him as 'the relaxed chap, who had a large nevus'. I boldly called the birthmark 'a thing' in my memory stories and noted that we had seen it.

After revisiting my narrated memories and the stored memory in my mind dozens of times and looking through numerous photographs produced by Finnish media houses, I came to the conclusion that this part of my story was not based on stored memory but was an element constructed by my adult mind. When writing my first memory story in 2016, I probably assumed that we must have been interested in seeing Gorbachev's birthmark because, as children, it was among those few things we knew about and associated with Gorbachev. It is also likely that I mentioned seeing the famous birthmark because it could authenticate my story, serving as proof that the person we had seen was really and truly Mikhail Gorbachev. Moreover, I may have wanted to add it for the sake of the story. Seeing the main star makes a nice climax, and using a visual symbol adds more to it. And, of course, it is possible that we actually had seen his birthmark. However, I do not remember the moment of seeing Gorbachev at all. There is no trace of seeing the man in my stored memory. Furthermore, in all the photos taken in front of the city hall, Gorbachev is wearing a hat. In all probability, we could not have seen his forehead and the famous mark.

For the purposes of studying memories in general, it does not actually matter if we saw Gorbachev's birthmark or not. What matters is that I wrote that way and made the past meaningful to myself by mentioning the birthmark. In this chapter, it is, nonetheless, worth noting the discrepancy between my recollections and other sources because it is relevant to the use of one's own memory in research. Because I have had the privilege of revisiting the memory in my mind to check if I remember the things as I committed them to paper, I have been able to identify those parts of my narratives that are more likely constructions introduced to comply with methods of storytelling. Studying one's own memories enables us to dig much deeper into human experience and the process of remembering than other types of sources; it illuminates the ways in which the mind makes connections between the lived past and the narrated past in the present.

Conclusion

In October 1989, on a Friday afternoon, the nine-year-old girl went home. She did not know it at the time, but the memories of this occasion lived on to eventually become an inspiration for her work. It would, however, take more than twenty years for her to even mention it to anyone (or that is how she remembers it) and more than twenty-seven years before she would start exploring the event that left traces in her memory.

Working with my own memory has been a rewarding, surprising, and instructive adventure. It has taught me about the mechanisms of memory and narration but also about the affective aspects of individual memory. This little experiment has shown me how powerful a tool memory can be and how it can generate so much new knowledge when activated, encouraged, and put into dialogue with other sources. It has also demonstrated how close we can be to our research topics even if not studying our own memories. When studying the contemporary world or recent history, scholars are, in many ways, embroiled and entangled with their subjects. Irrespective of the nature of the sources, a researcher cannot entirely distance herself from the research subject nor from the ways in which she or he explores it.

After deconstructing my memory stories and recognising the little additions which had entered my stories to make them narratively coherent, what remained was a few fragments. I remember that the visit happened on a Friday. I have a visual memory of us standing behind the rope and talking with the Soviet film crew. I do not remember with whom I was there, but I do remember having said 'Karelia back'. I remember wondering whether we would end up in the film or not. I remember that we waited for Gorbachev to come. I remember black cars, but I have no visual memory of seeing him.

These fragments may seem useless, marginal, and totally insignificant. However, without these tiny fragments I might have never become interested in the Cold War, state visits, and

Gorbachev, not to mention the scholarly works on Gorbachev's visit. Of course, I might have developed this interest anyway, but it is hardly a coincidence that a person who has experienced an event writes articles and organises an exhibition about it. Moreover, these fragments become extremely powerful when put together with others' memories and other types of sources. By collating my own memory with other sources on the same event, it became possible to locate discontinuities—places where memory ended and the story was continued with the help of imagination, reasoning, additional knowledge or collective memory. Together they form a much richer and denser picture of the past and can produce knowledge that would not otherwise have come to light. Instead of failing to capture the authenticity of the past, memory keeps the past alive through the people who narrate their memories in a way they find important and meaningful at that moment.

In this experiment I acted in two roles—those of observer and observed—which made the process very different from the usual research work I do. At times, it was difficult to separate those roles and to know whether it was the observer or the observed who was reacting and reflecting. This difficulty could probably be overcome by working only with narrated (written or oral) memory stories, but I very much wanted to analyse what was happening in my mind even if the two roles were sometimes bewildering and confused. My confusion became evident in the reactions and reflections that I noticed during the process, some of which were quite contrary to my scholarly training. An unexpected outcome of the study was the strong emotional attachment that I discovered I feel towards the fragments of my memory. Besides a general curiosity to know more, I approached the interviews with my two classmates with an expectation of finding confirmation for some parts of my own story. Although I had worked with memories and experiences before and knew that people remember past events differently, I still expected confirmation from them that the things I remembered had happened and were meaningful for them, too. I have also noted how, as a result of the long process of revisiting my memory, my story has become more important and more meaningful to me than it was before the memory was activated and I started to work with it.

In terms of the mechanism of memory and narration, this experiment has enabled me to see beyond the articulated memory. When working with others' memories, we are always working with the verbal and narrated forms of memory without access to the memory in mind, the fragments, flashbacks, recollections as they are before they are told to others in the form of a narrative. Exploring my own memory and comparing the written memory stories with the fragments in my mind allowed me to see how the non-verbal material is translated into a coherent story through narrativising and contextualising (see Keightley 2010). Each time of (re)telling the story, it takes a different shape depending on the audience, the cultural and social environment, and the political climate. The experiment also showed that it is not only the narrated memory that changes. I noticed that when challenging the memory with other sources (interviews, newspaper articles, photographs, etc.) new parts of the memory were activated; I could remember things that, earlier, I had not.

Finally, this chapter shows how our interest in knowledge production is related to our pasts, our experiences, and our memories. The urge to know and study comes from somewhere; it is situated in various larger and smaller moments in our lives, some of which we might forget for years until they find the right moment and are revived.

References

Abrams, L. (2010). *Oral History Theory*. London: Routledge, https://doi.org/10.4324/9780203849033

Anderson, L. (2006). 'Analytic Autoethnography'. *Journal of Contemporary Ethnography*, 35(4), 373–95, https://doi.org/10.1177/0891241605280449

Arnold-de Simine, S., and Radstone, S. (2013). 'The GDR and the Memory Debate'. *Remembering and Rethinking the GDR: Multiple Perspectives and Plural Authenticities*, ed. by Anna Saunders and Debbie Pinfold. Springer, https://doi.org/10.1057/9781137292094_2

Aunesluoma, J., and Rainio-Niemi, J. (2016). 'Neutrality as Identity? Finland's Quest for Security in the Cold War'. *Journal of Cold War Studies*, 18(4), 51–78, https://doi.org/10.1162/JCWS_a_00680

Eiranen, R. (2015). 'The Narrative Self: Letters and Experience in Historical Research'. *Private and Public Voices: An Interdisciplinary Approach to Letters and Letter Writing*, ed. by Karin Koehler and Kathryn McDonal-Miranda. Interdisciplinary Press

Gannon, S. (2017). 'Autoethnography', in *Oxford Research Encyclopedia of Education*. Oxford: Oxford University Press, pp. 1–21, https://doi.org/10.1093/acrefore/9780190264093.013.71

Kalela, J. (2012). *Making History. The Historian and the Uses of the Past*. Palgrave Macmillan.

Kaitasuo, P. (2019). 'Muistatko, kun Gorba kävi kylässä ja koululaiset tervehtivät vierasta kaupungintalon portailla?' [Do You Remember when Gorby Visited Oulu and School Children Welcomed the Guest in Front of the City Hall?]. *Kaleva*, 24 February, https://www.kaleva.fi/muistatko-kun-gorba-kavi-kylassa-ja-koululaiset-te/1732216

Keightley, E. (2010). 'Remembering Research: Memory and Methodology in the Social Sciences'. *International Journal of Social Research Methodology*, 13(1), 55–70, https://doi.org/10.1080/13645570802605440

Koivunen, P. (2016). 'Gorbatshovin vierailu Ouluun 1989—mitä muistan?' [Unpublished memory]. Written 29 June

—— (2017). 'I Wanted to See the Leader of the USSR—Oral Histories of Gorbachev's State Visit to Finland in 1989'. [Conference Presentation]. Association for Slavonic East European and Eurasian Studies annual convention, Chicago, USA, https://www.aseees.org/convention/2017-theme

—— (2019a). 'Gorba tulee, oletko valmis?' [Gorby is Coming, are you Ready?]. Exhibition announcement. Museum and Science centre Luuppi. Oulu, Finland, https://www.ouka.fi/oulu/luuppi/gorba-tulee

—— (2019b). Gorbatšovin Suomen-vierailu lasten silmin [Gorbachev's visit to Finland through the eyes of children]. *Idäntutkimus*, 26(4), 18–36, https://doi.org/10.33345/idantutkimus.88846

—— (2022). 'Neuvostoliiton uudet kasvot. Mihail Gorbatšovin vuoden 1989 Suomen-vierailu muistoissa' [The New Face of the USSR. Mikhail Gorbachev's Visit to Finland in 1989 in Collective Memory], in *Neuvostoliitto muistoissa ja mielikuvissa* [Remembered and Imagined Soviet Union], ed. by A. Helle and P. Koivunen. Finnish Literature Society, https://doi.org/10.21435/skst.1480

'Mihail ja Matti Oulussa' [Mihail and Matti in Oulu] (1989). *Liitto*. 28 October

Miettunen, K. M. (2014). 'Muistelu historiantutkimuksen haasteena ja mahdollisuutena' [Remembrance as a Challenge and Opportunity for Historical Research], in *Muisti*, ed. by Jani Hakkarainen, Mirja Haartimo, and Jaana Virta. Tampere University Press, pp. 167–77

Millei, Z., Silova, I., and Gannon, S. (2022). 'Thinking Through Memories of Childhood in (Post) Socialist Spaces: Ordinary Lives in Extraordinary

Times. *Children's Geographies*, 20(3), 324–37, https://doi.org/10.1080/14733 285.2019.1648759

Portelli, A. (1998). 'What Makes Oral History Different?', in *The Oral History Reader*, ed. by R. Perkis and A. Thomson. Routledge, pp. 63–74

Ritvanen, J. M. (2021), *Mureneva kulmakivi: Suomi, Neuvostoliiton hajoaminen ja YYA-sopimuksen loppuvaiheet 1989–1992* [Crumbling Cornerstone: Finland, the Disintegration of the Soviet Union and the Final Phase of the FCMA Treaty 1989–1992]. Annales Universitatis Turkuensis, University of Turku

Silova, I., Piattoeva, N., and Millei, Z. (2018). Childhood and Schooling in (Post) Socialist Societies. *Memories of Everyday Life*. Palgrave Macmillan, https://doi.org/10.1007/978-3-319-62791-5

'Sinitakit tuskailivat kun Oulu hullaantui' [Policemen Were in Trouble as the City of Oulu Went Crazy] (1989). *Uusi Suomi*. 28 October

Vizit M. S. Gorbacheva v Finliandiiu. Tsentral'naia studiia dokumental'nykh filmov (1990). Net Film, https://www.net-film.ru/film-9805/

Winkler, I. (2018). 'Doing Autoethnography: Facing Challenges, Taking Choices, Accepting Responsibilities'. *Qualitative Inquiry*, 24(4), 236–47, https://doi.org/10.1177/1077800417728956

Rua Liga Dos Comunistas[1]

José Cossa

They had just moved to the city because black Mozambicans could not live in the city before independence, but there was a new government. The earliest episode he remembers must have been when he was 4 years old, going to 5. He woke up very early as usual, perhaps around 5:30 AM, and was very excited about going out on the street, at sunrise, with his family to join the rest of the neighbors in cleaning their street named as Rua Dr. Ângelo Ferreira. He lived with his mom, dad, three siblings (he was the youngest of two boys and one elder sister), his aunt and uncle and their 10-year-old daughter, a cousin, and his paternal grandmother. He remembers carrying a broom and noticing that everyone else also carried one and this made him feel as being a part of something big and important; something that even adults were a part of. He was among the youngest children, one of the smallest bodies on the street that day, so he and other children carried child-sized brooms. This was different from where they lived before and sweeping a tarred street was different from sweeping an unpaved sand road also.

He remembers the campaigns to mobilize people to get up and clean the streets and the rationale that cleaning was their responsibility because the streets were theirs now. Yes, there was a municipality service responsible for cleaning the streets and they did clean the streets, but there was an additional responsibility expected of the citizens of a newly independent nation. The kids, the boy and his friends, even re-named their street, 'rua liga dos comunistas' (communists' league road) to counter the colonial name, 'rua dr. Ângelo Ferreira.' Anyway, he has no idea who came up with the idea, but they all agreed that such was a

---

1   This is a childhood memory produced as part of the Reconnect/Recollect project discussed in the introduction to this book.

suitable name. It didn't last long and was never made official, even though the kids painted the name on the sides of the street pavement/sidewalk.

He remembers that they would all wake up early and go to the streets with brooms and everyone seemed enthusiastic about the task, although in hindsight there might have been some discontent folk. The boy's street used to be very clean then and he has no idea when this mobilization and action ended, but it was still during Samora Machel's time (the first president of independent Mozambique). He was very fond of Samora and still is; he doesn't think there will be a better president with such a commitment to the country.

The boy remembers also watching people march on the streets as they were on their way to the farms in Gaza province (he was in Maputo, the capital city, and Gaza is the next province north) to harvest rice and how enthusiastic people seemed as they marched and sang. He is not sure if they went by bus, trains, or planes, but he knows they went and he knows some family members went too, but he cannot recall if both his parents or just one of them went. This was an adults-only affair. The boy holds these memories fondly because he remembers that when both the cleaning and the harvesting were no longer a thing, he started seeing dirty roads and heard that the rice was being exported to other places or not produced at all. He started seeing some garbage accumulated in various parts of the city (and became worse after Machel died and never seemed to get better) and they started eating rice from other countries, some of which felt like eating plastic because they were used to eating their home grown organic rice. Community work was important back then and people seemed to have clarity as to why they needed to work together for the country. They had cleaning days in school (kids loved it because they could hangout after school. They still got the job done because they had teachers supervising and motivating them to complete the tasks. The teachers set them examples by working with them. It was such a fun time!

3. Passing Bye

Hanna Trampert

This chapter retells an autobiographical journey of Hanna Trampert, an artist who was born in Poland during the Cold War but frequently visited her family members in the Eastern borderlands of Germany. Growing up in a divided world, the themes of borders, freedom, and fear have accompanied Hanna throughout her life and have also been reflected in her artwork. This chapter is a reflection on Hanna's work since 2019. Inspired by her participation in the Reconnect/Recollect project, it focuses on the theme of connection(s). The experience of working with childhood memories has created an opportunity to see—and make visible—the existing connections and entanglements that have always existed despite walls and borders.

My parents come from the Eastern borderlands of Germany, a territory lost to the Soviet Union after World War II. In the 1950s, my parents emigrated to Gdynia on the Baltic Sea in Poland, where I was born in 1963. Most of my family stayed behind the border, and we visited them every year. These journeys were associated with complicated procedures: applying for invitations and passports, standing in line, enduring long daytime and nighttime train journeys with frightening border controls. The visits to the beloved grandma and aunts were very warm, but they were also very demanding. The towns and villages looked unlike Baltic Poland, the smells and the dishes were different from those at home, and many women wore headscarves. There was so much to watch and observe. Although I did not dare to speak in the foreign language, I learned Russian passively on these visits and, later, in school, I already knew everything taught in language lessons. In socialist Poland, my father was a party member and often told us that silence was golden, that it was best not to say anything outside of home. In 1986, the borders were closed, and travelling to the West became illegal. The theme of borders, freedom, and fear have since accompanied me and have also been reflected in my artwork.

My participation in the Reconnect/Recollect memory workshops in Berlin and their interest in childhood memories set something in motion that caused a change in my thinking about boundaries. I have noticed that not only is silence golden but so, too, is talking. Both the narration and sharing of the small, seemingly unimportant moments from my childhood and the showing of the memorabilia during the workshop produced an outgrowth echoed in my paintings.

The mood in many of my earlier works might be described as one of being 'behind the wall'. In the new works created after the workshop in Berlin, the theme of connection(s) began to play a role and was reflected in a different mood. I see new relationships with myself and others. Being part of a group caused the walls to fall away and new communities and dialogues to emerge in their place. In some pictures, this shift is reflected in the childlike lightness, the beauty of nature, and the tangible quality of light-heartedness. I was able to participate in this project as a non-English speaker, for which I am grateful. This new experience showed me that it is possible to belong despite a language barrier. With the help of interpreters and translators, I have become a part of this project, and my paintings speak for themselves. Here I show some examples of my works from 2019 onwards.

Fig. 3.1 Hanna Trampert, *Was uns verbindet*, 2019, 80×60 cm.

The first artwork of the project Reconnect/Recollect was created after our initial, online exchange of childhood memories. It is an assemblage with ball bearings that symbolise a movable and smooth connection with other countries and continents. At this early point, I already felt part of this far-reaching program. My signature logo on the artwork—the girl's face—is one of these connections.

Fig. 3.2 Hanna Trampert, *Travel in Space and Time*, 2019, 100×100 cm.

This artwork was created based on the memory workshops in Berlin, and it tells about our meeting, our stories, and our memories. The piece is a collage made with my old stamps and my photos of Gdynia, Vilnius, and the trains. It captures the journeys, the connections, the tracks, the faces. Maybe you see the tunnel that appears in the ghost-train story and the light when you leave the tunnel. The history of the train was told by the GDR historian Anja Werner and the West Berlin social anthropologist Sarah Fichtner (see Chapter 15). The image has its dynamics, has many layers of experience, is circular, like recurring memories, like the time clock. Part of the red colour in the image stores the light during the day and glows at night. This is a symbol of the memory project: it is a form or process that makes old memories visible.

Fig. 3.3 Hanna Trampert, *End of the Day*, 50×100 cm.

Women and children form a small community walking at sunset. The piece has a cheerful mood and light colours.

Fig. 3.4 Hanna Trampert, *Together*, 2019, 70×90 cm.

84   (An)Archive: Childhood, Memory, and the Cold War

Together (Figure 3.4) is the cover picture for my exhibition 'Expedition Mensch', which took place in 2020 at the Catholic Family Education Center Ehrang e. V. I felt the need to represent physical contact, the touching of people's hands.

Fig. 3.5 Hanna Trampert, *Memory 1*, 2020, 100×100 cm.

As if in a vehicle or a boat, memories are on the move. They are subject to constant transformation, especially when they get to the surface. Connections build up and collapse. In the background, there is a quiet person who is remembering and contemplating. She has a benevolent look, a smile. The colours here are fresh and intense, matching how children see and experience the world. Many colourful objects cause the picture to look closed and all-encompassing at the same time. Viewers have the impression of passing by, of flowing, as well as of going into the depths. Maybe it is the world, the continents connected by blue waters, or maybe a river or sea journey? 'It's a psychological painting of the unconscious,' Zsuzsa Millei reflected.

Fig. 3.6 Hanna Trampert, *Memory 2*, 2020, 100×100 cm.

This piece represents the brain's building of memory pathways or the subconscious. It also describes the human experience in the twenty-first century of changing time.

Fig. 3.7 Hanna Trampert, *The Girl with the Balloon 1*, 2020, 70×90 cm.

The act of giving childhood an importance, a justification, has a very special and significant impact on adult life. This is what happened for me in the Reconnect/Recollect workshop: something changed and continues to change so that I feel as light as a balloon.

Fig. 3.8 Hanna Trampert, *The Girl by the Sea*, 2020, 70×90 cm.

Here, it is as if the girl is going back to the Baltic Sea, to where her migration from Poland began. The water beckons benevolently towards us or towards itself. In the eddies, different times of day on the sea are visible.

Fig. 3.9 Hanna Trampert, *The Girl with the Balloon 2*, 2020, 70×90 cm.

In *The Girl with the Balloon 2* (Figure 3.9), the girl is older. She is relaxed and her gaze follows the balloon, which floats far in the sky over the Baltic Sea.

Fig. 3.10 Hanna Trampert, *Friends 3*, 2021, 50×60 cm.

Here, people are depicted in nature. They are connected by the thread, helping each other. This work, as all of my work, was created intuitively. It represents my good experiences with the Reconnect/Recollect project. Helpfulness and openness pass from one person to another like a rope.

Fig. 3.11 Hanna Trampert, *Self-Portrait*, 2021, 50×60 cm.

This, the last picture inspired by the Reconnect/Recollect project, was created shortly before the conference in Berlin in which I participated. The woman (me) faces the same direction as the viewer, and a connection is created: me and the viewer are now a 'we'. As my view wanders from the west to east, it ponders history and the neighboring countries; it crosses borders. The symbolic blue surface dissolves, becomes water. Moments and memories of childhood fly over my shoulder. Temporal and spatial separations cease to exist.

Breakfast Across Borders[1]

Stefanie Weiss

She goes down a stone staircase. She wears pink pajamas, shorts with a shirt, and has long hair. The light enters the room through the dining room window on the left side, the living room area and the stone fireplace are still in darkness. The floor is almost black. She turns right and then again to the right and enters the kitchen, which is large and wide. The sun begins to enter through the window above the sink. The stove is at the bottom of the kitchen. There is a long L-shaped bar covered with tiles painted with blue birds, in the middle a wooden table. Her place is the one with the wall behind, she does not like the open space behind her. She approaches the cupboard under the left side of the stove, takes out a blue pewter pitcher to boil water, from the top drawer takes a thermos can that her mother brought on the return trip from Germany, which they left after the German grandmother died. Then she goes to the big cupboard in the shape of a triangle and takes out a coffee filter from a green and red cardboard box that says Melita. She opens the top drawer again, takes out a white porcelain filter that has stripes inside and at the bottom has been dyed with the color of coffee. She puts the porcelain filter on top of the white thermos can from which she already had removed the lid, puts the Melita filter inside the porcelain filter that belongs to the grandmother and is one of the things they carried across the sea. She brings coffee from the cupboard, which is in a can of Lebkuchen. She likes the smell when she opens the can. Then she pours five tablespoons in the filter. Now she goes to one of the drawers and takes out four oval wicker tablecloths, puts one on each side of the round table, mom's place, brother's place, dad's place and her own place. She takes out four medium plates of the Cornieware dishes that her mother bought in San Antonio Texas and that 'does not break'.

---

1   This is a childhood memory produced as part of the Reconnect/Recollect project discussed in the introduction to this book.

The plates have a green line that goes around the edge and then is surrounded by small flowers; now she takes out four coffee plates from the same tableware and puts them on the upper right side of the plate in each place, then goes for the cups and puts them on top of the coffee plates. Now she takes out four forks, four knives and four small teaspoons. Meanwhile, her mother has gone down, they greeted each other, kissed each other on the cheek. She felt her mother's large, warm chest in the hug. Her mother has begun to prepare machaca with egg. For that, she is cutting onions into strips, then putting them to fry in the pan and it smells great. After that, the mother is threading the dried meat they bought last time they went to visit the grandparents in Monterrey. The meat was bought at a greenhouse in the great-grandmother's village where the meat hung from a clothesline. The brother comes down and says hello, he sees what each one is doing and starts to chop a melon. The door of the house opens, it is her father who comes in with a smile and a bag of bread. He takes out a basket and puts the bolillos and sweet bread in there. The water is boiling now. This is what this family does every weekend, they can change roles in preparing breakfast, but they will maintain this breakfast get-together as an important thing across borders.

4. The Other Side of the Curtain?
Troubling Western Memories of (Post)socialism

Erica Burman

I interrogate my historical and current positionings in this chapter by recalling memories of growing up during the Cold War but on the other (Western) side of the so-called Iron Curtain. Focused on a specific example from my minoritised but otherwise quite privileged background in the north of England, I explore what returns to me now as either topicalised or occluded by, presumably, the cultural-political construction of the Cold-War period that dominated my own place and time. Specifically, I attempt to retrieve my memories of what I knew and understood about the 'Save Soviet Jewry' campaign in the 1970s, and consider what it these might indicate about how now-former Soviet and allied communist countries were perceived. During this process, I encounter memorial gaps and obstacles and address the temptation to fill these in and to elaborate upon my recollections from my current geopolitical, chronological, and biographical position. What emerges is the impossibility of 'looking back' without also reflecting on the 'now' and how it shapes the perspective from which the review takes place.

My prior interests in the geopolitical contextualisation of children and childhood, especially via the approach I have called 'Child as method' (Burman 2019a and 2019b), were what initially led the research team devising the Post-socialist Childhoods project to involve me in its proposal and design from an early stage. It has engaged and fascinated me ever since. While convinced from the outset of the relevance and significance of the project even then, what has been less clear (to me, as perhaps also other participants in the project) is how I am positioned in relation to it.

This chapter is the outcome of my exploration of this positioning. I see this question of my relationship to the project as (auto)biographical and historical as well as general and particular, since my singular subjectivity must reflect wider sociocultural features past and present, even if it is not absolutely determined by these. Further, this personal-political history necessarily interpellates, as well as is interpellated by, my narrative-accounting process here. This piece of writing takes the form of a memoir but also (I hope) offers some analytical reflections on the conceptual-political issues set in play by such accounting processes. I also use it to instantiate, or respond to, calls to decolonise subjective as well as material practices by interrogating a small enactment of received hegemonic stories of the Cold War within my own childhood, which was lived in a (capitalist) 'Western' country as opposed to a (state socialist, or 'communist') 'Eastern' one.

Whether this effort succeeds in disidentifying with the normative positionings associated with my context is a question I must leave to the reader, alongside whether such a project is, indeed, possible. At the very least, I hope this chapter illustrates some indicative disjunctures between the individual and sociopolitical 'border thinking' of the kind called for by feminist commentators who have drawn on postcolonial debates specifically to explore post-socialist conditions (Tlostanova et al. 2016; Gržinić et al. 2020). My aim, moreover, is to contribute to an awareness of how the Cold War figures within other, both earlier and contemporaneous, colonial dynamics, thereby highlighting the relevance of the third element that Chen (2010) identifies in his key postcolonial cultural-studies text *Asia as Method*: after decolonisation and de-imperialisation, we must 'De-Cold War'.

While working with the Post-socialist Childhoods project, I have wondered much about how and where the Cold War appeared in my childhood. I was born in 1960 and, so, grew up during its peak period (so to speak). Therefore, the analytical starting point must be the question of 'how', rather than 'whether', it impacted on my childhood. In addition to identifying overt references and events, the task here is one of excavating normalised assumptions that have been naturalised into absence, into the social unconscious (as group analysts put it (see Hopper 2003; Dalal 2001)), or into what might have been called, in less poststructuralist or postmodern days (or, in Marxist terms), 'ideology'.

This point also prompts me to speak of another commitment, one shared (I think) with others on the project team. I sought to bring a socialist as well as a feminist consciousness to bear on the project material, including, here, on my own memories and memorial-accounting processes. The current context of late, racial capitalism (Bhattacharrya 2018) proclaims that this system has won, that 'there is no alternative', even as its necropolitics produces new disposable labour forces (from and in Eastern Europe, Asia, and Africa). Formerly communist states, notably Russia, are hurtling into what Gržinić et al. (2020) aptly call 'turbo capitalism'. The search for new markets and goods to extract and exploit, both within and beyond national borders, seems endless.

Yet, I do believe there are alternatives, both current and to be forged in the future, as there have also been at some earlier historical moments—even as I have no illusions about state-socialist practices of the past. After all, socialism cannot be practised in one country and so, in the context of the stranglehold of the West, it was perhaps unsurprising that so-called socialist countries (as also many other countries across the world) slid into nationalism and, from thence, into authoritarianism. In making this point I am in no way sanitising or exonerating the evils of Stalinism, its physical and psychological regime of brutality, terror, and oppression. But, just as the Post-socialist Childhoods project has generated an anarchive of 'memory stories', tracing the diverse as well as myriad ways the Cold War entered into and configured the participants' childhoods, so too must my exploration confront how the context of my childhood under Western capitalist conditions structured and reflected contemporary assumed meanings of the 'East'.

I am conscious of the claim, often repeated in discussions of antiracist or decolonial practice, that no one seems to inhabit the position of the oppressor. So, let me say now that, as a child of the West, I clearly have benefited from the (demise of the) Cold War, even as I feel repugnance at the neocolonialism, and the intensifications of and inventions of new forms of racism, this has enabled. Yet, if intersectionality is taken as a starting point, then complexities, conflicts, and contradictions must be at play—at the level of subjectivity as also within political economy—that can, perhaps, form the basis for a renewed politics of engagement. Just as no one is entirely a 'victim', no one ever only inhabits a position of dominance, even as the privileged consequences of such positioning must not be forgotten or displaced.

In particular, as children, we have all been helpless and dependent on others. How we have dealt with those experiences—which must include terrible fear and anxiety—is a moot political point, however. This is the point Fanon (1958/2008) makes at the opening and closing of *Black Skin, White Masks*: that the 'tragedy' of the adult is shaped in childhood. Nevertheless, he understood that we can transform even the most negative or traumatic of childhood experiences through deliberative reflection and action. Solidarity and collective action is forged via recognition of and identification with the oppression of others. So, my attempt here is to unearth, bring to the fore, both complicities and resistances but also to stay with the sense of uncertain, partial, and absent knowledge.

A Significant Aside

As already mentioned, I have struggled to recall specific instances or tangible examples of how the Cold War impacted in consciously experienced ways on my childhood. I must assume, therefore, that these impacts are structured into other classed, gendered, and racialised incitements, experiences, and sedimentations. Only one material instance has come to mind, and so I will run with this and see where it leads.

But let me first set out the frame. I grew up in Liverpool, within a small Jewish community. By the 1960s, Liverpool was no longer the great English port it once had been and, notwithstanding the Beatles and football, was a poor and declining city. Its real heyday was during slavery, when the port was a major transport point (see, for example, Williams 2013), though as a child I did not know about that. The port location was important though, as the point of my family's arrival to the UK. Both of my grandfathers were first-generation immigrants to Britain, coming in the 1890–1920 period when many Jews from Eastern Europe arrived on boats in search of a better life, and to escape from poverty and pogroms, that is, economic and political persecution. They, like the desperate Syrians, Afghanis, Kurds, and Somalis who now risk— and often lose—their lives crossing the English Channel in tiny rubber dinghies, were fleeing from oppression but would have been classified formally as economic migrants. As my dear dead friend and comrade, the immigration lawyer Steve Cohen, put it: 'It's the same old story' (1987). Moreover, until Brexit, many Eastern Europeans continued to come to the UK as economic migrants once European borders opened for business with the so-called 'free movement' of labour.

I say my family came from 'Eastern Europe', rather than being more specific, because, like many Ashkenazi Jews,[1] my grandparents and their families had lived in the region at a time when the borders between Lithuania, Belarus, Ukraine, Poland, and Russia were in flux. Of course, this heritage nuances my engagement with the Post-socialist Childhoods project in various ways. Moreover, while both my grandmothers were British-born, their parents had also come from similar regions. Had my grandfathers not migrated then, it is likely that I would either have grown up under state socialism or else—depending on how my forebears had fared during Nazi occupation of these countries and the Nazi industrial-scale genocide of Jews—not have been born at all. This latter scenario undoubtedly coloured the political context of my childhood, since I was surrounded by migrants and the children of migrants, including direct refugees from Nazism. Their constant refrain

---

1   Jews are typically identified into two main categories: Ashkenazim refers to Jews originating from Central and Eastern Europe, and Sephardim to those originating from Spain, Portugal, and North Africa. A more recent term, Mizrahim, usually now designates Jews of non-European background, including those from the Middle East, Africa, and further east. There are other named Jewish communities, including Georgian and Mountain Jews, and Bene Israel Jews from India. Shifts in designations and categorisations are due, in part, to the massive migration and displacement of Jews after the Second World War, as well as to the advent of the State of Israel and its immigration policies.

was 'It couldn't happen here' and 'how wonderful Britain is', but this sentiment was also interestingly tempered by an insistence that 'the British are so slow and cold-blooded that we would have time to escape if things got bad…'. So, maybe not so wonderful, but Britain was at least safe—for the time being.

Safety and security were, therefore, provisional and discretionary. The dominant narrative, then, was the typical one of the grateful immigrant who can pass for white in white-dominant societies: don't cause trouble, don't draw attention to yourself, don't stand out as different. (It is worth recalling that, during the Second World War, many Jewish refugees from Nazism were treated as enemy aliens in Britain and interned in camps, often alongside Nazis. So, fear of standing out, of being noticeable, can be said to have had some basis.) This extended into religious practice, wherein, to this day, a prayer for the British Royal Family is said at each of the morning, afternoon, and evening services, as written into the 'authorised' prayer book used by all mainstream Orthodox synagogues (or what in the US is called the United Synagogue Jewish movement of Ashkenazi communities), and the US version has an equivalent Presidential/Congressional prayer. This prayer-performance of loyalty to the British state was, it should be noted, also accompanied by a prayer for the State of Israel (later versions also included the Israeli Defence Forces), and, unlike many other prayers, each were recited in both Hebrew and English. As Sarna (1998) notes in relation to US Jewry (but addressing a longer and more widespread phenomenon), these texts clearly indicate a longstanding and important political history; the inclusion of such secular devotional inscriptions into services practised by Jewish communities across the world dates from at least the seventeenth century.[2]

---

2   Sarna writes, 'The practice of praying for the welfare of the sovereign was common not only in Antiquity but also in mediaeval Christendom and Islam. Jewish prayers nevertheless stand out as expressions of minority group insecurity. In one case, for example, Jews added to their prayers a special plea for "all of the Muslims who live in our country". Another Jewish prayer book contains a special blessing for the welfare of the Pope.' (p. 206) Tracing the vicissitudes of the canonical prayer to the (American) state from its inception in the mid-seventeenth century onwards, he also addresses how the prayers reflected and accommodated to the establishment of the State of Israel: 'As so often before, so too here, liturgy sheds light on an issue of central importance to American Judaism: the immensely sensitive political and moral question of how to balance national loyalty with devotion to Zion' (p. 223).

Here, then, was a prime exemplar of the dual-ideological structuring of mainstream Anglo-Jewish identity. Oriented around compliance and obedience to the British state, these prayers also enacted a performance of concern around the State of Israel. The latter, during my childhood, was seen as a metaphorical place of safety, or perhaps for curious visits, as much as for migration. Indeed, those contemporaries and friends who made *Aliyah*—those who, literally, 'went up' to go and live in Israel— were looked upon by the community as misguided if not deranged, and usually as 'losers' who had nothing better to do. This attitude was reflected in the practice of sending off children who had not achieved well at school to Israel for a year or more: a 'gap year' of expedience.

Now I find myself perplexed and distracted from my original theme. Surely, this chapter, on my relationship to the Cold War, is not the place to enter into greater detail about the changing relationship British Jewish communities have had with Israel and Zionism? And yet, it seems one colonialism casts its shadow over another.[3] I must return to the present for a moment to note, first, that British Jewish communities' current (presumed) support of the apartheid State of Israel is a recent historical phenomenon. Second, the British Board of Deputies, the self-appointed political 'representatives' (i.e., not at all 'representative') of the (presumed monolithic) British Jewish community, were initially opposed to the Balfour Declaration which first proposed a Jewish state in historic Palestine. They objected on the grounds that such a state might undermine the political position of British Jews by appearing to divide or reduce their loyalty to Britain. This was of a piece with the ways the Jewish elites (some of them Sephardis long settled in the UK) were, at that time, attempting to socialise the newly arriving 'Ostjuden' (Eastern European Jews) by encouraging them to look and sound as

---

3   This chapter was first drafted in 2020, long before the current (at the time of going to press, early 2024) now already months- long bombardment of Gaza by the Israeli state and its armed forces (alongside acts of terror, mass arrests, and the demolition of houses and institutions in the West Bank). I hope its exploration of the emergence, contingency, and variability of British Jewry's Zionist commitments may work to help understanding of how and why such commitments may remain, even as also of how they could change. Equally, the current configuration of Euro-US power in supporting the Israeli state, even in suppressing calls for a ceasefire and—as I write this—attempting to silence calls for Palestinian solidarity, should be read in the context of misguided responses to historical complicities within the Nazi genocide of Jews.

English as possible. Their methods included disallowing the speaking of Yiddish in the Jewish schools and requiring Yiddish first names to be changed into English upon arrival (Burman, personal communication 2021; Williams 1985).[4]

Why do I have to say this? Because somehow these points have acquired greater focus as I have worked with these ideas. The key point is that, in my early to middle childhood, the political movement of Zionism was really quite remote to mainstream British Jewish community life.[5] I feel I can say this with some authority, as, when I joined a Zionist youth group at age nine, I recall encountering a great deal of suspicion and bemusement at my passionate engagement. This was before the 1967 war had really made an impact on the collective psyche of the Jewish community. Such youth groups were exhibitions of what Hakim (2012) calls 'Popular Zionism', that is, 'primarily a (highly charged) affective disposition practised on the planes of everyday life, pop cultural consumption and cultural identity' rather than some informed political commitments or analysis (p. 302).[6] Clearly, there is much to be said

---

4   The categories of black and white were and remain much at play within Jewish communities, as well as between Jewish and black communities. This is because black Jews and many Sephardic Jews encounter racism on the basis of skin colour inside as well as outside the communities. In April 2021, a 'landmark' report acknowledging this issue was published by the British Board of Deputies: https://www.bod.org.uk/bod-news/board-of-deputies-publishes-landmark-report-on-racial-inclusivity-in-the-jewish-community/. A similar internalisation, so to speak, of wider dynamics can be seen in the ways the categories of East and West functioned within and between different 'waves' of Jewish migrants at a specific moment as a differentiator of class and civilisational status. 'Westerners' (migrants from central Europe, for example, Germany) were considered to be more highly educated, intellectual, secular; while 'Easterners' ('Ostjuden') were regarded as working class, possibly tradespeople, and uneducated. These class and cultural distinctions between Jews were so profound as to be almost racialised (see Williams, 2010).

5   For a more general review, see Kahn-Harris and Gidley (2010) and https://www.jewishsocialist.org.uk/resources/js

6   Hakim concludes that, 'Up until 1967 it had been respectable (in differing degrees) for British Jews and their institutions to be anti- and non-Zionist. The reason this changed after the war [...] is because although during the 1960s British Jews were experiencing unprecedented measures of status and power, both socio-economically and within Britain's racial hierarchies, they still felt vulnerable to anti-Semitism. This produced a contradictory affective economy within the assemblage that was reinforced in the ways that Jewishness was being coded in popular culture at the time. The successful attempt by Zionist institutions in coding the 1967 war as a (super-) heroic Israel fending off its annihilation and the genocide of its Jewish population resolved these contradictions by reflecting the increased status of British

about when and how I came to understand that Palestine was not an empty land, and that the Israeli state had expelled, dispossessed, and massacred Palestinians to take occupation of this region.[7]

All this is for another book perhaps, but others echo my own experience of having been drawn to the Zionist youth-group scene because it had less stupidly gendered activities than the other religious groups. Some commentators highlight the incipient feminism structured into and by such youth groups, with their focus on outdoor activities, camps, and nightwatches. They were a kind of Jewish version of the Scouts or Girl Guides which, because these were actively Christian forms of colonial adventuring, I would have been neither admitted into nor allowed by my family to join (see Griffiths 2021; Meinhard 2006). Here, exemplified, is the intersection of gender with nationalism, echoing other literatures on gender and imperialism, including how, in nineteenth-century Britain, when these groups were established, being a colonist could be promoted as a feminist enterprise (Amos and Parmar 1984; Chaudhuri and Strobel 1992; Ware 2015).

Yet, what I want to highlight here is how, firstly, the engagement with the Zionist youth group marked my introduction to politics, specifically to a socialist politics. We were taught explicitly about different models of society and its structures. Indeed, we were taught about the various different Zionist positions on whether the founding of a Jewish state would allow Jews to form a nation like all others, with different classes of people and including criminals and prostitutes (yes, I think I recall those examples), or whether it would somehow be 'better' and more equal. The particular organisation I joined (Hanoar Hatzioni) did not promote a politics as leftwing as those of some other Zionist groups (for example, Habonim and Hashomer Hatzair, which were associated with many of the original kibbutzim in Israel), but it was certainly allied to a socialist project of equality for all (all Jews, that is, as the land of Palestine was configured as empty and awaiting cultivation to make the desert blossom etc.).[8]

Jews in British society whilst also making them feel protected against the threat of anti-Semitism (which was, paradoxically, at an historic low).' (p. 299)

7   Given this history, it is perhaps unsurprising that solidarity with Palestinians in challenging the Israeli Occupation is a key site and outlet for my political activity now.

8   The origins of the Zionist slogan 'A land for a people for a people without a land', interestingly, are multiple or contested. This notion, which has powerfully

And so now a second reflection on the community's reaction to my ostensible Zionist fervour emerges: perhaps it was this socialist politics that attracted suspicion, as much as the expressed commitment to, or psychic investment in, a 'foreign' State.

Another apparent diversion follows. Clearly, there is a class issue here, and one that I sense was intensified within a small, self-preoccupied Jewish community that perceived itself as peripheral and constantly in crisis. Growing up Jewish in Liverpool was, presumably, very different from doing so in London, which had large, visible, and vibrant working-class Jewish areas, or even in other more populous North-of-England cities with substantial Jewish communities, such as Manchester or Leeds (where the class backgrounds and affiliations of these communities were more radical and aligned with different migration trajectories from different parts of Eastern Europe). Demonstrating loyalty to the British state meant not being a burden to it.[9] Poor, working-class Jews did not seem to exist in the community I grew up in, an invisibility that, of course, feeds antisemitic stereotypes about Jews and money, along with the other antisemitic, racist tropes associating Jews with capitalism. It is, however, relevant to note that a key, perhaps unique, feature of antisemitism as a form of racism, is that Jews are seen as both a capitalist and a communist threat. Well, racism is not rational so the contradictions are difficult to acknowledge (as I have discussed in Burman 2018).

Of course, there must have been many poor Jews, and, dimly, I can retrieve some wisps of conversations and references by relatives, even about other relatives! But their presence was hidden, and they were, perhaps, also excluded from many of the visible markers of Jewish observance (buying kosher food, synagogue membership, etc.) through lack of money. The long history of Jewish social services and support organisations that ran in parallel with the more-prominent Christian ones comes to mind. As a grateful, good minority community, it 'looked

---

reverberated for many years with Christian Zionists as well as Jews, of course erases the existence of Palestinians and their longstanding habitation and corresponding claims to the territories of Palestine.

9   This is rather graphically supported by Hochberg's (1988) account, which documents how, between 1881 and 1914, it was Jewish-community policy to send back to Eastern Europe any Jews who applied for relief: 'It was a matter of historical pride to the community, as well as prudent politically, to be able to take care of its own' (p. 49).

after its own'. This was work performed especially by Jewish women (Marks 1991).

Surely this presented image of a self-sufficient, prosperous community discloses a deep insecurity and anxiety wrought from its own all-too-recent and precarious class transition and fragile hold on upward mobility? But more than that, the erasure or cutting off from working-class movements severed other links too. Now I am reminded of Alexei Sayle, who also grew up in Liverpool not so long before me. His comedy career relies on his stories of his Jewish communist (Stalinist parents who were members of the Communist Party of Great Britain and their (largely misguided) activism), albeit that, even as he lampoons his parents, he remains leftwing and socialist but not in any party (after a brief spell in a Maoist group).[10] But, they were working class (I subvocalise this word as I write it, suddenly hearing myself inflect the 'a' of 'class' with a northern-English, if not Liverpudlian, accent...).[11]

Mining my childhood for traces of 'politics', I identify the Zionist youth group as one key arena wherein exploration and self-expression, as well as political education, were taught. Yes, individual self-expression was discouraged by the broader community, another way to avoid attracting notice. I can feel again that sense of liberation and self-assertion fostered by the youth group, the relief of claiming individuality in marking myself apart from family affiliations and allying with what was a minor, nonnormative, position. Although the group I had joined was less left wing than other Zionist organisations, at least it had some such politics. More to the point, it was the only such group in Liverpool (though I recall we did meet up with some of the *Habonim* members from Manchester sometimes for joint activities).

It was only decades later that I heard from my mother about friends in the community who had been communists, including some that had lost jobs because of their political affiliations (as a minor British reflection of McCarthyism). It was a long time later that I learnt that

---

10 For a sociological analysis of Jewish membership of the Communist Part of Great Britain, see Heppel 2004.

11 While 'RP' (Received Pronunciation) English may be perceived as neutral, it is, in fact, middle class. Regional accents in the UK are associated with working-class status. Liverpool has its own accent, or dialect, Scouse, which uses short vowels, as opposed to the longer drawn-out version used in the South of England and RP.

my father had (rather briefly) been a member of the party in the 1950s. When my mother told me this, she also reported my father being asked by his comrades if my mother was a member too, and he supposedly replied 'No, but she is very intelligent'! Nevertheless, it seems that marriage ended my father's communist activism, whether because of likely disapproval from his parents-in-law, disinterest on the part of my mother, or the demands of being the breadwinner. Or, perhaps, he left out of disillusionment in the wake of news of Stalinist atrocities. Which, or how many, of these reasons apply remains unclear. He had died before I was able to ask him.

A Particular Window on the 'East' in the 'West': 'Save Soviet Jewry!'

All this may seem a long way from reflecting on Cold-War childhoods. And also from the project of memory work, with its commitment to specificity and deepening understanding of the moment and context of each memory generated. So I am frustrated by the generality of the memory traces I retrieve. Yet, the very vagueness or lack of specificity seems to speak to a normalised absence of culturally foundational assumptions that is also in need of interrogation. Further, I am convinced that class and gender statuses, such as identified above, but also immigrant insecurities that modulate minoritised or racialised status, impinge on configurations of the Cold War as structured into a minoritised middle-class, white childhood lived in a particular location within 'the West'. One example is the blue-and-white-painted, gold tin collection box for the Jewish National Fund that could be found in every Jewish living room I knew in my hometown. It held change set aside for the buying of land to make a Jewish state in historic Palestine (see https://www.jnf.org/menu-3/about-jnf),[12] yet I cannot recall the contents ever being collected. Omnipresent but largely inactive, then, this tin suggests how subtle or unconscious the coding of political affiliation might be.

---

12   The Jewish National Fund (JNF), which was set up in 1901, remains implicated in very direct dispossession of Palestinian lands and links with military actions. Active campaigns demand that it should be stripped of its charity status: see www.stopthejnf.org

The only instance I can dimly recall from my childhood where the Cold War explicitly figured was a campaign to 'Save Soviet Jewry'. Even so, this is a general memory of a phrase, rather than an event or situation, although I have a sense of attending or hearing about fundraising activities or even meetings as part of the backdrop of family and community life in the 1970s and 1980s. Such memories are hazy, and it has been hard to ward off the desire to check out facts and dates before writing this. Without doing so, I maintain the sense that this campaign was a national (and likely international) mobilisation of Jewish communities in support of 'Soviet Jews' who were 'trapped' in communist countries (principally the USSR), sometimes imprisoned as dissidents for applying to leave, or otherwise deprived of rights. In my mind's eye, I can see grainy images, photocopied faces of men and women, features indistinct, in leaflets and posters, around whom campaigns were being organised. The meetings, coffee mornings, and other fundraising events paralleled those for Zionist causes. In my memory, these were as much social opportunities for catching up with friends and relatives, including exchanging the latest gossip, as serious political business. Some people, likely, were very actively involved in this cause, but such commitment washed past me. I have the sense that the campaign started in the 1970s and continued into the 1990s, but this could equally be just because this was the period of my middle childhood and adolescence—a period when I was more likely to notice such things.

Now I feel rising within me questions about the nature of the 'oppression' suffered by the 'Soviet Jews'. The key point, it seemed, was that they wanted to leave the USSR but were not allowed to do so. The mobilisation was, I assume, to exercise political pressure on both the USSR and other countries and also to generate money to support those lucky enough to get out. From my vantage point now, I feel some suspicion about this campaign, not least because the destination for the Jews permitted to leave was Israel. Even the category 'Soviet Jew' raises doubts as I have the sense that it is widely acknowledged that many Russians who were able to 'get out' to Israel by claiming to be Jewish were, in fact, not Jewish. Probably mistakenly, I also dredge up some association between activists politicised by the 'Save Soviet Jewry' campaign who then became rampant political Zionists. But, on the other hand, there is no doubt that Israel was promoting the immigration of Russian (supposed-) Jews as a way of populating the (expansionist and ethnonationalist project of the) nation state. Yet, that invites the questions: what does, or did, it mean to be Jewish? How did one claim this status in Russia, after generations of marginalising the identities of religious and cultural minorities?

This takes me to the proud history of Jewish revolutionaries and the little I know about the Bund (Jewish Workers Party), about Jewish activists in the October Revolution, about minority rights in the Soviet Union, and about Lenin's promise of a Jewish autonomous region within the USSR. I learned, from a documentary I saw only around ten years ago, that this region was eventually established in 1934 and called Birobidzhan. It is in Siberia, near the border with China, and, according to my memory of this film, is now entirely populated by non-Jewish but Yiddish-speaking people.[13] And, while some of my (more often male) Jewish socialist comrades occupied themselves with learning Yiddish as part of their revolutionary heritage, my main association with the Bund now is a visit to its headquarters during my first-ever trip to the US in 1991. The organisation was based in a crumbling tenement block in New York's Lower East Side. Its small and dusty office was full of Yiddish newspapers and pamphlets written in both Hebrew and Roman characters. Somehow it seemed significant that this building also housed the American Group Psychotherapy Association (I was, at that time, first becoming interested in group psychotherapy).

At any rate, reflecting the overtly socially conservative ethos of my community (but noting the history of communist and socialist affiliation this suppresses), the affect I retrieve surrounding the term 'Soviet' suggests something repressive. The name and the feeling of brutality it evoked effectively stood for the whole of Eastern Europe at that time (notwithstanding the many different politics, and politics of Jewish communities, within these). On the other hand, I retrieve idealised representations of the Shtetl, the Heim, picturing the Eastern European

---

13 According to a 2017 *Guardian* article, efforts to revive the Jewish character of Birobidzhan are now being made. As most Jews were purged under Stalin and the remainder left at the fall of communism, the garish iconography that gives Birobidzhan the flavour of a 'Jewish Disneyland' is, doubtless, an attempt to attract tourists as well as new settlers to this remote region (Walker, para. 22 of 30).

village backlit with nostalgic images akin to those of the musical *Fiddler on the Roof* (which I remember seeing, around age twelve, in a packed Liverpool theatre) and Chagall paintings (which my mother particularly liked).

Writing this now makes me remember Bruno Bettelheim's (1986) harsh critique of Chagall's glowing, quasi-mystical representations of Jewish communal life in the villages of Eastern Europe. While Bettelheim's suggestion that these contributed to the Jews' delayed flight from destruction and extermination may be hyperbole, at the very least, Chagall's paintings do perform a noxious romanticisation of poverty.[14] Yet, such colourful images contrast with the stark black-and-white photocopied campaign posters of unrecognisable faces, rendered anonymous through poor reproduction as well as alienness. They are just faces, of individuals not families, and they are disembodied. This contrast seems to reiterate the presumed difference between 'the old days' and 'modern-day' supposed bleak and brutal Russia. During a visit to Moscow and St Petersburg in the 1990s, I was surprised to see the beauty of the architecture, including from the Soviet era.

It seems curious that 'Save Soviet Jewry' is the only explicit memory I can generate of the Cold War. Of course, I was aware of the Arms Race, and so on, and a supporter of CND. And, in the late 1960s, my aunt married a Hungarian-Jewish emigrée (I remember this distinctly because it was my long-awaited moment to be a bridesmaid). Most of his relatives had been exterminated in the Second World War, but he maintained Eastern European business connections, especially in Hungary, after coming to Britain in the late 1950s or early 1960s. My aunt has stories of her travels with him that include many Cold-War tropes, but these I have heard only recently.

Back to the blue-and-white Jewish National Fund tin and the 'Save Soviet Jewry' campaign. One feature common to both is how charity,

---

14 It is worth recalling that Chagall was inspired by the allied revolutionary project in Russia and was appointed Commissioner for Fine Arts in his native Vitebsk. He founded The People's Art School there, and key avant-garde figures such as El Lizzitzki and Kazimir Malevich taught at the school as part of a short-lived project to create a form of leftist art expressing the revolutionary values of (as one exhibition put it) 'collectivism, education, and innovation' (see: https://thejewishmuseum.org/index.php/exhibitions/chagall-lissitzky-malevich-the-russian-avant-garde-in-vitebsk-1918-1922)

or rather the performance of philanthropy, is a demonstration of class identity and status: one identifies as a giver rather than as one in need. A second is that both were institutionally-sanctioned mobilisations that signified some communal transnational affiliation and solidarity that transcended citizen loyalty to the 'host' nation-state. It may be (as I hinted above) that the two mobilisations, Zionism and support for Soviet Jews to leave Russia, had greater political alignment than I realised at the time. If so, then, perhaps, it is important to stay with the possibility of their separation, or disaggregation, as much as with their connection. That is, it is noteworthy that there had been two such movements beyond mere nationalist conformity to the British state, even if—in the light of the fall of communism—Zionism has now emerged as the only such expression for many British Jews.

Thinking about it now, it is easy to draw the conclusion that the 'Save Soviet Jewry' campaign was a perfect demonstration of British Jewry's commitment to the capitalist West. Bound up with loyalty to Britain was loyalty to the West, against the (communist) East. What better way to manifest trustworthiness to a suspicious state, and to ward off the memory of working-class Jewish communist and socialist activism! Here, as is the experience of so many minority communities, class interests meet migrant assimilationist politics. On the other hand, those of us politicised ('radicalised'?) in Zionist movements did not only become army fodder for the Israel Defence Forces or fundamentalist settlers in the Occupied West Bank. Many of the people I first met at Hanoar Hatzioni camps, I encountered again in the Jewish Socialist Group,[15] which has long called for the decentring of Israel from Jewish communal identity and revives radical Jewish histories across the world, most notably from Revolutionary Russia, and even in short-lived UK Jewish feminist movements. I discern similar or equivalent histories among fellow Jewish activists in other socialist and Palestine-solidarity organisations. So, this political trajectory is clearly not only mine.

Questions surface: what does it mean that it seems I first encountered the term 'dissident' in relation to the 'Save Soviet Jewry' campaign, that is, as an anti-communist trope? Was I able to reshape or rework my understanding, or is the term still invested with this Cold-War association? In a supposedly 'post-political' era, when resignation,

---

15   https://www.jewishsocialist.org.uk/about

passivity, and apathy prevail, I find myself clutching at even perhaps-misguided moments of collective organisation and transnational affiliation. I suppose the key issue is what kind of political imaginaries were, and can be, fostered from diverse and contradictory resources.

Here, at least, I recognise one key asset that my geopolitical, embodied experience has brought to the Post-socialist Childhoods project: a desire to attend to minoritised cultural, ethnic, and religious positionings and to disrupt any sense of homogeneity of Eastern-European populations, as elsewhere, whether Roma, Jewish, Muslim or any other minority affiliation (including diverse embodiedness and sexualities). My 'heritage' (or geopolitical cultural positioning) has generated in me a constitutional suspicion of all nationalistic claims of universality and uniformity that work to suppress and oppress marginal groups. Asking questions to disrupt what I heard as generalised assumptions has sometimes felt uncomfortable, inappropriate even. Such questions may well have been ill-informed, and I have learnt so much through the process of engagement in this project. But I also hope that, clumsy as they may have been, and shaped by a political subjectivity forged from the West rather than the East, my questions helped to further expose some key tropes and tenets structuring both the narratives of Cold-War childhoods and their interpretation.

I acknowledge that the examples I have discussed here are recalled signifiers (and, in the case of the JNF box, a material object) rather than a memory story or retrieved narrative of personal experience as is more usual for memory work. Yet, as is also the case with memory work, I am trying here to excavate that which has been assumed and normalised. But what I have relayed are such pervasive, enduring, and implicit features of the cultural-political life of my childhood that it would be disingenuous to try to pin the analysis onto a single episode or event.

Layers of complicity coexist with potential resistance, and collective political amnesia intersects with personal repressions to the extent that one cannot disentangle which arises from which (see, for example, Williams 2010). What remains from this process is an enduring sense of the fragmentariness and instability of memory as well as a deep uncertainty about the validity of my own commitments, strongly felt though they may be. The myriad layering of experience, of years passed and subjective defences acquired since and at play now, render this account as unreliable—and in places as obscure to me—as it must be to others. I am an other to myself, and this estrangement has to be acknowledged and embraced as a necessary component of any decolonial, De-Cold War process. Interrogation, rather than exoneration, is the starting point for further exploration. As Scholz (2011) put it,

> The unconscious is not a reservoir of eternal topics, released from the laws of time and space. Unconscious life has a special relation to time and has its special media … embodied memories and values, the significance of family talks, and … externalizations such as books, museums, and rituals, as well as places (p. 365).

She further distinguishes between what she calls communicative and cultural memory to highlight how 'personal memories emerge from, and are based in, collective memories' (ibid.).

Whether I have disidentified, or rather which kinds of re-identifications I have now installed, is not for me to say. I do, however, hope that I have indicated some of the existing borders and bordering practices that are at play in the disruption if also reiteration of prevailing East/West binaries. I inhabited a Cold-War childhood to the extent that I was constructed and produced as its normalised other, situated 'outside' to peer in through its curtains. Nevertheless, my recollections of the felt experiences of those times relationally and correlatively disclose my own and other Western-majority and -minority positionings, both then and now. The Cold War was fought on many fronts, within and between Europe and the Americas, but also across Asia and Africa. As Chen (2010) noted, its legacies pose urgent subjective as well as geomaterial challenges, and—to extend his point—interface with the forms, effects, and affects of its more recent renewal across the globe.

And Now, the 'Facts'...

After the struggle with memory retrieval and the mining of the encounter with the contradictions of the past, I now offer some broader historical account of the 'Save Soviet Jewry' campaign and its relationship with Zionism, as a way of also illuminating my process here. While not-quite following the instructions for memory work (although I did try thinking through these stories from the third person, as well as the first), my 'method' here was one of attempting to stay with recollected past representations or memory stories. Now, however, having written the above, I have allowed myself to 'check' the 'facts' of the campaign. This causes me to think of Deborah Britzman's (2012) notion of 'after-education', perhaps because she topicalises both the (retrospective) temporality and the complex and fantasised interpersonal and singular relationships involved in teaching and learning. My reflections here on my own 'memory stories' (a term coined by the Post-socialist Childhoods Project) arise from and were provoked by joint work but are necessarily forged 'after' it, by me as a singular, geomaterially, and historically positioned subject.

Here, therefore, are some choice samples of what the internet says about the 'Save Soviet Jewry Campaign', corresponding to the murky filaments of feeling and personal history narrated above, much of which was news to me…

On the 'Save Soviet Jewry' Campaign

First, this campaign appears to have been initiated and driven from the USA, beginning in the early 1960s. So, the UK was, really, a minor player. Clearly, the Cold-War politics of US-USSR relations figured prominently both in the US and USSR's governmental responses to why and how the issue of Soviet Jewry was taken up by the US.

Second, the 'Save Soviet Jewry' campaign is tied to the self-image and status of the US Jewish community, including its intersection with other local antiracist struggles. This is indicated in a review for the (US) Jewish Book Council by Bob Goldfarb, in which he claims that 'the struggle to save Soviet Jews in the 1960's marked a decisive shift by many Jewish Americans from African-American civil rights to a specifically Jewish cause' (2011, para. 3 of 4). Discussing the American Israel Public Affairs Committee, he continues,

> The success of Congressional lobbying led to AIPAC's immensely influential role as an advocate for Israel on Capitol Hill. And the end of the Soviet Jewry campaign after the fall of the Soviet Union has left the American Jewish establishment in search of another unifying theme for the past two decades (Ibid).

Goldfarb, perhaps subject to a dynamic present in most minority communities, overestimates the political clout of this lobbying group.

His observations are suggestive in relation to the move to Zionism alongside and especially after the Soviet Jewry campaign.

Another revealing comment in a particularly motivated account of the movement comes from a relatively recent article in *The Times of Israel*. Dr. Shaul Keiner, associate professor of sociology and Jewish studies at Vanderbilt University, is quoted as saying that the campaign 'was the height of American Jews' sense of empowerment as American Jews' (Gher-Zand 2019, para. 17 of 29). The overall narrative seems to be that the campaign was a victim of its own success since, once successful (in the sense that Soviet Jews were able to emigrate by the early 1990s), the campaign was forgotten. However, some recent scholarship makes the contradictory claim that Soviet Jews continue to exercise a key cultural and material influence globally (Shneer 2021).

Third, as I dimly discerned, the link between demanding the right to leave the USSR and wish to relocate to Israel was structured into the project from the outset. Those who sought the freedom to leave the Soviet Union were called 'Refuseniks' but also 'Prisoners of Zion' (Gher-Zand 2019, para. 7 of 29). More significantly, the campaign was explicitly mobilised by the Israeli state as a strategy for managing the 'demographic problem' of maintaining a higher proportion of Jewish people in the Israel/Palestine population, according to the history produced by the American Jewish Historical Society. However, other accounts highlight the tensions or disagreements that arose when some of the 'Refuseniks', once granted permission to leave, 'dropped out' or changed destination halfway through their journeys. Instead of carrying on from Vienna to Israel, they elected to go to the US or to other countries (Lazin 2005). Indeed, Goldfarb opens his review of the history written by Gal Beckerman by noting that 'the chair of the Jewish Agency, Arieh Dulzin, declared in 1976, "our first duty is not to save Jews; we must save only those who will go to Israel"' (2011, para. 1 of 4). This argument was, however, overruled by federated Jewish organisations.

Finally, I have vague recollections of other Cold-War figures whose plight penetrated the Jewish community of my childhood. I remember the name Sharansky and the slogan 'Let my people go'; I also remember Yevtushenko's poem 'Babi Yar'. Not quite able to recall the details of these, however, I did not mention them above. More comes back now, of course….

References

American Jewish Historical Society (n.d.). 'Timelines of the American Soviet Jewry Movement', https://ajhs.org/holdings/timelines-of-the-american-soviet-jewry-movement/

Amos, V., and Parmar, P. (1984). 'Challenging Feminist Imperialism'. *Feminist Review*, 17, 3–19

Bettelheim, B. (1986). *Surviving the Holocaust*. Flamingo

Bhattacharyya, G. (2018). *Rethinking Racial Capitalism: Questions of Reproduction and Survival*. Rowman and Littlefield

Britzman, D. P. (2012). *After-education: Anna Freud, Melanie Klein, and Psychoanalytic Histories of Learning*. SUNY Press

Burman, E. (2018). 'Brexit, "Child as Method," and the Pedagogy of Failure: How Discourses of Childhood Structure the Resistance of Racist Discourse to Analysis'. *Review of Education, Pedagogy, and Cultural Studies*, 40(2), 119–43, https://doi.org/10.1080/10714413.2018.1442082

—— (2019a). *Fanon, Education, Action: Child as Method*. Routledge, https://doi.org/10.4324/9781315108896-1

—— (2019b). 'Child as Method: Implications for Decolonising Educational Research'. *International Studies in Sociology of Education*, 28(1), 4–26, https://doi.org/10.1080/09620214.2017.1412266

Chen, K. H. (2010). *Asia as Method: Towards Deimperialization*. Duke University Press, https://doi.org/10.1515/9780822391692

Chaudhuri, N., and Strobel, M. (eds). (1992). *Western Women and Imperialism: Complicity and Resistance*. Indiana University Press

Cohen, S. (1987). *It's the Same Old Story: Immigration Controls Against Jewish, Black and Asian People, with Special Reference to Manchester*. Manchester City Council.

Dalal, F. (2001). 'The Social Unconscious: A Post-Foulkesian Perspective'. *Group Analysis*, 34(4), 539–55, https://doi.org/10.1177/0533316401344011

Fanon, F. (2008). *Black Skin, White Masks*. Grove Press (original work published 1958)

Ghert-Zand, R. (2019, 22 December). 'Once Heroes of US Jewry, Soviet Refuseniks are Largely Forgotten. Not for Long'. *Times of Israel*, https://www.timesofisrael.com/once-heroes-of-us-jewry-soviet-refuseniks-are-largely-forgotten-not-for-long/

Goldfarb, B. (2011, 26 September). 'Book Review: Gal Beckerman, *When they Come for Us, We'll be Gone: The Epic Struggle to Save Soviet Jewry*'.

Jewish Book Council, https://www.jewishbookcouncil.org/book/when-they-come-for-us-well-be-gone-the-epic-struggle-to-save-soviet-jewry

Griffiths, J. (2021). *Empire and Popular Culture*. Routledge, https://doi.org/10.4324/9781351024822

Gržinić, M., Kancler, T., and Rexhepi, P. (2020). 'Decolonial Encounters and the Geopolitics of Racial Capitalism'. *Feminist Critique: Eastern European Journal of Feminist and Queer Studies*, 3, 13–38, https://doi.org/10.52323/365802

Hakim, J. (2012). *Affect and Cultural Change: The Rise of Popular Zionism in the British Jewish Community after the Six Day War (1967)* [Doctoral dissertation, University of East London]

Heppell, J. L. (2004). 'A Rebel, not a Rabbi: Jewish Membership of the Communist Party of Great Britain'. *Twentieth Century British History*, 15(1), 28–50, https://doi.org/10.1093/tcbh/15.1.28

Hochberg, S. A. (1988). 'The Repatriation of Eastern European Jews from Great Britain: 1881–1914. *Jewish Social Studies*, 20 (1–2), 49–62

Hopper, E. (2003). *The Social Unconscious: Selected Papers*. Jessica Kingsley Publishers

Kahn-Harris, K., and Gidley, B. (2010). *Turbulent Times: The British Jewish Community Today*. A and C Black, https://doi.org/10.5040/9781472548771.0004

Lazin, Frederick A. (2005). *The Struggle for Soviet Jewry in American Politics: Israel Versus the American Jewish Establishment*. Lexington Books

Marks, L. (1991). 'Carers and Servers of the Jewish Community: The Marginalised Heritage of Jewish Women in Britain'. *Immigrants and Minorities*, 10 (1–2), 106–27

Meinhart, C. J. (2006). 'Good Christian Boys: Scouting for Masculinity'. *Journal of Philosophy and History of Education*, 56, 116–20

Sarna, J. D. (1998). 'Jewish Prayers for the US Government: A Study in the Liturgy of Politics and the Politics of Liturgy, in *Moral Problems in American Life: New Perspectives on Cultural History*, ed. by Halttunen, K., and Perry, L. Cornell University Press, pp. 201–22

Scholz, R. (2011). 'The Foundation Matrix and the Social Unconscious' in *The Social Unconscious in Persons, Groups, and Societies, Vol. 1: Mainly Theory*, ed. by E. Hopper and H. Weinberg. Karnac Books, pp. 365–85, https://doi.org/10.4324/9780429483233

Shneer. D. (2021, 8 December). 'Saving Soviet Jews and the Future of the Global Jewish Diaspora', *Oxford Handbook of the Jewish Diaspora*. Oxford University Press, pp. 540–C27.S10, https://doi.org/10.1093/oxfordhb/9780190240943.013.33

Tlostanova, M., Thapar-Björkert, S., and Koobak, R. (2016). 'Border Thinking and Disidentification: Postcolonial and Post-socialist Feminist Dialogues'. *Feminist Theory*, 17(2), 211–28, https://doi.org/10.1177/1464700116645878

Walker, Shaun (2017, 27 September). 'Revival of a Soviet Zion: Birobidzhan Celebrates its Jewish Heritage', *The Guardian*, https://www.theguardian.com/world/2017/sep/27/revival-of-a-soviet-zion-birobidzhan-celebrates-its-jewish-heritage

Ware, V. (2015). *Beyond the Pale: White Women, Racism, and History*. Verso Books.

Williams, B. (1985). *The Making of Manchester Jewry, 1740–1875*. Manchester University Press

Williams, B. (2010). 'Heritage and Community: The Rescue of Manchester's Jewish Past'. *Immigrants and Minorities*, 10 (1–2), 128–46, https://doi.org/10.1080/02619288.1991.9974756

Williams, G. (2013). *History of the Liverpool Privateers and Letter of Marque: With an Account of the Liverpool Slave Trade*. Routledge

Smearing the Portrait[1]

Lucian Țion

The break was coming to an end. It was the long break—the one that all students had in the middle of the school day between 10:10 and 10:30 in the morning. They had just finished a short soccer game in the school yard before they started to go back to the classroom in a haphazard crowd. The game exhausted them, and even though the ball was almost flat and the ground covered in cement, as usual, the boys gave it all. Some were panting heavily from running, others were playing it cool.

When they entered the classroom the sun had just moved to the other side of the building, so the room felt a little bit cooler. The girls were sitting at their desks, or on their desks sometimes, as the boys reentered. And the usual haggling and teasing restarted immediately thereafter. That was the way school children had always amused themselves, they thought at the time, and this gave them a feeling of belonging.

The next class was math and comrade Stancu was a very strict teacher. Not the usual walk-in-the-park class as it was with comrade Ana, the drawing teacher or comrade Andrei who taught geography as if he couldn't care less whether the kids went away with any knowledge from his classes or not. Stancu had a pair of brown-tinted glasses and always wore the same slightly discolored brown work-gown. This gave him an intimidating air, and made math look like an enormously important subject in the eyes of the kids. They were all secretly fearing him, although, of course, none would ever admit to it. And they were waiting for him with a mix of anxiety and anticipation on that day, as well.

Only that day, for some reason, Stancu was late. Sometimes he would stay behind a little longer with the others in the teachers' lounge; other times he

---

1 This is a childhood memory produced as part of the Reconnect/Recollect project discussed in the introduction to this book.

would be busy marking papers until a few minutes after class would start. Or at least so he said. The kids didn't really care what the specific reason was: All that mattered to them was that he wasn't there on time, which meant a few extra minutes in which the boys could horseplay around, pulling their classmates' ponytails or simply picking their noses.

George was an unusual type. His long curly hair made him look like a girl, but the curses that came out of his mouth reminded one of the uneducated son of a garbage collector or a bricklayer. His uniform would always carry stains of some nature or another, while his pioneer's tie was so worn out as to actually look torn. And it was no easy feat to tear a pioneer's tie. No matter how many times the class-mistress threatened him with bringing his parents to school; and no matter how many phone calls she actually made to his parents, this didn't change. In a week or two, George's outlook would soon return to the dilapidated state with which everyone was familiar: that of a boy coming from a difficult social background that was making his way through life largely on his own.

That day, while Stancu was being unusually late, the boys in the back of the room—always the unruly ones—bored with teasing the girls who were starting to put up something of a legitimately powerful self-defense, were beginning to turn on each other rather than continuing to harass them. Soon enough the fight turned into a full-out war between five or six of the boys who were using everything that came within reach as projectiles to be thrown in the enemy's general direction. Pens, entire pen-holders, rulers, erasers and notebooks were all flying around with threatening speed, when George, catching sight of the sponge used for wiping the chalkboard, made a dash for the sink at the corner of the room.

Covered in chalk dust, the sponge soon turned into a heavy mush of white mud, which, when thrown with precision, could in fact become a quite dangerous weapon. The others had barely noticed George's tactics and continued to fight each other with more conventional weaponry when George raised the sponge above his head to draw attention to himself and the potential asset he was holding. Gradually, signaling to each other loudly, the others stopped playing, still holding onto the random book they were just about to throw a minute ago. Now they were all watching George and questioning themselves what was to be the boy's next target.

But George made an unusual gesture: Instead of picking a classmate he had a grudge on, he made an about-face, and, with the sponge still dripping colored liquid to the floor in the middle of the room, he stood facing the portrait of the *supreme leader that was hanging, as in every classroom in the school, on top of the blackboard. Then, without missing a beat, he arched his arm behind him and threw the sponge into the picture on the wall.*

The water started to evaporate almost instantaneously when comrade Stancu entered, brown glasses and brown gown almost preceding him in the classroom. The kids made a speedy return to their desks, attempting to erase any traces of their game in the process. But as the seconds wore on, a grayish-dark splotch of freshly dried choke-water was becoming more and more visible on the portrait of the leader. Stancu demurred for a second, then, following what must have been the eye-line of the students, turned around to the portrait of Ceaușescu

By that time, the leader's smile had turned into a disgruntled frown.

In revenge for his punishment, which was a very low grade in general conduct and a long talk with the parents, George was gifted with the revolution: Only a few weeks after the smearing of the portrait, while school was out for vacation, the crowds gathered in the streets and removed the leader. As if by chance the first class after the holidays was math, and George was late, as usual, for the first day of school. Entering the classroom, he first bid Mr. Stancu 'good morning', and then, as if nothing in the world mattered more, he swiftly glanced in the direction of the portrait.

The spot where the leader stood on the wall was still visible, but the leader's face was gone. George felt an onrush of relief, but then, almost simultaneously, and unexpectedly, one of sadness. The feelings succeeded each other too quickly for George to pay attention. He was invited to sit without the usual reprimand and the class resumed, almost as if nothing had happened. And before he knew it, things were back to normal. As if the kids were just returning to school from a usual vacation; as if the outline of the leader's portrait on the wall had always been just that: nothing more than a simple outline.

5. You Can't Go Home Again... Especially if You Have Never Had One

Madina Tlostanova

Starting from the premise that any childhood is existentially tragic, this fictionalised memory reflects on the last Soviet generation of children as a lost generation. This chapter is written as a memory stream based on free associations, and it dwells on the major leitmotifs and recurrent sensibilities that have shaped the author's experience as a member of this generation. Following her personal trajectory, the memory stream refers to the symbol of the vertical, to the sense of being lost both literally and symbolically, to specific ways and strategies of hiding in her own world and rejecting the outside reality. These personal paths combine with more general patterns of double consciousness and redoubling of the world that generated a cynical framework in its late-Soviet children's version: an urge to make their own escapist forms of alternative realities and internal emigration models in the decade just before *perestroika*. The chapter touches upon key late-Soviet oppositions that children of the 1970s learned to identify from early on in order to survive. It also considers the ethnic-racial and religious differences that affected the lost generation's internal erosive processes.

> I must go back to my childhood to die there.
>
> Sergei Paradzhanov

Although there are dozens of sociological taxonomies attempting to divide recent generations, my gut feeling tells me that the last truly Soviet generation was the children born in the late 1960s and early 1970s. It is a lost generation in the sense that we were born too late to manage to root ourselves in the dying Soviet system. Because this system collapsed precisely when we were entering adulthood, we did not have a chance to find a place within it, to become one of those who belonged, or to take the role of the 'janitors and night watchman' mentioned in Boris Grebenschikov's well-known song.[1] Yet, we were also born too early to adapt to the impending age of wild capitalism with its completely different value system. Stuck between the two epochs, this generation, with its diverse and most-unusual life trajectories, still shares a cynical and all-encompassing doublethink and doublesense. I refer not to the Orwellian (1949) understanding but, rather, to a very mundane expectation set by the lying that was so ubiquitous in the late-Soviet era—a feeling so viscerally represented in Vladimir Sorokin's (1994) nauseating *The Norm*. This enormous bunch of sickening lies penetrated everywhere, turning children into hypocrites that accurately predicted or, perhaps, felt what was acceptable or unacceptable to say and where. Such survival skills festered the young souls, burnt them from inside; they made us look for and create different escapes and outlets.

At the end of the Soviet regime, everyday life had almost lost the sticky fear and the sense of walking on the edge that characterised life in the Stalinist era. But instead, we were left with viscous despair and doom to which children learnt to adjust early on. Somewhere in the entangled knots of this double consciousness, of this false-bottomed world, we nourished a sense of homelessness, unsettlement, uprootedness and non-belonging, an alienation from the world, from the social context and from ourselves and our lives. Therefore, many of us are no strangers to restlessness and disidentification. From our earliest years, we became

---

1 'Generation of Janitors' from the album *Equinox* by Aquarium and Boris Grebenschikov (1987). See, for example, 'Поколение дворников', uploaded by Akvarium—Topic, 18 November 2014, https://www.youtube.com/watch?v=mM35HDtrNQw

aliens in different ways and to different degrees, we have lived unsettled lives. Perhaps that is why my own and my contemporaries' memories so often focus on efforts to reconstruct, rebuild, and remodel a home space where we might feel a sense of inner peace and balance with the world. So, our childhood memories frequently repeat stories of various games based on the creation of alternative spaces or other worlds. As in many other childhoods, these spaces were often associated with freedom, however transient and secret. The wish, however, was not just for a freedom from the grown-up world of responsibilities, parental control, and boring duties; this is clear from the experience of our parents who often felt the same conflict and aversion. A major part of our lives—adults' and children's, material and spiritual—was expropriated by the rotting Soviet regime, and it is from this that we wished to be free. This is perhaps why we loved so much to 'play house' and to design different models of houses that allowed us to dream of other lives. Some children fashioned them with the help of curtains thrown over the backs of the chairs to create a semblance of a tent, others made small copies of real houses using different blocks and building kits. I could never become the architect my father once dreamed I might because I had absolutely no drawing talents and would not be able to pass the entrance exams to any architectural institute. Yet, the urge to design imaginary living spaces attracted me from very early on. In my peony-wall-papered nursery, there was never a single doll but instead lots of houses that I assembled from components of several GDR kits, following my own designer's fantasy rather than the attached specification. The building kit was supposed to imitate standardised socialist panel constructions, but I came up with non-symmetrical houses of varied heights with multiple balconies and terraces and sloping roofs, which looked completely different from the miserable lined-up, five-storied apartment complexes crowding the main streets of our town.

 A kind of internal or psychical emigration is my first and foremost memory and sensibility. Somewhere towards the early teenage years it had channeled into the more conscious choice of future-life strategies that would let me avoid almost entirely any contacts with Soviet ideology and let me 'leak through' it into my imagined home, my imagined self. Later, this refusal to take any part in political life—a stance that was so typical for the late-Soviet intelligentsia and took the form of passive,

Bartleby-like protest, and that I interiorised through my family and environment—prevented me, for a while, from collaborating with critical Western colleagues. They, because of their completely different experience, were not allergic to ideology and politics in general; they genuinely believed that they were capable of really changing something through their struggle and, therefore, that it was worth engaging in and writing about.

But all that came later, after the incredibly long pre-*perestroika* childhood and the crisis years that left many of us in the situation of the 'minimal self' in its Soviet rather than the American version that Christopher Lasch (1985) would write about later in his controversial book *The Minimal Self: Psychic Survival in Troubled Times*. Nevertheless, in both cases, this self arose out of austerity and survival in crisis conditions wherein ordinary relations stopped working. It is a bare selfhood—one devoid of personal history, friends, a family, a sense of place. Our lost generation had lost this sort of settlement very early on, before we had managed to entirely shape our identifications and inclinations, and, hence, we looked for and created some substitutes instead.

Double existence had become so habitual and mundane by the 1970s that children were not even bothered by it, and it almost did not matter. Each of us quickly learnt to lie and pretend or, let us say, feed into the game everyone else was playing; we learnt to be actors and feel at home in this pervasive mimicry. Besides, the regime of the increasingly senile Brezhnev had, by then, largely replaced the previous massive bloody and deadly repressions with imprisonment, commitment to a psychiatric clinic, or exile. And yet, the double existence had its poisoning effect on every minute of our lives. Even the organisation of space in my own home displayed the same all-penetrating double logic, an array of confusing, contradictory messages that I never stopped to reflect upon but learnt to decipher intuitively. Take, for instance, our enormous home library that occupied the walls of all the rooms, including the hall, floor to ceiling, in our spacious and airy apartment. The library was strategically shelved by my mother with the same duality in mind. The upper, unreachable shelves carried pre-revolutionary and foreign-published books; sometimes soiled, home-bound typewritten texts borrowed for one night. At eye level, one could admire lavish art albums that had been printed abroad, the tastefully designed translations of so-called foreign literature, and some selective Russian classics. My father's solid and corpulent Soviet editions of the complete works of Lenin, Hegel, and Marx were exiled to the bottom, invisible shelves. Was this arrangement a reflection of our ideological preferences? Perhaps.

Sometimes, one could spot on one of the middle shelves a brightly coloured propagandistic book denouncing a famous dissident in a catchy title, while, on the invisible top shelf, this very dissident's half-blind texts were carefully nested away from an accidental guest's notice. We treasured many Soviet books that denounced various 'bourgeois cultural phenomena' such as modernist and generally non-realistic styles in art, cinema, or literature, because it was from these books that we could get at least some information about and some usually bad-quality images of the artists and cultural phenomena that was otherwise inaccessible to us. Thus, second hand, via the cautious Soviet critics, we often acquired knowledge and awareness of a cultural world beyond what was usually possible to read or see. In my earliest childhood, I loved to sit under the large, glass-covered coffee table, slowly leafing through enormous colourful albums of impressionists, Bosch, Chagall—all brought from abroad. But not only that. Among my favourites were also the ridiculous but well-illustrated books by Soviet critic Kukarkin that were published with remarkable regularity and invariably denounced the bourgeois mass culture (Kukarkin 1985). Equipped with politically correct introductions by Yakovlev, the future ideological architect of *Perestroika*, the texts of these mediocre books did not give any food for thought. But I was enormously attracted by the reproductions of pop art and abstract-impressionist works they contained and, most of all, by the many stills from Western horror films and thrillers, which were out of reach of the ordinary Soviet people in that pre-video-player era. These stills were always accompanied by indignant authorial comments such as 'The characters of the horror films have different faces for every taste, or rather, for any type of psychopathology' (Kukarkin 1985, p. 417), but the author was clearly enjoying his taxonomy of Western cinema monsters. Already then, I noticed that Viy and the witch—characters from the technologically naïve and clumsy Soviet horror film based on a story by Nikolai Gogol—were really different from the aliens, vampires, and zombies depicted in Kukarkin's books. For one thing, Pannochka (the witch) and Viy were much scarier. I remembered this very well from watching the film in the local, gloomy movie theatre 'Victory'. The place itself perhaps added to the horror affect. It left a strange impression of incongruence: the vaguely constructivist compact building dissonated with a set of oversized imperial columns attached to its façade and two disproportionately large, ominously realistic human figures adorning its roof (these, it turns out, were early works by a future famous Canadian sculptor Leo Mol [Leonid Molodozhanin]). Did all of this induce cognitive dissonances in my growing mind? Hardly so. Rather, it taught me to easily incorporate into my worldview quite different, eclectic, and at times contradictory things.

Pinning onto my white starched apron a 'Little Octobrist' star—mine was a plastic, cherry-coloured one with a black-and-white photograph of an angelic Lenin instead of the more-common orange metal ones—I could not help imagining a different face, one of the senile Lenin with crazy, hollow eyes that I had seen in some book that belonged to my parents. Yet, it felt almost normal to stand in the militarised school line and observe all of the nonsense with which we were fed. This situation multiplied and repeated again and again. After lessons were over, I used to go to a music school, which was based in an old merchant's house that survived the years of massive Soviet construction. My choir class met in its former ceremonial hall—one frequented by the ghosts of the ex-owners who were probably executed in their own yard so that I could almost hear the rustle of their fluffy skirts. The choirmaster made us sing mostly hideous Soviet songs, such as 'Love, Komsomol, and the Spring'. However, as soon as she was called to quickly answer the phone in some far away teachers' room, I would immediately jump to the tall 'Red October' piano and start playing and singing Edit Piaf's 'Hymne à l'amour' to the utter delight of my choirmates.

My childhood, like so many others, was also full of dread. This phase of life is seldom discussed in such grim terms, perhaps because what follows on from it is so often a transition from bad to worse. So, we apply an illusion of happiness to at least the start of our lives. I believe, though, that childhood is the most hopelessly tragic time in any life. It opens up an existential abyss that is hard to overcome because, as Sergei Paradzhanov (2004) so graphically put it, 'from the balcony of one's childhood', everything is seen too seriously, too irrevocably. In my particular childhood, the external social world was extremely and permanently hostile, and this hostility only acquired additional overtones, nuances, and depths as I grew older. Hence, it was necessary and, in fact, lifesaving to keep this world at a distance at all times. Yet, what I also remember as a leitmotif of my childhood sensibility was a discordance of feeling. My moods and dispositions would quickly change from absolute grief to joy and then boredom and back. This intense psychic fluidity was a contrast to the deadening slowness and stillness of time that was controlled by invisible machines of power disciplining human lives. It was the time of the dying empire, creaking with all its ungreased gears. But, then, I was not aware of it. My childhood world so easily switched from major to minor, from beautiful to ugly and scary, from the safety and nonchalant freedom of the cosy old flat to the treacherous threatening falsity of public spaces and institutions.

The outside world was non-homogenous and diverse and, in its turn, was divided into more and less hostile spaces. For instance, there was a clear difference between the provincial world and that of the cultural capital, between different spaces inside and outside, beyond the Soviet borders, at its borderlands, and even within them. And one learned quickly to differentiate all the nuances between Armenia and Estonia, between Moscow and Sofia, Leningrad and Dresden. The frequent trips to various places, including several socialist countries in Eastern Europe, were always tastes of freedom and temporary liberation from the drag of my habitual double existence. But they were short. And one had to return to the well-ordered and sluggish childhood life. My first sixteen years were spent in what was conventionally referred to as a provincial place, but this North Caucasus province was not very calm, boring, or culturally impoverished. In some elements, it even outstripped Moscow; it had its own musical, theatrical, and literary underground—one to which I had access from very early childhood thanks to my mother. This was not, however, the kind of province that Brodsky (2010) recommended when writing, 'If you were destined to be born in the Empire, it's best to find some province, by the ocean' (para. 4 of 9). No ocean was nearby, although pale vacationers flocked anyway to our town in the summer months from all over the Soviet Union. With their trade-union vouchers in hand and plans in mind to spend twenty-four days at a sanatorium or a spa hotel, they used to ask the local people in the street: 'Could you tell us, please, what is the way to the sea?' Once, I answered very seriously that they should follow the famous hiking route through the mountains that would take them first to the 'blue lakes', then along Cherek River to the glacier Shtulu, and finally to the Gezevtsek Pass, which is the easiest way to get to Georgia. And then, I added, you just go down to the mountain resort Shovi to take a bus to Kutaisi or Poti. There you have your Black Sea. 'It would take you a week!' This I had to shout after the frightened holidaymakers as they retreated to their usual peaceful mineral water 'drinking paths'.[2]

Our late-Soviet province was not that backwards, it was still penetrable. Seeds of another life, other voices, came through; bits of entirely non-Soviet trajectories and unbelievable nodes of forgotten histories and erased memories suddenly emerged in the measured space of the congealing Soviet existence that was rapidly turning already then into a decoration, a theatrical set ready to gather dust in some warehouse or on a museum shelf. Meanwhile, life turned out to be much broader and more multifaceted than its allowed external manifestations. Perhaps the most crucial and disturbingly persistent sensibility of my childhood was the everyday inevitable struggle with the dichotomy of the same and the other, of belonging and exclusion. I had no universal key to solve this problem and sometimes it led to amusing mistakes.

One of them I remember quite well, although I was not yet four years old. In the early spring, when the sun shines so ruthlessly but the snow still lies around in sloppy, thick patches, I was standing in line with my mother in the bakery that was on the ground floor of our apartment complex. As always happens in small towns, we bumped into an acquaintance—a professor of pathology from the medical school of the local university. But I was soon distracted from her strange, fixed gaze. I had noticed some weird-looking, unfamiliar, high-and-narrow cakes and asked my mother to get me one. Strangely, my mother refused to buy it, and she whispered that it was an Easter bread and that we

---

2 'Drinking paths' were a local slang used to define the ways connecting sanatoriums and multiple mineral water springs located throughout the resort area. Holidaymakers were routinely prescribed to take mineral water from different springs several times per day depending on their ailments. These people could be immediately distinguished from the locals as they busily followed the drinking paths, often sloppily dressed between different sanatorium treatments.

did not need it at all. I peered closer at the strange bread that had immediately become much more interesting and mysterious and read aloud its tag: 'spring fruitcake'. Like many children, I used to read out every bit of text I saw. My mother whispered again, 'They only say that it is fruitcake but, in fact, it is an Easter bread. I will explain it to you later'. But I was already moving forward and continued reading out loud the inscriptions on all the cardboard boxes that were stacked in the corner of the shop. One of them, for some reason, did not make any sense; it refused to form any word no matter how hard I tried: 'Uedeta?' 'Rotgauipu?'[3]

The pathologist, with her typical soft sarcasm, asked me: 'So you have not mastered the Latin alphabet yet, have you?' I proudly replied: 'I read only in Soviet.' This comment was a product of the internal contradictions and the unstable divisions of same/other that, already then, excluded me and made me an alien in any cultural group, even in this, my presumably native, space. At barely four years of age, I already knew that we were not Russian but Soviet, that our country was the USSR and not Russia, and that I myself was not Russian even though Russian was my native language. Why is something I would figure out only later. Moreover, if the inscriptions were printed on cardboard boxes imported from abroad, then texts on those produced in the USSR should, indeed, have been called Soviet and not Russian. So formally, politically, what I had said was all correct. Except it was not. Theatrical Soviet multiculturalism stumbled in the face of this Easter bread: it had been renamed a fruitcake in a presumably secular bakery in a Muslim republic as the enforced use of the Russian language and alphabet suppressed any internal diversity and usurped its external representation. What I had yet to learn, then, was what to do when the language is Russian but the culture is Soviet and if, in all of these intersections, there was still a place for me.

The Caucasus itself was perhaps the most important element of the lighter side of my childhood. It smelled sweet and pungent, and it offered astounding colours and tastes. The small town of my childhood was surrounded on all sides but one by the unbelievable beauty of the high mountains. How I miss this Caucasian vertical from my present

---

3   Attempts at reading the words 'Vegeta' and 'Potraviny' as if they were written in Russian/Cyrillic.

place in Nordic Europe, with its flat and meagre landscape. Yet, this verticality had its own dark dimension—one strangely connected in my perception with an early realisation of the flow of time, not my own, but historical. I was no more than five. I remember a strange sensation of the trees and thick bushes of the mountain forest slowly going vertically upwards and disappearing from the frame of my vision while we gradually descended from the alpinist camp where my family liked to go from time to time. Our 'Volga'[4] with passengers on board, was slowly descending, laid up on the old vehicle elevator at the Doctor's Mountain Pass,[5] the elevator travelled very slowly, creating the impression in my impatient childish perception that we were crawling down endlessly. And then, the beautiful but monotonous landscape was interrupted by two human figures right next to the side window of our car. They were slowly struggling down the narrow staircase on the right side of the elevator. A man and a woman. Very old. Both were breathing hard, and it was somehow immediately clear that they were foreigners—anyone in the Soviet Union, including the small children, could immediately tell foreigners from locals.

My mother mused, 'I wonder how they managed to climb up in the first place? It is way too steep!' My father asked for the elevator to be stopped and, opening the window, inquired in the only foreign language he could speak a little of, which was German, if they were fine and if they wanted to 'ride' in our car instead of walking. Surprisingly, the white-headed and blue-eyed old lady answered him in German: 'We came to visit our son's grave. He served in the 'Edelweiss'.[6] And then

---

4 'Volga' or GAZ-24 is a famous Soviet car that was manufactured by the Gorky Automobile Plant (GAZ) from 1970 to 1985.

5 Doctor's Mountain Pass is a jokey name for the high vertical rock at the beginning of the Adyr-Su gorge that is necessary to climb to get to the actual gorge where two alpinist camps have functioned for many decades. Visitors to these camps invented the name to convey the idea that anyone who can manage this pass should be given a doctor's approval to become a mountain climber. The place is famous by its unique vehicle elevator which was constructed in the 1960s to bring cars and vans to the plateau top. The vehicles are placed on the large platform which moves along the rails up and down based on the funicular principle. Passengers are asked to leave their cars and use the 360 steps staircase on the side of the elevator.

6 The name refers to 'operation Edelweiss', a plan by the German Wehrmacht during World War II to gain control over the entire Caucasus, thereby capturing the oil fields, cutting off the Soviet army from strategic resources, and preparing the foothold for the future attacks in the Middle East and Asia. Fierce battles took place at many mountain passes in 1942, and German regiments did not manage to

she froze as if waiting to be rebuked. According to the safety rules, the passengers had to leave the car while it was transported up and down on the elevator and use the narrow staircase on the side. But that time the vehicle elevator had to endure, along with the heavy 'Volga', an additional five adults and myself. My father beckoned them inside as I held the following conversation with my mother:

Mom, and why is their son buried here?

He fought and he was killed.

When?

In 1942, just as your grandfather.

You mean they are fascists?

No, they are Germans, and they are parents whose son was killed in the war.

I was silent and brooding while we continued moving down at a snail's pace. It occurred to me that the war, which had managed to bronze itself into monuments and Soviet apocrypha, took place so long ago. Yet that 'long ago' shattered into pieces when I looked at the old man and woman who were sitting in our car as if nothing had happened. Then I realised that only thirty-something years had passed since the war ended. 'They were enemies?'—I hesitated—'no, even worse, they were the enemy's parents'. But my mother repeated, 'They came to visit their son's grave. There are many such graves around. Heavy fighting took place here.'

I do not know how to combine this 'heavy fighting' with the festive Caucasus of my childhood. The setting was far from ideal, but it had sunny and hot summers when one had to take the shady side of the street not to get burnt. It had long, dry, and breath-taking autumns, the astounding beauty of which was interrupted only by the annoying necessity of going back to school. Our small town had a marvellous spa-and-resort suburb with a huge old park, cosy hills, and beautiful lakes; it was full of fruit trees gone wild or, perhaps, that had once been grafted

---

get to Transcaucasia. Subsequent events in Stalingrad and elsewhere led to Hitler's decision to order the troops to retreat, and the North Caucasus was soon recaptured by the Soviet army.

according to the old Circassian technique.⁷ Here and there, one could find wooden mansions in the eclectic, intricate, provincial art-nouveau style; these were later remade into summer houses for the communist-party elite, kindergartens, sanatoriums, and Soviet institutions. There were so many things there that, later, completely disappeared from my life: the huge and extremely sweet watermelons that were left to cool in the cold water of mountain rivers at every picnic, the endemic fear of mosquitoes (oh, that horrendous Caucasus malaria!), the appallingly deep sounds of some Eurasian water bird that was spending its winters in the swampy valleys of the Caucasus, the spread-out mulberry tree in the nearby street of adobe houses, the old tree that perennially blackened the pavement underneath it with abundant fragrant berries, the sense of utmost calmness and unity with the universe while swiftly slaloming down the gentle Elbrus slope under the just-starting snowfall all by myself, and the pungent taste of wild medlar. There was also a trembling and seemingly unsafe chairlift which made its way over the old park. This long-unused chairlift that remains in place for lack of resources to dismantle it, often visits me in my dreams. I think it is that state of being in between heaven and earth so literally embodied in a small, rusted chair that attracts me so much; it is my most organic condition, for I am a bird whose home is where it sings its song.⁸ I sing my songs for the loved ones and since there are no left, I have no home anymore.

As a strange, human version of a cat who likes to crawl into narrow enclosed spaces with a controlled entrance, such as a box or a bag, the child me loved my own room as a space where I could hide from the double reality, at least for a while. Mine was the only room in our apartment that had a solid white door with no glass panels, through which it could have been possible to look inside. My privacy was strongly protected by this heavy oak door and by my own fantasies. Falling asleep and slowly waking up, I liked to trace the designs on the

---

7   In pre-colonial times, Circassians developed a culture of forest gardens in which they not only cultivated certain edible plants in the wild forest but also grafted the wild plants found in the woods with domesticated ones. Their idea was to create a paradise on Earth where everyone would always find fruit to satiate their hunger. After colonisation, most of the forest gardens were destroyed, abandoned, or cut down.

8   This is from an Uzbek proverb about a quail. There is a tradition of quail-song competitions organised by the bird-owners.

peach-coloured wallpaper painted with impressionistic peonies that looked pale and withered. I have never slept better than on my parents' huge, old, 1960s ottoman that was put in my nursery when I turned three. I could not live without my old and simple record player and my vinyl records. These included 'Radio Nanny',[9] little flexible blue disks that came in the popular magazine *Krugozor* [The Outlook] and played 'melodies and rhythms of the foreign variety music',[10] and my favourite green disk 'The Bremen Musicians' with Muslim Magomayev[11] astonishingly singing all parts except the princess.

    The best thing ever was to get sick and stay home alone. It was such a wonderful, feverish excuse to avoid the public spaces of the Soviet country—kindergartens, schools, and, a few times, even the pioneer camps where my parents tried to send me, hoping in vain to teach me some collectivism so that I could survive later. My rejection of school had nothing to do with studies or learning as such but with the school itself, its atmosphere of control and discipline, all-penetrating falseness and cynical demagogy, humiliation, and restriction of freedoms. The very time that moves so slowly when you are a child was being devoured in large chunks by the meaningless abyss of school that I hated honestly and wholeheartedly from the beginning to the end. Therefore, my enormous ottoman with a dozen pillows, a small mountain of books, and a vase of fruit was such a desirable alternative. Oh, the books! They were always around, and they could change everything. Yet, it was not clear at all how to leave this book world for the real one with its unknown laws and enigmatic characters called people. To complicate things even more, most of the books I used to read as a child were not Russian or Soviet. They were translations of world literature, some but not all of which was written specifically for children. When my illness would take over me and my eyes closed, I would start inventing endless stories about myself in the future, playing out different life scenarios. None of these came true. When, during *perestroika*, my parents finally changed the

---

9   Radio Nanny was a Soviet educational program for elementary school children produced by the all-union radio station. The broadcasts, which continued for almost twenty years, were released on vinyl disks.

10   *Krugozor* was a Soviet literary and musical magazine with flexi-discs which was published from 1964 to 1993. The Soviet audiences eagerly awaited each new issue because they hoped to get some new recordings of popular music from elsewhere in the world that was otherwise hard to find in the USSR.

11   Muslim Magomayev was one of the most famous and beloved Soviet pop and opera singers in the 1960s, 70s, and 80s.

old furniture in my room to a new set, it became a different space, and I felt that my home had been taken away from me. I could not imagine that it was only my first, small rehearsal of losing a home, of parting with, in fact, saying goodbye to a notion of belonging somewhere, anywhere at all.

In the endlessly multiplying and complicating opposition of sameness and otherness, a very specific child's stumbling point is the everlasting fear of getting lost. My experience varied depending on the situation of the internal or external alien space and on the degree of existential alienation it evoked. When I was seven, for example, I lost my way in a new neighbourhood in Varna. We were visiting our Bulgarian friends, and I begged my mom to let me sneak out to get an exotic—or so it seemed to a Soviet child—raspberry ice-cream. Although I did not know where to go, at first, I was not even scared. I was peeking into the windows of indistinguishable block houses until I spotted what seemed to be an exactly identical living room to the one I had left half an hour ago. It was, indeed, the same room with the same furniture and a set of the same adult heads and one curly child's—could it be mine? Did it mean I was there and, at the same time, looking at myself from the outside? Or, was I not me?

Being lost could also have a strange biopolitical aftertaste. When I was ten or eleven, my mother took me to Moscow during the winter break. While she was doing her medical examinations at the oncological centre, she managed to get tickets for me and the daughter of her old friend to attend the so-called Kremlin New-Year matinee called, simply, 'Yolka'.[12] Tickets for this performance, as with so many other things in the Soviet Union, were extremely hard to get. My memory has not retained any traces of the miserable New Year show or the taste of candy from the 'gift' that was packed in a weird, red-plastic Russian cottage.[13] What I will always remember, though, is the frozen Kremlin yard to which several thousand children were taken immediately after the performance at the Kremlin State Palace. It was very dark and cold. Only several spotlights were illuminating the yard. In its centre, the militia men cordoned off a large circle, putting up some barricades to prevent thousands of parents from entering. Then, they let the children walk

---

12   Yolka, the Russian word for 'spruce', is a colloquial, metonymic compression used to name a matinee organised usually for children around the New Year holidays.

13   Gift, here, refers to a standard, nicely packed set of candy and fruit that children traditionally receive at the 'Yolka'. Most were packed in plastic bags, but rarer sets came in hard plastic containers in the form of houses, rockets, and Kremlin towers.

around the circle, periodically chasing us with loud orders. Parents were calling their children's names when they thought they spotted their child among hundreds of others. We walked faster and faster, hoping that, any second, we would be found, we would be definitely found. Then, it would be possible to leave this children's flock as it marched obediently to an unknown but sinister fate. Many youngsters were crying. A couple of smaller ones slipped on the ice and fell into the snow. Yet, the militia men were standing around the outside of the circle, as if guarding children from their parents. At first, we were focused and serious; our eyes feverishly searched for moms, dads, grannies. Well into our third lap, we started to panic. Grown-ups, looking out from behind the militia men's backs, hollered discordantly in hoarse, almost hysterical voices: 'Misha! Katya! Natasha! Vasya! Dima!' Yet, no one seemed to be found. I even wondered for a moment if they paired us with the wrong set of parents. Tall and strong men forced their way to the first row, pushing the weaker mothers and grandmothers away. Shorter adults could not squeeze in at all. When we went into the fourth lap, I thought that we would never be picked up. Perhaps our parents just failed to come and collect us, but why? My imagination was drawing a terrible picture: the militia men would take us to an orphanage where we, those unclaimed by our parents, would solemnly check in and never leave. I could almost sense the smell of trouble, the horror of communal existence, the bedside tables shared by ten people, the open shower cabins and toilet stalls, the indescribably rancid taste of larvae-infested soup, and the rough surface of faded bedding that had known too many tenants. At this point, I lingered a bit and the close-by militia man immediately yelled: 'Get a move on! Don't stop!' The Kremlin yard made one feel decidedly uncomfortable. One could clearly feel here the clanking of the power's gears—one wrong step, and you are under its treads. And then, we were found! My mother's friend, who came to pick us up but could not see from behind the taller people in front, started calling to us in a very loud voice. She did not shout her own daughter's name, which was a common one in Moscow in the early 1980s. Instead, she shouted my strange and obviously not-Russian appellation, correctly sensing that I was probably the only one there who was called so.

Like many years ago, I am sitting in a small, red, wooden chair with a white number—38—on its back. The chair is slowly moving almost vertically up through the air, slightly vibrating as it passes the towers of the chairlift system and periodically freezing up between heaven and earth. It is a different chairlift in a different country, and it is perhaps the best realisation of the state of unsettlement that has become my real authentic 'home' ever since I can remember. In my old mobile phone, there is still a contact 'Dom' [Home]. But now, there is no one there, and there cannot be if I am not there myself. I cannot call myself, or can I? And it is not a home anymore. It is time to change this incongruous name for something else, for instance, 'my old number' or, perhaps, give it some nickname or literary pseudonym. Against all odds, however, one humid and cold April night, my telephone rang. On its screen, the caller-ID read 'Dom'. I froze, but when my finger finally swiped with some delay on the green receiver, I could make out only some strange, almost-inaudible rustling and static silence on the other end of the line. I felt the stillness and emptiness of the dusty, abandoned not-a-home-anymore, where I cannot go back to just as I cannot return to my vanished childhood. This time, my vertical movement is upwards, as in the imagined scene of Sergei Paradzhanov's unfinished last film *A Confession*. In it, his dead ancestors, whose graves were destroyed to build a city park, become unsettled and run to the famous Tbilisi funicular to head to its upper station as a symbol of their ultimate ascension. And I am thinking once again of the exile from childhood as our first home and of the ways we can or cannot return there in order to die and be buried by our restless spirits—ancestral or not.

References

Brodsky, J. (2010). *Letters to a Roman Friend*, trans. by A. Kneller. Russian Poetry in English, https://sites.google.com/site/poetryandtranslations/joseph-brodsky/letters-to-a-roman-friend

Kukarkin, A. (1985). *Burzhuaznaya massovaya kultura* [Bourgeois Mass Culture]. Izdatelstvo Politicheskoi Literaturi

Lasch, C. (1985). *The Minimal Self: Psychic Survival in Troubled Times*. WW Norton and Company

Orwell, G. (1949). *Nineteen Eighty-Four*. London: Secker and Warburg.

Paradzhanov, G. (2004). *Ya Umer v Detstve* [I Died in my Childhood]. Documentary film. Paradzhanov Film Studio

Sorokin, V. (1994). *Norma* [The Norm]. Tri Kita

Smuggling Jewelry[1]

Tatyana Kleyn

'Smuggling Jewelry', a memory-story video by Tatyana Kleyn.
https://hdl.handle.net/20.500.12434/644c3d3b

It was a big day for her, just five years old at the time. She didn't know it, but her life and her family would never be the same. It was a chilly February day in the Soviet Union as they arrived at the airport as one family unit. It was time to leave the cramped home that everyone had ever known in Riga and venture into the unknown with the new status of political refugee. She could sense that a major event was taking place, but she doesn't recall anyone explaining the gravity of it to her: that her life as she knew it would become a distant memory among forgotten places and spaces. Under a homemade red wool sweater was a family heirloom of a yellow and burnt-orange amber necklace. The family hoped that her young age would permit her to act as the vessel to circumvent strict guidelines about what could and could not be taken out of the country by refugees leaving for greater freedoms and opportunities. She was given clear instructions by her mother not to say anything about the 'contraband' that hung from her body and which she was tasked with smuggling across the border.

---

1   This is a childhood memory produced as part of the Reconnect/Recollect project discussed in the introduction to this book.

© 2024 Tatyana Kleyn, CC BY-NC 4.0   https://doi.org/10.11647/OBP.0383.21

She was anxious about what was to come, but she kept her emotions hidden so as not to create more strain for her parents who she sensed were already undergoing tremendous stress. So, she simply followed the directives as they went through the in-depth screening process. In tow were also two animals, one living and another living in the girl's imagination. There was an unnamed but most special pink teddy bear in her arms. It had already seen a few good years and was a bit worn and dirty to show for it but, nevertheless, was her prized possession. Her mom warned her that airport security guards may cut it open, with the idea that they may suspect something hidden inside that the family was trying to smuggle out. Not overly phased, she responded that if that happened, they could just sew the bear back together, thereby bringing it back to life and to wholeness. Luckily, it stayed in one piece and the prized jewelry, albeit meager by some standards, made its way via a five-year-old vessel to Italy and eventually to their new home in the United States.

The other animal was Charley, a black Great Dane whose presence often brought strangers to ask if he was a small pony or a big dog. He was her grandparent's 'favourite child' who ate home-cooked meals (albeit dog food was not readily available in the Soviet Union), had numerous photo albums devoted to him, and won dozens of medals that were displayed for all to see from the dog shows he had entered. But Charley didn't have the same fortune as the teddy bear. Once the family arrived in Italy, they learned that dogs could not easily be brought to the United States. Given Charley's prominent status, one thing was clear: he would not be left behind. The family had to scramble to come up with a plan that resulted in her grandparents rerouting to Germany, where they had friends. Charley would, of course, go with them and the rest of the family would continue with their original plans to the United States. It was five years later they would all be reunited as a family.

Smuggling Jewelry 137

Photograph of Tatyana with her family in her birth city of Riga in the Soviet Union, 1977. From Tatyana Kleyn's family archive.

Photograph of Tatyana, her aunt Doris, and Charley the Great Dane. Riga, 1977. From Tatyana Kleyn's family archive.

Sleepy Smuggles[1]

Sarah Fichtner

She crossed and sensed the border with her eyes closed many times, half asleep, on the backseat of her parent's car. She must have been 6 or 7. Hearing the voices of the border guards from a distance (that's how you hear when you are supposed not to hear, when you're actually asleep, right?): 'Open the trunk. … Could you get out of the car, please? … Everyone! The child, too.'

'But don't you see, she's fast asleep!' she heard her Mom plead. 'Please don't make me wake her up. I'm so glad that she is FINALLY asleep.' She heard her Mom sigh.

The girl was not really sleeping. She noticed the flashlights outside intruding through her eyelids. She smelled the gasoline evaporating from the turned off engines nearby. Her heart was beating fast, adrenaline rushed through her body, but she was not afraid. She heard her parents' voices, reassuring. They were standing outside, negotiating with the border guards. The guards did not insist on waking her up. They understood. What exactly had they understood? It didn't matter. Everyone played their role. She felt safe. And complicit. They had succeeded, again.

When they reached their friends' house in East Berlin, her parents got out the books and the newest issue of the political magazine 'Der Spiegel' from underneath her seat. The presents had been protected through her seemingly innocent sleep. She felt very proud and everyone was happy.

---

1   This is a childhood memory produced as part of the Reconnect/Recollect project discussed in the introduction to this book.

6. The Power of Other Worlds: Civilisational Frames and Child-Adult Intimacies in Socialist Childhoods

Jennifer Patico

This chapter draws on childhood-memory narratives from Cold-War socialist and early post-socialist settings to problematise the east-west civilisational hierarchies that often frame accounts of socialism's 'less developed' material and consumer worlds. In the narratives, children's encounters with commodities from abroad speak not only or directly to the significance of east/west, socialist/capitalist hierarchies in their lives but also to children's relationships with the adults closest to them and children's affective experiences of their own maturation. Exploring these dynamics brings scholarship on socialism and post-socialism into fresh conversation with contemporary childhood studies and other work that theorises how selfhood and intimacy take form in and through specific moments in political economy. To bring the falsely simple oppositions of east/west and adult/child into the same analytical frame is to begin building more nuanced, nimble understandings of how macro-level political economic boundaries can be integral to children's most intimate forms of self-knowledge.

Afterwards, usually at nights, she would spend hours, looking again and again, secretly looking at the forbidden world. She did it at night because she did not want anyone to know; she felt shameful about this kind of stupid wasting of time. She thought she would not be able to explain to her parents why she did it. For her it was clear that she was attracted by attractive people demonstrating attractive objects, and that did not require any explanations.

In the passage above, a contemporary adult remembers her 1960s childhood in Northern Ossetia, a Russian republic that was part of the Soviet Union. What gave the young girl, about ten or eleven years old at the time, such secret and shameful enjoyment late in the night? She was poring over French clothing catalogues that had been brought home by her parents who had been working abroad. The images therein spoke not only to her own aesthetic desires and not only to a larger political economy—revealing a Soviet girl's imagination of the abroad as a space of attractive and mysterious difference—but also, as this brief excerpt hints, to the intricacies of a girl's evolving relationship with her own parents.

Socialist consumers' desires for, and perceptions of, the world on the other side of the Iron Curtain certainly have been considered in previous scholarship, not to mention popular media. However, as Gille and Mincyte (2020) have observed, scholarly and journalistic treatments too often impose a simple civilisational logic onto socialist subjects' experiences and perceptions, assuming

> a linear and even teleological view of development and modernization that permeates the *differences* between Western consumer society and socialist central planning into *hierarchy*—that is, into a register of inferiority and superiority, expressed as lower and higher stages of development or modernization. (p. 219, emphasis in original)

That is, such works assume a unilineal, progressive, modern, and capitalist scheme of development in which the economies of countries such as the United States appear to be at the forefront, whereas those in socialist settings are framed as less developed and sophisticated, less modern, and more backward in relation to that specific teleology (see Burrell 2011; Patico 2008). Such assumptions are belied, however, by a deeper understanding of the consumer politics of socialist-bloc countries.

Although the commodity shortages that dominated US media representations of the Soviet Union in the later twentieth century were indeed common, focus on these obscures the region's distinct consumerist modernities. Throughout the region, internally-produced comforts from perfumes to televisions were enjoyed and touted as evidence of increasing standards of living and the superiority of socialist life; they were cultivated as part of the experience of a socialist middle class (Gille et al. 2020; Patico 2008). The consumer experiences of late-socialist citizens were not ones of pure deprivation, then, but were more complex stories of both fostered and frustrated consumer desires and intermittent access to exotic items from further afield, such as the young girl's French clothing catalogues.

This is not to say that similarly hierarchical civilisational logics have not been part of emic cultural schema in socialist and post-socialist worlds. During the early years of Russian post-socialism, I found that many—particularly members of the downwardly mobile, educated, 'older' middle classes, among whom I was conducting ethnographic research in St. Petersburg—were all too likely to place themselves into a developmental hierarchy that situated them as behind and below the 'west' in terms of the sophistication of their material environments and their consumer repertoires (Patico 2008). Such local talk often treated market-driven development and expanded consumerism as inevitabilities yet also framed such development as a road on which they had fallen behind. In the late 1990s, as these post-socialist consumers experimented (for better and worse) with a deluge of goods and media from around the world, they often referred to their material circumstances as subordinate to those of the imagined west: explicitly, by disparaging their level of 'civilisation', or somewhat more implicitly, by jokingly describing their conditions in Russia as 'like Africa' or by asking me whether I, the American, might like to see their unrenovated apartment windows for the sake of enjoying some 'exotica' (Patico 2008). Such discourses were self-orientalising, describing a new reality or new consciousness of being materially and technologically 'behind'—even as their ironic tones also suggested that Russians were thought to be worthy of something more 'civilised'.

Burrell (2011) notes that depictions of socialism from within the (former) socialist bloc often thematise sensory experiences, with perceptions of colour primary among these: 'Colour and visual life … and in particular the denotation of a 'gray' communist bloc—are almost ubiquitous in accounts of socialism across the Soviet Union and eastern Europe' (p. 148). Observations about the grayness of socialist life, about the colourful nature of life in the west by contrast, and about post-socialist transformation as a colourising process have constituted collective symbolic reference points (ibid., p. 149). These framings of colour, while rich with sensory and 'civilisational' meaning, do not lend support for the straightforward use of un-usefully neat civilisational hierarchies as analytical models for the material realities and perceptual schemes of life in socialist Europe, however. For, as recent scholarship has highlighted, such hierarchical models reinforce a simplistic view of the relationship between desire and politics, assuming, for example, that the pleasure in imported goods experienced by socialist citizens was based in 'envy, as a desire for capitalism', which Gille et al. (2020) call 'a logical fallacy' (p. 12). They go on to say that 'many have written about how it was the illicitness of Western goods that made them all the more desirable, not necessarily that they were lacking in the East or that they were better' (ibid.). Scarboro (2020), referencing Crowley and Reid, adds that the role of pleasure in late socialism is underexamined because our existing histories emphasise the dynamics of 'need, command, and shortage' rather than those of 'luxury, leisure, and pleasure' (Reid and Crowley 2010, p. 10 as cited by Scarboro 2020, p. 192).

My point here is not to argue that the pleasures of socialist life have been painted unfairly and now must be represented in a more positive manner. Rather, I highlight this scholarship to posit that we must continue to seek for new, less top-down, more fluid ways of looking at the materialities of socialist life, at experiences of the east-west Cold-War divide, and at how socialist and post-socialist citizens have imagined and utilised the abroad or the west in the course of inhabiting and conceptualising their everyday worlds. Even as east-west dichotomies and related sensory images were salient in the everyday, affective experiences of the Cold War and its aftermath, we can ask more nuanced questions about how these were embedded in social contexts and triggered social effects that transcended conventional framings of the Iron Curtain per se. This chapter attends, then, through close readings of Cold-War memory narratives, to some of the ways in which material and sensory experiences of the 'other side' served consumers as a means of knowing the world at large, of making sense of it, and of participating in relationships very close to home.

In particular, I examine how civilisational logics are linked in memories of socialist and early post-socialist childhoods to frames of intimacy, desire, and relationship of various kinds. These themes are salient in special ways in the lives of children, for whom such material encounters are also part and parcel of their coming into knowledge of adult sensibilities and expectations within their immediate social worlds. In these contexts, commodities do not have predetermined, referential meanings linked only or mainly with the political significance of the east-west divide. Rather, consumption of these goods was part of a 'process of objectification—that is, a use of goods and services in which the object or activity becomes simultaneously a practice in the world and a form in which we construct our understandings of ourselves in the world' (Miller 2005, p. 27). Material encounters with the 'west' or with an 'outside' were, for children of the Cold War and early post-Cold-War years, precisely bound up with their affective experiences of their own maturation and of their perceptions of the adults closest to them. I take up these memory stories to consider how civilisational imaginations were lived intimately, not least inasmuch as they helped to define the contours of post/socialist childhood and adulthood—which, again, is not to say that the hierarchies were real in the teleological ways capitalist triumphalism would have us believe (see Yurchak 2006).

To do so, I draw from childhood memory narratives generated by adult participants in a 2019 workshop in Helsinki, Finland, in which those who had spent their childhoods in socialist and early post-socialist European locales shared personal memories alongside others who had come of age in the United States, Finland, and elsewhere during the same era. Participants offered individual stories and then worked in groups to draw out more detail from one another, striving to prioritise the most immediate sensory and emotional aspects of these childhood episodes and to avoid, to the extent possible, any overlay of adult analysis. While the memories inevitability were filtered through the consciousnesses of adult minds and post-Cold-War experiences, the attempt was made to focus in on those details of the memories that seemed closest to the episodes as they had been felt and perceived in the immediacy of the moment, so that we as adult researchers might learn from our own and others' stories about Cold War life in fresh, possibly unexpected ways. Indeed, the goal of this technique was to break free, to the extent possible, from 'normative, constitutive forms of discourse' about the Cold War (Davies and Gannon 2012, p. 359) and to dwell not on reconstructing individual subjects and their psychologies but in painting the material, sensory and social contexts of lives as remembered—and to see what meanings and themes arose from the collective process of telling and analysis, understanding that the speakers, their past selves as remembered, as well as 'the physical, relational, and discursive space of the memories' and 'the physical, relational, and discursive space inside of which the memory work is done' are 'always-emergent entities' (ibid., p. 362).

The Helsinki memory stories were prompted by a focus, agreed upon by the group members in advance, on the broad topics of leisure time and materialities. The particular analytical threads I have taken up in this paper are among those that rose to the surface from a broad analysis of all the memories shared by fifteen adults in Helsinki; they were echoed by narratives from other workshop sites of the larger project, and one of these stories is also included in my analysis. I focus here on a select few narratives that nicely condense the ways in which childhood memories from socialist and early-post-socialist contexts interwove accounts of fascination with the commodities and textures of faraway places with the emergent, fraught relationships between children and adults—speaking through, but not only about, the politics of Cold-War commodity consumption.

The story that opened this chapter is that of a girl who grew up in Northern Ossetia, in Soviet Russia, in the 1960s. Her family had relatively unusual access to distant places and their commodities: her parents, both medical doctors, travelled to Algeria to work for two years, while she was left at home with her grandmother. Writing in the third person, she recalls:

For her it was a country in the faraway Africa, and the first question: Why are children not allowed to go with the parents? She could not imagine living without parents and felt sad about parting with them. […] Her grandparents […] loved her dearly, but sometimes she would cry at nights when thinking about Mother.

Yet the girl found that nice things came of this arrangement as well, as her parents began sending packages with items that intrigued her, with unheard of and unseen things like practically transparent underwear made of nylon!

Or clothes that do not get wrinkled. Now Algeria seemed to be a country with incredible and beautiful things.

Even more exciting things appeared when her parents finally returned home. The girl learned that the special items were not from Algeria but had been ordered from French mail-order catalogues. She was unfamiliar with catalogue-shopping as a concept, but her parents had brought the catalogues home with them, and these were a source of great interest for the girl.

They turned out to be very thick big colourful books with fascinating pictures on very thin pages. That was a real wonder! The catalogue had photos of everything—clothes, household appliances, even wallpaper and curtains, and everywhere—beautiful people.

For the girl, what jumped out from the pages were both consumer novelties and people, themselves visually attractive.

Other workshop participants conveyed similar impressions of the co-constitutive attractiveness of both things and people from the U.S. and western Europe. For example, a young girl growing up in Poland in the 1980s corresponded with penpals in the United States.

The photos are colourful, what is rarely used in Poland, because the colour films are very expensive. Pictures have such a smooth texture and they even shine gently. They are printed on Kodak paper, with Kodak logo on the back side. The quality of the photos is stunning to her. There are no such pictures in her photo album. The campground owners sent her a family photo from the pier. There are 7 people standing on the wooden platform by the sea. For her they look like from a show. They are dressed nicely, and their clothes are so colourful.

As an adult today, she remembers how struck she was by the colourful clothes worn by Americans in photos she received by mail, as well as the smooth, shiny quality of the Kodak paper on which the images were printed.

A speaker from a related memory-project workshop who grew up in 1970s and 1980s Romania described having observed tourists on visits to the Black Sea who walked 'nonchalantly, smiling, laughing, in their colourful clothes'. Her memory story contrasted foreign tourists' 'inner confidence' with locals' colourlessness and subdued affects.

I could spot 'them' from miles away: they were walking nonchalantly, smiling, laughing, in their colourful clothes [...]. As a child, I perceived a certain superiority of the human race in the way they were holding their heads up, walking straight and talking their language loudly, English, German, French, as if they really wanted to be noticed. There was something in the way they were holding their bodies, an inner confidence.

After passing them on the street, my nostrils would be in heaven. Today I can explain that smell: the detergent they used for their clothes, the shampoo, the body wash, the perfume, all mixing in a heavenly concoction, lingering in my olfactory memory for ages. Luxury items we didn't know existed. We wore gray, brown and black clothes, all the same, walked quickly, heads down, we were quiet, just a mass, with no distinctive qualities; we didn't want to attract attention. As a child, my impression was that they looked so different that they could even be from another planet.

These memories intermingle the materiality of unfamiliar, colourful, and glossy, sweet-selling items with the bodies and selves of 'superior' and 'confident' people from alien places.

Decades later, a young girl in Romania had a similar sensory experience of the 'away' as accessed through material commodities. A child of the early-post-socialist years, her understanding of these fabulous objects was mediated less through glossy magazine pages than through television advertisements. Today, in her early thirties, she recalls a birthday party in Bucharest, 1998. She was celebrating a friend's birthday, together with a group of girls whose mothers had become acquainted in the maternity ward. Hence the girls in attendance all were just about eight years old at the time. She remembers that she and the other girls had been confused by their parents' requirement that they 'dress up' in their school uniforms—white shirt and blue skirt—for the party; the young girls found it unnecessary to dress up 'among themselves', though they were accustomed to dressing up for special occasions. Still, 'they accepted this dressing up without a fuss'. Yet, one of the girls attending dressed differently.

Only Irina was wearing a yellow T-shirt
She stuck out among them
The girl whose mum was a stewardess,
The girl raised by her grandparents

The girl who'd eat bananas at all meals.

Though the memory story does not offer direct analysis of the family's situation, a connection is suggested among the facts that Irina had a mother who travelled for work, that her family had different rules about dressing up, and that she enjoyed 'bananas at all meals', which most likely was understood an unconventional privilege since bananas were seen rarely in state-socialist countries prior to their marketisation (Patico 2008). Meanwhile, two other girls attending the party had an aunt living abroad who would send them 'all kinds of nice things'.

Shiny things, nice smelling things, pink things
Things you only saw on Cartoon Network, never in a shop.
Their aunt would send them from France.
She had left just before the Revolution
She would send all kinds of toys and clothes and useful stuff.
Like Pampers.
When the girls were babies it was difficult to find Pampers in Romania.
Mariana the aunt would get them from social shops or from aids for poor people.
Cool clothes, dolls, Polypockets […] everything smelled so incredibly nice.
Like candies, like cuteness
Like sugar, spice and everything nice.

This memory portrays the girl's awareness of basic consumer scarcities in early-post-socialist Romania (Pampers were sent to this family from a relative who had migrated to western Europe, though it is not entirely clear whether this would have been known to the young girl at the time) as well as her attraction to 'cool clothes' and dolls that smelled 'like candies, like cuteness,' which seemed to be the stuff of foreign television ads rather than of everyday reality.

Such exotic and appealing items were becoming accessible to some local families through various means, however, so that they now became inserted into the young girl's material experience. As the story continues, the narrator describes the girls' mutual enjoyment of these items as they 'without any plan in advance […] spontaneously' painted their faces with makeup sent by the French aunt.

And as that makeup covered more and more of their faces,
The more satisfied they were

As if they had discovered something
As if they had done something forbidden
As if they were innovative and daring.
[...] Their blue faces looked a bit sinister
But what does that matter in front of the fun they had?

Her experience of the makeup is collective and raucous, but she is aware of something transgressive in her enjoyment of these things, something that feels distinct to her generation. She describes their faces 'innovative and daring' and even 'sinister', but notes that this was excusable given the fun they had. The transgression, perhaps, is central to the enjoyment; as noted above, Gille et al. (2020) have pointed out that the illicitness of goods from the west was perhaps a key part of their appeal, even apart from any supposed superiority or exoticness of the products. As such goods became more accessible, this memory story suggests, their sensory pleasures were bound up with the sense of something still illicit, something with a complex moral valence.

Returning to the first story, the Soviet girl looking at the French catalogues shared that sense of transgression and moral ambiguity, here amplified by the secrecy she attaches to her involvement with the images.

She did not want to be interrupted while enjoying the photos, so until the time she had a room of her own, she seldom looked at the catalogue pages. But afterwards, usually at nights, she would spend hours, looking again and again, secretly looking at the forbidden world.

Not only does she describe a feeling of pleasure in absorbing those pages, but she recalls a sense of shame. Somehow this activity of hers did not seem to have an understood or excusable place in her social world, despite the fact that the idea of being attracted to pretty things and people seemed natural enough to her.

She did it at nights because she did not want anyone to know, she felt shameful about this kind of stupid wasting of time. She thought she would not be able to explain to her parents why she did it. For her it was clear that she was attracted by attractive people demonstrating attractive objects, and that did not require any explanations. She also knew that her parents used the catalogues in real life: they selected some goods which they bought. She often asked herself a question:

What would you select from this page? It was always a hard question, how to select the best from the best.

Though these pages connected the girl tenuously to a world far away, she was aware that her parents had more tangible connections to it. They, at least, had been abroad and had managed actually to order things from these catalogues; and, perhaps in part for this reason, the girl finds her own fascination with the pages to be somehow awkward and possibly wrong. She wonders how one would possibly choose which items were best, and she posits her parents as people who must know the answers; yet the questions do not seem to be ones she feels ready to ask. Her parents, she fears, would not understand her absorption, her 'stupid wasting of time'. Her sense of transgression, then, is not necessarily triumphant or particularly rebellious in her memory but connected with feelings of shame, ambivalence, and compromised intimacy. (On ambivalence experienced in the use of imported commodities, see also Gille et al. 2020.)

Additional stories from the same two individuals (those who enjoyed the French catalogues and the girls' makeup party) paint further aspects of how goods from abroad provided opportunities for fascination but also for fraught exchanges with the adults whom children feared to disappoint or, alternatively, whom they suspected of ill intent. The Soviet girl recalls travelling to the Pioneer summer camp Artek, which was in the Crimea and known to be exclusive:

it was next to impossible to get there, it was supposed to be for the most of the most active pioneers and the best pupils [...] a dream of every Soviet child.

Due to her excellent grades, she was able to attend, but she ultimately was disillusioned by the experience: the camp activities were more boring and regimented than she had expected and she was placed in a group of younger children, without her friends.

A small break in the monotony comes when a 'foreign delegation' visits the camp.

We [the campers] were warned that if the guests offered them anything, not to accept, since the gift may be poisoned. She was excited as she had never seen foreigners before, and she expected it would be very interesting to meet them. But she remembered little of the meeting (there was just some concert), as they did not communicate, there was just a group of elderly people. At the end of the meeting the foreign delegation went to the bus, and before the doors closed, one of them threw out 2 colourful packs which looked like packs of candies. The Pioneer Leader caught the packs, told the children that the candy was sure to be poisoned, and assured the children that she was going to throw the candy away. She never believed these words! She was absolutely convinced that the Pioneer Leader took the candy for herself!

The story of the foreign delegation amounts to one more way in which the camp promised to be exciting but ended up being disappointing. Moreover, the girl experiences a lack of trust in the adult world here that is entangled with her close encounter with rarefied foreign gifts: she is convinced that she is being misled by the Pioneer Leader who claims that candy from foreigners is dangerous. The woman simply wanted to keep the candy for herself, the girl is sure, suggesting the growing child's understanding that imported items were coveted as such—and also that one's coveting was sometimes to be hidden, and potentially socially divisive.

By contrast, the Romanian girl's second memory is about disappointment in her own behaviour in front of adults. She is in an urban park with her grandparents, Bitu and Bita, playing with a colourful ball received from her grandmother's family in Bulgaria. She is about four years old.

– Take care with the ball, Bitu says.
– I will, I will, she replies,
Thinking that Bita doesn't nag her
With observations all the time.
– Look around
There's no one here,
Nothing can happen, she reassures Bitu.
The park was indeed deserted as autumn creeped in.

But then the unexpected happens: she kicks the ball hard and a dog appears and carries it away. They attempt to chase down the dog and retrieve the ball, but to no avail.

The ball is gone.
Deflated. Forever.

The dog owner deeply apologizes
He offers to get her a new one
There is nothing
New
That can replace
The old.
Such a rainbow
Ball was virtually impossible to find.
–I told you to be careful, scorns Bitu.
The girl is sorry for the ball.
It really had a short life, not enough time to enjoy it.
But, more.
She feels inescapably embarrassed.
For not taking good enough care
Of this special gift coming from Bulgaria.
She hates to disappoint them.

The memory conveys the shame of a young child who has been told to be careful but evidently has not been careful enough. The result is the loss of a precious item from abroad, which only adds to the girl's dismay in having disappointed her grandparents. As in the other stories, she is aware that the imported item has value as such, and she is aware that the management of it is part of her evolving relationship with her adult caretakers.

Taken together, these memories convey the sensory power for children of unfamiliar, colourful images and items from abroad, as these were experienced during and soon after the Cold War. The items in question did not come only from the Euroamerican 'west' but also from places slightly closer to home (such as Bulgaria) or via detours (such as Algeria). Encountering or receiving things outside of the accustomed local channels was an impactful experience, the commodities providing pleasure in their fresh material characteristics as well as fodder for imaginings of other ways of being. In these scenes, commodities from abroad are shown to be media for imagining unfamiliar worlds and pleasures, to be sure, acting as something like what Burrell (2011) has called 'provenirs' (p. 145). These are items linked not, like souvenirs, to remembered experiences, but rather primarily to a particular construction of a place (the west) [... that] could also simultaneously act as 'avenirs', tapping into aspirations about what life in the future could look like [...]. They managed to encapsulate the imaginings of another place and the yearnings for another time yet to come, a potentially enchanting, and in the context of the socialist regime, politically subversive, combination.

The children's memories do not thematise east/west boundaries in any explicitly political way, but they convey the awareness that 'here' did not have the lovely-smelling and colourful things that 'there' had, tapping into a sense of the unknown or poorly understood elsewhere and future.

More importantly for this chapter, the stories also reveal how that gap mattered and had force in their immediate social worlds—and not only because, as has been more discussed in the literature on socialist consumerism, the coveted items could be used for strategic exchange, display, or prestige (for example, Ledeneva 1998). Rather, amidst all this idealisation and fascination, the material things undeniably are 'anchored into the private space of home, disrupting and reshaping special occasions and everyday activities' (Burrell 2011, p. 149). More specifically, they appear as tied to the emergent confusion and shame children feel as they navigate adult expectations and gaps in their own understanding. The girl in the park shrugs off her grandfather's warnings, but she is embarrassed terribly when she loses the Bulgarian ball after all. The girl at camp, slightly older, throws her judgement on adults and their disappointing behaviours: they try to cast visions of danger where there may not be any, perhaps for their own selfish ends. The same girl's earlier story, too, points to lapses of information and communication with adults: she enjoys the catalogues privately, with a sense of transgression and wrongness, not knowing exactly how it might be that her parents have managed to interact with the catalogues in a more routine and savvy way.

Indeed, if adults helped to circulate these items to children, they are not necessarily remembered as informative guides to the goods' local and translocal contexts or significance. Instead, the narrators recall themselves as children uncertain, ashamed, or without clear information about the acceptability of their own desires and how to manage them. In these remembered experiences, commodities speak not directly nor only to civilisational hierarchies, but more meaningfully to child-adult power dynamics, to sensory pleasures, and to the relationships among those.

In examining the material worlds of state socialism and its aftermath, then, we need to look beyond the surface of seemingly self-explanatory models of civilisational hierarchy—even as such discourses were persuasive in their own ways in the everyday lives of people both 'east' and 'west'—in order to understand how material connections to the abroad held social and emotional power close to home, shaping and shaped by the most intimate relationships, such as those between children and their caregivers. By exploring those dynamics, we can bring scholarship on socialism and postsocialism into fresh conversation with contemporary childhood studies and with other work that theorises how selfhood and intimacy take form in and through specific moments in political economy (Cook 2004; Faircloth 2014; Illouz 2007; Patico 2010, 2020). For example, recent scholarship in childhood and parenting studies has critiqued the seeming self-evidence of the category of the 'child'. Such work draws attention instead to the historical construction of the child, to the co-creation of salient understandings of childhood and adulthood, and to the ways in which these constructions tend to reflect broad social anxieties and political, economic or environmental pressures (see, for example, Katz 2008; Morgenstern 2018; Rosen and Faircloth 2020).

Likewise, we can ask how the seemingly self-evident and hierarchically organised categories of east and west, capitalist and socialist, cannot be taken for granted as 'actually existing' in any simple sense, even as they are unquestionably salient in experience, potently reflective of larger political realities, and lodged in the materiality of commodities and the affective immediacy of confusing desire. Post/socialist Europe's modernist consumer lifestyles, while distinct from those experienced elsewhere and at other times, were not in any sense the child of the 'West's' adult capitalism, though this logic tends to be smuggled into conversations about Cold-War and post-Cold-War economic development.

Putting these two falsely simple oppositions—east/west, adult/child—into dialogue with one another provides leverage to trouble both of them and to build more nuanced, nimble understandings of how macro-level political economic boundaries are bound up with children's (and adults') most intimate forms of self-knowledge. This is true not because they structurally determine children's experiences in straightforward ways but because they are context for the material stuff through which children (and adults) come to know their own relationships and movements in the world, their own pleasures and disappointments. Bringing these quiet, ambivalent moments to speak back to those civilisational frames is another kind of (productive) transgression, one that offers up what Anna Tsing (2013) has called the 'rough edges' that become 'a purchase point for both intellectual and political work in and across post-industrial economies' (p. 39).

References

Burrell, K. (2011). 'The Enchantment of Western Things: Children's Material Encounters in Late Socialist Poland'. *Transactions of the Institute of British Geographers*, 36(1), 143–56, https://doi.org/10.1111/j.1475-5661.2010.00408.x

Cook, D. T. (2004). *The Commodification of Childhood: The Children's Clothing Industry and the Rise of the Child Consumer*. Duke University Press, https://doi.org/10.1515/9780822385431

Davies, B., and Gannon, S. (2012). 'Collective Biography and the Entangled Enlivening of Being'. *International Review of Qualitative Research*, 5(4), 357–76, https://doi.org/10.1525/irqr.2012.5.4.357

Faircloth, C. (2014). 'Intensive Parenting and the Expansion of Parenting', in *Parenting Culture Studies*, ed. by E. Lee, J. Bristow, C. Faircloth, and J. MacVarish. Palgrave Macmillan, pp. 25–50, https://doi.org/10.1057/9781137304612

Gille, Z., Scarboro, C. and Mincyte, D. (2020). 'The Pleasures of Backwardness', in *The Socialist Good Life: Desire, Development, and Standards of Living in Eastern Europe*, ed. by C. Scarboro, D. Mincyte and Z. Gille. Indiana University Press, pp. 1–24, https://doi.org/10.2307/j.ctv11vcfvf

Gille, Z. and Mincyte, D. (2020). 'The Prosumerist Resonance Machine: Rethinking Political Subjectivity and Consumer Desire in Late Socialism', in *The Socialist Good Life: Desire, Development, and Standards of Living in Eastern Europe*, ed. by C. Scarboro, D. Mincyte and Z. Gille. Indiana University Press. Indiana University Press, pp. 218–37, https://doi.org/10.2307/j.ctv11vcfvf

Illouz, E. (2007). *Cold Intimacies: The Making of Emotional Capitalism*. Polity Press

Katz, C. (2008). 'Childhood as Spectacle: Relays of Anxiety and the Reconfiguration of the Child'. *Cultural Geographies*, 15(1), 5–17, https://doi.org/10.1177/1474474007085773

Ledeneva, A. (1998). *Russia's Economy of Favors: Blat, Networking and Informal Exchange*. Cambridge University Press

Miller, D. (2005). 'Consumption as the Vanguard of History: A Polemic by Way of an Introduction', in *Acknowledging Consumption: A Review of New Studies*, ed. by D. Miller. Routledge, pp. 1–57, https://doi.org/10.4324/9780203975398

Morgenstern, N. (2018). *Wild Child: Intensive Parenting and Posthumanist Ethics*. University of Minnesota Press, https://doi.org/10.5749/j.ctv175sm

Patico, J. (2008). *Consumption and Social Change in a Post-Soviet Middle Class*. Stanford University Press and Woodrow Wilson International Centre Press.

—— (2010). 'Kinship and Crisis: The Embedding of Economic Pressures and Gender Ideals in Post-Socialist International Matchmaking'. *Slavic Review*, 69(1), 16–40, https://doi.org/10.1017/S0037677900016685

—— (2020). *The Trouble with Snack Time: Children's Food and the Politics of Parenting*. New York University Press, https://doi.org/10.18574/nyu/9781479835331.001.0001

Reid, S. and D. Crowley. (2010) 'Introduction: Pleasures in Socialism?' in *Pleasures in Socialism: Leisure and Luxury in the Eastern Bloc*, ed. by D. Crowley and S. Reid. Northwestern University Press, pp. 3–51, https://doi.org/10.2307/j.ctv43vtgm

Rosen, R., and Faircloth, C. (2020). 'Adult-Child Relations in Neoliberal Times: Insights from a Dialogue across Childhood and Parenting Culture Studies', *Families, Relationships and Societies*, 9(1), 7–22, https://doi.org/10.1332/204674319X15764492732806

Tsing, A. (2013). 'Sorting Out Commodities: How Capitalist Value is Made through Gifts'. *HAU: Journal of Ethnographic Theory*, 3(1), 21–43, https://doi.org/10.14318/hau3.1.003

Yurchak, A. (2006). *Everything was Forever, Until it was No More: The Last Soviet Generation*. Princeton University Press, https://doi.org/10.1515/9781400849109

The Door[1]

Khanum Gevorgyan

In 5, 4, 3… she will hear the front door open, and his heavy footsteps will echo in their already 50-year-old, partially renovated yet so warm house. In 3, 2, 1… he will open the living room door, where everyone is waiting for him with tearful eyes, including his three children that do not really realize why he was wherever he was. At exactly 0, according to her counting at least, he will drop his duffel bag wrapped with a few packs of tape. At the time, she thought the tape wrapping was meant to make it easier for him to carry the bag because of the many handles it had. However, now that she has had a fair portion of the world in her pocket, she understands that it was meant to keep the bag safe from those who would try to open it or throw it so hard that the bag breaks. After zero is a scene engraved in her memory forever.

He was a father of three, her—Khanum, being the oldest. Although in the past 2–3 years, he had seen his kids only four months a year, no one could blame him. No one could complain. Neither his wife could voice her longing towards a husband hardly seen, neither the children could cry out for his presence. That was a normality at their schools, neighborhoods, and even family gatherings, where the barbeque could no longer be made by the fathers of the family, so mothers had to get a crash course and teach themselves.

Russia had become the fathers' land. The mothers' land Armenia was forced to face not only longing for a loved one but also challenging house tasks, upbringing, and teaching children, and the economic challenges, which were portrayed in her childhood memories as the exchange rate boards that gave her mother a horrifying feeling. The only public display of longing allowed was screaming, 'Airplane! Bring my father back!' every time an airplane was seen

---

[1] This is a childhood memory produced as part of the Reconnect/Recollect project discussed in the introduction to this book.

in any part of the sky. Only children screamed. With mothers' encouragement, the screams were sometimes so loud, they would deafen one's ears. One day, her father would be in one of those airplanes, landing in Armenia, and hearing her voice, he would fly faster, get home faster, open the doors faster...

There was no need to count after zero. Not only because she did not know about negative infinities, but also because a few seconds after zero, she was hugging her father. He would always kneel on the floor, open his arms wide like an eagle and wait till one of his children was courageous enough to hug a stranger so familiar. She was not always the bravest. However, after the three of them were in his arms, everything else would go silent, at least for her. She would not hear or see her grandma drying her eyes, her uncle screaming, 'Someone, give me coffee!' or her mom crying, having 'Armen', her father's name, on her lips. Nothing else mattered, aside from the taped duffel bag full of Russian chocolate. The next stop after her father's embrace would be the bag full of chocolates and gifts. The three of them literally made a jump towards the bag and ripped the tape apart, while their father was hugging the rest of the family members.

The siblings, excited with their gifts and the unlimited amount of chocolate, were planning on which candies they were to take to school and share with classmates to show off their father being back from Russia. The happiness was cut short, however. The mother, Azniv, rushing from the kitchen with a huge kompot² jar in her hand ordered the kids to put all the chocolate in the jar, so she could keep some for the New Year table. This was the mark of winter for the children because from then on, they would go on a secret mission to find this jar and destroy the chocolate way before the New Year's Eve. The best part about this was that they worked individually. If one found the jar hidden in mother's wardrobe or behind the kitchenware, they would never share the secret to make sure the chocolate lasts longer. They were wise children...

There was also a lot of Armenian chocolate in the vase just beside the hidden jar. If chocolate had feelings, the Armenian one would be desperately heartbroken because it was considered nothing compared to the Russian one. It is not like Armenia did not have Alonushka or the animal looking chocolates or Rosher. Culturally, everything from Russia was considered to be a luxury, something more quality than everything else in Armenia. That is why Khanum and her

---

2 'Kompot' (In Armenian: կոմպոտ)—homemade juice usually made in summer and kept till winter.

siblings were always proud when going to school after the day their father came home.

December was a month of celebrations. Her father's arrival always overlapped with New Year and Christmas celebrations, so even if the airplanes never landed from Russia, this period would still be a celebration. At least that is how Khanum thought at the time because her life was surrounded only by laughter and happiness then. She never asked questions and only enjoyed the gifts left by her pillow or under the Christmas tree from the Winter Grandfather.3 So did her younger siblings. If they were lucky that year, Winter Grandfather would get them whatever they asked for in their letter. If not, Winter Grandfather was so kind that even in those years that he was poor, he would still leave a bag of chocolates and fruits for the kids. Perhaps because a child's heart was too keen on disappointment. Winter Grandfather wanted them to have a joyous childhood. Winter Grandfather was no one other than Azniv and Armen, whose wealth depended on how much Armen had earned in Russia or Azniv managed to save in Armenia.

Disappointing. So many lives depended and depend on Russia.

The logical continuation of the December celebrations was the setting of the Christmas tree. The Christmas tree they owned was huge. It was tall, almost reaching the sky, as Khanum remembered. It had beautiful ornaments in yellow, red, green, and blue. They even had some fancy ones: a Christmas tree ornament, a Winter Grandfather ornament, a snowflake, and even a star. The best thing about this tree was that it was the first thing their family bought and owned by themselves. It was an achievement, like buying a house, or a piece of land. For their family, that Christmas tree was a sign of their independence despite everything that had happened in their life. That Christmas tree still decorates their house. It has already been at least 15 years but neither the tree nor their family wants to let go of the memories.

That year, decorating the Christmas tree was extra special because their father agreed to take photos with the tree. The old-time serious father, who usually would prefer to be in the shadow despite his shiny personality and disliked being photographed, had agreed to take a silly photo, where two of the red ornaments were hanging from his ears. Quite an achievement for children with limited time with their father, not only because he would soon-enough leave

---

3 'Winter Grandfather' (in Armenian: Ձմեռ Պապիկ 'Dzmer Papik')—an equivalent of Santa Claus in Armenian Christmas and New Year celebrations.

for Russia, but also in a literal sense. Surprisingly, those silly photos became the last ones of the happy December.

Putting up the Christmas tree also marked the beginning of New Year Preparations. Every New Year seemed the same besides the fact that the Christmas tree became smaller and smaller with each year passing by. The New Year preparations for the female kids in the family were very smooth. Khanum does not really remember how she ended up writing to Winter Grandfather in the kitchen, instead of the living room. The worst is, she never understood why her brother was not sharing her faith in letter-writing with doughy hands. With the Christmas tree growing smaller, Khanum and her sister started sharing more responsibilities alongside her mother in cleaning and cooking. From December 27th to the 31st, Khanum, her mother, and her sister worked in the kitchen like ants preparing for the long winter. Many dishes and salads were made, many recipes were uncovered, and many failed. The kitchen used to smell like an actual restaurant kitchen and the cooks smelled like a mix of their dishes. The women in the house prepared for the New Year for four-five days in a row and no one dared to question why they were alone. Khanum does not recall when exactly she started asking her brother for help but one day the response was that "he is a man" and "men do not cook." Khanum thought and went with the idea, burying the resentment in her heart because going against traditions far too rooted meant disappointing her family. As the oldest child, she could not endure that pain. They worked in the kitchen for hours, sometimes even forgetting to grab a bite. To add to the restaurant vibe, her brother or father would scream occasionally asking for coffee. Then another fight would flame in the kitchen between the sisters because none of them liked making coffee.

Meanwhile, her father would lie on the couch watching a movie and her brother would entertain himself with dangerous experiments that now shape his profession. This memory hurt Khanum deeply. She resented cooking and baking from those days onward, especially seeing not only her mother in horrible shape after those celebrations but also all the women she saw. Everyone was tired. Everyone had cooked for a whole week before the New Year to make sure they get enough rest and not cook for a few days afterward. This was a dream vacation for many women in her surroundings and she hated this. Everyone was in their righteous place at the time, wherever they were perceived to belong, were not they?

Many Christmas tree years later, the order in Khanum's family started to change. 2008 was already in the past and even though airplanes were still a means to show longing, at least exchange rate boards in the banks were no longer *a threat. Their family also managed to purchase the second thing they fully owned: a house, where the role division was challenged. However, the financial difficulties and the ambition to bring a better, stable future for his family cost Armen his life. The red ornaments stopped being earrings for him and Khanum and her family members stopped waiting for open doors or Russian chocolates.*

Photograph of the author and her father in a military uniform, n.d. From Khanum Gevorgyan's family archive.

Holding a photo in her hand that brought back all these memories, Khanum remembered that she does not really remember. Memories fade away and the worst is, sometimes one is unable to distinguish between real memories and memories that our minds create to compensate for the time lost with a special someone. In this photo, where Khanum is sitting in her father's lap, with his military beret on her head, she is way younger than she was in her memories. What is fascinating, Khanum bears no memories of this photo, because after spending days thinking about the photo and the time it was shot, she failed... failed to remember or perhaps the memory did not exist to remember.

Memories are not only pieces of recollections but also puzzles to understand the past and its consequences. In her book titled *Remains of Socialism: Memory and the Futures of the Past in Post-socialist Hungary*, Maya Nadkarni (2020) highlights the transformation of the notion of 'nostalgia'. At one point in history, nostalgia named a physical illness experienced by those away from home, but, in the modern cultural understanding, the term describes not an individual's pain but his or her longing for a past to which it is impossible to return (Nadkarni 2020, p. 106). Nadkarni believes that nostalgia is a result of loneliness and exile from the present and a yearning for a much more sensible, authentic, soulful past (ibid.). Nostalgia does not have to revolve around 'virulent nationalism', as Svetlana Boym calls it (cited in Nadkarni 2020, p. 106), the yearned-for past may still be individual. However, nostalgia related to memories of life within a particular socio-political situation may be shared by many. The details might not necessarily be the same, but the longing and the reasons for hate and love may overlap.

My home country's socio-political situation mirrored itself in my childhood memories through which I could understand myself as a child of the 'independence generation'.[4] The events in the memories took place in December across the years from 1998–2014 and in various villages and the capital of Armenia. As the socio-political situation did not differ much in centralised Armenia, the settings in each memory have not been specified. In 1988, after *Perestroika* began, many Armenian revolutionaries and politicians started campaigning for the unification of Armenia and Nagorno Karabakh, a disputed region at the time populated with Armenians and Azerbaijanis. The Independence Movement of Armenia started with unification protests and demonstrations all around Armenia (De Wall 2003). The result of this

---

4   'Independence Generation' is a term used to describe the generations coming after the fall of the USSR and the independence of Armenia. Children from 1994 onwards are a part of the independence generation because of the First Nagorno Karabakh War (1988–1994). See more: https://library.fes.de/pdf-files/bueros/georgien/13149.pdf

was the Nagorno Karabakh (now the First NK) war. The combination of the 1988 Spitak Earthquake, which increased poverty and homelessness in Armenia and compounded the national anger and victimisation still felt in response to the 1915 Armenian Genocide (Steiner 2021), and the NK war coincided with the dissolution of the USSR. Armenia, now a post-Soviet country, was in chaos. I was born in 1998 when the war had been over for four years and Armenia was independent; however, the cost of the war, the consequences of the Spitak Earthquake, and the paused economic situation after the collapse of the Soviet Union did not ensure a worry-free life for any married couple in Armenia, my parents being one of them. Until age 14–15, I was quite unaware of the past and how much it had affected my present, including my family.

My father, Armen, was an NK war veteran and carried the psychological and physical pain of the war. As Jens Qvortrup highlights, children are not outside the zone of political influence even when politics are not directed specifically toward them (2008). '[M]uch of what happens to childhood, towards forming and transforming childhood and much of what influence childhood and their daily lives is in fact instigated, invented or simply taken place without having children and childhood in mind', therefore, children become non-targeted, yet political objects (Qvortrup, 2008, p. 12). My siblings and I were non-targeted objects of politics. Neither the war nor politics—not even our family—was meant to direct our mindset towards one or another way, however, every lived experience shaped our fragile personalities. Despite our wish and anyone's intent to pass on national pain and political emotion, we grew up with it and were very much influenced by it. The photo I mention in the last paragraph of my story, which I remember portraying my father in his military uniform and me, ended up being just a photo with no memories of it remaining. Nevertheless, it always brought back memories and awakened vengeance in me against Azerbaijan, the enemy country. As the oldest daughter of an NK war veteran, I always felt that hating is my responsibility, although no one ever told me so. The photo reminded me that, just like the beret in the photo, my father gifted me his legacy and I have to proudly keep it. I must, thus, avenge those who left such deep scars on my family and country. That was the general discourse in all childhoods, veteran or not. The burden was especially heavy on the boys. I can only imagine how children on the other side felt (feel). This shared political emotion also contributed to the romanticisation of the military, wars, and veterans. The financial challenges that my parents faced afterward were all negative results of the war. Despite the war being over, my childhood was still full of transferred war memories. Although vengeance has long left my heart, the actuality of memories inherited from my family and the memories I was unfortunate enough to create during the second NK war, in 2020, prevent me from being hopeful.

After the Spitak Earthquake, the collapse of the USSR, and the NK war and its aftermath, Armenia was not the safest country in which to live. Democracy was fragile and the blockade made living challenging. My father, who continued to work for the National Army, soon enough left his post and took the same road as many other Armenian fathers: he became a work migrant in Russia to be able to care for his family. Migrant workers were often known as 'people who go to *khopan*',[5] and Russia had become the equivalent of *khopan* as many Armenians would choose Russia as their destiny (ILO, 2009). In my memories, my family's financial difficulties were portrayed through the New Year and Christmas gifts that I would get from Winter Grandfather, which, sometimes would be nothing but fruits and candies as these were already purchased for New Year and did not require extra spending. At some point, my siblings and I started guessing the pattern of our gifts based on daily conversations that we heard from our parents and the amount of money we would save or the amount of work we would do on our house in later years. Soon enough, my childhood also became filled with adult worries, and I started carrying the worry of not being a burden.

The first year we bought the Christmas tree, it was nothing but a sign that there was hope that we may be able to catch up with the rest of our classmates and neighbours in having a brand-new Christmas tree. However, as time passed, the Christmas tree became more of an emotional symbol—a door to the longing for the past and the nostalgic feelings and the *déjà vu* that it gave every year during its decoration. As mentioned in the memory, that same Christmas tree is now fifteen

---

5 *Khopan* (in Armenian: խոպան) is Armenian slang used to define people who leave Armenia for abroad to become cheap migrant workers. According to the ILO, Russia is the top host country for Armenian migrant workers (2009).

(or perhaps more) years old, which may speak of two things: the sustainability of the household and the financial challenges that kept the Christmas tree the same for years despite its growing deterioration.

We had the tradition of saving chocolate and putting it on the New Year table to feel fancy. Despite the economic situation in the newly independent Armenia, many Armenians continued to aspire to the heights of development at the core of the USSR: Moscow. Anything from Moscow was a luxury. As Nadkarni mentions, 'the Western standard of living became the benchmark of the "normal" through which the Hungarians developed consumer consciousness' (2020, p. 108). The same happened in Armenia. Before consumer tastes in the country were westernised, they carried proud sentiments of their Soviet past, giving Russian products special treatment and looking at the local ones with prejudice. Many of my classmates, as mentioned in the memories, would have brand-new shoes, coats, and phones, and would bring chocolates to share with others. These products and this gesture were viewed as something fancy that not many could afford. That was how children romanticised the idea of *khopan*, despite knowing what it entailed, what their fathers had to go through. Continuing the consumer consciousness, the memories of the two chocolate jars—the Armenian and Russian—show how much was each valued through the eyes of children with no knowledge of political happenings.

My memories show how I resented gender inequality, even as a child. The clear role divisions put forward unhealthy expectations for both sexes to meet. As shared through the memories, my father was a migrant worker who left his family in the Spring and came back only in Winter for a few months. He worked for various construction companies in Russia, and the work was often physically punishing and, sometimes, exploitative. My father came back from Russia exhausted, in bad shape, and with little money that our family had to use to make ends meet. My mother could not contribute to the household income because my extended family did not consider it acceptable at the time for a woman to work outside the home. Although my mother had ambitions to work as a teacher, she was forced to become a housewife. This was the fate of many Armenian women and girls at the time who did not dare to question their situation. My father, as the sole financial provider of the family, could not afford to stay in Armenia.

As the memory tells, sometimes New Year preparations were very hard on women. While men had the opportunity to rest in Winter after working hard in the other seasons, women were never given the same chance. They worked the whole year, busy with housework, yardwork, the upbringing of their children, and other matters. New Year brought extra work: a whole week of just cooking and cleaning because the tradition was so. This was a shared social difficulty that many families carried. Gender inequality and role distribution very much depended on individual families. One family in the city-centre of Yerevan was conservative to the degree that its womenfolk were prohibited from leaving the house alone, while many families in villages did their best to ensure that both their male and female children received equal education. Therefore, I dare not say that women faced this social challenge only in villages or small towns. The worst thing about the gender inequality was the presumption that it would naturally continue, as when, for instance, my brother would rest while his sisters cooked. Gender roles are rooted in everyday life in Armenia. It is unfair for both men and women. Nevertheless, many people fight against this every day despite the challenges posed because of the latest war, the on-going skirmishes, and the lack of male soldiers in the country. There have been growing equality movements in Armenia and other social developments—both had an immediate effect on my childhood and youth. In 2006, when I was a first grader, a foundation, the Children of Armenia Fund, launched development programs in Armenia, beginning in the village of Karakert, where I was raised. Many other non-profit organisations joined them, offering hundreds of students an opportunity to explore the world outside their families and villages. Although my memories do not detail this transformation, this social and political change was at the core of Armenia as a former Soviet republic.

Thanks to this project, I was able to travel back in time and understand the reasons why my memories of these years feel so nostalgic. While feeling nostalgic about certain things is harmless, after analysing my own memories and understanding how unintentionally politicised my childhood was, I understand the importance a memory carries. Memories can work as puzzle pieces to reconstruct the past and at the same time an opportunity to review our actions and the way we build the presence of children nowadays and in the future.

References

De Waal, T. (2003). *The Black Garden*. New York University Press

International Labour Organization (ILO). (2009). *Migration and Development: Armenia Country Study*. Yereva, Armenia

Nadkarni, M. (2020). *Remains of Socialism: Memory and the Futures of the Past in Postsocialist Hungary*. Cornell University Press

Qvortrup, J. (2008). 'Childhood and Politics'. *Educare*, 3, 6–19, https://ojs.mau.se/index.php/educare/article/view/1291

Steiner, P. (2021). *Collective Trauma and the Armenian Genocide: Armenian, Turkish, and Azerbaijani Relations since 1839*. Hart Publishing

7. Growing up in Cold-War Argentina:
Working through the (An)archives of Childhood Memories

Inés Dussel

This chapter sets out to present some exercises on childhood memories from Cold-War Argentina. Combining written texts with drawings and pictures, it seeks to navigate the tensions between an 'I' of personal memories and a 'we' emerging in the collective-biography workshops. It invites a journey through an (an)archive of childhood memories produced in the interstitial space between memory and forgetting, not looking for healing but trying to 'excavate a wound'. What does one remember from one's childhood? Where or when does a childhood start and end? Do traumatic events cast their ominous shadows on every recollection of the past? Do these memories speak about the past or about the present in which they emerge? Memory seems to be a tricky lane, which morphs as one moves. The text aims to work through these memory exercises and materials to discuss how we connect with children's memories and experiences.

It all started at a conference: a casual discussion over some German beers about the worst thing our parents had done to us when we were children. I am not sure who suggested that topic or whether my old 'let's-not-talk-about-this-issue' reflex might have been there, but the warmth and the beer must have helped me to move beyond it. Talking about our childhoods turned out to be a good ice-breaker for strangers coming from post-socialist and South American countries who did not otherwise seem to have much in common except for being of a similar age and having jobs at universities. We soon realised that there were many connections among our experiences of juggling with repressive regimes and the upbringings our parents managed to perform amid those circumstances. For the record, I think I won the contest for the worst parenting experience when I told my new friends that my sister and I had been left alone when we were eight and six years old. Our parents had departed after telling us not to worry if they did not come back that night: they were going to a demonstration and might be jailed; but, at any rate, they would return the next day (a confidence that soon turned out to be a gross miscalculation).

That night of German beers, I immediately felt that this new group could be part of an imaginary community I founded with some Argentinian friends: the club of those permanently damaged by progressive parenting. We were little fighters or pioneers, having been taught autonomy and self-sufficiency since we were very young. We shared similar stories of early internationalisms and solidarity, a sense of feeling responsible for the world. We also shared an awareness of a certain gravity or solemnity in our demeanours, which, though we had learned to laugh about it, still caught us from time to time. The effects of these early marks on our adult life were not discussed there, but none of us seemed to cling onto some grievance against our parents, with whom we could now relate to as adults who had gone through quite difficult times themselves.

Sharing our memories, we could see that our childhoods were punctuated by a pressure to conform or, if not, to be ready to pay the price for the deviation. Consequently, they were also marked by several clandestine rites. Our parents had imbued us, through subtle yet sharp training, with an ability to read situations and decide what could be said where, or what could be shown to whom. True, this distancing and calculation is not exclusive to growing up in repressive regimes. Migrant children experience some of these feelings, as do children whose identities make them feel marginalised and who learn very quickly to deal with the visible and invisible borders that make them stand out. All these experiences or 'scenes of instruction', as Veena Das (2015, p. 61) calls them, are ways in which children learn about the politics of the world, about their place in it, about what is just or unjust, about the boundaries of the sayable and the visible in their communities, and about the role of secrets and silences.

Reconnecting and recollecting children's memories is a way to make these learnings visible and audible, to reflect on the political ontology of childhood, and to try to inscribe these experiences in collective memory exercises. The notion of an (an)archive is, with all its confusions (Ernst 2017), appropriate for these kinds of recollections, as this new archive does not intend to organise a historical narrative in a sequence of events but rather to decentre history and to discuss the forms in which memory emerges or is called out. Its ways of operation are more related to montage and resonance than to the order of the librarian.

This project is, as the reader might have noticed, intensely personal, and this text is an exploratory exercise on how to inscribe our (my) own memories to nurture a collective (an)archive about children's experiences. It builds on previous experiences, particularly on the writings done by children of the disappeared and of exile (Alcoba 2014; Arfuch 2018; Blejmar 2016; Pérez 2021; Robles 2013; among many others) but also on exhibits such as 'Hijxs. Poéticas de la Memoria' (Biblioteca Nacional Mariano Moreno 2021), organised by the National Library in Argentina in 2021. In particular, this exhibit dealt with a multiplicity of records to produce a multimedia digital repository of voices, images, and texts related to the political collective H.I.J.O.S.[1] The exhibition, which united works by photographers, writers, filmmakers, and painters, sought to pose questions that could act as gateways for new aesthetic and political memory practices and could define new territories for memories: the everyday and the banal, the street, the space between past and present.

---

1 'H.I.J.O.S.' literally means offspring, or someone's children, in Spanish, and it is an acronym for Hijos por la Identidad y la Justicia contra el Olvido y el Silencio [Children for Identity and Justice and against Forgetting and Silence]. This association was founded in 1994 by children of the disappeared, jailed, or sent into exile by the dictatorship. At that time, H.I.J.O.S. organised successful demonstrations and artistic gatherings in front of the homes of the perpetrators. It put up signs along the road reading 'Beware, a committer of genocide lives nearby' and sprayed on the walls of their houses graffiti—called *'escraches'*—thereby outing the offenders. The emergence of this collective on the public scene renewed the participation of young people in human-rights demonstrations in the late 1990s, after years of declining numbers. With the introduction of laws against amnesty and impunity and the reopening of the trials against the perpetrators, its role changed (for a chronicle, see Pérez 2021). Remarkably, the collective includes a significant group of artists: photographers, writers, playwrights, filmmakers, and painters.

Following their lead, this writing experiment attempts to navigate the tensions between an 'I' of my personal memories and a 'we' that speaks of the workshops of collective biography in which these texts were produced. As William E. Connolly (2022) says in his writing about his adventures as an academic from the working class, 'the "I" can become quite a crowd' (p. 5), full of intertextual dialogues and echoes from other people's memories. The 'I' understood in this way is never an individual but a singular perspective or point of utterance. This remark is important because, when it is considered as a self-sufficient, self-contained person, the 'I' can obscure the many folds within which memory emerges and takes shape, becoming the support of a de-politicised and reified version of the past and of a historiography that is only concerned with the intimate sphere, without problematising and historicising it (Traverso 2020).

And yet, this text wants to experiment with an 'I' that presents a recollection of memories, one deeply defined by a singular history that happens to be my own. I am aware of the risks such an experiment entails but also hopeful of the new paths it can open for historical and pedagogical inquiries. I grew up in Argentina during the 1970s and 1980s, under one of the worst military dictatorships of that era—although that ranking is hard to make. Firmly aligned with the Western rhetoric and practices of the Cold War, the Argentinian Junta performed a brutal repression of leftist activists that closely followed the playbook of the counterinsurgency developed in Africa, Southeast Asia, and Latin America in the 1960s and early 1970s.

Important to the Cold-War context for Argentina is that US foreign policy towards Latin America was to actively support military juntas and right-wing governments that violently repressed left-wing political parties. As is well-known in the cases of Brazil, Chile, and Argentina, the US actively helped right-wing governments come to power and hold on to it through dictatorships in order to forge strong alliances against the communist world.

In Argentina, the brutal persecution of dissidents rested on a clandestine repressive network of detention centres and extermination machines that created a new figure: 'the disappeared' (Pérez 2022, p. 19). People thus named were neither alive nor dead; they were names split from bodies, spectres who haunt the living (Gatti 2014; Pérez 2022). Culturally, the dictatorship was conservative and traditionalist. In the name of Christianity, it banned modern mathematics because of its set theory and meetings larger than three persons. Authorities also prohibited long hair for boys and blue jeans for everybody in schools, kisses on the street, and anything that had a scent of the 1960s (Pineau et al. 2006).

My family was a target of this repression, first from the paramilitary groups that threatened leftist activists and paved the way for the military coup, and, after 1976, from the dictatorship. We went into hiding for almost two years, during which time my father got ill and died, and my uncle and his family had to flee into exile. My grandparents' house and my own were assaulted by military troops in search of my father and my uncle. As part of our clandestine life, we had to move frequently, and my sister and I had to change schools to avoid being traced. Once we got into a relatively stable safe house, we were told to walk home from school by different routes in order to avoid being followed by the secret police. From a distance, it seems incredibly naïve and risky to trust the safety of a family to an eight-year-old girl, but that is how many families and their children lived in those days (Oberti 2015).

Not surprisingly, I repressed my memories of the repression for a long time, despite years of psychoanalytic therapy and involvement in political movements for democracy and human rights. I struggled, I still struggle, with how to talk or write about these memories—in which tone, in which format—and ask myself whether more memories are needed in the collective anarchive, and how my personal recollections relate to broader politics of memory. These have been ongoing questions for many years, much earlier than the talk about bad parenting that opens this text. While writing a secondary school textbook on human rights in 1996, I read an interview with a survivor from a concentration camp in Buenos Aires who said that he didn't want to be defined solely by his experience in a clandestine jail; he wanted to move on, be a physicist (as my father was), be like anyone else, because otherwise the repressors would have won. I connected instantly with this feeling that one should not be defined by 'them'. I felt that, however much we seemed to have no choice in deciding which experiences shaped us, he and I and so many others had to struggle to make room for a choice, to make room for another option in the way we define ourselves. Looking at this interview again now, it still amazes me the extent to which the language of winning or being defeated permeates so many daily actions and positionalities for those of us who were directly touched by these events and who were the targets of the brutal repression.

Indeed, in these memory exercises, my own positionality is implicated, but is this not always the case? I have not yet been able to feel comfortable about sharing these memories; there is always an annoying internal voice that prevents me from doing it: you will sound too selfish, too confessional, too victimised. Maybe what has made me take a further step here is that this chapter is part of a collective project—one that forced me to think again, to think otherwise, about memory and forgetting, about childhood and memory, and to see myself in the mirror of other childhoods, different yet at the same time connected to mine. When writing these pages, I found a quote by Maurice Blanchot (2002): 'Whoever wants to remember himself must entrust himself to forgetfulness, to the risk that absolute forgetfulness is, and to the beautiful chance that memory then becomes' (p. 263). Perhaps this is my beautiful chance to give a form to my memories in the company of others to whom I can entrust myself.

Childhood is a Foreign Country

What does one remember from one's childhood? Where or when does a childhood start and end? Do traumatic events cast their ominous shadows on every recollection one might have of that past? Do these memories speak about the past or about the present in which they emerge? Memory seems to be a tricky lane, which morphs as one moves. As I walk that path, I keep in mind Benjamin's 'Excavation and Memory,' a short piece from 1932, in which he sees memory 'not [as] an instrument for exploring the past, but rather a medium' in that quest (Benjamin 2005, p. 576). He uses an analogy of archeology: one who wants to excavate the past through memory should always 'mark, quite precisely, the site where he gained possession of them' and give 'an account of the strata which first had to be broken through' (ibid.).

Hannah Arendt, in her introduction to Benjamin's *Illuminations* (1968), also refers to excavation but uses the metaphor of the pearl diver to talk about memory work. Conferring on them a materiality, she describes memories as things that sink into the depth of the sea, dissolve themselves, '"suffer a sea-change" and survive in new crystallised forms and shapes' (p. 50). The diver 'bring[s] them up into the world of the living as "thought fragments", as something "rich and strange"' (ibid.), thus the image of pearls.

Rereading these takes on memory, I would say that 'thought fragments' is a pretentious name for my memory exercises and yet, at the same time, fits with their episodic quality and the invitation they extend to think through or along them. What definitely does not feel right is the metaphor of the pearl diver. One undertaking memory work, as Pérez (2022) analyses, is more of a ghost-buster, someone who has to deal with the marks of a biopolitics that produced spectres or phantoms (such as the disappeared), that operated in the dark a clandestine repressive apparatus, and that confined many of us to secrecy, hiding, lying, masking. In this kind of search, the diver might have the impression of swimming in a viscous substance full of detritus rather than a pristine sea (but which sea is pristine?). Can pearls be found in that detritus? Are pearls the best metaphor for thinking about memories, which are more fragmentary and episodic than the complete image of a found pearl? What I would like to retain from this metaphor, however, is the possibility of finding beauty in memories forged in an era of terror, cruelty, and long-lasting trauma. The work done by H.I.J.O.S. gives me some hope that something poetic, something that carries a sense of justice and love, can emerge out of it.

As to the strata in which my memories emerge, I would say they are made up of layers and layers of politics of memory and forgetting, of scenes of justice and impunity, of melancholy and joy. In Argentina, there was a boom of memory studies and memory narratives after the dictatorship, in the 1980s and 1990s. It was, at first, mostly dominated by writing from a generation of activists and militants who had suffered jail, kidnapping, and torture (Jelín 2002), linked more or less loosely to a more general obsession with memory (Huyssen 1995) and to the age of testimony in Latin America (Beverley 1996). Memories from the next generation, their children born in the late 1960s and the 1970, emerged afterwards, in the mid-1990s. This wave was related to the work done by H.I.J.O.S., which was organised in 1994, and involved contributions from children of the disappeared as well as of victims of repression both in Argentina and abroad.

Moving from the mothers of the disappeared to their children was a generational relay, but it also brought other shifts in the politics of memory in Argentina, the effects of which have become more visible in recent years. After years of silence and shame, after years of seeing their parents demonised and repressed, these children-become-adults overturned the silence by getting together and speaking out, doing research on their disappeared parents and making their stories visible and heard. They also started to articulate their own observations of the earlier time and to talk about their own position, their own wounds, their own claims. Many of them have used a playful tone and have experimented with different genres (films, photography, theatre, novels, blogs, animated movies, video games) to produce a new take on Argentina's traumatic past (Blejmar 2016).

Certainly, it was a mostly urban, highly educated, psychoanalysed group that actively engaged in H.I.J.O.S.; however, their quest to 'reverse the mark of the sign' (Pérez 2021, p. 126) is an important one for all families affected by the repression because it involved working through mourning and melancholy and being able to produce a different encounter with the past. Perhaps more importantly, their work poses several questions about identity and memory, about childhoods lost and regained (can they be regained?), and about what is achieved in the process of reconstituting one's identity after facing the traumatic past. Memory and forgetting are not mutually exclusive opposites; there are 'muddier gray zones of partial recognition […that are] harder to trace' (Stoler 2022, p. 117). For Stoler, one needs to look at 'the space in between', that is, the 'interstitial space [that] is shaped by what form knowledge takes, neither wholly remembered nor forgotten' (p. 126).

Looking for this interstitial space, without fully wanting to unveil some hidden truth or to shed light on others but with the gut feeling that the journey is valuable if done collectively and pensively, I embark on my exercises of memory. Here, I consider four memories that I wrote in the third-person voice during the collective-biography workshops organised by Mnemo ZIN that are discussed at length in other chapters of this book. I put these texts together with pictures and drawings from that earlier time as a way of accounting for the tensions present in the 'translations of the visual to verbal, from the visual act of witnessing to the stench, to the screech, to the silent and unseen and unheard' (Stoler 2022, p. 136). My aim is to work through (a verb to which I will later return) these materials to see if something else can be grasped about children's memories of traumatic events and particularly of my own trajectory. Mariana Eva Pérez (2021) says that 'all *hijis*[2] are fans of the past' (p. 23); maybe my historiographical passions can also be included in that category.

---

2 Pérez refers to H.I.J.O.S., the collective of which she was a part, as *hijis*—a pun that denotes a deconstructive play with language (Arfuch, 2018).

7. *Growing up in Cold-War Argentina*   175

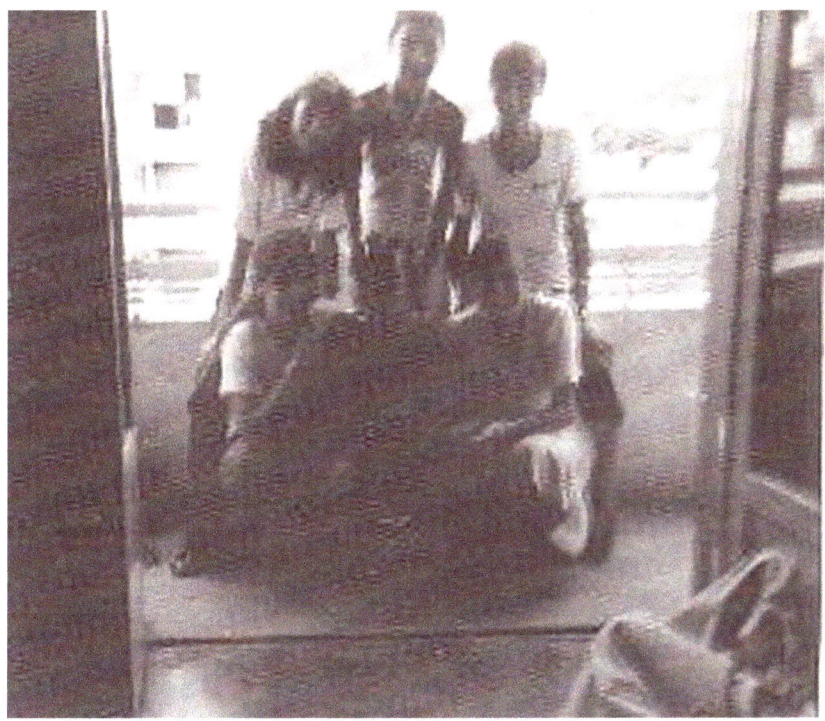

Fig. 7.1 Photograph of Claudia, Diana, Fabiana, me, and two unrecognised friends at my place, Buenos Aires, circa 1978. From Nano Belvedere's personal archive.

I start with a photograph sent to me a couple of years ago by Nano, a primary school classmate (Figure 7.1). I like that it is blurred and grayish: the qualities align well with the texture of my memories, which I am afraid will appear sharper and more clear-cut than they actually are as a result of translating them into writing and of my own clumsiness in that process. The photograph shows me and some girlfriends on the balcony of the apartment in which my family lived. From the light and the clothes, I deduce that it was taken in summer. We are smiling and this is an important sign: not everything in my childhood was gloomy and sad. It may have been the end of our time together at primary school, from a year in which we felt grown-up because we were going into secondary school. We were happy but also sad because the transition meant we would be parting ways.

The memory that follows is from an earlier date and is related to the drawing I made in 1975 of a colourful boat that sails on the sea

(Figure 7.2)—the sea of pearls, maybe? I have written *mar* [sea] three times, twice on the sails and once on the ship's hull. This repetition suggests that words needed to be inscribed and remembered.

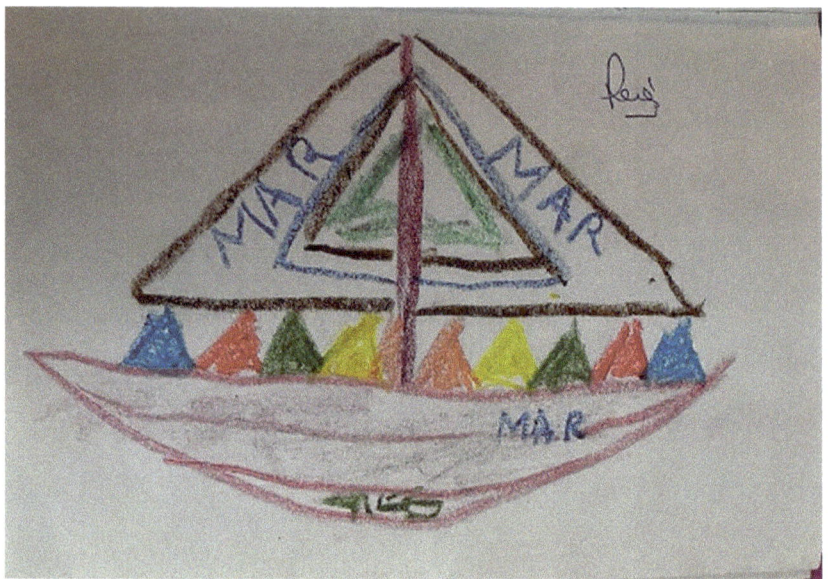

Fig. 7.2 Inés Dussel, untitled drawing of a sailboat, 1975.

Sailing Away

She might have been eight. The flat was on the first floor in an orange-brick, unpretentious building in the corner of a busy avenue. It was a small two-bedroom apartment, but felt like paradise after several months of constantly shifting places, sometimes every two weeks. Her parents decided to go into hiding after receiving several death threats, and while they continued working and her sister and herself kept going to school, everybody was under big stress.

She had to change schools and was told to be extra careful on her way home, checking out if she was followed by the secret police (which, not too secretly, used to wander around in green Ford Falcons and donned dark sunglasses and almost mandatory moustache). She felt it was hard but she knew there was no room for complaints.

This flat was supposed to become more permanent. They had to keep the window shades three-quarters down all the time, so as not to be seen from the outside. Her family spent most of the time in the kitchen, which looked to the inside of the building. It was there where they had breakfast, maybe coffee and mate,[3] dined, and listened to the radio (Radio Colonia, a Uruguayan station that supposedly had less censorship). The kitchen felt like the only cozy place in this apartment.

She decided the living room was to be her playground. This room had a tiled floor and the dark shades were scarcely interrupted by electric lights; all in all, it felt cold, but she tried to make it her own place. The play she remembers more vividly was when she put her toys in the sofa and pretended she was sailing away with all her beloved ones. She could spend hours doing this after she came back from school. She would play with the toys, particularly a pair of elephants (Babar and Celeste, from one of her favorite children's books). She imagined that she was the captain of the boat, steering the wheel and sailing towards distant lands.

Another play she recalls is making a tent above the dining table. She is unsure of why she preferred to produce it above and not under the table. She put two or three chairs up the table, which she remembers as involving some challenge, and then covered them with sheets or blankets. She climbed on the table and brought her toys. She remembers an orange bed sheet that created a warm light inside her tent. She thinks she kept this particular construction for a couple of days, and her mom was not too happy but let it be, as they used to be in the kitchen. Her memories are of her alone, but her sister might have joined her in the tent too. It was her space, where she felt at home.

Here is another drawing of a house/home [*casa* in Spanish] (Figure 7.3) that I found in the same notebook as the previous drawing. The house does not resemble any of the places where we lived during those years. Its windows are adorned with what seem to be closed curtains, and the two-panel wooden door is also closed. The word 'casa' is repeated on both panels of the roof, as if she needed to make sure this was it.

---

3   *Mate (yerba mate)* is an Argentinean drink that one sips with a straw.

Fig. 7.3 Inés Dussel, untitled drawing of a house with a gabled roof, 1975.

Radio Talk

As far as she can remember, her father loved three things: physics, politics, and music. He listened to classical music most of the time, and also folklore. Her mother also liked music, but she brought other tunes: protest singers like Joan Baez, Nana Mouskouri or Mercedes Sosa, and Nacha Guevara, an Argentinean cabaret singer who was quite provocative. The mother used to play one of her songs to her daughters, which made them laugh a lot: 'Don't you marry girls', a funny, fast tune that advised young women to prefer good sex, short flings, and economic independence to the boring, depressing prospect of a fat and old husband (she later discovered the lyrics were from Boris Vian).

Among her father's possessions, there was a tape recorder, a big-sized, reel-to-reel, high fidelity device. The tapes were mostly music, but from time to time he recorded some sounds at home. She remembers being interviewed by her father when she was four or five, but she recalls just his voice making questions and not their content. Was he interested in how she felt, or what she thought, or what she knew? No way to ask him now.

At some point her sister figured out how to handle the tape recorder and started playing with it. She felt lucky to be invited in. As the radio was always on, the girls were familiar with the style of the programs. They used to pretend to be radio anchors, sang songs, made silly comments, imitated the ads and the chants they heard in the street demonstrations. They could play for hours, re-recording the tapes if needed. She had lots of fun.

One particular piece delighted the family. In it the girls pretended to interview the president, the first woman to be named president after her husband, Juan Domingo Perón, passed away in July 1974. Isabelita Perón—that was her name— was a lousy president, very weak, and her term saw the growth of the paramilitary violence against popular movements, and soon after there was a military coup. Isabelita's tenure was the time when her family went into hiding because of threats from the far right. The tape-recorder came with them to their safe house and was a good source of joy, particularly when they pretended they interviewed people. Her sister, two years older, decided who played which character each time. In the interview with Isabel Perón, the older sister took the mic (the girl remembers it as a small, quite modern device) and pretended to be the journalist; the little girl had no option but to be the lousy, weak President. Both girls had a long conversation about what the President was doing, the journalist being always on the offensive and the weak President becoming almost speechless. The girls knew the names of several ministers of the cabinet and brought them into the conversation. One question of the smart journalist still hangs in her memory: 'President Isabelita, tell me, why are you sooo bad?' At that point of the interview, everybody laughed. She doesn't remember what she answered, but she was happy to participate in the plot, even if she played the villain. She felt so proud that the family enjoyed it, and that her parents knew that she was on their side.

When I read this text to my stepdaughters, they were surprised to hear that I was so politicised at a young age and that I knew the names of the cabinet ministers by heart. Such experience seemed quite unlike their own childhoods, but politics was always present when I was growing up, for better or worse, for as long as I can recall. We listened to the radio and read the newspapers every day, and we were taken to street demonstrations and to political meetings, where I remember I had no trouble falling asleep. I never questioned it: that is how it was. We were trained to be *pequeñas combatientes*, 'little fighters' (Robles 2013), learning skills that would become crucial in the years that followed.

Maybe what went unnoticed by my stepdaughters is the fact that I wanted to be on and by my parents' side, but that solidarity came at a high price. Here is a photograph from what I think might be one year later, when we were already hiding from paramilitary threats (see Figure 7.4). We had recently started to attend this school, so I am surprised to find myself in the centre of the scene [wearing a dotted red jumper pink and blue], together with my older sister [the tall person behind me in red], who came with me as we had to stick together most of the time (probably for safety reasons?). My smile seems a bit forced, and my sister is definitely not smiling.

The event was one of my classmates' first communion, a Roman Catholic rite of passage very commonly observed by families in my generation. I am not a Catholic and was always pointed at by my teachers because of it. One of the questions we were asked at the beginning of every school year, which I assume was related to bureaucratic form-filling, was about our religion. Throughout primary school, I was the only person in my age group to declare herself an atheist—an immediate marker to the school that something was very wrong with my family. Yet, maybe for that very reason, I was perceived as exotic by my classmates. I remember that they came to ask me 'how children were made', assuming that my modern, hippy-looking, fan-of-Boris Vian mother would talk about such issues with me. They were right: she did. '*Don't you marry, girls, don't you marry. Have sex and have fun.*'

Fig. 7.4 Photograph of a Catholic friend's celebration of communion, Buenos Aires, 1975. Author's family archive.

Compañeros

She was in her 6th grade in a primary school. They had brought a TV on the last stages of her father's cancer, which left him deaf and extremely weak. Her father died in June 1976 but the TV stayed with them, and she spent most afternoons watching soap operas. She even watched adult soap operas with serious drama that played at night prime time; her classmates, whose parents were much stricter, envied her freedom to do as she wished.

At that time, she spent a lot of time writing short stories that imitated what she saw on TV. She remembers one particular story about a murder in a hotel, which she signed with the name of the male writer of a soap opera she followed. She liked to give sophisticated names to her characters, with less common first names and patrician surnames. She was not particularly proud of her stories; she knew something was not quite right in them, but she liked to try out new words and imagining farfetched plots.

It was May, and at school it was time to celebrate the 1810 revolution that led to independence from Spanish rule, as was done every year. She decided she would write a theater piece for that date, and that she would give it to her teacher to see if it could be played as part of the school's civic ceremony. She had a brief and unusual moment of total confidence. She sat down and wrote a four-page text in which she portrayed the actions of the leaders of independence. She imagined clandestine meetings in the Jabonería de Vieytes—the place where 'the patriots' supposedly met—to conspire against the Spanish oppressors; she narrated what happened in popular assemblies in which the revolutionary leaders would address other people as 'compañeros' (comrades) and speak about revolution and making this a better world. The piece ended with the masses marching towards victory in the Plaza de Mayo, Buenos Aires' central square. She was beaming with happiness.

Her mom came from work, and the girl must have sensed that something was not quite right because she decided to show it before handing it to the teacher. Her mother smiled at the beginning, but her face soon turned serious and worried. What would her teacher think if she spoke about revolution? Moreover, all the joy about people marching in the Plaza and the compañeros: how would it sound in those dark days? The mother did not need to give an order. The girl folded the pages, took them to her room, and hid them in a drawer.

Self-discipline was essential for clandestine lives. In fact, several militants were caught by the military when they broke the code by visiting relatives or by sharing too much information with the wrong people. Historian Alejandra Oberti (2015) has studied the affective life of female militants who joined the guerrilla movements. She found that these movements had published behavioural codes and rules, and that there were cases in which militants were put on trial and punished because they had broken them with queries about maintaining their family and sexual life while in hiding.

One such code for militants, issued in 1972, specifies that 'the children of the revolutionary' should share all aspects of their parents' lives, including running their risks. 'Special protection to children should be sought as long as it doesn't get in conflict with the superior interests of revolution' (Ortolani, cited in Oberti 2015, p. 41). An image of a Vietnamese mother breast-feeding her baby with a rifle by her side is praised as beautiful and as 'a symbol of this new revolutionary attitude towards our offspring' (ibid.).

It is not easy for me to read these rules, to picture myself in these images. Yet, it helps me to understand the seemingly unquestionable order of priorities with which I can connect. Mariana Eva Pérez, whose parents were kidnapped and disappeared when she was fifteen months old, calls such offspring 'princesas montoneras' [revolutionary princesses] and writes a poem that plays with a well-known children's rhyme, *Arroz con Leche*:

> these girls
> knew how to sew and embroider
> but the part of going out to play, they owe you that
> because they were to be responsible for everything too soon
> for what they remembered and for what they had forgotten
> *O cursed spite*!
> Princesses from the wrong tale
>
> (Pérez 2021, pp. 21–2, my translation, emphasis in the original (a quote from Hamlet)).

I found a drawing from those years in which I sketched a two-faced apple (Figure 7.5).

7. *Growing up in Cold-War Argentina* 183

Fig. 7.5 Inés Dussel, *Apple = Two Faces*, drawing, 1977.

I always struggled with noses in my drawings, and this doodle shows it. The image, however, tells of the duplicity I was forced to endure, of the double life I felt I was living. One eye seems shy and alert; the other one, the one that seems to hide behind the first one, is more vivid and bright, and it is accompanied by what seems to be a smile. I am surprised that the writing is in English, a language that I did not feel comfortable with at that time. Maybe language was also a way of hiding who I was. The line 'two faces' is repeated three times, the second one cut in half, the third one blurred. It seems that I tended to repeat words; maybe the fear of forgetting or getting lost was always there, or maybe I was not able to work through my wounds, a topic to which I return in the final section of this chapter. Compared to 'mar' and 'casa', the verbal repetitions in this drawing introduce some changes: I must have felt the need to write about the duplicity and at the same time to deny it, to erase it.

More on Compañeros

It was the year of the military coup; she knows it because she remembers Miss (Señorita) Susana was her 5th grade teacher, and that was 1976. 'La señorita Susana' was nice, warm, and seemed to know her way around the class; she must have been in her 40s or 50s, as she had grown-up children. Her husband was involved in a football club that the girl liked, and that made the girl feel close to her teacher.

The class was usually quite participatory. Miss Susana asked children about their opinion and made them write a lot, which the girl liked. The atmosphere was relaxed, and children wandered around the space freely and noisily.

The girl sat in the first rows of the classroom, perhaps because she wanted to be a good student, but it also might have been related to her shortsightedness, as she later discovered. One day, she heard two boys fighting behind her back. One of them was the son of a military officer, and the other boy's father was a journalist who worked at a popular newspaper. The boys were shouting at each other, but nobody seemed to care. At one point, the son of the officer cried: 'Your father is a Peronist!', referring to the political party that had been overthrown by the military coup and that was proscribed at that time. The son of the journalist replied, quite annoyed: 'No, my father is not a Peronist, he is a Montonero!'. The class went silent. Montoneros was a group from the Peronist left which had moved into a guerrilla group ('armed struggle', it was called those days) and was considered a terrorist group by the military ('los subversivos'). The girl knew that because her father had belonged to that group, and for a moment she stopped breathing. She realised that it had caused a similar effect on everyone: the class was unusually silent and they were all frozen.

Miss Susana also stopped doing whatever she was doing, but reacted quickly and talked to the whole class: 'Hey, all of you, this boy is talking nonsense. Don't you worry, he doesn't know what he's talking about. Please go on with your work.' The son of the officer insisted: 'He said his father is Montonero!' And the teacher silenced him at once: 'He is a boy. He doesn't know a thing. Stop it.' The girl looked down to her notebook. It was not easy to continue working, but she tried. She loved Miss Susana even more than before.

The next year, the son of the journalist did not come back to school. The girl feared the worst. Thirty years later she met him at a school reunion and asked him about his father: he had survived the dictatorship.

In Argentina, teachers are called *'señorita'* or 'miss', no matter how long they have been married and how many children they have. Their sexuality and personal lives are forever trapped in a figure that is always young, single, and chaste (Fernández 1998). But Miss Susana inhabited that figure in her own way. I think about her gesture, her reassurance that we were just children and not little fighters (as some of our parents were convinced), and I am still moved today. In that context, being 'just' boys and girls produced a different space that protected us.

Those minor gestures of solidarity and care were not unusual, and maybe it is in them that flashes of hope can be found. Around 2006, I shared a panel with one of the Grandmothers of Plaza de Mayo,[4] who worked as a teacher when her pregnant daughter was kidnapped. She told us that, when she got news of the abduction, she was at the school and could barely stand still. The school principal, who was married to a member of the police, told her to come to the schoolyard and raise the national flag, as a sort of act of humiliation and a sign of defeat to the 'national' forces. The soon-to-be Grandmother of Plaza de Mayo felt as if the floor beneath her was opening. A colleague of hers stood up and told the principal that she would take her place. It took great courage to confront the school principal and, by proxy, the police, and to show solidarity; most people looked down and pretended not to see or hear. Thirty years later, the Grandmother could still remember the scene.

Here is Señorita Susana with the whole class (Figure 7.6). Again, I find myself centre-stage in the photograph, and I continue to be surprised by that, since I remember myself hiding and trying to go unnoticed. Memory is indeed a tricky and confusing lane. Miss Susana is in the upper-right corner.

---

4 The 'Abuelas' [Grandmothers] is a civil association that was founded in 1977 by relatives of disappeared people in order to search for kidnapped children who were given up for adoption and had their identities stolen during the dictatorship. So far, the group has found 137 children, but hundreds more are still missing. See: https://abuelas.org.ar/idiomas/english/history.htm

Fig. 7.6 Photograph of the author's fifth-grade class in Primary school, Buenos Aires, 1976. Author's family archive.

Working Through Memories

I feel a little dizzy writing these memories, maybe because I have this old reflex of not exposing myself, not showing or saying much about those years. But now it is done. I want to think that my journey through this interstitial space between memory and forgetting is not looking for healing but, maybe, excavating a wound (Hartman 2007), with the hope that, in the end, there will be an 'elsewhere' where my generation can stop being 'the orphaned princesses / of revolution and defeat / in the eternal exile of childhood' (Pérez 2021, p. 22).

To be honest, I do not feel eternally exiled into childhood, and my history differs from those of several H.I.J.O.S. whose parents disappeared when they were toddlers. I was lucky that I could grow up with my mom and, some years later, also with a stepdad. Instead of permanent exile, I think of my childhood as having been cut short by traumatic events that required me to act as an adult from very early on. But what the Reconnect/Recollect project has implied all along is that childhood is not a fixed category; we cannot assume that childhood is an unburdened, free-of-rules time in which children wander happily. Childhood is so much more than that, as this book attests: it is so complex and multi-layered, so much part of a common human experience and, yet, so singular. As said before, children are not passive receptors of the world but inhabit it and take part in it with their words, views, and actions. In that respect, my childhood was not different from, and in a way was even more privileged than, many other childhoods that take place in diverse contexts. Making sense of the world, deciphering it, placing oneself in it, blending in or standing out, showing or not showing, are dilemmas that each child has to walk through, to work through.

A final comment on this verb I repeated throughout these pages. I borrow it from psychoanalysis, where it is used to refer to the elaboration of a trauma. In a short piece called 'Remembering, Repeating and Working-Through', Freud (1950) proposed that the analyst should help the patient to process and interpret his or her memories in a way that connects, reorganises, and rearticulates the remembrance into the ego or self. 'Working through' means giving time to converse about memories and also organising an intermediate region, maybe something similar to the interstitial space between memory and forgetting to which Stoler (2022) refers.

Memories demand work. They are not immediate pathways to the past and will never be. If there are any pearls, they will have to be dug and sought with passion and interest, with time and patience. Memories are not mirrors in which we can recognise ourselves, or mental places where we are able to grasp the past 'as it really happened', as historians following the Rankean tradition would assume if they considered memories a relevant source. Recollecting memories does not have to provide the stage for an unbounded ego that replaces the transcendental modern collective subject with an individual one. Instead, the process can be a way to account for the ways in which our histories, while deeply personal, are entangled with other human and non-human beings, with tape recorders, writing pads, photos, spaces, and voices.

Moreover, as the work done by some H.I.J.O.S. in Argentina shows, if memories are worked-through, they may open up a different relationship with the past, perhaps making 'room for other realities, other narratives' and even 'for subscribing to other regimes of truth' (Stoler 2022, p. 136). The past is not out there to be recognised as a single causal line that determines our present. Instead, the past might be more productively approached as 'a contemporaneity [...] vital and potent in this present' (ibid.). In that respect, childhood memories, even if they are blurred images or distorted mirrors, can be very helpful in understanding the vitality and potency of that past among us. If worked through, if taken pensively, if connected with other fragments and inscribed in different series, these memories can make some room for an 'elsewhere' that allows us, collectively, to elaborate our traumatic pasts.

Without Whom...

I borrowed the title of this section from a book by Ann Laura Stoler (2022), whose work on archives and racialised pasts has accompanied me throughout the years. 'Without whom' seems so much more appropriate than 'acknowledgements' to allow me to recognise and give back to the intellectual and affective networks that make memory exercises possible. This experiment would not have been possible without Zsuzsa, who took me by the hand and made me laugh and think, and stayed with me when tears came and also when they went away, and without the Mnemo ZIN collective, whose creative energy took me on the ride. Without Leonor Arfuch, my dear friend who recently passed away, who read a preliminary version of some of these texts and urged me to write more and work through my memories: this text owes more to her than I can verbally account for, and for many reasons I wish she was still here to read it and critique it. Without the H.I.J.O.S. and without all those who try to deal with traumatic childhoods through writing and art, particularly my friend Julia but also other 'hijis' (Pérez 2021) whom I have scarcely or never met: Mariana Eva, Raquel, Laura, Verónica, Albertina, María, Lucila, Félix, Julián, María Inés, and so many others. Without Verónica, my sister, who endured me through childhood and cared for me even when she was as fearful and scared as I was. Without my mom and stepdad, who were there to lift me up and help me go places. Without Pato and Ale, my friends who listened, asked questions, criticised, and listened again. Without the Seminaria Fuera de Lugar at my department, where we also started writing and thinking about academic work and life through collective exercises of memory. Without Norma, another experienced listener and guide in the workings on memory and the self. Without Antonio, whose love, joy, and optimism gave me the platform, the earth, the sea in which and from which I could dare to excavate. Without Ana, Mariana, and

Amalia, who also make part of that earth, my world, and who taught me about childhoods in more ways than I could have ever imagined. To all of them, *gracias totales*.

References

Alcoba, L. (2014). *La Casa de los Conejos*. Edhasa

Arendt, H. (1968). 'Introduction', in W. Benjamin, *Illuminations: Essays and Reflections* Schocken Books, pp. 1–51

Arfuch, L. (2018). *La Vida Narrada. Memoria, Subjetividad y Política*. EDUVIM, https://doi.org/10.7774/cevr.2016.5.1.19

Benjamin, W. (2005). 'Excavation and Memory', in *Selected Writings, Vol. 2: 1930–1934*, ed. and trans. by M. Jennings, H. Eiland, and G. Smith. Harvard University Press, p. 576

Beverley, J. (1996). 'The Real Thing', in *The Real Thing: Testimonial Discourse and Latin America*, ed. by G. M. Gugelberg. Duke University Press, pp. 266–86

Biblioteca Nacional Mariano Moreno (2021). *Hijxs. Poéticas de la Memoria*. Biblioteca Nacional

Blanchot, M. (2002). *The Book to Come*, trans. by C. Mandell. Stanford University Press http://www.sup.org/books/title/?id=1459

Blejmar, J. (2016). *Playful Memories: The Autofictional Turn in Post-Dictatorship Argentina*. Palgrave Macmillan, https://doi.org/10.1007/978-3-319-40964-1

Connolly, W. E. (2022). *Resounding Events. Adventures of an Academic from the Working Class*. Fordham University Press, https://doi.org/10.5422/fordham/9781531500221.001.0001

Coria, J. (2006). 'El Sentido de la Historia'. *El Monitor de la Educación Común*, 6, Quinta Época, 30–8

Das, V. (2015). *Affliction: Health, Disease, Poverty*. Fordham University Press, https://doi.org/10.5422/fordham/9780823261802.001.0001

Ernst, W. (2017, May 17). 'Good-Bye "Archive": Towards a Media Theory of Dynamic Storage'. [Lecture at Lusitanean University Lisbon]. Museum of Contemporary Art, https://www.musikundmedien.hu-berlin.de/de/medienwissenschaft/medientheorien/ernst-in-english/pdfs/archive-good-bye.pdf

Fernández, A. (1998). '*La Sexualidad Atrapada de la Señorita Maestra: Una Lectura Psicopedagógica del ser Mujer, la Corporeidad y el Aprendizaje*'. Ediciones Nueva Visión.

Freud, S. (1950). 'Remembering, Repeating and Working-Through', in *The Standard Edition of the Complete Psychological Works of Sigmund Freud*. Hogarth Press, vol. 12, pp. 147–57

Gatti, G. (2014). *Surviving Forced Disappearance in Argentina and Uruguay: Identity and Meaning*. Palgrave Macmillan

Hartman, S. (2007). *Lose Your Mother. A Journey along the Atlantic Slave Route*. Macmillan

Huyssen, A. (1995). *Twilight Memories. Marking Time in a Culture of Amnesia*. Routledge, https://doi.org/10.4324/9780203610213

Jelín, E. (2002). *Los Trabajos de la Memoria*. Siglo XXI de Argentina Editores

Oberti, A. (2015). *Las Revolucionarias: Militancia, Vida Cotidiana y Afectividad en los Setenta*. Edhasa

Pérez, M. E. (2021). *Diario de una Princesa Montonera: 110% Verdad*. Planeta

—— (2022). *Fantasmas en Escena: Teatro y Desaparición*. Paidós

Pineau, P., Mariño, M., Arata, N., and Mercado, B. (2006). *El Principio del Fin: Políticas y Memorias de la Educación en la Última Dictadura Militar (1976–1983)*. Ediciones Colihue

Robles, R. (2013). *Pequeños Combatientes*. Alfaguara

Stoler, A. L. (2022). *Interior Frontiers: Essays on the Entrails of Inequality*. Oxford University Press, https://doi.org/10.1093/oso/9780190076375.001.0001

Traverso, E. (2020). *Passés Singuliers: Le 'Je' dans l'écriture de l'Histoire*. Lux Éditeurs

Searching for Childhood Gummi Bears[1]

Nadine Bernhard

I was born in 1981 in East Berlin and thus lived the first eight years of my childhood in the GDR. After reunification, I lived still in Berlin, but now in the Federal Republic of Germany. The division of east and west (Germany) has been an important experience that has been part of my life and identity ever since. It seems that this is prevalent in particular in Germany where the division between east and west is reproduced continuously in education, politics, media, and everyday life. When, in a Reconnect/Recollect workshop, I saw another participant's photo of a bear, I was moved to think of a family holiday in Poland in 1991, where we children could buy milk ice cream (called Lody) in the shape of this bear. It tasted wonderful. The memory of sweets is the association that leads me to a memory that I now share with you.

Every year in spring, there was a little fair in the parking lot in front of their high-rise building. They lived on the 23rd floor. The fair had only a few stalls, but for her as a child it was huge. When she was 5 or 6 years old, she was also allowed to go to the fair alone and she divided the pennies she got or saved by collecting paper and glass. One half of the money she wanted to use for the one-armed bandit and the other half for sweets. Her favorite sweets were big

---

1   This is a childhood memory produced as part of the Reconnect/Recollect project discussed in the introduction to this book.

© 2024 Nadine Bernhard, CC BY-NC 4.0   https://doi.org/10.11647/OBP.0383.24

soft gummi bears in the shape of the rabbit and wolf.[2] *She loved these sweets and tried to save them by dividing them up for the following weeks/or days. Unfortunately, not long after 1990, these gummi bears were no longer produced. Still, today she tries new varieties of soft gummi bears in the small hope to find the taste again. But she has never been lucky.*

---

2   Ну, погоди [Well, Just You Wait!]. My mother still has dishes with the motives of the rabbit and wolf and I remember vividly how my sister and I always argued who would get the plate or the cup.

8. The Secrets:

Connections Across Divides

Irena Kašparová, Beatrice Scutaru, Zsuzsa Millei, Josefine Raasch, and Katarzyna Gawlicz

---

Childhood memories are filled with secrets. Secrets have a potency to connect, to cross, or to create a divide between people, generations, places, ideologies, borders, and geopolitical relations. They are agents of movement and action, despite the fact that they may be locked away in a person's mind, heart, or body. A slight hint—a sensual intake, a word, or a shared memory may trigger the re/emergence of a secret. The ethnodrama presented in this chapter is created from memories shared during a collective memory workshop in Berlin in 2019 and is embellished with fictional characters, additions, and dramatisation to allow the reader to engage, make sense, or affectively connect to childhood secrets of the Cold War.

Secrets! We all accumulate them throughout our lives. Some of them last only for a short while, bursting into the open rather quickly. Others remain buried, permeating our lives in their embodied entrails and contributing to our becoming. Private and intimate, they must be watched over and protected. No secrets are, however, either forgotten or inactive. They spice up the reservoir of our feelings and can act spontaneously when we least expect them to. In this chapter, we aim to capture the life of childhood secrets during the Cold War, especially as these connect, cross, or create divides between people, generations, places, ideologies, borders, and geopolitical relations. We do this by dramatising and adding fictional elements to our childhood memories in an ethnodrama.

We, the authors of this chapter, first met in September 2019 in Berlin, as part of the collective memory workshop of the Reconnect/Recollect project. During the workshop, we shared our childhood memories from the Cold-War period. These memories recounted events that spanned the former state-socialist countries in East-Central Europe. To our surprise, secrets appeared in many memories, including accounts of very private bodily experiences and, at perhaps the opposite extreme, of participation in political activism. These memories, embedded in secrets, not only tell about singular, individual, or culturally specific experiences; they resonated across the participants´ recollections, connecting their bodily sensations and evoking different facets of their lived experiences, including the emotions and tensions that surrounded them.

We were fascinated by the power of secrets to connect people across time and space. This chapter is an attempt to share our fascination with the reader. We want to draw readers into the bridging and bonding potency of secrets and hope that, by sharing childhood secrets in a dramatic form, we will also trigger the emergence of readers' childhood memories. First, however, we present a short exploration of public-private secret dynamisms from a theoretical perspective. For this, we brought together reflections from the fields of sociology, anthropology, history, and childhood studies. This theoretical framing is followed by the introduction of childhood memories, including the way we gathered and analysed them to create an ethnodrama, which constitutes the final part of our contribution. The plot of the script is a fiction, comprising childhood memories of secrets and imaginative elements. The combination aims to foreground the mechanics of secrets and the tensions these create.

Theoretical Anchor

Secret is a multisensory phenomenon, expressed across a plurality of domains, such as everyday talk, folklore, semiotic spaces, journalism, humour, and many others (Jones 2014). Charged with social tension, a secret creates, mediates, and controls social relations and colours their nature by modulating the ratio of knowledge to ignorance (Simmel 1906). A palpable aura of risk emerges from secrets. If a secret is not private, those who know it may understand its meanings differently—a situation that leads to tensions. Revealing a secret can also have consequences. As such, it becomes an active agent. The secret shapes understandings and acts without one's control; it may even act without one's knowledge or without knowledge of what others might do upon learning the secret.

A secret itself can be considered as an affair that occurs in a liminal or bordered space of existence. It happens when boundaries or norms are crossed, reality is split open, and emotions are stricken. Admitting the existence of any such fissure could lead to undesired or feared changes (for example, a mother does not confront the children who stole flowers from people's gardens for her). To prevent a change taking place and to hold onto the foregone reality, a secret is born. The secret functions as a hanging bridge, uncertain and shaky, operating as a connection or an uncrossable division. With a secret's coming into being, the former consistency of the self is interrupted as life starts to deviate from its original course.

Secrets are also paradoxical, in at least two ways. The first paradox resides in the individual or collective nature of a secret. A secret's existence, while often concealed from all but one individual, emerges and is sustained through relations. One cannot keep a secret from him or herself but only from others. Thus, every secret, even when held by a single individual, is nevertheless relational because it exists only in relation to others from whom the secret is kept.

The second paradox intertwines two notions: that secrets are constitutive of one's life and, at the same time, that one's life (in modern societies) is transparent or holds no secrets. First, a secret can be a decisive and constitutive moment in one's life. It shapes the emerging individual while, at the same time, shaping society and its norms, hierarchies, categories, relations, and materialities. As such, a secret has creative and productive agency over the trajectory of every human life (Birchall 2016). Each child, for instance, needs a secret hiding place, a 'space of shelter and safety, where one can withdraw from the outside world' (Van Manen and Levering 1996, p. 23). The secret place can be a space of contemplation, 'an asylum in which the child can withdraw to experiment with a growing sense of self-awareness affecting growth of the inner, spiritual life' (ibid.). In our memories, listening in on radio channels from Western European countries, such as Radio Free Europe; playing with the body of a deceased person before the funeral in a Church; entering someone else's room and playing with others' possession; or smoking or drinking in secret are examples of such personal secrets.

Second, as Simmel (1906) was already arguing over a century ago, Europe has a moral distaste for secrecy. With the collapse of the feudal world order and the emergence of socialism and early capitalism, transparency became a virtue. The absence of secrets was associated with religious and/or intellectual rebirth and purity that few could fail to praise. As members of societies espousing this moral code, children are taught about the undesirability of secrets. Yet, they are also taught that some secrets need to be kept. These can refer to the private life of a family or community or be public secrets. Sometimes secrets become embedded in the culture and show themselves in language conventions. For instance, the longstanding notion that some secrets carry sinister connotations is enshrined in proverbs such as the Czech ´Co je šeptem, to je čertem´ [what is whispered becomes the Devil himself] (Gable 1997). In such cases, shared norms regulate a secret's open existence, meaning that, while a secret may be known by a group of people, it may not be pronounced publicly. A veil is drawn over the secret. If whispering to preserve a secret is publicly detected, whispering is also publicly condemned as sinister behaviour that prevents transparency and supports conspiracy. The social norm that publicly condemns secrets may also be expressed as ridicule through jokes and humour, as folklore, or in games (Jones 2014). Its expression is learned by children from an early age together with its norms. Such secrets in our childhood memories emerged as we were made to smuggle money and goods across the East-West borders; as we kept Western goods hidden (Kent cigarettes, Bravo or French fashion magazines, French scarves), hid a disagreement with the socialist ideology; or we knew that only the façade of buildings was refurbished leaving the building otherwise in ruins.

Our childhood memories recount personal and public secrets, including even those secrets that must be kept forever as they would mean incarceration for those involved. Personal secrets were known by friends of family; the latter were sometimes not really secrets since they were known by many people but were, nevertheless, kept as secrets. These public secrets were often related to norms accepted by society such as, say, stealing from socialist cooperatives or cheating in exams. If cheating happened in secret but with the knowledge of the teacher who pretended not to notice, for example, the facade of the norm was maintained despite being (unofficially) broken. As children, we had to come to terms with this kind of duality: not having personal secrets yet knowing how to uphold public secrets. This type often involved some kind of disrespect for the regime, which led to corruption as a form of resistance, such as when employees stole raw materials or end-products from state-run factories. During the communist Czechoslovak times, there was even a popular saying *'Whoever is not stealing from the state is stealing from their family'*, which appeared in public discourse in the same way as popular wisdom and proverbs. A public secret involves the risk of public acknowledgement and consequential punishment for breaking the norm (Taussig 1999). Consequently, a public secret occupies the squeezed middle in political arenas:

> On one side it is challenged by calls for transparency and openness; on the other it is trumped, in moral terms, by privacy [...]. Citizens are commonly said to have a 'right to privacy' but not exactly a 'right to secrecy'. (Birchall 2011, p. 8)

If private lives become inspected for secrets, that is where a totalitarian space begins (Derrida and Ferraris 2001). Our childhood memories of socialism demonstrate similar paradoxes.

Under socialist reality, transparency was associated with the possibility of all citizens taking part in running the country economically, politically, and ideologically. Transparency was theoretically assured by concentrating power in the hands of people, who were encouraged and rewarded for watching over each other. Snitching, once merely an expedient obtrusion, became a necessary group-protective activity. As such, it became a symbol of regime-collaboration and was despised by those who opposed its repression (Van Manen and Levering 1996). Despite this focus on exposure, secrecy was vital in socialist regimes (Fitzpatrick 1999). The obsession with secrecy, which had its origins in communist parties' experiences as illegal and persecuted movements before they took power, invaded government and party practice. It led to the development of a culture of secrecy and of political organisations characterised by what they did not share (Verdery 2014). This also had an impact on people's everyday lives. In a society where people could be arrested for loose tongues (their own or those of people around them), where 'the walls have ears', families turned inwards. They kept, sometimes even from their own children, information, opinions, beliefs, values, or modes of existence that clashed with public norms. From a very early age, children learned the importance of secrets for the survival of their families, and secrecy became an intrinsic part of their lives (Figes 2007).

Debates about transparency and secrecy are ongoing in the social sciences. This chapter aims to contribute to such discourse by recognising the plurality of and paradoxes inflicted by the presence of secrets. It explores secrets in childhood memories as social agents from a relational perspective, while paying attention to the time-spaces and socio-material entanglements that enabled secrets to bond people together across socialist borders.

Creating an Ethnodrama

We have gathered all memories about secrets that were produced in the collective-biography workshops (Davies and Gannon 2006) and included in the archive on the project website. Our final selection included twenty-two memories that portray personal, group, or public secrets. We each read them carefully, over and over again, afterwards making inferences about the memory and responding to the following questions: What is the nature of the secret in the memory? How does it create / draw on relations? How does it operate in the memory? What does the memory reveal about a secret? After several collective discussions about our responses to these questions, thinking through the variety of Cold-War contexts across the region these memories recounted, and reading across multidisciplinary literature in anthropology, education, history, and childhood studies, we arrived at the conclusion that we would like to highlight the ways in which secrets relate to, create, maintain, and disrupt different divisions. We understand division in multiple ways, including age, gender, generation, family, place, Cold War, borders, ideologies. We also wished to bring into our analysis the emotional and affective aspects of secrets, as we felt that, even from the temporal distance of the present, looking back on the secrets still produced visceral reactions within our bodies.

We took childhood memories of the Cold War from the narratives of adults in which they make sense of remembered fragments, feelings, sensations, and dialogues but do not recreate the events that took place. In other words, memories are not historical truths, even though they refer to historical events and conditions. Memory stories mix imagination with the above-listed narrative elements (Keightley 2010), and they are written by adults with the intention of intimating a child's way of being in the world (Millei et al. 2019). In some ways, memories and secrets operate similarly. Both lie dormant, helping to orient the person in everyday life without taking full shape and intensity, until there is an intention or necessity to revive them. Then, they move the memory- or secret-teller and the listener with an affective force, creating relations, emotions, visceral reactions, and bringing to the fore other memories.

How, we wondered, could we capture in our writing the moment of the emergence of affect in the most expressive way? We wanted to show readers the secrets' dynamism and real-world effects with all their consequences, including the sparking of emotions, curiosity, doubt, fascination, and anxiety. To fulfil these intentions, we turned to ethnodrama—a methodology that fuses research of participants' experiences, including the emotive elements of the stories (data), with the artistic techniques of theatre (Saldaña 2011). Ethnodrama is a mode of exploration that recounts the insights gained through analysis in a written script for a dramatic play that can be performed by actors. Like the memory stories, an ethnodrama is not a direct representation of the world (Richardson 1997). Nonetheless, its techniques allow for the creation of engagements with an audience that are similar to how a secret operates.

The plot of our ethnodrama, entitled *Secrets*, is based on several memories. Fictional elements, borrowed from other memories in the archive, provided the missing glue that allowed us to build our characters and to develop tensions. We fused the narrators of these different memories into five characters, switching their genders, and giving them names typically used across East-Central Europe. While writing their storyline, we paid special attention to how secrets facilitate both conflict and reconciliation. As the ethnodrama incorporates analysis of the memories, we do not offer further analytical remarks or discussion to conclude the chapter. We wish, instead, to leave the readers to be affected by the story as though by a secret—with intrigue, tension, and emotions.

Secrets

Characters

HANNA: a thirteen-year-old girl from the East (socialist country) who is cheeky, street smart, and brainy. She is the cousin of JÖRG.

MARIA: her friend, a thirteen-year-old girl from the East who is timid at home but wild in public and has her own views.

JÖRG: a fourteen-year-old boy from the West (Western European non-socialist country). HANNA's cousin, he feels superior to her because he thinks he knows the world better than she does. He dresses well and loves to play Nintendo.

MOTHER: the mother of HANNA and aunt of JÖRG. An exhausted, busy person, she trusts her daughter but is an authority and demands respect. She is from the East.

AUNT: the mother of JÖRG and aunt of HANNA. She is from the West.

RADIO HOST: male voice.

Act 1.

A flat in an apartment block, somewhere in the East: Radio Free Europe

In the back of the stage positioned in the middle, a white sheet hangs dividing the two parts of the stage diagonally. Posters from Bravo Magazine of Sinéad O'Connor and Enya are projected upon it, as if pinned above the bed. Evening. O'Connor's song 'Nothing Compares 2 U' is playing. On the left side of the stage, the light goes on, revealing cupboards across from the bed.

HANNA and MARIA (*sing in chorus as they search in the cupboard for cigarettes*). Noooothing compaaaaares.... PU-IUUUUU.

MARIA. Where does your mother keep them?

MARIA (*finding a pack*). They will notice we took one, look it is not even open!

HANNA. Do you think they will be mad? I am so scared, we shouldn't do this.

MARIA (*lighting the cigarette*). They said these are better than the Carpati. But they taste horrible!

HANNA. Grandpa smokes Carpati. He loves Kent, he says it is better quality. You know, from the West.

MARIA. I was so embarrassed last week when my mom slid it into the doctor's pocket. I would never be able to do that

(*Girls put the cigarettes under the mattress and continue smoking. 'Take Five' by Dave Brubeck starts to play.*)

RADIO HOST. Dave Brubeck's 'Take Five'—the importance of this band can't be stressed enough... (*voice fades out*).

Act 2.

Somewhere in the West

Right side of the stage lights up where there is a family in the living room listening to the radio. On the white sheet a journey across the border is projected. The radio plays pop music.

AUNT. Did you hear that Dave Brubeck visited East Germany and Poland?

HANNA. Mommy, who is Dave Brubeck?

JÖRG. Gosh, how can you be so dumb?

AUNT. A famous US jazz player. Do you know his saying: 'No dictatorship can tolerate jazz?' (*Switches off radio and moves to turntable.*) Let me put the vinyl on... Dave Brubeck band, Jazz fights communism.

(*Music starts.*)

HANNA. I know this song! They played it on the West German Radio!

AUNT. Amazing, right?

MOTHER (*mumbles to herself*). Don´t you put such ideas into her head, jazz and stuff. (*Out loud:*) But anyway, let's finish packing now.

(*MOTHER spreads bills of Western Marks into the fake bottom of the suitcase. HANNA hands her mother two copies of Bravo magazine.*)

AUNT (*fastening an antique medallion around HANNA´s neck*). Let me put this on you. It belonged to your great grandmother, it is yours now, Jörg will not wear it. Family treasure.

HANNA (*puzzled*). Thank you.

MOTHER (*wiping away tears*). Here, Hanna, put these two pairs of jeans on, they are too skinny for me to wear. First your pair and then the one for Olga that is bigger.

HANNA (*pulls off her old trousers and is not concerned about JÖRG staring at her and then pulls on the two pairs of jeans*). It looks ridiculous. I look ridiculous!

JÖRG. Yeah, you look like an elephant.

HANNA. I don't care, I just want the jeans.

MOTHER. Act normal at the border. They won't search a child.

HANNA. I'm not a child. I don't look like a child.

MOTHER (*looks at the fake bottom of the suitcase, to herself*). It's still visible, they will find it.

AUNT hands over a vinyl with Madonna to HANNA, she receives it with great joy. They add it and some cans of pineapple, chocolate, and coffee into the suitcase. MOTHER finishes packing and closes the suitcase.

MOTHER. So, see you Jörg in the summer at Balaton.

MOTHER and HANNA walk behind the curtain.

Act 3.

MOTHER's and HANNA's flat.

The left side of the stage is lit up. MARIA and HANNA sit at the dining table. They are drinking lemonade out of the bottle.

MOTHER. Did you do your homework?

HANNA. Yes, we had to write an assignment about building socialism. I've written three and a half pages!

MOTHER. Really? What did you write about? Show me! (*Taking the paper that HANNA hands over, reads*:) 'When I am older... we will all be free from imperialist oppression... Nelson Mandela is free... We have cars for everyone... I will love jazz, the music based on improvisation so that socialism does not become a dictatorship.'

Are you crazy, Hanna?! You can't write this! Your father will lose his job!

MARIA. Why?

(*MOTHER rips out the pages from the book.*)

MOTHER. Arghhh, I am late ... I'll be back in a couple of hours. Go sunbathing, or swimming. The weather looks lovely. Don´t sit in front of the TV, there's nothing on...

HANNA. Mom, where did you put those French fashion magazines?

(*MOTHER leaves the stage. Girls look for the magazine and find some scarves.*)

HANNA. Wow! I've never seen them. So beautiful!

MARIA. I wish we could take them to the Balaton.

HANNA. I think they make these in France.

MARIA. Is it next week that your cousin is coming?

HANNA. Yes, they're going to stay with us for almost a month. Can you imagine? My mother wants to spend more time with her sister since grandma died, I guess. They could have left Jörg at home.

MARIA. What's he like? Does he smoke?

HANNA. Jörg? No, he's a weirdo. He doesn't speak much, you know, the kind who thinks he knows everything better. He's in his room all the time, just playing Nintendo.

MARIA. Do you have a picture of him?

HANNA. Why are you interested? He is not a boyfriend material?

MARIA. Don't be stupid. Show me.

HANNA. You will have plenty of time with him at the Balaton. They have rented a fancy house for all of us to fit there.

MARIA. Awesome!

HANNA. I'm glad you are coming along, it will be fun, you'll see.

(*Light dims.*)

Act 4.

Lake Balaton

Light comes up on the left side. JÖRG is frantically looking for the girls in front of a solid fence. HANNA and MARIA are behind the fence.

HANNA (*crouched*). Get down! He can see us!

MARIA. Ok, we lost him.

HANNA. Let's go see the bike race! Maybe we will be on TV!

MARIA. Whaaaat! Is the TV crew there?

HANNA. Yes! How could we get to the very front?

MARIA. Easy! You saw how they painted the front of the houses? We could get around there, backyards are always open. To get to the front, we will run around the back. The foreign delegations will be in the front too.

HANNA. They did a bit of lift up for sure, this street used to look like a dump.... Well, it is still a dump from the back. Yack!

MARIA. Wait, my leg got stuck in this shit. What is this? Hell. What a mess.

HANNA. Some paint. Careful, there is some broken glass there and rubbish that looks suspicious.

MARIA. Yeah, the same paint they used for the front of this house, look.

HANNA. Bright and shiny on one side and dirty, stinky, and full of rubbish on the other side. What a shitty place, huh?

MARIA. Hey look, Jörg is coming...

HANNA. Shit, he saw us. Let's hide in the church.

(*Lights go off for a moment. The church interior is projected on the sheet.*)

HANNA. Come on, I have something to show you. Now you have a chance to sniff and touch a corpse.

MARIA. That is disgusting, I will never do that.

HANNA. It's not a big deal. I've done it many times. Come and see! (*they walk over to a corpse laid out on a table*) Look at the face, how clean and beautifully prepared he is, smells like perfume!

MARIA. The flowers are nice. Are they from wax paper? I would love to have one of these...

HANNA. Touch, here, just the face, it is OK.

MARIA. It freaks me out.

HANNA. How about a hide-and-seek? The corpse is the base.

(The lights go off and on. The girls run into JÖRG on the town bridge. It is raining. An old Bravo magazine wet on the pavement.)

MARIA. Look! A new Bravo! Oh—look—Sinéad O'Connor's new album on the cover!

JÖRG. This place looks familiar. I have seen it somewhere already… Was it not on TV?

(HANNA picks up the wet magazine and it falls apart.)

HANNA. Such a pity! All ripped up! Damn!

MARIA. This is the bridge that….

HANNA. Shhhhsss

JÖRG. What is the story?

HANNA. Oh, we can't tell you, sorry, no way! Maybe in a hundred years.

Act 5.

On the Beach

Lights off. Behind the sheet only silhouettes are visible. Balaton beach is projected on the sheet. Murmurs in German, Hungarian, Czech, Romanian, and Polish merge with the sound of children screaming and splashing water. Naked people on the beach on projection.

HANNA. It's sooooo hot. I'm dying. Can't wait to get into the water.

MARIA. Race you.

(The girls and MOTHER start to undress, giggling.)

JÖRG. What are you doing?

HANNA. What do you mean? Why are you shouting?

JÖRG. Why are you taking all your clothes off?

MARIA. Huh?

HANNA. What do you mean?

JÖRG. Don't you have bathing suits?

HANNA. Why would I need it? Nobody's wearing them.

AUNT. Oh. Sorry Jörg, I forgot about you. This is a nudist beach. We used to come here with our parents. You and I can keep our bathing suits on. It's no problem.

JÖRG. But... But...

HANNA. Weirdo.

MARIA. Yeah. Such a weirdo...

JÖRG. Whatever!

MARIA. Do you wanna come with us? In the water?

(The girls run off.)

JÖRG *(to MOTHER)*. Auntie, I have something to tell you. The girls are really strange. Could you please tell them to behave normally? Aren't you worried?

MOTHER: What do you mean?

(Lights off.)

Act 6.

In the Balaton House

Light comes up, girls are in Jörg's room playing Nintendo.

MARIA. This is so cool! One more round? We are getting really good at this! I bet we would beat Jörg!

HANNA. Yeah—if ever. He would kill us if he found out.

MARIA. Why is he so annoying? He is your cousin after all.

HANNA. He is so protective of his stuff, so careful about his Nintendo, his clothes, his hair, his majesty. He is boring. No fun at all.

MARIA. But he smells really nice.

HANNA. Yes, it is his cologne, Aramis. Dad says perfumes are for girls. But I like it too. I wish men here would use it too. I hate their smell.

MARIA. I hate him, he snitched on us and now we're grounded here at home for the day! He will be at the party for sure tonight.

HANNA. Would your mom let you go to the party? My mom is so strict, she thinks I am a baby.

JÖRG (*appearing at the door*). What the fuck are you doing? Get out!

Act 7.

The Balaton Party

An opened window is projected upon the white sheet.

MARIA. Make sure the knot is really tight, I do not want to fall down into the bushes!

HANNA. Yeah, yeah, don´t worry... He's such an ass to go without us.

MARIA. He wanted to go alone. Fair enough.

HANNA. Why are you defending him? Do you love him or what?

MARIA. I'd give him a chance. He has nice clothes and smells nice and we would look cool with him.

HANNA. Did you bring the cigarettes?

MARIA. Yeah, sure. You look so nice with the scarf!

HANNA. French, it can't look bad.

MARIA. Did you see how cute he looked when he came into the room and shouted at us? It was nice that he did not snitch on us again...

HANNA. He looked like Boris Becker.

MARIA. Oh I love him!

HANNA. Ok, let's go to the beach. Jörg will be so surprised!

MARIA. Do you think he will wear his perfume?

HANNA. He better do…

(Lights go off, the three youths are behind the curtain smoking together, girls acting drunk, hugging each other, picking some flowers on the way home. They pick up the Bravo magazine.)

(Light comes up in front of curtain. MOTHER comes into the kitchen and picks up the flowers left on the table and smiles. Silence. Light dims slowly.)

THE END

References

Birchall, C. (2011). 'Introduction to "Secrecy and Transparency": The Politics of Opacity and Openness'. *Theory, Culture and Society*, 28(7–8), 7–25, https://doi.org/10.1177/0263276411427744

—— (2016). 'Managing Secrecy'. *International Journal of Communication*, 10, 152–63, http://ijoc.org/index.php/ijoc/article/view/4399/1528

Davies, B., and Gannon, S. (eds). (2006). *Doing Collective Biography: Investigating the Production of Subjectivity*. Open University Press

Derrida, J. and M. Ferraris (2001). *A Taste for the Secret*, trans. by G. Donis. Polity Press (Original work published 1997)

Figes, O. (2007). *The Whisperers: Private Life in Stalin's Russia*. Macmillan

Fitzpatrick, S. (1999). *Everyday Stalinism: Ordinary Life in Extraordinary Times: Soviet Russia in the 1930s*. Oxford University Press

Gable, E. (1997). 'A Secret Shared: Fieldwork and the Sinister in a West African Village'. *Cultural Anthropology*, 12(2), 213–33, https://doi.org/10.1525/can.1997.12.2.213

Jones, G. M. (2014). 'Secrecy'. *Annual Review of Anthropology*, 43, 53–69, https://doi.org/10.1146/annurev-anthro-102313-030058

Keightley, E. (2010). 'Remembering Research: Memory and Methodology in the Social Sciences'. *International Journal of Social Research Methodology*, 13(1), 55–70, https://doi.org/10.1080/13645570802605440

Millei, Z., Silova, I., and Gannon, S. (2022). 'Thinking Through Memories of Childhood in (Post) Socialist Spaces: Ordinary Lives in Extraordinary Times. *Children's Geographies*, 20(3), 324–37, https://doi.org/10.1080/14733285.2019.1648759

Richardson, L. (1997). *Fields of Play: Constructing an Academic Life.* Rutgers University Press

Saldaña, J. (2011). *Ethnotheatre: Research from Page to Stage.* Routledge, https://doi.org/10.4324/9781315428932

Simmel, G. (1906). 'The Sociology of Secrecy and of Secret Societies'. *American Journal of Sociology*, 11(4), 441–98

Taussig, M. T. (1999). *Defacement: Public Secrecy and the Labor of the Negative.* Stanford University Press

Van Manen, M., and Levering, B. (1996). *Childhood's Secrets: Intimacy, Privacy, and the Self Reconsidered.* Teachers College Press

Verdery, K. (2014). *Secrets and Truths: Ethnography in the Archive of Romania's Secret Police.* Central European University Press, https://doi.org/10.1515/9789633860519

Open Coffin[1]

Irena Kašparová

She is excited. There is a funeral in the church of her father today, the corpse will be displayed in the open coffin as usual. She has prepared an exciting challenge for her friends, she wants to tease them, she wants to play a daring game, be a brave and hero girl in their eyes. They have two hours prior to the funeral. Under the oath of life not to tell anybody, she asks them to come in secret, should they want to see the dead body, should they want to touch the dead body, should they want to sniff the dead body. She has done it herself several times, more than she can remember. She knows the dead body is not dirty, nor cold, it smells of cologne and there are plenty of waxed flowers around it, so it is beautifully decorated in its Sunday clothes. She is not scared and she enjoys the feeling of power of that knowledge. Other children do not know what she knows, perhaps they have not seen the dead person before, they are afraid of the dead body, they are afraid of the church, they are afraid of the funeral. She feels powerful and at the same time wants to share her power with her friends. She does not want to be different any longer. They all come after school, sneaking in the church once the body is displayed. One by one they look at it, they touch it, they smell it. Their initiation is completed. For the rest of the afternoon they all play hide and seek in the church. The corpse is the base.

---

1 This is a childhood memory produced as part of the Reconnect/Recollect project discussed in the introduction to this book.

© 2024 Irena Kašparová, CC BY-NC 4.0   https://doi.org/10.11647/OBP.0383.25

9. Mysterious Cotton Pieces:
Childhood Memories of Menstruation

Katarzyna Gawlicz and Zsuzsa Millei

> This chapter explores the memories of menarche of three girls who grew up in socialist countries in the 1980s. We use Kopytoff's theory of the cultural biography of objects and Rogoff's theory of guided participation to intimate the girls' ways of knowing and practising menarche in relation to objects and significant others. Objects carry cultural meanings and, as such, taught girls about practices and feelings associated with menstruation and helped them to navigate their periods. The memories analysed here demonstrate that girls' everyday experiences in state-socialist and capitalist countries were quite similar and that children on the Eastern side acted as knowing subjects rather than passive victims of 'indoctrination'.

Menstruation and menarche (the first menstrual period) are deeply personal experiences and cultural phenomena. As such, they have attracted considerable attention in research, including how girls come to know and practise menstruation from their own perspectives (Burrows and Johnson 2005; Orringer and Gahagan 2010; Piran 2020). Menstruation as a biosocial and cultural phenomenon is often associated with secrecy, shame, and fear, and this is consistent across different geographical contexts (Uskul 2004). These associations have been attributed to the institutionalisation of the menstrual taboo by major patriarchal religions (Patterson 2014). Menstruation is also a biological marker of the end of the female human's juvenile period; bleeding and abdominal pain signal the arrival of her reproductive stage. In traditions such as

Hinduism and Judaism, menstruation is codified within larger coming-of-age and purity systems that have been instrumental in controlling women's sexuality and in constructing women as 'bearers of tradition and responsible for the wellbeing of the family, society, and religion itself' (Cohen 2020, p. 126). With the nineteenth-century development of patriarchal medical discourses came a perception of women's bodies as medical maladies and of women as incapable of properly handling menstruation without medical surveillance (Patterson 2014). In modern societies, medicalisation objectified the human body in general, but the female body became subject to further objectification, with girls themselves looking at their bodies as objects of beauty and sexualisation (Kovácsné and Szeverényi 2006). As Brumberg (1998) argues for the US context, perceptions of menarche shifted in the twentieth century: what had been a maturational event turned into a hygienic crisis that required the intervention of the medical field and sanitary-product industry, the latter contributing to the commercialisation of young women's bodily processes. Feminist writers point to misogyny as the source of the negative perceptions of menstruation (Steinem 2020). They have exposed the role that religious and medical discourses, perpetuating menstrual stigma and commoditising women's bodies in capitalism, play in silencing a positive and open menstrual dialogue (Patterson 2014).

Despite cultural and social changes, menstruation remains a taboo in public life. A 'menstrual etiquette' requires women to hide any evidence of menstruation (Laws 1990), and the appearance of commercially sold menstrual products reinforces this message (Ginsburg 1996). Even the term menstruation is replaced with a range of euphemisms, such as 'aunt', 'period', 'the curse', or 'being on the rag' (Ernster 1975; Ilnicka 2020). The surrounding secrecy and silence in modern societies often leave young women unprepared for their menarche, which puts them at risk of having a possibly challenging, negative experience. Young girls from different cultures tell about fears of leaking and being discovered, of being ashamed, of being sick, or even of dying as a result of their periods (Burrows and Johnson 2005; Donmall 2013; Sommer 2009). The shame of menstruation and the perception of menstruating women's bodies as deficient are perpetuated by advertisements that, while bringing the issue to the public sphere, links women's emancipation with the use of products that make their bodies socially acceptable and reinforces the need for women to have a 'blood-free ... body' (Sitar 2018, p. 784). However, menstruating bodies often leak or 'bleed through', revealing the menstruation and initiating action. The negative social perception of menstruation, in which menstrual blood is viewed as an abomination that taints women's femininity and differentiates them from the normative male body, leads Johnston-Robledo and Chrisler (2020) to interpret it as stigma. Menstruation is not talked about publicly, except under specific circumstances, such as in private settings, biology classes, or a doctor's office (Johnston-Robledo and Chrisler 2020). Consequently, women go to great lengths to conceal it (Ginsburg 1996; Koutroulis 2001), and menstruation remains 'more like a hidden than a visible stigma' (Johnston-Robledo and Chrisler 2020, p. 184), one associated with shame, dirt, and disgust (Burrows and Johnson 2005; Koutroulis 2001). Mothers can play an important role in the negotiation of menstruation's onset (Lee 2008; Uskul 2004). As Donmall (2013) explains, 'menarche is a crucial time of both identification and separation/individuation from the mother, which may be made more or less difficult by the mother's own experience of menstruation and/or feelings about her femininity' (p. 213). This is reinforced in the memories we explore; they suggest that mothers are sometimes the people children feel least able to confide in about menstruation.

Acting as a counterforce to shame and stigma are feminist menstrual activists. They draw on cultural and spiritual perspectives that range from the essentialist to the radical as they engage in a variety of actions to reclaim menstruation as a significant, valuable, and positive experience. Their work has included interpreting menstruation as a source of embodied knowledge and power, challenging the pathologisation of women and the medicalisation and commodification of their bodies, reclaiming menarche and the menstrual cycle as a rite of passage and a source of pride and community, and drawing attention to the roots of menstrual stigma (Bobel 2010; Bobel and Fahs 2020). Menstrual art (Fahs 2016; Green-Cole 2020) has also contributed to the increased public visibility of menstruation outside of the commodification framework. Studies about menarche carried out in Western societies demonstrate that the experiences of menarche are changing. Lee (2009), for example, found that predominant view of the onset of menstruation during the 1980s was negative, associated with shame, embarrassment, and unpreparedness; whereas, later, it was regarded with ambivalence or even as a positive experience.

In this chapter we explore menstruation through the analysis of childhood memories written by women who were growing up in state-socialist countries during the 1980s, a time when consumer products, including menstrual hygiene products, were scarce (Feinberg 2022; Sitar 2018; Ulč 1989). The lack of female hygiene products could be interpreted as a geopolitical message concerning the status of women in states purportedly devoted to gender equality. Slavenka Drakulić (1992), a Croatian feminist writer, recalls:

> The big midtown auditorium at CUNY was almost filled. I was to give a paper on the [...] subject: women in Eastern Europe. But before I started my speech, I took out one sanitary napkin and one Tampax and, holding them high in the air, I showed them to the audience. 'I have just come from Bulgaria', I said, 'and believe me, women there don't have either napkins or Tampaxes—they never had them, in fact. Nor do women in Poland, or Czechoslovakia, much less in the Soviet Union or Romania. This I hold as one of the proofs of why communism failed, because in the seventy years of its existence it couldn't fulfill the basic needs of half the population.' (p. 124)

The shortage of menstrual hygiene products as a consumer good was compounded by their cultural invisibility. While in some state-socialist countries, newly available sanitary pads and tampons featured in advertisements (Sitar 2018), in others they gained this kind of public visibility only after the turn to a market economy. Poland, for instance, aired its first TV commercial for sanitary napkins in the early 1990s, and the decision to do so stirred great disconcert (Lamek-Kochanowska 2020). The perception of menstruation as a private matter that should be kept secret was perpetuated in handbooks on sex education for adolescents. For instance, a popular Polish self-help book for girls, though providing a thorough introduction into the physiological dimensions of menstruation and menstrual management, emphasised that 'it is not good manners to flaunt this "ailment" of yours. Menstruating is a personal and intimate matter' (Kobyłecka and Jaczewski 1991, p. 25). It also urged its readers to make 'a colourful, unembarrassing pouch' for menstrual-care products as it is 'unhygienic' to carry them loose and 'it can always happen that someone knocks down the school bag, the content scatters and [...] nothing terrible happens but it can be a bit unpleasant' (ibid., p. 95). Moreover, although sexologists and other experts provided sex education (some even fairly progressive) in youth magazines and handbooks, the popular media still constructed an ambivalent or negative image of changes related to puberty (Kościańska 2021; Stańczak-Wiślicz et al. 2020). The result was that mothers and daughters almost never discussed menstruation nor issues related to sexuality and the body (Ilnicka 2020). At best, some mothers might have provided the relevant literature but left their daughters to read and apply the information (Korolczuk 2019). In this way, the sense of secrecy surrounding menstruation was retained even in the family environment.

The childhood memories of menarche we explore are set in this sociocultural context. The limited availability of menstrual-hygiene products and their near-invisibility in public life restricted girls' exposure to open communication about the phenomena of menstruation. Nevertheless, girls still encountered a variety of menstrual objects at home, and these inspired conversation about associated practices, gave hints, and ignited imaginations. We suggest that, by paying attention to and interacting with menstruation-related objects and other people's way of handling them, girls developed understandings of menstruation and its practices as well as of culturally prescribed feelings about these, including shame. Before introducing the memories, we turn next to the theoretical frame we use to highlight object-relations and their roles in sense-making.

Exploring Menarche through Childhood Memories

The memory stories analysed in this chapter exhibit the themes commonly identified in menstruation research, such as feelings of shame, embarrassment, disgust, and fear; a sense of the need to retain secrecy about menstruation; and the consequent use of a range of concealment practices. However, rather than taking up these well-researched themes, we are interested in what these stories tell us about how girls know and practise menarche in relation to objects and significant others. We acknowledge the particular situatedness of the events in the countries of the Eastern bloc (namely, Poland, Latvia, and Hungary) during the late-socialism period (1980s) by focusing on the experiences and objects that are present in the memories and those that are absent. We explore how the girls learn by paying attention to the ways in which their mothers and other women handle menstruation and by carefully investigating, experimenting with, and sensing menstrual-management objects.

The theoretical framework for our analysis draws on Kopytoff's (1986) theory of the cultural biography of objects and Rogoff's theory of guided participation (Rogoff et al. 1989). Kopytoff assumes that, rather than functioning univocally as commodities, objects can be imbued with various meanings and functions that change in time and space, thus they have their own histories. In complex societies, he observes, 'publicly recognised commoditization operates side by side with innumerable schemes of valuation and singularization devised by individuals, social categories, and groups' (Kopytoff 1986, pp. 79–80). Individuals can reiterate public-use or commercial discourses around objects, but they can also use them to serve their own needs or desires, thereby changing the objects' functions and meanings. Objects accumulate such classifications and reclassifications over time. For example, since antiquity, cotton wool has been used to provide warmth and comfort in the form of clothing and blankets. With the invention of machines to create cotton pads and balls, however, cotton wool acquired a protective function; it started to be used in medicine to cover wounds, as wrapping in the transportation of breakable items, and in the beauty business for cleansing and sanitary products (Baines 2015). The expanding industrial use of cotton wool during the twentieth century inspired a variety of personal uses as well. As the memories of menarche explored here will show, children notice objects and take in both their 'official' and 'unofficial' meanings.

Children learn in a variety of ways. They may be explicitly taught in educational settings but also by books and the media. However, they also obtain information more implicitly, by observing others; this is the method by which they most often find their way in social life. We emphasise the learning about culturally important activities that takes place in pairs or groups, that is, when children watch or act together with their more-experienced peers. This indirect style of learning is complicated and often incomplete, hence the recognised need for explicit instruction (Rogoff et al. 1989) on already complex topics (which led to the inclusion of sex education in schools). Children learn informally in shared activities via participation or 'keen observation of events directed to others' (Silva et al. 2010, p. 898). Although Rogoff et al. and Silva et al. focus on such learning-through-watching as it occurs in indigenous communities of the Americas, they maintain that it occurs in all communities. We suggest that children might learn this way in all situations, but especially those that involve taboo subjects or those from which they are excluded and so must participate secretly. What children learn through observation of their peers and others orients their actions when somewhat unexpected events arise, such as the menarche. Children also observe objects, exploring and repurposing them as they learn from them. Through the analysis of memories, we aim to show how children might learn about menstruation through keen observation of the people and objects around them and how this learning prepares them to act when menarche occurs.

We selected three memories of menarche that we shared in a collective memory workshop (Davies and Gannon 2006) held in Berlin in 2019 as part of the Reconnect/Recollect project. Participants were asked to respond to the prompt: 'Bring a childhood memory about secrets'. Because everyone in the workshop was about the same age, we surmise that the events these memories recount took place during the 1980s. The workshop was structured so that, after each individual shared her memory, the group explored it through questions that helped other participants make sense of the experience. It is noteworthy that, in the subsequent rewriting of their memories, individuals added details of bodily texture, object descriptions, and sensations to the stories. In the process of sharing, questioning, and rewriting the memories in a group setting, they ceased to belong just to the individual and became collective. This shift was marked verbally in the stories as authors switched from the first to the third person. We were surprised that three of us brought memories of menstruation to this workshop, so we decided to explore them further in this chapter by asking how they relate to the geopolitical context of the Cold War and its particular conditions within the three former state-socialist countries in which their authors grew up.

We contrasted and juxtaposed the memories, paying special attention to the protagonists of the stories and to bodies, objects, and their relations, as well as to liquids, smells, emotions, and affects. Our exploration can be conceptualised as an 'analysis through discussion'

(Gordon et al. 2000; Lahelma et al. 2014; Millei and Lappalainen 2020). Being both insiders and outsiders of cultures helped us to notice similarities and differences in the stories, especially those related to geopolitical and economic contexts. We combined the theories and the literature about menstruation and menarche with our interest in the historical and geopolitical differences of experience. We identified actions as these occur in relation with others, and we identified objects laden with meanings and emotions. Aware of how objects and social relations interplay in a symmetrical manner, we sought to attribute equal importance to both. Sørensen (2013) explains that a focus on sociomaterial processes 'highlights "doings" in contrast to "sense"' (p. 118), that is, it draws attention towards the situation and its events, which can cause emotions and intuitions to be overlooked, and emphasises children's keen observation and 'doings' in those events. Applying this principle helped us to look holistically at how humans, objects, spaces, feelings, and affective relations contribute to children's knowledge of (and knowledge of how to act in) the partly unexpected and emotionally intense situations of menarche and menstruation.

Menstruating

The three memory stories featured here provide insights into the ways in which young girls experience their menarche. They specifically focus on how objects and affects entangle in these experiences, which we indicate in the sub-headings of the analysis below. We include excerpts that particularly illustrate this entanglement, but the full stories can be found in the online memory archive of the Reconnect/Recollect project (https://coldwarchildhoods.org/memories/). The title of each story is given at the end of its excerpt.

Re-signification and Affect

They had never talked about menstruation or sex or the body at home; she only learned about it at school. But she knew well what to do when on her period. Her teacher had talked about it, and she knew where her mom kept the cotton wool. She tried using it herself, but she didn't like that too much. She had also noticed how her mom would regularly put a piece of blood-stained cotton wool in the coal stove which they had in the kitchen, sometimes to burn it right away, sometimes just to keep it there until it was the time to light the fire. Sometimes she would even take the used cotton out of the stove just to see what it looked like and then put it right back in with the feeling of repulsion. The blood on the cotton had dried and turned brownish, and she found it disgusting. ('Blood on the Sheet' n.d.)

This memory tells of two parallel sources of information about menstruation. The girl learns about it at school but also through keen observation of her mother and through the re-signification of objects associated with the process: the cotton wool, blood stain, and coal stove. She explores the objects marked with brown bloodstains, and feelings of repulsion and disgust emerge. Would she be disgusted by her own blood? And, is it the blood itself that disgusts her or the realisation of the menstrual process that came through observation of this new use for cotton wool? Watching her mother burn the stained cotton without talking to her about it, the girl learns to associate menstruation with concealment. The used cotton wool is put in a place deliberately meant to be out of sight, where it can be destroyed without a trace. Disposal of these signs of bodily functions coupled with the mother's silence about the process surround menstruation with a sense of secrecy even within the family (Koutroulis 2001). Would the girl's experience change if there were other objects involved, objects with other uses and with other kinds of affective charge? Would visibility of and easy access to sanitary pads or tampons place menstruation in a different light? Would seeing TV commercials for 'Always' lend it the intended glamour, for example, or would seeing dozens of brands of pads displayed on drugstore shelves make it seem ordinary? Perhaps not, as the mother made the cotton wool disappear in silence, she might do the same with those commercial products, too.

The sight of bloody cotton wool and the silence around it makes menstruating repulsive and disgusting to the girl. She may liken the dried blood, brownish on the shrinking cotton, to dirt and, therefore, associate menstruation with uncleanliness (Burrows and Johnson 2005; Koutroulis 2001). The experience foreshadows the forthcoming experience of menarche, signifying it as dreadful even before it happens.

Blood, Pain, and Fear

The day the girl got her first period, she thought she was going to die. It was right after she got back from school and her parents were still at work. The girl was at home all alone. In pain. Something was wrong, but she was not quite sure what. An unfamiliar pain in the stomach—extending into her lower back—the pain she had never felt before. [...] Then the blood. Both on her panties and on the toilet paper. The feeling of horror that something is really really wrong.

What was happening to her? Was she dying? Life cut so short. Her parents' expectations never met. Panicking, she tried to call her mother at work, but there was no answer. She was going to call her grandmother next. If she did not answer, she would have to call the neighbors. Oma picked up. The girl began to speak, her voice trembling and her tears running down her cheeks: 'Oma, I think I am dying. There is blood in my panties and it is not stopping. I am in horrible pain, too. I think I am going to die. I am afraid. I am so sorry'.

Oma responded calmly, with a smile in her voice—a smile that could be felt through the telephone line. It was the girl's first period! 'Period? What is it?' the girl asked. Oma explained. Perplexed, but finally relieved and now more relaxed, the girl knew then that she was not going to die that day. Period. ('Not Going to Die. Period.' n.d.)

The girl is overwhelmed by the pain and blood of her menarche that she experiences while home alone. She panics. The sight of blood and feeling of pain might be taken by the girl as an injury to the body; they give her a feeling of horror and evoke a fear that her death is imminent. Her concern is for herself, as she seeks help to deal with the potential injury, but it is perhaps even greater for the others who might suffer as a result of her loss. In trouble, she reaches out to her mother and then grandmother, perhaps instinctively knowing that they are the ones who can help in this case, as girls in various cultures do (Uskul 2004). She makes contact with the supportive grandmother by phone and receives an explanation and reassurance. The sudden onset of pain, the blood on the panties and toilet paper, the feeling of incapacitation due to assumed injury, and the accompanying overpowering emotions make the menarche an immense experience. This is not unusual. As Fahs (2016) notes, the first encounter with one's own menstrual blood can create 'an oddly paradoxical association of death and life simultaneously intertwined' (p. 35), as it opens the reproductive phase of a woman's life. The memory story continues as the girl links her grandmother's explanation with other observations:

As the news began to slowly sink in, fragments of information she learned before (but never pieced together) began to slowly assemble in her mind:
An older girl in her school choir, leaving a puddle of red blood on her seat after she got up to sing one day.
Her little dog Čina in heat several times a year, sometimes leaving traces of blood on the floor and furniture.
An older friend refusing to swim one day when everyone else was swimming.
A 'Soviet Encyclopedia of Young Woman' given to her a few months
before, but never opened.
Mysterious cotton pieces and pads periodically left by someone in the bathroom.
Periods.
Now, the girl had one too.
Not going to die.
Period. ('Not Going to Die. Period.' n.d.)

The girl had stored up some keen observations—of blood on the choir seat or furniture, pieces of cotton left in the bathroom, girls not swimming for some reason, being given a book about young women— that now acted as clues about significance of menstruation. Triggered by her new experience, they flooded her memory to help her make sense of her blood and pain. She perhaps overlooked, ignored, or misunderstood these observations when she first made them. At the time of menarche, however, the realisation that this happened to others, too, brought calm. The girl regains her sense of control and finds a new place in the world, among other women.

Trouble-Making Objects

She woke up in the morning; it could have been Saturday. She had gotten her first period a few months ago. Her mom didn't know about it, or at least she had never revealed it to her. She tried to break the secret and tell her about it. One day she went to the kitchen where her mom was doing something, lingered there for a while gathering her strength, but there was something in her mom's reaction to her presence in the kitchen that turned her back. […] She would always sneak out of the bathroom carrying a used pad in such a way that nobody would notice it, and then hide it somewhere in her room and burn it only when nobody was home to get rid of the evidence. But that morning when she woke up, she realised that there was blood on the bed sheet. The fact that she had gotten her period could not be hidden any longer, and the thought of the imminent act of disclosing something that she knew was not supposed to be talked about made her nervous. She felt she had to tell her mom about it; she knew her mom would notice it. ('Blood on the Sheet' n.d.)

Taking another excerpt from our first story, blood on the bed sheet becomes a proof or a witness of the girl's menstruation, problematically forcing her to reveal her secret. She has tried to talk about menstruation before when it involved only the staining of cotton wool but remained silent, and her mother, too, remained silent while disposing of her own stained cotton wool. The blood stain on the sheet, however, is very different. Even if she became quite experienced with hiding and burning blood on the cotton wool or a pad, she could not destroy the bed sheet in the same way: it needed to be cleaned by an expert hand, her mother's. The secrecy surrounding menstruation in the home makes it probable that the girl has had no experience of what her mother would do in this case. Unaccustomed to talking about blood stains with her mother, she is uncomfortable about being compelled to do so now. The blood on the sheet works in complex ways, therefore, simultaneously forcing the girl to act and inviting her to take control rather than passively waiting for mother to find the stain. Though pressed to reveal that she has started menstruating, she may be relieved of the burden of secret-keeping. The blood on the bed sheet may be simultaneously doing her a service and a disservice.

In contrast to the other memory wherein the girl reaches out to her mother and grandmother, here, the sense of secrecy and disgust prevents this girl from speaking and compels her to hide both the fact of her menstruation and its physical evidence. Another girl, in our third story, does the same:

She was in her unique pair of jeans bought in Yugoslavia on her family's regular cross border shopping trip. [...] She was sitting in the 3.a primary class's school bench in a border town in Hungary, first row just before the teacher. She felt a sudden rush of warmth between her legs. Her underwear has a brown line already. She saw it when she went to the toilet in the morning, and now this [...]. Hopefully it is just drops of pee. If it was blood, it might have soaked through to colour the pants. She already hid one pair of those precious pants with blood marks between the legs. She hid it up in the cupboard's top shelf in her room, way way in the back so her mother doesn't find it, rolled up disappearing in the middle of other grown out clothes. Mother liked cleanliness. She pre-washed every item before she put the clothes in the washing machine. She asked when she found the underwear with the brown line: is this blood? The girl explained she could not hold the poo, so it got coloured. It sounded not too believable, who poos in pants at her age, but better than admitting the blood. She could not have borne her mother's look again, examining the stain, and asking more questions. What if she would find out, even the thought of that made her body shrivel. The solution remained a piece of toilet paper wrapped around the bottom part of the underwear. A tear off of the cotton wool placed in her pants would show. Skirt, that might hide it, but she could not wear those. The other problem is where to dispose of the cotton wool so her mother doesn't find it. The toilet paper did not work the time when the other pair of jeans got bloody. Oh, I hope mother never finds that bloody one, when she cleans. ('Blood on the Pants' n.d.)

Although toilet paper had soaked up a little blood and could be gotten rid of easily by flushing it down the toilet, it could not protect her clothing from an increased flow of blood. Her stained pants attest to her menstruation and, as such, must also be somehow disposed of. As in the previous memory, the daughter's relationship with her mother has prevented her from revealing her menstruation. She hates to be found out and goes to great lengths to gain control over the repeated situation. Clothes partly become her ally, by covering the blood, but they also create the risk of exposing the signs of her period. Blue jeans, underwear, and toilet paper keep the blood from revealing itself. In socialist countries, jeans represented the ideological power of the West, and Levi's, Wrangler, and Lee were everyone's top choices. Youth wanted to emulate the look of film and rock stars. This girl's pair had come all the way from Yugoslavia, but others were either smuggled or sent by relatives who lived in the West (Stearns, 2017). That she would hide the precious blue jeans, therefore, shows the severity of what is at stake: the girl would rather give up the soiled jeans by hiding them in the top of the cupboard than make the arrival of her period known to her mother. This is reinforced by her lie that the stain on the underwear is faeces and not blood. She considers it the lesser of two evils to be shamed by poo—opening herself to being labelled as a baby or disabled person, or simply disgusting—rather than by menstrual blood. The mention that she was not able to wear skirts perhaps indicates that she was not fully comfortable with the female fashion assigned by society. If so, menstruation, another aspect which makes her body more female, might be adding to her feelings of discomfort.

The focus in this excerpt is on disguising menstruation from others but also from herself. Because the bloodstain is irregular and brown, she can identify it as poo and, in this way, can cause the evidence of what is happening with her body to disappear in the washing. If the blue jeans, blood, and stained toilet paper can be out of sight, outside the range of recognition and discovery, the period can also be out of mind. As the girl who experienced pain, this girl might want the menstruation to go away, so it does not happen to her. And, like the other girl with the bloody bed sheet, she also actively seeks ways to make the evidence disappear, trying to refuse any thoughts associated with the period. All of these young women might be feeling the stigma of the menstruating woman (Johnston-Robledo and Chrisler 2020), but blood and its trace, the brownish stain, operates differently in this story. In line with Julia Kristeva's notion of the abject, the stain 'signifies not the living, life-giving, pulsating, alive woman (as actual menstrual blood might do) but, rather, the decaying, dying [...] woman' (Fahs 2016, p. 35). The girl refuses to become comfortable with her blood, to identify it with a kind of life-giving and life-taking female identity. In the Lacanian psychoanalytic tradition, the emergence of subjectivity is linked to an understanding of genital difference that happens in a phallocentric discourse. Thus, it is a masculine and perhaps biological discourse that informs the ways in which young girls understand what is happening to their bodies and how they form their identities, which might lead them to a refusal of their body and their genital configuration (Irigaray 1977). This experience is also shaped by the role of the mother—her discourses, actions, and subjectivity—and the child's attitude and construction of a female identity (Donmall 2013). The menarche is a time of intensive feminine subject-formation; it is underpinned by a separation from the mother even as it is overshadowed by the mother's experiences and feelings about her own womanhood.

With the onset of menstruation, girls find themselves balancing between childhood and adulthood, trying to find the right place and identity for themselves. Womanhood comes with the stigma of 'mess, dirt and shame, potentially reflective of feelings about sexuality' (Donmall 2013, p. 213). The three girls in our stories negotiate this liminal state differently. They either actively take steps to make signs of their evident entry into womanhood disappear (and reinterpret them as a non-gendered excretion), or give in to the overwhelming anxiety, fear, and pain. Feeling themselves petrified, half-dead, and exposed, they are unable to take any other action than seeking an adult's assistance in an attempt to comprehend their changed bodily and mental state. The menarche appears as a power that takes something away from the girls, be it their ability to move freely and feel healthy in their bodies (Piran 2020), or precious items, such as blue jeans now stained with blood. With the experience of menarche comes then the challenge for the girls to negotiate loss. Girls also learn that menstruation carries within it the possibility of failure. Since bleeding cannot be controlled, 'women learn to see menstruation as inherently disappointing, frustrating, and difficult' (Fahs 2016, p. 36).

Objects and Refuge

She approached her mom; she was standing in the door to her room, embarrassed and uncomfortable, her mom in the hallway, so they were talking across the doorstep, and she was sort of hiding behind the door frame, in the safety of her room. She told her mom that she had gotten her period. She made it sound as if it had happened for the first time. Revealing the secret of having kept it secret for so long was unimaginable. Her mom told her, matter-of-factly, seemingly emotionless, that there was cotton wool in the bathroom that she could take and use. The girl reacted as if she hadn't known and was just learning about it, even though she felt so experienced already and completely confident how to go about her period. ('Blood on the Sheet' n.d.)

The door frame, standing between rooms, represents liminality. Talking across the doorstep crosses the borders between revelation and secret-keeping, acknowledgement and denial, becoming a woman and remaining a child. The way the girl physically approaches her mother is also symbolic of the half-hidden truth in her disclosure:

although she admits to having a period, she does not admit that she has kept secret both her menstruation and all the observations and emotions associated with it. In this way, the secrecy of menstruation is partially maintained. Positioning herself in the liminal space by the door frame, between the openness of the corridor and the safety of her own room, she is out there, visible to her mother, but also hiding from her, keeping her distance, securing her own space. There is no crossing of the doorstep, no physical contact, no revelation of the complete story, no emergence of the girl as both competent and vulnerable, independent and not wanting to be alone, able 'to share her experiences with her mother as a growing adolescent whilst still receiving comfort as a child' (Donmall 2013, p. 209). The door frame enables the girl to retain her strong, knowledgeable, independent self, rather than identify herself as a daughter relying on her mother. The process of 'identification and separation/individuation from the mother' (ibid., p. 213) that happens at menarche is manifested here in the girl's acquired independence and self-reliance in handling menstruation, the limited communication about menstruation between the girl and her mother, and in their physical separation emphasised by the door frame and step. Standing in the doorstep also represents the threshold of the transition, and what this change might produce for the child. Maybe there is joy in keeping a secret of her own, in the feeling that she holds adult knowledge while still being a child. Maybe there is joy in belonging and relating in a new way to her mother in this shared secret. If so, revelation of the secret may cause this joy to dissipate.

Although the mother offers a few instructive words, her emotionless response to the situation upholds the silent taboo around menstruation. The memory suggests that, in the absence of words, a complex affective landscape exists between the mother and daughter. Both probably suspect that the other knows more, and yet they both decide to keep quiet. The negative affective charge of menstruation and the secrecy surrounding it encourage reticence. Menstruation has been like an elephant in the room that no one sees; however, by acknowledging its existence with the minimum of words, both feel eased. The mother does not need to talk about menstruation and the girl can keep her experience a secret and retain her innocence as a child. At the end of the day, the girl knows how to manage the situation anyways.

Objects and Menstruation

In this chapter, we set out to explore childhood memories in which narrators tell about their experiences of menarche and menstruation within the geopolitical context of the late Cold War. Rather than focusing on children's sense-making, which is the dominant way of exploring children's construction of knowledge, we paid attention to objects and the ways girls keenly observed their female counterparts. We wanted to show that even when explicit knowledge is not offered by mothers, teachers, or different forms of media, children learn about menstruation. They learned about it by noticing objects that carry cultural meanings. As these objects gained new uses or disappeared in order to conceal their use, they also helped the girls to navigate their periods.

Researchers increasingly consider childhood memories to be a productive way of studying childhood. As a method, it overcomes concerns that adults are less able to intimate children's experiences in research and therefore not well positioned to interpret their actions and words and takes advantage of the fact that every researcher was once a child (see Horton and Kraftl 2006; Hohti and MacLure 2022; Silova et al. 2018). However, working with memories has its own concerns. Memory stories are not close recreations of events and include the interpretations of the narrators that draw on knowledge they have accumulated during their lives (see, for example, Burman and Millei 2022).

As the overall Reconnect/Recollect project seeks to explore childhood experience within the geopolitical context of the Cold War, we set out in this chapter to study menarche and menstruation in relation to geopolitics and the relative unavailability of menstrual products across some state-socialist countries. The longing for these products one might expect to see does not appear in the memories studied here. Moreover, it is also apparent from our analysis and the review of literature that the menstruation experiences recalled in these memory stories are very similar to those of girls in 'western' countries and in other eras of the twentieth century. Although 'the Cold War' carries the assumption of great divides, these observations of similarity offer evidence of the opposite: the divide, at least in terms of children's experiences, may have been largely imaginary. The assumption of difference might be cultivated by public figures and researchers who understand divisions in ideological terms and view children as objects of ideological socialisation. These memories demonstrate not only that children's everyday experiences across state-socialist and capitalist countries were quite similar but also that children on the Eastern side were knowing subjects rather than victims of so-called 'indoctrination' (Silova et al. 2018).

The absence and silence of the mothers in these memories contributed to secrecy around menstruation. In socialist states, policies of compulsory employment, which were linked to women's liberation and equality, caused most mothers to be absent from the home during work hours. How this imposed maternal absence shaped girls' experiences of the menarche and menstruation in state-socialist countries requires further research. Here, we can only discuss some tentative relations by drawing on previous research. First, menarche and menstruation are portrayed as an experience that the girls go through on their own and that is usually not shared even with other women. This observation is in line with research that demonstrates the secretive character of menstruation as something that is kept in hiding, not spoken about, a taboo (Ginsburg 1996; Laws 1990; Piran 2020). Mothers did not seem to prepare the girls (enough, if at all) for the eventual experience. Previous research shows that unpreparedness and mothers' indifference toward menarche contribute to girls' negative experiences of the onset of menstruation (Uskul 2004). However, the girls in the memories analysed were also able to mobilise menarche in agentic ways that brought forth the feelings of independence and competence. And, perhaps because mothers might experience menstruation as a stigma, which they themselves need to hide, and as an uncomfortable topic related to sexuality to discuss especially with children, they might expect children to learn through keen observation rather than through direct conversation.

Second, although female emancipation featured prominently on the agendas of Eastern European communist-party ideologues, it was narrowly construed and, in general, failed to remove mechanisms of male domination (Fodor 2004). The mechanics of menstruation might be covered in a 'Soviet Encyclopedia of Young Woman', for example, but not the feelings or identities it might evoke. Some women used the phrase 'bleeding through', 'giving language to their menstrual blood that has crossed a barrier, pushed through a boundary, ruptured the existing social order' (Fahs 2016, p. 38). As in the excerpt where the girl stood in the door frame that represented the boundary between the binaries of adult and child, woman and girl, public and private, girls have bled through not only their literal underwear and pants but also 'transformed the boundary between public/private, self/other, and animal/human' (ibid.). The phrase 'bleeding through', if proudly accepted in public, represents the rupturing of the existing social order. However, that 'bleeding through' is associated in these memories with shame might indicate that secrecy around and the hiding of the female body's secretion of blood remained the general practice despite the egalitarian intentions of state socialism.

References

Baines, E. (2015). *History of the Cotton Manufacture in Great Britain*. Cambridge University Press, https://doi.org/10.1017/cbo9781316144633

'Blood on the Sheet'. (n.d.). *Memories of Everyday Childhoods: De-colonial and De-Cold War Dialogues in Childhood and Schooling*, https://coldwarchildhoods.org/portfolio/blood-on-the-sheet/

'Blood on the Pants'. (n.d.). *Memories of Everyday Childhoods: De-colonial and De-Cold War Dialogues in Childhood and Schooling*, https://coldwarchildhoods.org/portfolio/blood-on-the-pants/

Bobel, C. (2010). *New Blood: Third-Wave Feminism and the Politics of Menstruation*. Rutgers University Press, https://doi.org/10.36019/9780813549538

—— and Fahs, B. (2020). 'From Bloodless Respectability to Radical Menstrual Embodiment: Shifting Menstrual Politics from Private to Public'. *Signs: Journal of Women in Culture and Society*, 45(4), 955–83, https://doi.org/10.1086/707802

Brumberg, J. J. (1998). *The Body Project: An Intimate History of American Girls*. Vintage

Burman, E., and Millei, Z. (2022). 'Post-Socialist Geopolitical Uncertainties: Researching Memories of Childhood with "Child as Method". *Children and Society*, 36(5), 993–1009, https://doi.org/10.1111/chso.12551

Burrows, A., and Johnson, S. (2005). 'Girls' Experiences of Menarche and Menstruation'. *Journal of Reproductive and Infant Psychology*, 23(3), 235–49, https://doi.org/10.1080/02646830500165846

Cohen, I. (2020). 'Menstruation and Religion: Developing a Critical Menstrual Studies Approach', in *The Palgrave Handbook of Critical Menstruation Studies*, ed. by C. Bobel, I. T. Winkler, B. Fahs, K. A. Hasson, E. A.

Kissling, and T.-A. Roberts (pp. 115–29). Springer Nature, https://doi.org/10.1007/978-981-15-0614-7_11

Davies, B., and Gannon, S. (eds). (2006). *Doing Collective Biography: Investigating the Production of Subjectivity*. Open University Press

Donmall, K. (2013). 'What it Means to Bleed: An Exploration of Young Women's Experiences of Menarche and Menstruation'. *British Journal of Psychotherapy*, 29(2), 202–16, https://doi.org/10.1111/bjp.12016

Drakulic, S. (1992, January 13). 'How We Survived Communism and Even Laughed'. *Publishers Weekly*, 239(3), 39, https://link.gale.com/apps/doc/A11866509/LitRC?u=anon~ac645e5candsid=googleScholarandxid=77516866

Ernster, V. L. (1975). 'American Menstrual Expressions'. *Sex Roles*, 1(1), 3–13, https://doi.org/10.1007/BF00287209

Fahs, B. (2016). *Out for Blood: Essays on Menstruation and Resistance*. State University of New York Press

Feinberg, M. (2022). *Communism in Eastern Europe*. Routledge, https://doi.org/10.4324/9780813348186

Fodor, É. (2004). 'The State Socialist Emancipation Project: Gender Inequality in Workplace Authority in Hungary and Austria'. *Signs: Journal of Women in Culture and Society*, 29(3), 783–13, https://doi.org/10.1086/381103

Ginsburg, R. (1996). '"Don't Tell, Dear": The Material Culture of Tampons and Napkins'. *Journal of Material Culture*, 1(3), 365–75, https://doi.org/10.1177/135918359600100305

Gordon, T., Holland, J., and Lahelma, E. (2000). *Making Spaces: Citizenship and Difference in Schools*. Springer, https://doi.org/10.1057/9780230287976

Green-Cole, R. (2020). 'Painting Blood: Visualizing Menstrual Blood in Art.', in *The Palgrave Handbook of Critical Menstruation Studies*, ed. by C. Bobel, I. T. Winkler, B. Fahs, K. A. Hasson, E. A. Kissling, and T.-A. Roberts (pp. 787–801). Springer Nature, https://doi.org/10.1007/978-981-15-0614-7

Hohti R., and MacLure M. (2022). 'Insect-Thinking as Resistance to Education's Human Exceptionalism: Relationality and Cuts in More-than-Human Childhoods'. *Qualitative Inquiry*. 28(3–4), 322–32, https://doi.org/10.1177/10778004211059237

Horton, J., and Kraftl, P. (2006). 'What Else? Some More Ways of Thinking and Doing "Children's Geographies"'. *Children's Geographies*, 4(1), 69–95, https://doi.org/10.1080/14733280600577459

Ilnicka, V. (2020). *Uniesienie spódnicy. Seksualne doświadczenia i kobieca moc.* [*Raising the Skirt. Sexual Experiences and Women's Power*]. Wrocław

Irigaray, L. (1977). *This Sex which is not One*. Cornell University Press

Johnston-Robledo, I., and Chrisler, J. C. (2020). 'The Menstrual Mark: Menstruation as Social Stigma', in *The Palgrave Handbook of Critical Menstruation Studies*, ed. by C. Bobel, I. T. Winkler, B. Fahs, K. A. Hasson, E. A. Kissling, and T.-A. Roberts (pp. 181–99). Springer Nature, https://doi.org/10.1007/978-981-15-0614-7

Kobyłecka, W., and Jaczewski, A. (1991). *O dziewczętach dla dziewcząt* [*About Girls for Girls*]. (7th edn). Warszawa: PZWL

Kopytoff, I. (1986). 'The Cultural Biography of Things: Commoditization as Process', in *The Social Life of Things: Commodities in Cultural Perspective*, ed. by A. Appadurai (pp. 64–91). Cambridge University Press, https://doi.org/10.1017/cbo9780511819582

Korolczuk, E. (2019). *Matki i córki we współczesnej Polsce* [*Mothers and Daughters in Contemporary Poland*]. Kraków: Universitas

Kościańska, A. (2021). *To See a Moose: The History of Polish Sex Education*, trans. by P. Palmer. Berghahn Books, https://doi.org/10.2307/j.ctv2tsx8vf

Koutroulis, G. (2001). 'Soiled Identity: Memory-Work Narratives of Menstruation'. *Health*, 5(2), 187–205

Kovácsné, T. Z., and Szeverényi, P. (2006). Egyéni és társadalmi vélekedés a menstruációról [Individual and societal views about menstruation]. *LAM*, 16(8–9), 806–09

Lahelma, E., Lappalainen, S., Mietola, R., and Palmu, T. (2014). 'Discussions that "Tickle our Brains": Constructing Interpretations through Multiple Ethnographic Data-sets'. *Ethnography and Education*, 9(1), 51–65, https://doi.org/10.1080/17457823.2013.828476

Lamek-Kochanowska, A. (2020). 'Chleba i podpasek! O ubóstwie menstruacyjnym' [Bread and Sanitary Napkins! About Menstrual Poverty]. *Równość*, 3, 15–9

Laws, S. (1990). *Issues of Blood: The Politics of Menstruation*. Macmillan

Lee, J. (2008). '"A Kotex and a Smile": Mothers and Daughters at Menarche'. *Journal of Family Issues*, 29(10), 1325–47, https://doi.org/10.1177/0192513x08316117

—— (2009). 'Bodies at Menarche: Stories of Shame, Concealment, and Sexual Maturation'. *Sex Roles*, 60(9–10), 615–27, https://doi.org/10.1007/s11199-008-9569-1

Millei, Z., and Lappalainen, S. (2020). 'Learning Nation in Early Childhood Education: Multi-Sited Comparison between Pedagogies of Nation in Australia and Hungary'. *European Education*, 52(1), 33–47, https://doi.org/10.1080/10564934.2019.1691015

'Not Going to Die. Period.' (n.d.). *Memories of Everyday Childhoods: De-colonial and De-Cold War Dialogues in Childhood and Schooling*, https://coldwarchildhoods.org/portfolio/not-going-to-die-period/

Patterson, A. (2014). 'The Social Construction and Resistance of Menstruation as a Public Spectacle', in *Illuminating How Identities, Stereotypes and Inequalities Matter through Gender Studies*, ed. by D. N. Farris, M. A. Davis, and D. R. Compton (pp. 91–108). Springer, https://doi.org/10.1007/978-94-017-8718-5

Piran, N. (2020). 'The Menarche Journey: Embodied Connections and Disconnections', in *The Palgrave Handbook of Critical Menstruation Studies*, ed. by C. Bobel, I. T. Winkler, B. Fahs, K. A. Hasson, E. A. Kissling, and T.-A. Roberts (pp. 201–14) Springer Nature, https://doi.org/10.1007/978-981-15-0614-7

Rogoff, B., Mosier, C., Mistry, J., and Göncü, A. (1989). 'Toddlers' Guided Participation in Cultural Activity'. *Cultural Dynamics*, 2(2), 209–37, https://doi.org/10.1177/092137408900200205

Silova, I., Piattoeva, N., and Millei, Z. (eds). (2018). *Childhood and Schooling in (Post)Socialist Societies: Memories of Everyday Life*. Palgrave Macmillan, https://doi.org/10.1007/978-3-319-62791-5

Silva, K. G., Correa-Chávez, M., and Rogoff, B. (2010). 'Mexican-Heritage Children's Attention and Learning from Interactions Directed to Others'. *Child Development*, 81(3), 898–912, https://doi.org/10.1111/j.1467-8624.2010.01441.x

Sitar, P. (2018). 'Female Trouble: Menstrual Hygiene, Shame and Socialism'. *Journal of Gender Studies*, 27(7), 771–87, https://doi.org/10.1080/09589236.2017.1304860

Sommer, M. (2009). 'Ideologies of Sexuality, Menstruation and Risk: Girls' Experiences of Puberty and Schooling in Northern Tanzania'. *Culture, Health and Sexuality*, 11(4), 383–98, https://doi.org/10.1080/13691050902722372

Stańczak-Wiślicz, K., Perkowski, P., Fidelis, M., and Klich-Kluczewska, B. (2020). *Kobiety w Polsce 1945–1989: nowoczesność, równouprawnienie, komunizm* [*Women in Poland 1945–1989: Modernity, Equal Rights, Communism*]. Kraków: Universitas

Stearns, P. N. (2017). *Childhood in World History* (3rd edn). Routledge, https://doi.org/10.4324/9781315561363

Steinem, G. (2020). 'If Men could Menstruate', in *The Palgrave Handbook of Critical Menstruation Studies*, ed. by C. Bobel, I. T. Winkler, B. Fahs, K. A. Hasson, E. A. Kissling, and T.-A. Roberts (pp. 353–56). Springer Nature, https://doi.org/10.1007/978-981-15-0614-7

Sørensen, E. (2013). 'Human Presence: Towards a Posthumanist Approach to Experience'. *Subjectivity*, 6(1), 112–29, https://doi.org/10.1057/sub.2012.31

Ulč, O. (1989). 'Czechoslovakia: Realistic Socialism?'. *Current History*, 88(541), 389–92, 401–04, https://www.jstor.org/stable/45316271

Uskul, A. K. (2004). 'Women's Menarche Stories from a Multicultural Sample'. *Social Science and Medicine*, 59(4), 667–79, https://doi.org/10.1016/j.socscimed.2003.11.031

Soviet Feminism?[1]

Nadia Tsulukidze

It happened at school. She was 11 or 12 years old. The teacher was too late for class and the whole class was happily jumping around. Some boys even went into the hall and her friend and her followed them. They were laughing loudly and having fun, when suddenly a Russian language teacher appeared. She was not teaching their class, but she had a bad name among students. Everyone was scared of her and hated her. She grabbed the kids by the arms and pushed them into the classroom. 'You are girls!!!', she screamed. 'Do you think this is appropriate behavior for girls?' 'Well', the girl said, 'you are a woman, do you think grabbing us by the arms and pushing us into the classroom is an appropriate behavior for a woman?' The teacher became even angrier and yelled at the girl, pointing her finger right into her face: 'who are you to talk to me like that?! Who are you, ha?!' The girl answered with a calm voice, telling the teacher her name. The whole class broke out in laughter. Their class teacher, who followed them inside, got furious and screamed at the whole class: 'Why are you laughing? Do you hear her name for the first time?' Her classmate answered with a smile: 'Of course not, but it was the first time we heard it spoken out at such a perfect occasion!'

She has been coming back to this memory very often and thinking about the teacher and her question. 'Who am I?' became a central question in her artistic work.

Feminism in the Soviet Union is an interesting topic. On the one hand, it was ok as a woman to drive a tractor and work in the *kolkhoz*, but, on the other hand, any sexual behavior and expression of individuality

---

1 This is a childhood memory produced as part of the Reconnect/Recollect project discussed in the introduction to this book.

was seen as a threat to the communist regime. Female hero figures were Mothers of Nation, Mother of a Soldier, Khokhoznica (collective farm worker), Proletariat, etc., all very functional for the society, but not for their own pleasure. And in that sense, there may be many parallels to the religious icons in Christianity. Since psychoanalysis was banned, libido had to be controlled. The private space/body had to be sacrificed for the common good of the society. If one thinks of a communist party as a replacement for God, everything becomes logical. Hahaha.

10. Lift Up Your Arms!
Elite Athletes and Cold-War Childhoods

Susanne Gannon and Stefanie Weiss

This chapter turns to configurations of athleticism, child bodies, and the instrumental uses of sport as a form of soft power. We work with memory stories of children selected to become elite athletes within the diverse geopolitical timespaces of the Cold War in East Germany, Romania, and Hungary. We follow trajectories of selection, training, and injury as we trace formations of sporting subjectivities as discursive, affective, relational, and material. In close readings of each of the stories, we consider desire and longing for sporting success, the investments of state institutions and individuals in producing elite sporting bodies, and how we might think the body through ever-present risk and intimations of freedom. In our analysis, we introduce theoretical resources on risk, memory, and the carnal body to help us to think differently about the memories and processes of collective biography as a methodology.

Sporting excellence in the global arena was a central plank of Cold-War cultural politics, and significant state resources were invested in identifying and cultivating sporting talent. This chapter turns to memory stories of children who were part of this strategy in particular geohistorical junctures. Recognition of elite potential opens children to new opportunities, and their bodies are subjected to new instructional regimes and disciplinary procedures. They take up new desires and aspirations, join with others who are similarly selected, and become members of new communities. Children in elite sporting programs are trained to anticipate success, but they also experience numerous risks and disappointments. Their bodies, minds, desires, dreams, imaginings of possible futures are all shaped and profoundly impacted by the experiences and the procedures of sports training and competition.

Representing collective identity and embodying the desire of a nation, elite athletic programmes provide new perspectives on the Cold War from those who remember themselves through their sporting capacities and potential. Each memory story describes a specific moment in the elite sporting journey of the narrator as a child. Although the body (flesh, tendons, strength, dexterity, agility) may be the obvious focus of training, the memory stories reinforce the inseparability of bodies, affects and emotions, imaginings, and the material and sociopolitical contexts of children's lives. We begin by briefly outlining how the body is understood in collective biography and the theoretical resources we draw on to think through bodies, stories, and memories. We summarise current research on Cold-War sport and youth. We then present close readings of three memory stories of elite sporting childhoods. We conclude with our thoughts on contributions to research on Cold-War sporting childhoods and collective biography.

Bodies, Stories, Memories

The body has always been central to collective-biography and memory work, from Haug et al.'s instruction to 'choose a theme connected with the body' (1987, p. 13) through to Davies and Gannon's focus on 'writing *from* the body', since the memory is 'lodged in the body' (2006, p. 10). Bodies are not understood as discrete or intact entities but as discursive, affective, relational accomplishments that settle, momentarily, in particular configurations (Gannon et al. 2014). Memory stories evoked through and about the body, therefore, cannot be assumed to be reliable or truthful representations of any particular experience. Fragmentation, misremembering, artful reconstruction, and imagination are all at work in the processes of collective biography. The narrator is inevitably captured by multiple discontinuous temporalities. Hints and flickerings of the child subject that they feel themselves to be, that they come to recognise and reconstruct as their 'self', are pinned to a specific event or moment that is imbued with retrospective significance, layered with subsequent historicity, adult insights, habits of thought, and culturally available tropes and motifs. Collective-biography processes move memories from individuals into social spaces where these elements are opened up for critical consideration.

Memories of sporting prowess suggest themes of strength, power, submission, routine, pain, and disappointment. We are interested in tracing the specificities and detail of how these materialise in the memory stories, rather than generalising from them. Embodied or corporeal memories are organised into stories whose coherence relies as much on gaps, omissions, and exclusions, as it does on inclusions of particular details. We are interested not in the facticity of history but in how history works discursively and materially to produce certain embodied subjects in the memory stories. We are interested, too, in dissonances and inconsistencies that disrupt the seamlessness of any story.

Memory is always an ambivalent process, with the body both elusive and pivotal to what we can remember, how we remember, which details are arranged for narrative form and coherence, and which are suppressed. In collective biography, remembering is intensely social. Participants tell their memories to the group, write and rewrite them, guided by questions such as: 'How did it feel? How did it look? What were the embodied details of this remembered event?' (Davies and Gannon 2006, p. 10). Philosopher-psychoanalyst Anne Dufourmantelle (2019) says that the body is a puzzle, profoundly ambiguous. Our 'carnal being' exceeds the 'perceptible body', to include 'the thought body, the imagined body, the dreamed body, the body of the voice, the body of taste, the affected body, or the body overtaken by fever, jouissance, drunkenness, the body that migrates beyond the body in order not to suffer' (p. 75). The body is multiple, excessive, generative, and relational. In this project, sporting memories arise in dreams, visions, sensations: smells and sweat on the skin, gut-wrenching pain, the metallic taste of soup at a training camp, the sound of a coach shouting in your ear, or the ecstatic joy of victory all exceed reason and are impossible to contain in one small story. In Dufourmantelle's practice, participants tell stories about and from the body to a particular listener. The difference in the methodology of collective biography is that the audience and interlocutor for stories is the group rather than the individual analyst. For Dufourmantelle, memories lodged in the body, stories we tell ourselves and others, habituated narrative stances and perspectives, are always open to variation. The key tool of analysis lies in creating conditions for the subject to tell her story differently, reflecting back its dimensions, querying a detail or an angle, opening it up to variations. Collective-biography workshops provide this space, one where stories are interrogated to explore new angles and lines of variation, details come in and out of sight, and sensations echo and resonate. Working with the memory archive as we do in this chapter—writing around and through the memories, trying out different readings and interpretations—continues these processes. Despite differences of intent and process, including the intimacy of analysis compared to the collectivity of memory work, Dufourmantelle offers fresh conceptual tools to think through bodies, memories, and practices of collective biography. The relationality of collective biography, with interrogation by others as part of the workshop process, deepens our awareness that processes of remembering (such as in Cold-War contexts) are always embedded in social formations (Arnold-de Simine and Radstone 2013).

Dufourmantelle's theorising of 'risk' also offers us new ways to think through stories of children and sport as well as of the processes of collective biography. She asks readers to think of risk as a 'territory' to be 'traced' rather than as a discrete heroic act, as a 'certain manner of being in the world… a horizon line' (p. 2). Moments of risk can push us ahead of ourselves, opening us to chance and freedoms, determining future possibilities but also looping back to reanimate the past. In telling stories, we take the risk to surrender our memories and rehabilitate the collective experiences with a sense of freedom and strength. Collective-biography processes entail inherent risks, but these are productive and generative risks. We return to this reflection in our conclusion.

Children's Sport and State Socialism

We juxtapose three memory stories of child athletes at a time when the sporting body embodied the desire of the nation in the body of the child. The body is both a fleshy corporeal or carnal entity, as evoked in the memory stories, and a symbolic system implicated in geopolitics, part of the identity construction of nations. Bodies are points on which power operates, and from which power pushes back. We investigate processes of subjectification through which children are enrolled in state structures that cultivate athleticism and confer recognition, as each of the memory stories describes how a child takes up, negotiates and disavows desire for that subject position.

Configurations of athleticism and child bodies suggest the instrumental uses of sport. Sport was a 'major cultural phenomenon' in the Cold War, such that the 'liminality of sport made it both the hardest form of soft power and the softest form of hard power' (Edelman and Young 2019, p. 1). Although children's recruitment and participation were key strategies of state sporting apparatus, crucial for cultivating elite performances, their experiences as children rarely feature in historical analysis, except for those few who achieved global fame (for example, Nadia Comăneci). Yet, their accounts offer nuanced insights into how sport was experienced, felt, and remembered by child athletes beyond stereotypes of regimentation and disciplinary power. In Czech state socialism, Oates-Indruchova (2018) reexamines moments from her own childhood as 'epiphanies', arguing that children's physical cultures were egalitarian spaces where sporting participation was assumed, inclusive, and gender-neutral. Collective synchronised exercise (*spartakiad*) was a public ritual in which all Czech schools participated (Kaščák and Pupala 2018), and sport was integral to children's organisations such as Pioneers. Organised performances symbolised the literal building of communist ideals of strength and optimism through the bodies of children. In contrast to this egalitarianism, where all bodies had a place on the field of display, and where inclusion and mass performance were the point of the exercise, elite athletics had a different purpose and relied on differentiation and separation from the masses. They required different sorts of disciplines and temporalities, with training in the present pivoting on imagined futures.

Memory Stories

We selected memories from the archive that focused on children's bodies in training, shaping and being shaped by the desire of the state as well as of the individual. While the stories are written from a child's perspective, they are made sense of by the adult narrator who tends to compress the political and historical knowledge that makes each story tellable and interesting within this project. Although there are many stories about sport in the archive, the three we selected are of child athletes in East Germany, Romania, and Hungary: a rower, a gymnast, and a track-and-field athlete. Importantly, each child was selected for these sports because their bodies had certain dispositions. Being selected opened opportunities for specialist programs, schools, trips, and tours. The children moved into a new category of young person—one with potential, worthy of specific focused attention. Rather than foregrounding individualised or inherent talent, these stories suggest the labour that goes into making the elite sporting body. While they invite us to imagine bodily trajectories that are lived as limit, vigilance, and submission, there are also intimations of amazement, desire, and freedom. There is also, always, a shadow of precarity or risk—the body might fail, the child might lose their status and therefore part of their identity, they might be rejected as readily as they are selected. The three stories that we explore follow a sequence through from selection and training to competition and injury.

Selected for Rowing (East Germany)

She is sitting in class. It is a quiet morning. The class is organised into three rows of desks with six desks in each row. She sits at the third desk in the row next to the wall. Notebooks and pencils are uniformly laid out in the top-right corner of the desk in front of each child. The teacher, Mrs Lindner, is speaking and all the children have turned to face her.

When the door opens, everyone shifts their gaze to the door. Three adults come in. Mrs. Lindner interrupts her lesson and takes two steps towards them. They talk quietly to each other. They look serious. Mrs. Lindner turns back to the class and explains. These visitors are here to see if any of the children would like to join a rowing club in the south of Berlin. She asks all to stand up, next to the chair. The noise of moving chairs scraping the floor fills the classroom, breaking the silence in the room. The kids are standing and waiting for the next thing to happen. The strangers start to move along the rows of desks. They do not stop at the first bench, but they pause briefly at the second bench in her row. They are looking at Ivo now, her friend. 'You. Go over to the window' the woman tells him, pointing towards the teacher's desk. Then she takes a step back to make space for Ivo. He steps away from his desk, fills the gap the woman just made for him with his body and, without looking at the girl, hesitantly starts going to the teacher's desk next to the window. The strangers come to the girl and Holger. Holger is three months older than her, but visibly shorter. They don't look at Holger but they turn to her. The woman who was speaking to Ivo points at her: 'You. Go over to the window.' The girl tries to read the tone of her voice. Is this good or bad news? She does not have a clue. She does not know what will happen to her once she reaches the window, but she finds some solace in Ivo being there. So she starts walking towards him.

The three adults are walking from one desk to the next, and the little group of them at the teacher's desk grows to six people. When the three adults finish their round through the classroom, the classmates are allowed to sit down. The woman who told them to go to the window now tells them to stand in a line. Sensing the looks of the others, with no hint of what will happen next, they position themselves next to each other. The two men walk behind them, in the space between them and the wall where the blackboard is. 'Lift up your arms,' one of them says to Ivo, and she sees Ivo lifting up his arms. 'You too. Lift up your arms,' says the second man to the girl. She cannot look at Ivo to her right anymore. She lifts up her arms. Mrs. Lindner and the classmates are watching them standing there in silence with their arms lifted. She feels the fingers of the man on her shoulder, moving up the arms, the elbow and the wrist.

'Bend forwards,' he says, and a moment later, she hears the man behind Ivo saying the same. She bends forwards, assuming that Ivo would be doing the same by now. Again, she feels the fingers on her spine, pressing her vertebrae one after the other, starting at the neck and ending at the hip.

'Alright,' the man behind her says. 'Go and wait outside the classroom.' Together with Ivo, she leaves the room. Once the door closes, she asks him 'What are they doing?' Ivo explains to her that it has something to do with rowing. She knows what rowing is—she learnt how to do it during the last holiday. She can already row the boat with her whole family sitting in it. But what these three *adults did has nothing to do with rowing, she thinks. The door opens and Stefan and Antje, two of her classmates, come to join them.*

When the door opens again, not only do the last two children join them, but also the three adults. In the dark hallway, they tell stories about the rowing club, about the boats there, and the water, and that they will teach them how to row very quickly. They chose them because they were tall, the woman says. They can become really good rowers as their bodies fit well to the sport. She did not have any sense that her body would fit any sport. It had never occurred to her that in order to do a sport, one body is better suited than another.

This memory story opens with a meticulously ordered classroom—the children, the furniture, the notebooks are all lined up and in their proper places. Authority in the classroom is completely with the teacher, Mrs Lindner. It is a safe and familiar place. Abruptly, the power relations are disturbed when the door opens and unknown adults enter the room. Although the teacher introduces them as 'visitors', the children clearly see them as 'strangers' with absolute authority. Almost all the dialogue in the story comes in the form of imperatives/commands: 'You. Go over to the window... Lift up your arms... Bend forwards.... Go and wait outside the classroom.' Although the unnamed narrator observes everything that happens in great detail, this attention does not help her understand what is happening: 'She does not have a clue. She does not know what will happen'. When she does speak, much further into the story, it is only to ask 'What are they doing?'.

Although the children do not actively choose, there is a sort of mute agency operating through their bodies. The right body shape will get you chosen. The strangers map the children's bodies—with their eyes, looking for height, and then with their fingers, getting more specific and intimate. Initially, the woman steps back so Ivo can pass without their bodies touching but, as the story develops, there is no space between them as the adults begin to touch the bodies of the children. They start with arms, feeling perhaps for muscles, sinew, potential to be strengthened. We know no more than the child about what the man's fingers are feeling for. The fingers move down shoulder, elbow, wrist, down to all the vertebrae, one after another from neck to hip. It feels very invasive and there is no point when this child has the opportunity to say yes or no to any of it. The children are compliant and confused. Ivo has some idea of what this is about, and an image flashes into the narrator's mind of the pleasures of rowing on the last summer holiday. Outside in the corridor, there is more effort from the adults to explain what they have been selected for and imply how it might be enjoyable because they will be good at it. The child seems clear about two things by the end of the story—that what the strangers did to them in the classroom 'has nothing to do with rowing' and that sport is more about hierarchies of bodies and their fit to a particular sport than any other factor.

Being selected produces a double effect. The child did not know that she was good at a sport, nor if she wanted to be, but becoming an athlete (or being made into one by those prying adult fingers) is to become an object of desire of the state (as represented by these adults). The child will need to learn how to properly embody the desire that is invested in her. It might be confusing but also makes the child want something that she didn't already know she desired. This memory is told from the point of view of one who was selected, without knowing what is expected of her. The teacher offers an invitation, implying there is a choice ('if any of the children *would like* to join a rowing club…'), but the movements of the strangers around the room, pausing, looking, pointing, giving orders, clearly indicate that there is no choice. The invitation is contradictory because, in reality, it is about which body is suitable. The reconstruction of that moment allows us to experience the anguish of those who are being reviewed and finally selected, but it also leaves us open to the question of what happened to all those ´classmates that are allowed to sit down´, those who were not selected, who are `visibly shorter'. Where does risk lie—in being selected or not? We cannot tell, but we align with the narrator in the corridor in imagining the promise of the future. Dufourmantelle suggests that childhood can feel like 'hanging in wait for something to happen' where each event is infused with both disappointment and promise 'as if neither exists without the other' (2019, p. 67). The story of selection for training swirls with these feelings.

This story finishes before training begins, but we can imagine how this promised future might detract from other pleasures. Rowing the family on the lake in the summer holidays is likely to be in this child's past. From this pivotal moment onwards, rowing will take the child away from her family. It will be organised by the club, and will take place on their boats, and in their water. Rather than enjoyment and leisure, the goal now is speed, strength and the re-formation—through training—of this particular body into the generic rowing body. Our second story takes us into the thick of sport-training regimes, on a summer training camp for young gymnasts.

Gymnastics Training Camp (Romania)

She was awakened suddenly by a beam of light piercing through the windows. There were no curtains. Another 20 or 30 girls were sleeping in the same dormitory, on beds made of metal bars. It was a scorching summer day in a gymnastics training camp by the Black Sea.

For three weeks, the girls had done the same routine: waking up very early, eating breakfast, training, going to the beach, having lunch, more training, having dinner, sleeping. Those three weeks seemed like three years to her. She hated that routine and being away from her family. During 1974–1979, she trained as a gymnast at the primary school next to the block of flats where her family lived. With Nadia Comăneci's success at the Olympics in Montreal and her perfect 10 score, the dictator Nicolae Ceaușescu seized the opportunity to raise Romania's profile internationally through sports. A lot of talented girls were enrolled in free training programs throughout the country. She was one of them. She wanted to be like Nadia, all Romanian girls in the '70s wanted to be like Nadia. It was very hard work, with calloused palms, scratches, bumps to the head and blisters. And during summer camps, she missed her home dearly, her familiar surroundings, the food, familiar smells and faces.

A part of the routine was going to the beach as a group. She loved water, but she didn't have fond memories of going to the beach with the group of gymnasts. She didn't like the way children were exposed to water and sun at all. They were lined up on the beach like sardines, one next to each other, very close together, in three or four rows, and they were told when to turn: 10 minutes on their backs, 10 on their stomachs. A trainer would shout: 'Back now!', 'Front now!'. Her favourite position was on the stomach, as she could better protect herself from the sun that way. Then they were sent into the water, but in a very orderly and organised manner: a line of older girls would line up in front of the younger ones. The water was just up to their knees, but

10. Lift Up Your Arms!   247

nobody could go beyond the line of older children. Ten minutes or so in water and then back to our towels. She used to cry a lot in that camp, at night, in bed, quietly. She would write letters to her parents that she hated it and she wanted them to come and pick her up. But of course, by the time her letter would arrive home, it was time to leave the camp. That was the longest camp in her life.

This story takes us to a moment when Nadia Comăneci became a concrete object of desire and possibility for young people. The story opens and closes at the summer training camp, but the paragraph in the middle anchors it in a particular historical and geopolitical moment. The narrator says 'She wanted to be like Nadia, all Romanian girls in the 70s wanted to be like Nadia.' She anchors this desire precisely to the span of years when she trained as a gymnast, from 1974–1979. This girl was already well into gymnastics training by the time Comăneci achieved global prominence in Montreal in 1976, and became a socialist icon for the nation. Here the evocation of 'the dictator Nicolae Ceaușescu' and his inclination to 'seize' opportunities conveys a post-socialist sensibility and critical political awareness of what followed. Here wanting to 'be like Nadia' is only intelligible when geopolitics is part of the story. Whether explicit or implicit, all memories are infused with the sorts of tensions that come from writing from the perspective of a child, with the knowledge of an adult. Being 'like' Nadia in this memory, is a crucial qualifier because none of these girls can be Nadia. There is only, and can only ever be, one Nadia. Yet, the scale of desire is absolute, because it is shared by 'all Romanian girls'.

In contrast to the first story, this narrator has already taken up a sporting identity. Gymnast is the main identity she ascribes to herself during her six years of primary schooling. Woven through the story are glimpses of a homesick daughter, with the last lines telling us that she wants her parents to rescue her from the training camp. This is another impossible desire. Even though the letters do not serve their intended purpose, writing them means that she can express her anguish and therefore liberate herself to some extent from oppressive circumstances. Doufoumantelle speaks of running the risk of disobeying, which presupposes the ability to obey. Disobedience has nothing to do with whims and tantrums but, rather, supposes in the first instance being able to speak, to discover that it is possible to be loyal to oneself. The narrator takes the risk of accessing that inalienable place: 'that other space inside [...] the impregnable and universal space of her freedom' (Doufourmantelle 2019, p. 12). Here the girl is able to say that she no longer wants to be there. Even when the letter arrives days after she is already home, there is something liberating in the words and memory.

The framing story is the experience of the three-week gymnastics summer training camp by the Black Sea. If the figure of Nadia is remarkable for her uniqueness, and the child missing her family is also a particular individual subject, then the rest of the story is about the collapse of the individual into the group. From dawn when '20 or 30 girls' are all asleep in the same dormitory in the same sorts of beds, the story is about regimentation and the operations of power on children's bodies. The daily routine is the same with the repetition making three weeks seem 'like three years' or 'the longest camp in her life'. The marks of training are written on the body as 'calloused palms, scratches, bumps to the head and blisters' and we can assume that all the girls doing this 'hard work' carry similar physical marks. Perhaps all the girls are quietly crying in their beds at night but the perspective of the narrator does not allow any insight beyond her own unhappiness.

Regimentation carries through into the apparent daily leisure activity of 'going to the beach' which sits between scheduled training sessions. The girls are positioned on the sand like sardines packed tightly in a can. Their movements are controlled by instructors who tell them to turn at regular intervals to even out how their bodies are exposed to the hot sun. This is the opposite of relaxation, or of choice. Access, entry and exit from the water are regulated, within a hierarchy of older/young girls. Although water can be a medium for building strength, agility, and grace, here it does not have that purpose. This is just knee-high paddling amidst bodies restrained by other bodies.

The scene is vivid and detailed, easy to envisage, almost at times a parody. It does not make sense to ask whether these details were actually true but, rather, what versions of truth are suggested and what practices pertaining to bodies and sports do they gesture towards. The controlled exposure to sun and to seawater could be read in multiple ways. Perhaps gymnastics requires attention to the look as much as the strength of the body, with healthy suntanned skin desirable for high-cut barelegged gymnastics outfits. Perhaps it has nothing to do with appearance but is more about children who live in blocks of flats in cities and a general orientation to the health-giving properties of sun and sea. Would these city children have been able to visit the beach if they had not been invited to the training camp? There is no playing, no freedom, no choice and even though this is the seaside in summer, this is nothing like a summer holiday.

In our first and second stories, the children are developing skills, strength, and aspirations so that they might belong to the elite class of high-performance athletes. In our third story, the body fails and these dreams come crashing down. The communities of children that featured in the earlier stories are gone, and the immobilised child suffers an intensely private agony and grief.

Backpain (Hungary)

She was lying paralysed in bed. The toilet was 15 steps away so she only went when it was impossible to hold anymore. The pain was unbearable even with the strongest painkiller they prescribed her. Every step was agonising even if she moved very slowly trying to tense her muscles so they kept her lower back tightly in place. She felt despondent. Now she understood that she must stop competitive athletics. In the spring, they went to the doctor and then she had an appointment in the sports hospital in Budapest. They confirmed that the only way she could continue with competitions was if she had an operation strengthening her spine with screws in her lower back. The operation was very risky, and they only performed it if they deemed the person talented. She was 14 and her mother did not agree to the operation. She argued for a while, and her mother asked for a second opinion. Her decision stayed. The regional competition took place the day before. She did her usual combination: javelin, discus, shotput and long jump. She already felt the pain as she pushed off during the long jump and then on the way home sitting on the bus she could hardly bear the pain. By morning she could not move. Even the tiniest of movements came with shooting pain. As she was lying in bed there motionless, she slowly buried her dream of becoming an Olympic champion.

'No pain, no gain' is a familiar training slogan and mantra for elite sports stars. Pain is a necessary virtue, something to push through towards greater sporting achievements. Pain is linked to the idea of crossing thresholds as a body strengthens itself, becomes more agile, resists more. However, there is a difference between the pain of a body that is transforming itself in order to fit a particular sport that is different from the pain of injury. Here the carnal body manifests as 'unquantifiable pain' (Dufourmantelle 2019, p. 74). The injury rips, tears, paralyses her. The pain of injury alerts, prevents, stops her. The body is in a kind of suspension. For Dufourmantelle, suspension offers the chance 'to look with as much attention as possible at what is simply there, at what offers itself to you in the presence of things' (ibid., p. 13). Motionless, made still in her bed in the overwhelming presence of pain, the girl has no alternative than to confront her body's inadequacy to meet her desire to pursue elite sport. The story opens and closes with images of immobility and constraint: she is 'paralysed', every step is 'agonising', even the 'tiniest of movements'. There is a sort of separation of self from the recalcitrant wounded body, an interiority that transcends the exteriority of the body. Yet, Dufourmantelle says: 'There is no demarcation and no sign that allows you to say: here is the dead centre of interiority' (ibid., p. 76). From where does the narrator speak when there is no separation of self, will, body? This cleaving of body and self is even stronger here than in the previous memories. For Dufourmantelle, in the space of vulnerability 'your name gives way to this skin that bodies forth, that becomes a loving body, a tearful body, or a combatant body' (ibid.). Here, the triumphant body, the strong and agile body, becomes the broken body, and the narrator seeks to speak beyond that still place of pain that is all she is in the moment. The contrast between the ability of a body to move, even to break through regional and national borders and venture out into the world is confronting in this moment of immobility. It is worth wondering, then, what happens to this girl, how she confronts her own desire with the imminent obstacle. If the body is much more than the flesh, perhaps also there, in the pain and frustration of that interrupted dream, the foundations of inner strength are building that will enable her to go further and inhabit as yet unknown other worlds.

Memory, within the story, as it zigzags across time and place, is also an escape from the moment. This story's temporality is very different from the earlier chronological stories. It begins with the girl in bed unable to move, then jumps forward in time to the Spring visit to the sports hospital in Budapest, then backwards to the day before this one on the regional athletics field, then to the present frame of the story where she is again in bed, and at the same time far from there, in a possible future where she might have been an 'Olympic champion'. A dream that is now dead and buried. Everything is compressed to the immobilised body in the bed where the story starts and ends, with past and future suspended in the present.

The narrator suggests some possibilities of agency in this story, of desires that are blocked by others, by chance, by the body itself. She wanted the operation so she could continue with athletics, but this depends on her mother's approval. She clearly has talent—this operation is only offered to those who warrant its risk. It is a privilege that she feels she deserves, rather than a right that might be available to any child with an injured back. Yet, she has no agency over her body, its treatment, and her future, despite her Olympic aspirations. In this moment of suspense, it seems that 'in reality, the decision has already been made but no one knows it yet' (Dufourmantelle 2019, p. 13). If the body of the rowing child recruits her into elite sport, then the body of this child opts her out of elite sport.

Cold-War Sporting Bodies, Childhoods, and Collective Biography

The cultures of the Cold War cannot be understood without recognising the role of sport as a soft-power hinge between East and West and between high and popular cultures, or without acknowledging its global impacts and locally specific and national contours (Edelman and Young 2019). A 'false binary', or 'bipolar struggle' in the realm of sport between the Soviet bloc and the west is often assumed, but this view is simplistic and obscures subtleties and local variations (Edelman and Young 2020, pp. 28–29). Long before any sporting events attract attention in the public arena, there have been years of resource investment, training, and cultivation of athletes. For every sports person who reaches a public stage, hundreds more fall by the wayside. The children in these memory stories could be seen as casualties of this process. If they had not been selected and singled out as having talent and potential that separated them from their peers, they would not be disappointed. They would not have been undone by the risk of failure. The child in the final story will never be an Olympic athlete, her dreams are dashed, her body is literally broken. The child at the training camp will never be Nadia Comăneci, and, in the mundane present of the memory, she is homesick and lonely. The child selected for rowing has been removed from the routine of the classroom but also from the pleasure of rowing her family on the lake in summer. But on the other hand, it is important to recognise that the children are also beneficiaries of their selection. They had opportunities to leave home, to travel to other places, to be seen and appreciated, to become capable of cultivating aptitudes that they would not otherwise have found in themselves and of daring to dream of futures replete with potential. Through their participation in elite sports training, they experienced cultural, sports, and social programs that promoted collective life and an ethos that, in these individualised times, would be great to rethink.

Each memory story is also steeped in loss. They evoke the 'carnal body' of Dufourmantelle, encompassing thoughts, imaginings, dreams, tastes, affects, emotions, senses, and more (2019, p. 75). This expansive understanding of bodies forces us to think beyond any simple equivalence of bodies, experiences, and selves. The method of collective biography entails inherent risks that are simultaneously productive, generative, and disruptive. Risks arise in writing and rewriting memories, using the third-person pronoun, opening memory stories to collective analysis in workshops, and including them in an archive to be selected and reinterpreted by others. All of these strategies are risky because they distance or separate the memory from the narrator who experienced the event (Haug et al. 1987). The author may have become accustomed to telling and thinking their story in ways that are disrupted by the processes of collective biography. Alternative interpretations are produced, and potential meanings expand in ways that challenge habits of thought about one's own biography. Analyses diverge from the ways that the narrating subjects understood their stories. Collective-biography processes rupture habituated practices as memories are evoked and shared in critical social spaces and relations so that they each become more than a singular story. When working with collective-biography approaches to memories, something amazing happens that perhaps has to do with the fact that, in this way, we can cross the borders and erase the edges of what is mine or yours and run the risk of liberating the space of our reality and desire.

Approaching a different understanding of the Cold War from the perspective of childhood means taking the risk of putting our own memories at stake. It means playing at the limits of what we remember or think we remember. Memories written during the workshops become keys that, by letting emerge what is unique and particular to each participant's childhood, leads us to what has been lived in common and allows us to go deeper in understanding that moment in history that is materialised and embodied. The formation of elite athletes in the memories of children open those moments of history that are disregarded by conventional Cold-War histories. We wonder to what extent the so-called 'Cold War' (in all its multiplicities and variations) lives on in the body of these adults who revisit their childhood in such detail, evoking the child they imagined themselves to be, retrieving, arranging and organising their memories. Those thought, imagined, dreamed, remembered bodies of that time suggest a unique intimacy with history, as those girls and boys remember, decades later, from the territory of their own body, the moments of childhood that left traces of a remarkable time in history and humanity.

References

Arnold-de Simine, S. and Radstone, S. (2013). 'The GDR and the Memory Debate', in *Remembering and Rethinking the GDR: Multiple Perspectives and Plural Authenticities*, ed. by A. Saunders and D. Pinfold. (pp. 19–33). Palgrave Macmillan, https://doi.org/10.1057/9781137292094_2

Davies, B. and S. Gannon. (eds). (2006). *Doing Collective Biography. Investigating the Production of Subjectivity*. Open University Press

Dufourmantelle, A. (2019). *In Praise of Risk*, trans. by S. Miller. Fordham University Press. (Original work published 2015 as *Elogio del riesgo*), https://doi.org/10.2307/j.ctvnwbxf5

Edelman, R. and Young, C. (eds). (2019). *The Whole World was Watching: Sport in the Cold War*. Stanford University Press, https://doi.org/10.1515/9781503611016

Gannon, S., Walsh, S., Byers, M., and Rajiva, M. (2014). Deterritorializing Collective Biography. *International Journal of Qualitative Studies in Education*, 27(2), 181–95, https://doi.org/10.1080/09518398.2012.737044

Haug, F., et al. (1987). *Female Sexualization*. London: Verso

Kaščák, O. and Pupala, B. (2018). 'On the Edge of Two Zones: Slovak Socialist Childhoods', in *Childhood and Schooling in Post/Socialist Societies: Memories of Everyday Life*, ed. by I. Silova, N. Piattoeva, and S. Millei. (pp. 63–86). Basingstoke: Palgrave Macmillan, https://doi.org/10.1007/978-3-319-62791-5_4

Oates-Indruchová, L. (2018). 'A Dulled Mind in an Active Body: Growing up as a Girl in Normalization Czechoslovakia', in *Childhood and Schooling in Post/Socialist Societies: Memories of Everyday Life*, ed. by I. Silova, N. Piattoeva, and S. Millei. (pp. 41–61). Basingstoke: Palgrave Macmillan, https://doi.org/10.1007/978-3-319-62791-5_3

Losing Balance[1]

Tatyana Kleyn

She joined the Roy C. Ketcham (RCK) High School Gymnastics Team as a 7th grader who was still in junior high. Little did she know this team would become her life and her family for the next six years. It would take her around the world from Hawaii to Italy and even China, as the first high school team of any sport to compete in the communist nation. But it was a meet in Lakeland High School, just 45 minutes from Poughkeepsie, New York, where her high school was located, that would become a turning moment in her life.

It was her junior year, so she had already spent four years on the team, with 15–20 other girls depending on the year. But this family—until that day—had one thing in common. They were winners, they won every meet, every time. It was the expectation and the norm. That was until the Lakeland meet, where the abstract concept of defeat became a reality, and a very bitter one at that. The announcement of the final score was nothing short of a shockwave that ran through the girls as they assembled their belongings by the bleachers. They didn't know how to lose, how to act, what to do. It brought them all to tears, with their coach, Mr. Ross, yelling, 'You can't do that. Get on the bus!'

This was possibly the first time she cried in public as a teenager. But she was not alone. The nearly 20 sobbing girls boarded the bus, as a team, in their red, white and blue uniforms (the school colors, not to be confused with those of the US flag) and eventually sat in silence for the rest of the ride home. Although nothing was said, the uncertainty of this new moment penetrated the yellow school bus with the most uncomfortable upright seats. How did this happen to us? Who are we now? Where do we go from here? The questions

---

1   This is a childhood memory produced as part of the Reconnect/Recollect project discussed in the introduction to this book.

were to be answered, but one constant remained, the team—albeit cracked—
was still whole.

Photograph of Tatyana (back row, fifth from the left) with her gymnastics team
in Tiananmen Square. Beijing, China, 1989. From Tatyana Kleyn's family archive.

Adult Hospital Ward[1]

Irena Kašparová

She is in the hospital bed, waiting for tonsil extractions. There was no room in the children's ward, so they admitted her to the ladies´ rooms. The only child among five grown up ladies. No toys, no children´s books, no posters on the wall, no other children to play or talk to. Instead, there are plain white walls. Adult faces buried in novels sink in white hospital linen pillows. The buzzing of the neon lamps is only interrupted by soft conversations about knitting patterns and strawberry pesticides. She feels lonely. The ladies quickly run out of short informative polite questions to which she gives short polite informative answers. Nobody to talk to. She is terribly lonely. She wants to cry but nobody cries around here. Not here. Here are only adults. She was placed here, because she looks like an adult. She is a big girl, responsible, eldest, good girl. She is almost ten but everybody would guess she is older. She has a big tall body, too grown up for her age. She does not feel big inside her big body, but she wants to live up to the expectations. She must not cry, not here. She is a big girl in the adult´s ward. A nurse comes in the evening, handing each person a thermometer and medicine, asking each everyone: 'Did you have your stool today?' The girl panics. What on earth is she talking about? What is a stool? Surely, she does not mean the chair to rest one's feet after a long and tiring day!? Or a king's stool, the hereditary seat the sovereign occupies. What else on earth could this word mean? She is helpless, shy, ashamed for not knowing, not being the big girl. Apparently, 'yes' is the correct answer to the nurse's question, every woman answers yes, so will she. But what if she misses something vital? What if the stool is some kind of a pill necessary for her operation? What if it is some food or treatment that she needs in order to get better? She decides not to admit she

---

1   This is a childhood memory produced as part of the Reconnect/Recollect project discussed in the introduction to this book.

does not know the word, because that would point to the fact that she should not be here, that she is out of place here, the fact that she does not belong here, because the rest of the people all know what a stool is. So, she will pretend she knows also. The nurse writes this information into the paper and goes away. The girl feels relieved, hoping it is resolved once and for all. However, the situation repeats itself the next day, when the stool question comes up again. Thinking hard about what went on differently today, what may be a stool out of all the food she has eaten (or the others) or the actions she had performed (or the others), she is still clueless. She pretends again, but this time she is terrified of missing something vital. She is tense and stressed, her body starts sweating. Her bad conscience is biting her hard. She dares not to ask, not to betray the trust of all those who have chosen for her to be among the adults. She wants to comply, to keep up the facade, the mask, to stay in control. The mind is determined but the body betrays her. She develops diarrhea and fever and receives a pill to cure both. In the morning, they move her downstairs to the children's ward. She feels she is allowed to be a child again; she allows herself to cry.

11. Children on their Own: Cold-War Childhood Memories of Unsupervised Times

Nadine Bernhard and Kathleen Falkenberg

Childhood in formerly socialist countries is often depicted in research as 'organised' or 'uniform'—a perspective we challenge in this paper. Using collective-memory work, we analyse our own childhood memories from the late GDR and memories taken from the memory archive of the Reconnect/Recollect project, focusing on unsupervised times, when institutional access to child supervision was no longer available and adult supervision could not (yet) be guaranteed. With this focus, we broaden existing literature on post/socialist childhood, which mainly focuses on institutionalised settings. Our analysis finds three patterns of unsupervised times present across different memory stories—unsupervised times perceived as freedom and contentment, responsibility, and loneliness. These patterns show that unsupervised times created opportunities for important children's experiences to take place—from being creative to imitating adults, breaking rules, and building communities with peers and siblings. Additionally, we find many similarities across geopolitical boundaries that break down the stereotypical dichotomies of childhoods between the 'East' and the 'West'.

As it is often the case in qualitative research, this chapter started off as an observation, a self-reflective moment that happened to us while sharing memories of our childhoods in the former GDR (German Democratic Republic). Sitting together on a balcony in a now-hip neighbourhood in what used to be socialist East Berlin, chatting about particular memory stories we had written down earlier, we came to a realisation. We had not explicitly planned it, but many of the situations we recalled were ones in which we were on our own as children: enjoying ourselves alone or with other children, doing forbidden things while left alone at home. Feelings of loneliness and being overwhelmed also came to mind. This perspective on children being on their own, their struggles and experiences, was in stark contrast to the uniform picture typically painted in research and even the media about childhood in the GDR.

We started wondering why time spent alone as children left such a lasting impression on our personal childhood memories and what shared qualities of these recollections could be insightful for other memory stories of childhood in formerly socialist countries or Cold-War childhoods. These questions have led us to many fruitful conversations, helped us develop analytical concepts and turned a chat on the balcony into a new and ongoing research endeavour (see also Falkenberg and Bernhard, forthcoming). This chapter is, thus, an attempt to summarise our thoughts at this moment in time, knowing that this project is far from complete.

The starting point for our writing and thinking about childhood memories as a data source for research on Cold-War childhoods was the international, collaborative, and multidisciplinary project Reconnect/Recollect. As participants in a memory workshop in Berlin, we created our first memory stories, contributing to an ever-growing online memory archive[1] as a way of gaining insights into post/socialist childhoods. We believe that even though memories are selective constructions of the past, they can serve as fruitful sources for a more nuanced analysis of everyday life and childhoods in formerly socialist countries. Memory stories provide insight into childhoods in specific socio-cultural contexts and highlight the social structures that helped shape everyday life. At the same time, childhood memory stories and their details, emotions, materialities, embodiments, and sensations illustrate how memories are intertwined with notions of childhood

---

1   See https://coldwarchildhoods.org/memories/

prevalent in societies and wider socio-political matrices of power, divisions, and connections (Silova et al. 2018).

How children experienced everyday life is still a less frequently explored approach to research on Cold-War childhoods compared to the extensive literature on childhood-related institutions such as kindergarten, school, or political mass organisations, and their aim of creating the new, socialist person. In contrast to well-established narratives about a supposedly uniform state-organised childhood in formerly socialist countries, in our analysis, we focus on times of the day when institutional access was no longer available and adult supervision could not (yet) be guaranteed—for example, weekday afternoons before parents came home from work or weekend hours when children were sent out to play. We ask how these unsupervised times were spent and what limitations, rules and arrangements there were for these times of the day in order to reflect upon children's agency, the opportunities, challenges, and responsibilities 'being alone' comprised for children, and in which societal structures these were embedded. By analysing Cold-War childhood memories of unsupervised times, we take a perspective on 'social, economic, political, and cultural formations' and everyday spaces in which ignorance, 'dissent, transgression, and resistance' to official ideologies and mandates took place (Millei et al. 2019, p. 327).

After presenting our conceptualisation of unsupervised times, we will discuss several memory stories—some our own and some obtained from the memory archive—grouping them under three main topics: (1) unsupervised times perceived as freedom and contentment, (2) unsupervised times as responsibility, and (3) unsupervised times as loneliness. By including manifold memory stories with different geopolitical and socio-historical backgrounds into our analysis, we explore similarities and differences in the experience of unsupervised times for children—both across and within Cold-War related pictures of 'the West' and 'the East'. Finally, reflecting on our own work with the memory archive, we discuss the possibilities (and limitations) of the archive, seeking to shift the focus to connections and similarities between the 'East' and 'West' in various spheres of life (Millei et al. 2019). The approach of working with childhood memories offers the possibility of opening up existing structures that marginalise knowledge production from post/socialist spaces (Millei et al. 2019) and overcoming familiar but one-sided images of the Cold-War world reproduced through dichotomies such as capitalism/socialism, religious/atheist, imperialist/liberalist (Silova et al. 2017). Nevertheless, working with memory stories from a variety of places and times is a challenging task that requires nuanced contextual knowledge and reflexivity from the involved researchers. We thus conclude our chapter with a short discussion of these issues.

Conceptualising Unsupervised Times

German educational history research on GDR childhoods has so far focused mostly on childhood institutions like kindergarten, school or mass youth organisations and their role in educating socialist citizens. Such scholarship has often reduced children to passive recipients of ideological propaganda, depicting them as members of collective institutions, often in uniforms and/or at mass organisation events (for an overview see Geißler and Wiegmann 1995; Tenorth 2010). To our knowledge, there is a corresponding lack of international research on unsupervised, non-institutional times in Soviet or Cold-War childhoods, leaving a huge research gap with respect to how childhood was experienced outside of those institutions. Although perspectives from formerly socialist states that are not traditionally part of the hegemonic knowledge discourse on socialist childhoods are increasingly being published (for example, see Silova et al. 2018), these too often focus on childhood in institutionalised spheres, such as kindergarten and school (see for example, the papers included in a recently published Special Issue edited by Teszenyi et al. 2022).

The predominant perspective in research on GDR childhood postulates highly standardised life paths, resulting in a 'standard biography of children' in the GDR as compared to West Germany (Grunert and Krüger 2006, p. 65). It is this monolithic idea of GDR childhood—or childhoods in formerly socialist countries more generally—as 'organised' or 'uniform' that we wish to challenge. We focus on the hours of the day when institutional care had ended and other adult supervision was not available, a time usually referred to as leisure time, free time, or after-school hours in contemporary childhood studies (Sharp et al. 2006). Going beyond such research, we suggest applying the concept of unsupervised times to analyse childhood memories from socialist countries for several reasons.

Firstly, we understand unsupervised times as a productive irritation of the established view of a uniform, singular 'socialist childhood' mostly happening in institutional settings by highlighting the importance of non-institutional, everyday childhood experiences. These help to provide a more complex, more comprehensive picture of socialist childhoods (in plural).

Secondly, unsupervised times encompasses all of children's activities performed and experiences gained on their own as part of their everyday routines (on weekdays as well as weekends), including household tasks and chores as well as joyful activities like playing and relaxing, but not organised extracurricular activities like music lessons or sports. This differs from the concept of leisure time, which can be spent with parents or other adults as well.

Thirdly, while highlighting children`s independence, the concept of unsupervised times acknowledges their irrevocable connection to the adult world. Even though adults were not physically present in the memories analysed in this chapter, elements of the adult world still structured how the children spent their time. Examples of those relational connections include schedules and chores but also internalised norms of good and bad as well as parental influences on children's feelings and thoughts. The adult world is an absent presence that is tangible in all the childhood memories analysed for this chapter.

Finally, our concept of unsupervised children is related to negatively connotated ideas of 'supervised' childhoods as well. Supervision of children in socialist contexts evokes notions of control, a need to regulate children and put them under adult surveillance and guidance to integrate them into a collective in which they suspend their individual needs, wishes, and desires for the greater good. In addition to those negative notions, we discovered multiple layers of supervision built into unsupervised time, sometimes related to children's safety and well-being, as well as a complete lack of supervision when children were entrusted with a certain task. From a contemporary childhood-studies perspective, the notion of unsupervised children is often linked to a discourse of risk and fear, stressing potential dangers of unsupervised time for children's well-being and development. While the degree of adult supervision decreases as children become older and more independent, contemporary discourses regarding at-risk youth point to unsupervised time as a missed learning opportunity or a cause of higher rates of drug abuse (Badura 2018). However, recent research also emphasises the value of noninstitutionalised and unsupervised time for independent play as beneficial for children's social, emotional, and physical well-being (Rixon et al. 2019). Time to play alone has reportedly been decreasing in recent decades—especially in the global North—due to parental anxieties about children's safety (ibid.) and parents' desire to maximise their children's educational achievement via organised after-school activities. Even though unsupervised times seem more typical of the past and are often reflected upon as positive, we would like to stress that numerous structures in society and in individual families necessitate(d) unsupervised times. These structures include rates of female labour-force participation and a lack of adequate childcare opportunities, parental values, but also social inequality.

Following educational research on childhood and childhood studies, we understand childhood as a social construction and as a specific phase of life with its own social status (Mierendorff 2019). We conceptualise childhood as part of the social structure and its institutional and cultural context and are interested in these interrelations. Since childhood conditions within modern societies are highly diverse, we aim to reflect the heterogeneity of children's experiences and biographical diversity, thereby resisting ideas of a single, uniform childhood.

Memory Stories of Unsupervised Times

In this paper, we combine our own collective memory work on childhood memories in the former GDR with an analysis of memory stories collected through the Reconnect/Recollect project and saved in the memory archive. We understand childhood memories as an analytical perspective and as a data source. We recognise that memories—as selective constructions of the past, not a linear representation of the past or what 'really' happened—are constructed by those who tell them, shaped by the present, and modified by the accounts of others. Memories are, therefore, creations and, in some ways, 'unreliable' (Davies and Gannon 2006, p. 3). The employment of collective biographical processing of memories, that is, 'the shared generation and analysis of systematically recalled memories' (Millei et al. 2019, p. 2), is a productive and reflexive way to work with memories as data.

In our collective memory work and in the memory workshops, we followed the steps recommended by Frigga Haug (1991) as well as Davies and Gannon (2006) on collective biography. Central to each of these is the collective evocation and analysis of written memories on a delimited subject, for example, unsupervised times in our childhood, 'to explore the effects of structural, systemic, discursive and affective processes on the emergence of particular subjects, such as [...] the gendered subject [...] or the child subject' (Millei et al. 2019, p. 2). It is, thus, a collective research approach that attempts to work out overarching patterns of action and interpretation as well as subjectivisations through method-guided systematic work with memories.

Our own memories of unsupervised times were first written down and collected by each author individually. Then we read each other's memory stories, scanned them for inconsistencies, clichés, or standardised formulations and reformulated them if necessary. We paid particular attention to our own positionality as authors of those stories, reflecting on what kind of childhood experiences we can shed light upon—or not. In the subsequent analysis of our own stories, we discovered three patterns of memories related to unsupervised times: unsupervised time (1) perceived as freedom and contentment, (2) as responsibility, and (3) as loneliness. In a second step, we then analysed the Reconnect/Recollect memory archive to compare and expand the analysis of our own memories. Can we find similar or new overarching patterns? Do we find differences between socialist and non-socialist memories of unsupervised times? These were the questions that informed our analysis.

The archive consists of more than 250 memory stories collected, for example, during memory workshops, expositions, and conferences and written in several languages, but mostly in English. Thus, our starting point was our own language skills, enabling us to include all 237 memories written in German, English, or Spanish.[2] In a first step, we preselected all memories in which children were described outside of

---

2   In this paper, we refer to the database content published until February 2022. Memories included afterwards are not part of our analysis.

an institutional setting like school, kindergarten, or afterschool care and in which there was no clear adult supervision. Of these 111 memories, we decided in a final selection process to concentrate on memories depicting children up to age 12, with no adults physically present, and we restricted the memories to everyday life; recollections of special events like vacations or holidays were excluded. The age restriction enables us to focus on children rather than teenagers, who usually become more independent as they get older. Moreover, this age range is also in line with our own memories from the GDR. The final sample included 27 memory stories. Since these stories were written by other people and are not our own memories, we employed Grounded Theory methodology for the analysis of this data. Following basic recommendations (Corbin and Strauss 2015), we focused on distinguishing who does what, how, with whom, why, and where in those memory stories. In this way, we were able to identify overarching patterns and narratives revealed in the memories rather than examining every single memory story in depth, a necessary restriction given the rather large number of selected stories.

The memory stories we analysed came from 17 geopolitical entities.[3] The majority were from formerly socialist countries like Romania, Poland, or the GDR, but other countries such as West Germany, Australia, and Finland were also part of the selection. This allows us to look at childhoods during the Cold War in both capitalist and socialist countries. In the memories, the children were alone, with siblings, or with friends or peers. In analysing the memories from the archive, we could not detect a new overarching pattern that would expand our previous research—a rather surprising first result. However, the memories in the archives were not produced with a focus on unsupervised times, unlike our own sample. This might have had an effect. Nonetheless, our own analysis is strengthened by the fact that the three patterns we did identify are repeated in the memories from different contexts. Furthermore, thinking about collectively produced memory stories as data, we then decided to take advantage of the opportunity to examine the social structures represented in those stories. Social structures can be determined with respect to several foci, including gender relations,

---

3   Argentina, Armenia, Australia, Azerbaijan, Brazil, Czechoslovakia, Finland, West Germany/FRG, East Germany/GDR, Georgia, Kazakhstan, Poland, Romania, Russia, Serbia, Slovenia, and Yugoslavia.

family structures, urban structures, but we focused on knowledge structures, namely the narratives about unsupervised times represented in the memories. In the following, we present the three overarching patterns and the occurrence of typical narratives therein. We use our own memory stories to interpret these patterns in more depth, but we also incorporate examples from the memory archive.

Unsupervised Times as Freedom and Contentment

The first pattern refers to memories in which time spent alone as a child was perceived as freedom, as a period without (or at least with less) parental or institutional regulation. It is perceived as time that children can fill with activities of their own choosing. In the stories in the archive, the pattern of unsupervised time perceived as freedom and contentment could be found in stories describing the walk home from school or from other activities, stories about skipping school, how children played in- or outdoors or how children organised celebrations at their houses. This was the pattern that dominated in most of the analysed memories.

Nevertheless, the perceived freedom described in the memories takes place within a temporally and spatially structured, adult-driven day, leaving only small pockets of time. The result is a rather conditional freedom dependent on complex societal and familial arrangements.

In the memories about children being alone and enjoying themselves, moments of boredom give rise to new activities, as the following example shows:

[…] *she takes her Gummihopse [elastics or jump rope] […] out of her satchel, sets up the two wooden chairs in the children's room and stretches the rubber band under the chair legs. The distance between the bands is wider than if her friends were standing there, but she bounces happily back and forth, always thinking up new difficulties. She pretends to be in a competition and gives herself posture scores like in figure skating.* ('Gummihopse' n.d., East Germany/GDR)

Apart from the obviously playful activity the girl in the story invents for herself to pass the afternoon on her own, the story provides deeper insights into societal structures. The reference to figure-skating competitions is probably no coincidence since the sport became increasingly popular as a field in which GDR athletes were able to achieve international success during the 1980s. At the same time, competitions in general were a part of children's everyday experience: for example, schoolchildren were publicly awarded prizes for good grades, and competitions for the 'most beautiful schoolyard' were announced. In other areas of society, competitions served to honour particularly productive members of socialist society. The child's play in this example invites us to look into broader social mentalities and, thus, points beyond itself. A careful analysis enables us to understand how everyday life, even on a small scale, was shaped by societal structures.

In this brief snippet of a memory story, we can, furthermore, identify two narratives that appear repeatedly in other stories. We understand the term 'narratives' here as shared interpretations and understandings of children's actions described as typical of (unsupervised) childhoods. They are inseparably linked to socially shared ideas and scripts represented not only in these memories but also in research concerning children's development and socialisation into society as well as in contemporary societal discourses.

The first narrative is one of 'childhood as a time for creativity, playing, and trying things out with available materials'. In the memory archive, for instance, we found children playing intensively with mud, making watercolours out of what nature offers, or staging a fashion show with existing clothes. Thus, in contrast to the potentially more consumerist present, where children often play with store-bought toys, the children in the memories create something with the help of ordinary things. Following Gaskins et al. (2007), these representations reflect 'culturally accepted play'—a type in which children play together, often unsupervised by adults, in spaces not particularly structured for play, and with naturally available objects rather than store-bought toys.

In the story above, the girl is also creative and plays with everyday objects that are available. In place of friends, the child uses chairs to be able to do what she likes. She also imitates adults, who use scores to competitively evaluate actions. Here again, we can see how the norms of the adult world influence children's actions even in the physical absence of adults. 'Imitation of the adult world' is the second narrative we frequently found when analysing the memories. Research has often emphasised that children's growth and development are strongly dependent on their capacity for imitation. When children play, they often imitate adults by staging events they witnessed or stories they listened to (Noschis 1992).

This imitation of the adult world is also prominent in the following memory from the archive:

Every day, after school, on her way home, she would stop at her best friend's house where they played and played and forgot about time. They explored many forbidden things. Adult things. [...] They felt they could do just about anything together. One day, must have been in second grade [...] her friend told her she discovered a secret, a treasure behind the porcelain figurines displayed in the glass windowed cupboard in the living room: a packet of Kent cigarettes. The best cigarettes in the world. A rare commodity, not available to everyone, as they somehow sensed. [...] It was a Western brand, most certainly American, a symbol of privilege. [...]. I already tried one, and believe me, it's great, the friend confessed. Let's smoke one together. Oh yes, it will be so cool to do it! Let's smoke it at the balcony window and do the gestures like the women in the movies do, when they smoke. The passers-by will see us and be amazed how grown-up we are. ('The Secret' n.d., Romania)

With grown-up women from the movies in mind, the two girls try to imitate them to look cool and grown-up themselves. They anticipate amazement rather than astonishment from passers-by who see two young girls smoking. What we also witness in this memory is that the two girls are best friends and their doing something forbidden together creates an even stronger bond between them because they share secrets. The secret in this memory is particularly big because they decide to smoke not normal cigarettes but hidden ones from the capitalist West, a 'symbol of privilege'. The memory shows us that Western products were very rare in these families and perceived by the children as something extraordinarily precious. This feeling might stem from the children's observations of the silent gestures of adults. Alternatively, it might reflect the conversations they heard about Western goods in comparison to the more limited selection of Eastern-bloc products, thus reproducing the image of scarcity and low-quality Eastern products.

The memory also displays two further typical narratives. First, we see 'unsupervised childhood as a time to do forbidden things, share and keep secrets, break rules, and test the limits'. In childhood-development studies, these are important developmental steps for children in which they not only interact with and uphold or resist societal norms but also develop their identities (see, for example, Piaget 2015 [1932]; Valtin 2020). The second narrative concerns 'unsupervised childhood as a time of community and cohesion' with peers and siblings, often by sharing secrets. Children are described as learning and acting together, building communities, and attempting to belong. Again, siblings—and even more so peers—are widely recognised as playing an essential role in the children's development and their becoming independent from parents and other adult guardians (see, for example, Berndt and Ladd 1989; Hoffmann 2022).

Unsupervised Time as Responsibility

The second pattern within the memory stories highlights the conditional nature of the abovementioned perceived freedom. In our memories, afternoon time was often structured by various chores assigned to children, like cleaning the house, watching younger siblings, or running small errands. These tasks fulfilled several functions: children were taught to be independent early on and to learn important life skills. They were also expected to help out at home to relieve working parents (or, rather, mothers) from household chores. Furthermore, chores served as a form of control by parents or other adults: the assignment of tasks shrank to a minimum the period in which children were left to their own devices and, thus, might get into 'trouble'. These temporal and spatial limitations created what we term 'conditional freedom' for children. Through the chores and tasks they assigned, parents and other adults were still present in absence, indirectly controlling children's activities, as seen in the following example:

The girl is on her way back from school. Today she is supposed to pick up her little brother from kindergarten [...]. The brother is only two years younger, but in her eyes, he is still a baby. After all, she is already a schoolchild! The kindergarten is right next to the school [...] the kindergarten teachers are already waving at her. [...] One of the women calls her brother. He comes through the gate to meet her, they both wave again to the teachers and then they walk off together. Always alongside the fence, through the narrow path that leads to their housing block, passing the mountains of sand at the building site next to it. [...] But, oh, the little brother walks so darn slowly, constantly wanting to pick up stones and put them in his pocket or climb the mountains of sand. The girl pulls at his hand and wants to keep going. They shouldn't dawdle, Mum said. And at home Gabi, the nice neighbour, is waiting. The girl likes to be with Gabi [...] she will have something sweet for them. ('Kindergarten' n.d., East Germany/GDR)

It was quite common for older children to look after their younger siblings for some time in the afternoon, even though the provision of day-care slots and after-school care was quite comprehensive in the 1980s in the GDR (Kirchhöfer 2000). This is reflected in the matter-of-fact interaction with the kindergarten teachers in the story, who immediately call the brother and hand him over to his not-very-much-older sister. They do not question a young child of roughly seven years of age picking up an even younger child and sending both on their way home. It remains unclear from the story if the kindergarten personnel knew about the neighbour waiting for the children—someone who would start looking for them in case of emergency—but with both parents working, such a 'bridging practice' between institutional care and parental or other adult supervision was necessary for many families (Kirchhöfer 2000, p. 196). Maternal employment was strongly encouraged since the 1950s, a response to politically normative claims regarding gender equality as well as economic necessity, but it required care work to be re-organised. Other factors, like long commutes between state-assigned housing and the workplace as well as restricted opening hours for shops, also made it difficult for working adults to run everyday errands, meaning that a 'developed familial division of labour' (Kirchhöfer 2000, p. 194) was common and necessary.

In the memory story above, it becomes apparent that the older child takes over the adult role to a certain extent, and the narrative of imitating the adult world pops up once again. The schoolchild takes the younger child by the hand—and thus under her control—and leads him home. She has little patience for the younger child's actions, such as picking up stones. We can almost hear the adult voice in her head when she reminds him not to dawdle, not to waste time, a typical argument of adults. Only at the end of the story can a glimpse of the child be seen, with the hope of sweets and thus a reward for the successful completion of the care task. Fostering children's independence expressed great confidence in their abilities. But, of course, placing high expectations and sometimes excessive demands on children could also reflect an 'imposition of independence' (Kirchhöfer 1998, p. 194) that overburdened children, as other stories show.

The second pattern—of unsupervised times as responsibility—was rare in the memory archive. Running errands or taking care of siblings are typical examples. However, sometimes moments of responsibility could also be experienced as times of freedom, as shown in the following example:

She must have been in first or maybe second grade, around the age of seven. She was the eldest child in the family with three younger siblings, the youngest being a baby, causing the mother to stay, even stick to the house. So the older children had to do errands from time to time. She was often asked to do the shopping, thus going to the grocery store […]. Although it could be annoying sometimes, she could go out even if the weather was not so nice (to play outside for example). The family had to be careful with the money because the income was not very high and the family was big, which meant a lot of sharing. […] ('Pink Sweets' n.d., West Germany)

This memory story adds a twist to the second pattern, expanding our view. Again, the child in the story needs to take over household tasks to support her mother. As the oldest child in a big family, she is supposed to act more grown-up than her younger siblings. Under these circumstances, being responsible and having to do chores could actually turn into something enjoyable: for a little while, she could escape the constricting family setting, be on her own, take her time, and play outside, even if the weather was bad. These were moments of freedom, even though framed by a household task.

This memory story shows that we need to keep in mind that the identified patterns are meant to work as analytical categories; the goal is not to force the stories to fit one or another of these categories. As the story continues, it plays out one of the narratives mentioned earlier—the narrative of unsupervised times as time for breaking the rules:

One day she went shopping again and, in the supermarket, she was passing by the sweets which always looked so attractive and colourful; and she saw a bag of sweets open and spread on the shelf. Could she take them? Why not? An open bag would not be sold, and the pink colour was so seductive. Still, was it ok to take one? Well, it must be, no harm would be done to anyone. Yet, being caught while taking it was not something she wanted to experience. She must have looked around if anyone was near or looking, or maybe even waited until it was out of sight. When she was sure, she took one. Then, she went to the cashier and paid for the other things. How she got out of the supermarket is not a clear memory, but she must have hidden it. On the way back home, she ate it, yummy. At the same time, she knew she was doing something wrong and felt so embarrassed. She never told her mother or anyone else but promised herself never to do such a thing again. ('Pink Sweets' n.d., West Germany)

Several things can be highlighted here: It is a very mundane situation from today's perspective, but obviously an open bag of candy spilled all over the shelf makes quite an impression on the child in the story. Maybe sweets in general are something precious in her family and she does not get them very often since the family is on a tight budget. She is well aware of the limitations that come with their financial constraints.

Then, although the child is on her own in the shop, she debates with herself—in her mind—about whether or not to take the sweets. She knows the rules, she has internalised some adult norms about good and bad, about stealing, taking stuff without paying. Finally, she takes one sweet because she tells herself they would be thrown away anyway. The child already knows how supermarkets deal with damaged goods or broken packages. She understands basic mechanisms of commerce in capitalist countries, and with that knowledge, she finds a way to be ok with breaking the rule of not stealing. She observes the shop, waiting for the right moment, and then takes one, and only one, candy. Taking one rather than several or even the whole bag might indicate how highly she values this piece of candy. She does not dare to take more. We can see in the story that it is the child acting, debating with herself and then ultimately taking the sweets, but it is the rules and norms of the adult world that convert this small incident into something very memorable for the grown-up narrator even decades later.

Again, however, memory stories of unsupervised times as responsibility were quite rare in the sample from the archive. Maybe those times were not remembered or written down because the memory workshops focused on other main topics, meaning that other stories were more likely to be written down.

Unsupervised Times as Loneliness

We have seen that unsupervised time—although pre-structured and conditioned—can facilitate creativity, a sense of responsibility and independence in children. But at the same time, it can pose great challenges and lead to a feeling of being (left) alone or loneliness. This is the third pattern we discovered in our memories. In this pattern, we can see how much children are emotionally dependent on the adults caring for them, how vulnerable and desperate they might feel when those support figures are absent. But we can also see how children cope with loneliness and which strategies they find to cope with a situation, look for help, and find relief. The following story exemplifies this pattern:

'You're a big girl, you can manage to stay home alone for two hours. We'll be back soon,' says Mum, in a hurry to make it to the parents' meeting. [...] Mum said they'd all be back by 8pm, but time passes so slowly. At first, she keeps herself busy, but then she gets more and more restless. She has already put on her nightgown, just like Mum said. She keeps looking out the window over the balcony to see if anyone is coming. [...] She's a big girl after all, she tells herself, but she gets sadder and sadder. Feels alone and starts to cry. [...] she sits down in the hallway by the front door, hoping that this might help someone come faster. [...] Although she is at home, she doesn't feel safe or secure in the big flat, all alone. She has turned on all the lights, so the dark, green-painted hallway is no longer so scary. [...] She puts the key around her neck, opens the door to the apartment and sits down in front of the door near the staircases, sobbing. It makes her feel closer to the three lifts and therefore closer to her family [...] She doesn't care that she is sitting on the dirty doormat with her clean nightgown [...] She doesn't hear the lift opening. It is a neighbour coming home to his family who sees her crouching in front of the door, sobbing. He takes her over to his place and writes a note for her parents. The girl is ashamed and feels small, but at the same time is glad that she is no longer alone. ('Big Girl' n.d., East Germany/GDR)

In this memory, the child is left alone at home because of an important appointment. The reason is very understandable to the child, she also does not want to disappoint her parents and wants to be as 'big' as she is told she is. However, these rational reasons for being alone do not help the child cope with the situation for long. Soon, a primal fear of being alone in the world makes itself felt. The child in the memory tries to find ways to handle this situation.

To cope with her increasing fear, she constantly rethinks and optimises her strategies (turning on the lights, sitting in the hallway, putting on the key, waiting outside the door). In doing so, she does not completely surrender to her fear but faces it. And, while it is not her parents who find the girl in the end but rather the neighbour, the child gets help and relief through her actions.

We can also see how being trusted to be a 'big girl' can be overwhelming. The child tries to live up to this expectation but struggles. She is afraid and ashamed of being afraid at the same time. When she is rescued by the neighbour, she feels even more ashamed but also relieved. Even though the family was living in a 23-storey tower block, knowing the neighbours and helping each other was very common in the GDR. People were expected to form building communities (Hausgemeinschaften) that took responsibility for common areas and took turns mopping the stairs, for example, or taking care of the yard in front of the building. These state-mandated building communities often celebrated special occasions and held festivities together, but they could also feel like social pressure, as people would take notice of even the smallest changes in a family (Günther and Nestmann 2000).

The third pattern, of unsupervised times as loneliness, was rarely found in the archived memories. Again, this relative scarcity might be explained by the fact that those memory stories were collected from memory workshops focusing on different themes and moments in childhood. Nevertheless, there are some memories that speak of loneliness, fear, and feelings of abandonment, like children being scared of a storm and longing for their parents to come home, or the story about a child's anxiety after taking the wrong train during a subway journey. Again, loneliness arose in different ways and the children in the stories found different strategies to deal with these feelings. In the following memory story, the child finds a very creative way to deal with them:

[...] Her favourite place to play was in the long hallway around or under a middle size table. The table was covered with a mostly yellow-red tablecloth with fringes. It had Slavic ornaments and floral prints. It was silky to touch. She remembers the smooth feeling as she glided her fingers following the threads. She loved to play under that table, especially with the fringes of the tablecloth.

She remembers that she learned how to braid and kept practising until she ruined the fringes. It was lots of fun and never boring staying under the table. She remembers the inner layout of the table, the nuts and the screws. She used to open and fasten them. And she remembers talking to her imaginary friend under the table. As a child, she was alone a lot, as she was the youngest child in the family and the only girl, so she missed having friends. So, her 'friend' was a great company, she never felt alone. The friend did not seem to have a gender, emerged from the sentence 'Now we…'. She remembers daydreaming a lot under the table and sharing everything with this 'Bogus' of hers. ('Under the Table' n.d., unknown)

In this story, it is not her parents or another adult that the child is missing. She longs for friends and so invents one who appears every time she needs to share something with someone. Imaginary friends are quite common in early and middle childhood, fulfilling important developmental tasks for children, especially if real partnerships are not available (Gleason 2013). As the youngest child, the only girl in the family, and one who is often alone at home, the narrator uses this strategy to deal with feelings of loneliness. Here, too, we see the narrative of unsupervised times as a time for creativity arise again: the child invents an imaginary friend but also creates playful activities using what is already there—a table and a tablecloth.

Unfortunately, no geopolitical information is included in this story. Hints, such as the tablecloth with Slavic ornaments, could point to a socialist country of origin, but we cannot be sure about this, which makes it difficult to analyse this memory story in terms of wider societal structures. We will return to the challenges of working with other people's memory stories in our final conclusions.

Final Discussion and an Outlook

We would like to end with some preliminary conclusions. First, our analysis showed how the patterns of unsupervised times present in our memories of growing up in the GDR—unsupervised times as perceived freedom and contentment, as responsibility and as loneliness—can be found in different geopolitical spaces and times and are therefore useful analytical lenses. In general, we conclude that unsupervised time is mainly constructed as perceived freedom and contentment in the analysed memory stories, although times of loneliness and responsibility are portrayed as well. The narratives we found across these three patterns show that during unsupervised times, important experiences for children's development take place: for example, being creative, imitating adults, breaking rules, and building communities with peers and siblings. We have also seen that the memories reveal many similarities across geopolitical boundaries, indicating that working with childhood memories can help bring more nuance to the often-stereotypical dichotomies between childhoods in 'the East' vs. 'the West'.

Furthermore, children in the analysed memory stories are constructed as active agents who have experiences, decide to act, are autonomous, and, often, organise themselves. And although this 'child as actor' perspective is nothing new for childhood studies in general, for a long time, it was not fully applied to research on children and childhood in formerly socialist countries. In those contexts, children were seen, instead, as passive receptors of education or even indoctrination through socialist educational institutions. Our analysis shows, though, that the concept of children's agency calls into question traditionalised, stereotypical images of Soviet/socialist childhoods as indoctrinated, institutionalised, and controlled. It makes visible the space for autonomous action within children's everyday lives in socialist societies.

Finally, we want to share some methodological considerations. We see collective memory work as a fertile reflexive method to access less-researched aspects of childhoods, in this case unsupervised times. Moreover, the Reconnect/Recollect memory archive provides an opportunity to access perspectives that are more typically excluded from prevailing tools of knowledge production, such as voices from post/socialist spaces.

While the archive makes accessible memories from a wide variety of geopolitical spaces, working with it is also fraught with challenges. In our own collective memory work, we have thought about our positionality then and now, and we have a great deal of knowledge about the specific situations but also the region. However, this contextual information is often missing when examining others' memories from the archive. This lack makes it more difficult to draw conclusions about societal structures and influences. But, for this reason, it is also easier to find fairly generalised patterns and similarities, as we did. In working with the memory archive, we must take care not to, once again, construct a uniform picture of childhoods in which diversity across geographic spaces is lost. Subtle differences between memories and explanations of them are more difficult to identify, not only due to the lack of contextual information but also due to our own positionality as German researchers who cannot or can only with difficulty understand certain allusions and self-evident facts from other contexts that are part of the memories. Here, on the one hand, cooperation with the authors of the memories or with people from the respective regions could help. On the other hand, case studies and in-depth analyses of selected memories could be an approach to deal with these difficulties in further research.

References

Badura, P. (2018). 'Healthy Adolescence in the Context of Leisure Time: The Role of Organised and Unstructured Leisure-Time Activities'. PhD Thesis, University of Groningen, https://research.rug.nl/en/publications/healthy-adolescence-in-the-context-of-leisure-time-the-role-of-or

Berndt, T. J. and G.W. Ladd (eds). (1989). *Peer Relationships in Child Development*. John Wiley and Sons

Corbin, J. M. and A. L. Strauss (2015). *Basics of Qualitative Research.* (4th edn.). Sage, https://doi.org/10.4135/9781452230153

Davies, B. and S. Gannon (eds). (2006). *Doing Collective Biography. Investigating the Production of Subjectivity*. Open University Press

Falkenberg, K., and N. Bernhard. (forthcoming). 'Kinder allein zu Haus. Kollektive Erinnerungsarbeit als forschungsmethodischer Zugang zu DDR-Kindheiten', in *Der andere Blick auf »den Osten«. Zum Paradigmenwechsel in der Ostdeutschlandforschung*, ed. by S. Matthäus. Transcript

Gaskins, S., W. Haight, and D. F. Lancy (2007). 'The Cultural Construction of Play', in *Play and Development: Evolutionary, Sociocultural and Functional Perspectives*, ed. by A. Göncü and S. Gaskins. (pp. 179–202). Lawrence Erlbaum, https://doi.org/10.4324/9780203936511

Geißler, G. and U. Wiegmann (1995). *Schule und Erziehung in der DDR*. Luchterhand

Gleason, T. R. (2013). 'Imaginary relationships', in *The Oxford Handbook of the Development of Imagination*, ed. by M. Taylor (pp. 251–71). Oxford University Press, https://doi.org/10.1093/oxfordhb/9780195395761.013.0017

Grunert, C., and H. H. Krüger (2006). *Kindheit und Kindheitsforschung in Deutschland: Forschungszugänge und Lebenslagen*. Verlag Barbara Budrich, https://doi.org/10.2307/j.ctvhktjs2

Günther, J. and F. Nestmann (2000). 'Quo vadis, Hausgemeinschaft? Zum Wandel nachbarschaftlicher Beziehungen in den östlichen Bundesländern'. *Gruppe. Interaktion.Organisation. Zeitschrift für Angewandte Organisationspsychologie*, 31(3), 321–37, http://dx.doi.org/10.1007/s11612-000-0028-x

Haug, F. (ed.) (1991). *Sexualisierung der Körper* (3rd edn.). Argument

Hoffmann, N. F. (2022). 'Peergroups im Kindes- und Jugendalter', in *Handbuch Kindheits- und Jugendforschung I*, ed. by H. H. Krüger, C. Grunert, K. Ludwig. (pp. 895–924). Springer VS, https://doi.org/10.1007/978-3-658-24777-5_31

Kirchhöfer, D. (1998). *Aufwachsen in Ostdeutschland. Langzeitstudie über Tagesläufe 10- bis 14jähriger Kinder*. Juventa

Kirchhöfer, D. (2000). 'Arbeit der Kinder im Kindheitskonzept der DDR-Gesellschaft', in *Die Arbeit der Kinder. Kindheitskonzept und Arbeitsteilung zwischen den Generationen*, ed. by H. Hengst and H. Zeiher. (pp. 189–208). Juventa

Mierendorff, J. (2019). 'Kindheit(en) in modernen Gesellschaften', in *Handbuch Philosophie der Kindheit*, ed. by J. Drerup and G. Schweiger. (pp. 26–34). J. B. Metzler, http://dx.doi.org/10.1007/978-3-476-04745-8_4

Millei, Z., I. Silova, and S. Gannon (2022). 'Thinking Through Memories of Childhood in (Post) Socialist Spaces: Ordinary Lives in Extraordinary Times'. *Children's Geographies*, 20(3), 324–37, https://doi.org/10.1080/14733285.2019.1648759

Noschis, K. (1992). 'Child Development Theory and Planning for Neighbourhood Play'. *Children's Environments*, 9(2), 3–9

Piaget, J. (2015 [1932]). *Das moralische Urteil des Kindes*. Klett-Cotta

Rixon, A., H. Lomax, and L. O'Dell (2019). 'Childhoods Past and Present: Anxiety and Idyll in Reminiscences of Childhood Outdoor Play and Contemporary Parenting Practices'. *Children's Geographies*, 17(5), 618–29, https://doi.org/10.1080/14733285.2019.1605047

Sharp, E. H., L. L. Caldwell, J. W. Graham, and T. A. Ridenour (2006). 'Individual Motivation and Parental Influence on Adolescents' Experiences of Interest in Free Time: A Longitudinal Examination'. *Journal of Youth and Adolescence*, 35, 340–53, https://doi.org/10.1007/s10964-006-9045-6

Silova, I., Z. Millei, and N. Piattoeva (2017). 'Interrupting the Coloniality of Knowledge and Being in Comparative Education: Post-Socialist and Post-Colonial Dialogues after the Cold War'. *Comparative Education Review*, 61(S1), S74–S102, https://doi.org/10.1086/690458

Silova, I., N. Piattoeva, and Z. Millei (eds) (2018). *Childhood and Schooling in (Post)Socialist Societies. Memories of Everyday Life*. Palgrave Macmillan, https://doi.org/10.1007/978-3-319-62791-5

Tenorth, H.-E. (2010). *Geschichte der Erziehung. Einführung in die Grundzüge ihrer neuzeitlichen Entwicklung* (5th edn.). Juventa

Teszenyi, E., A. Varga Nagy, and S. Pálfi (2022). 'Re-Imagining Socialist Childhoods: Changing Narratives of Spatial and Temporal (Dis)Orientations (Special Issue). *Journal of Childhood, Education and Society*, 3(3), https://doi.org/10.37291/2717638X.202233252

Valtin, R. (ed.) (2020). *Zur Entwicklung sozialkognitiver und moralischer Konzepte I. Was Kinder über Geheimnisse, Petzen und Strafe denken*. Berlin, https://doi.org/10.25656/01:20627

Nokia[1]

Nelli Piattoeva

She is sitting on the trolley bus going home from the city center after walking or meeting her friends. She turned seventeen a few months before and she came home to Russia from Finland where she studies, to spend the school summer break with her parents. This summer she started living on her own and she bought herself a used mobile phone—a NOKIA. Its cover is dark violet with a barely visible black ornament. The phone has a short antenna and a very tiny, grey screen. She does not remember if this is the kind of color that she really wished for, but here it is, as the range of used phones on offer was probably not that wide. In any case this does not matter at all because she has a phone, which is the most expensive thing she has ever bought on her own, and this time she was not asking her parents for permission.

The trolleybus is packed, as always. She is standing next to many people traveling home from work to their apartments. She is carrying her mobile phone in her bag. She feels its presence all the time as the phone is heavier than anything else she has in that bag. There is no reason for her to carry the phone around: calling anyone from a Finnish phone number while visiting Russia, even if technically possible, would be way too expensive for her pocket. Someone next to her stands up to leave the trolleybus and she can finally sit down. She keeps the bag next to her, holding it tight, because a very precious thing lies in it undiscovered. No one around knows what a treasure she's carrying. Why not let them know? She seizes the moment, opens the bag, and takes the phone out, pretending that it just rang.

She presses the green 'answer button' and starts talking to an imagined interlocutor. It might be in Russian or Finnish, she does not remember anymore.

---

1   This is a childhood memory produced as part of the Reconnect/Recollect project discussed in the introduction to this book.

She pretends to engage in a very casual, relaxed way, while being very worried that she would soon be discovered. She talks for a minute or less and then 'hangs up', putting the phone back into the bag. She is not looking around, pretending that for her, talking on the phone on public transport is a mundane matter, nothing to pay special attention to. But, she hopes so badly to be noticed: she comes from a better world, she does not belong here. She is just visiting, even though, the truth is, that she's on an old, packed trolleybus traveling home like anyone else.

Blackberry Picking[1]

Rahim Rahimov

It was the late 1980s and he was around 8–9 years old in the town of Imishli in a Muslim-majority, Turkic-speaking Azerbaijan—a republic of the former Soviet Union. He used to go for blackberry picking during the summer with his parents, brother, uncles, aunts and cousins. They would do blackberry picking at a forest near the Araz river during the summer school holidays. The area was not far from the USSR-Iran border and the river was also a natural border for both countries. Iran was on the other side of the river, while this side of the river was also home to a Soviet military base.

The forest was made up of dense thickets of blackberry bushes. They wore dresses with long sleeves. The long sleeves protected their arms against spiky blackberry bushes pinching them. They also served as protection from bees. Alongside blackberry picking, he and his cousins played there, and had lunch. This lunch was hilarious in a party atmosphere, like a picnic, which was not very common to the community in particular at that time. And they played a hide-and-seek game but in a different way. They found blackberry bushes with bigger and ripe blackberries simultaneously picking berries and hiding there and others trying to find them.

Yet the ripe black and unripe red blackberries made him particularly joyful. The colorful berries represented a little but important shine to his child life, which otherwise might be characterized as not very colorful.

They went there in the afternoons and came back home in the evening. They all got on one big vehicle, which was normally used to carry produce to markets. The vehicle had two blue dolphins painted on its sides. Before going

---

1 This is a childhood memory produced as part of the Reconnect/Recollect project discussed in the introduction to this book.

for blackberry picking, they had arranged a kind of carpet on the vehicle floor to sit on.

On the way home in the dark, his mother pointed to the lights appearing in the dark at a distance, saying that maybe those are the homes of their extended relatives that were left on the Iranian part when the Soviet-Iranian border was shut, and the Araz river became the border or dividing line rather than only a river. By the way, the word 'Araz' symbolizes division for most Azerbaijanis and a lot of works are associated with Araz in the Azerbaijani culture, in particular, poems and literature.

At home, his mother as well as aunts would make jam and compotes from the blackberry. He was happy about that not because he liked the jam but because his dad liked it. This meant they would again go for blackberry picking.

12. Transcending the Border:
Memory, Objects, and Alternative Memorialisation in Cold-War Childhoods

Ivana Polić

By analysing adult-generated childhood memories assembled in the online memory archive of the Reconnect/Recollect project, this chapter looks at the multidimensional function of objects in childhood memories that challenge binary Cold-War, border-centred frameworks traditionally represented in scholarship of the time period. More specifically, it examines the role of objects in both trying to imagine or envision those on the 'other side' of the adult-imposed borders as well as ideas of 'self' as pertinent to this process. The rich spectrum of shared experiences points to the critical importance of childhood memory in decolonising the studies of lived and imagined childhoods in the second half of the past century and thus transgresses these borders to provide a platform for future research on childhood history and memory.

Under US President James Carter, the United States boycotted the 1980 Olympics. A boy remembers the news that day. He had already fallen in love with Russian novels, especially Dostoyevsky's work and this Tolstoy too. Now this news he watched with his father in the comfort of the family living room. He wondered about the USSR. What was this USSR? He thought, what is life there like? Similar, different? There was so much red on the screen in Moscow. Red was not just a colour, but a culture, or so it

© 2024 Ivana Polić, CC BY-NC 4.0   https://doi.org/10.11647/OBP.0383.12

seemed. Communism, what was this belief system? Was it so different? It was intriguing to imagine himself in this other place. [...] For unknown reasons, the so-called 'other' fascinated, did not repulse and terrify him [...]. The love of books, already extant, grew exponentially [...] they offered thoughts of distant lands, distant times, and of a world unexplored. ('Love of Books' n.d.)[1]

Shared by one of the participants of the Reconnect/Recollect project, this testimony might at first glance be considered unexpected or unusual in many ways. As a child growing up in the 1980s United States, this was the memory one of the participants chose to share as part of the effort to remember the pivotal moments of his childhood as contextualised within the broader geopolitical climate. That the memory mentions clear indicators of the Cold-War atmosphere is perhaps not as surprising, given the omnipresent political and media language that permeated public domains on both sides of the Iron Curtain (Peacock 2014; Rawnsley 2016). However, despite the strong ideological content that surrounded the child in the given moment, the response that it evoked in him turned out to be exactly the opposite of division, borders, or antagonism. On the contrary, it was the feelings of interest and curiosity about the 'other side' that emerged as a guiding force behind not only that moment in the participant's childhood but also the signpost for narrating this memory in adult life.

An aspect that ties this memory together with others that exhibit a similar trajectory is the centrality of objects. Namely, in these adult-narrated stories, objects are the prompts that propel participants towards actively seeking knowledge about 'the other' and, in many stories, become the central points of the narratives. This chapter seeks to explore these kind of objects—ones that invite alternative narratives of interconnected experiences that do not fit into the predominant 'East vs. West' paradigm. In doing so, it approaches childhoods that took place in the second half of the twentieth century as interconnected

---

1   See https://coldwarchildhoods.org/memories/ for the online memory archive. When using excerpts from participants' personal memories, I include the title of the memory story from which it was taken. Many memories are written in the third person so as to facilitate their contextualisation.

rather than separate and isolated research spheres. It shows that borders on which the geopolitical world insisted and the associations which saturated the public sphere did not always and necessarily translate into children's worlds, hearts, and minds. Moreover, the interrelationships between autobiographical memories and objects as integral components of those memories accentuate the similarities of human experience in those turbulent times. Such connections ultimately challenge the idea of lived childhoods as pertinent to national boundaries and open up space for further cross-cultural and transnational research on the histories and meanings of childhoods.

Consequently, this chapter aims to address the following questions: What is the significance of everyday objects for the alternative memorialisation of 'the other' that troubles traditional, polarised Cold-War historical accounts? What is the connection between objects and children's idea of 'self' as envisioned through such object-centred memories? Finally, how can adults' recollections contribute to de-colonising the study of childhood and bring together various alternative and contradictory narratives, ideas, and stories that otherwise do not fit into the official, Cold War-dominated research framework?

Two main sections constitute this chapter. The first briefly lays out the approach of memory as a method to understand lived childhood experience, and it also situates the contribution within and as a response to the existing scholarship on lived childhoods in the Cold-War period. The second section starts by delineating alternative narratives of 'the other' and how these might be brought together through the interaction with and meaning ascribed to everyday objects of material culture. It then focuses on the idea of 'self' that also emerged in the process of constructing knowledge of 'the other' in the participants' various cultures. Taken together, these findings have the potential of opening up further possibilities in the wider scholarly effort to decolonise the study of childhood memory, childhood experience, and identity writing.

Research Approach and Methodology

Within the broader body of English-language scholarship pertaining to the historical periodisation of the Cold-War era (1945–1990), studies on childhood history and childhood experience remain fairly scarce. These works often attend to the relationship between the idea of nurturing patriotic young citizens and its integration into educational programs in the United States during the 1950s and 1960s (Grieve 2018; Hartman 2008; Holt 2014; Kordas 2015). Most anchor their methodological approaches in Western standards of 'normative' childhood and pedagogical and developmental principles. On the other hand, rare studies of socialist childhoods tend to adopt a top-down perspective, considering the ways in which the state envisioned and moulded young patriots through education and daily governance to be a kind of ideological indoctrination (Kelly 2007; Kirschenbaum 2013; Peacock 2014). An even smaller body of work compares childhoods across cultures and national boundaries (Bronfenbrenner and Condry 1970), while only a few scholars so far have explored alternative narratives and bottom-up reactions that challenged the socialist, state-crafted image of the child (Aydarova et al. 2016; Peacock 2014; Raleigh 2013; Winkler 2019).

In rethinking these binary frameworks over the past decade, scholars have increasingly turned to memory as a method for 'de-colonising' childhood studies. Memory, including in the form of collective biography, offers space to living subjects' own accounts of daily moments that complicate the bipolar, geopolitically-conditioned narratives (Silova, Piattoeva, Millei 2018). The power and strength of collective memory work comes from the connections and meanings forged between particular fragments of memory rather than from the establishment of a uniform past-present trajectory (Ouma 2020, p. 43). Because such non-linear narration allows for a rich variety of memory snippets, it helps participants to resist reaching for the prevailing Cold-War binaries and, therefore, asserts itself as a tool for studying 'counter-hegemonic' memorialisation (Boehmer 2000, p. 756, cited in Silova, Piattoeva and Millei 2018, p. 7). This chapter, by rejecting and de-constructing the border as a methodological starting point

(Mezzandra and Neilson 2013), explores the interconnection between the variety of childhoods as lived on both geopolitical poles.

Memories collected through the Reconnect/Recollect project serve as the main bulk of sources for this study. In 2019, the project held collective memory workshops online and in four different locations: Helsinki, Mexico City, Berlin, and Riga. Attendees included researchers and artists who grew up on both sides of the so-called 'Iron Curtain' during the historical designation of the Cold-War era and the decades after. They shared memories from their childhoods via academic discourse, art (travelling exhibitions, visual art, and performance), and collective (auto)biography. In doing so, participants created dialogue that enabled them to build many bridges across multiple divides (such as East and West, socialist and post-socialist) and to recognise commonalities in the meanings within their lived childhoods. The childhood memories in written format were then archived online and are publicly available through the project website (https://www.coldwarchildhoods.org). This chapter's analysis centres on memory stories wherein narrators describe the many ways/visions/imaginations through which they constructed their ideas of those living on the other side of the geopolitical divide. It is concerned with the definition of borders and the cognitive efforts to transgress them.

Many archived memories that present non-binary views of 'the other' or 'the other side' feature objects, such as different types of books, radios, cassettes, televisions, clocks, or pieces of clothing. The observation that these objects in most cases appeared central to the participants' formation of their memory stories prompted this research.[2] This chapter calls attention to the role of objects in memories in general, and in alternative memorialisation in particular. My analysis combines the definitions of objects advanced by Elizabeth Wood (2009a) and Richard Heersmink (2018). Wood (2009a) sees objects as physical things (including those not necessarily intended for consumption by children) that, with engagement over time and in particular contexts,

---

2 Memories referring to the post-1990 decades were not included in the research for this chapter as its scope is the period when Cold-War propaganda about the opposing blocs was being actively disseminated in private and public spaces via various mediums.

enable individuals to configure a sense of self (p. 153). Heersmink (2018) extends this definition by emphasising 'evocative' objects—those most closely linked to 'past personal experiences' that 'trigger and sometimes constitute' emotionally imbued autobiographical reflections (p. 1830).

The argument I make is twofold. First, merging these two approaches, I regard the exchange between the narrators and the objects in their stories as 'experiential transaction[s]' (Wood 2009a, p. 155) wherein the different 'intrinsic' (rather than simply external) meaning of the objects for each participant is what makes these objects 'evocative' over time (to Heersmink 2018, p. 1830). In that sense, I make the case that objects serve as 'technology of memory' (Wood 2009a, p. 157) insofar as they shape the trajectory of these memory stories: it is precisely through these deeper interactions with artifacts of material culture that the child-subjects forged the relationships of meaning that help us to understand the focal points of the adults' memory stories. Second, I argue that the engagement with objects conditioned two critical aspects of alternative memorialisation: (1) perceptions of those on 'the other' side of the Cold-War imposed borders; and (2) the participants' ideas of the 'self' as contingent upon the process of learning about 'the other'. These findings stress the significance of objects in memory stories as guideposts that interconnect these two identity markers in memory studies pertaining to childhood experiences.

Envisioning 'the Other' and 'Self' Through Objects in Memory Stories

Throughout the workshops that aimed to bring into conversation people who grew up divided by a variety of Cold War-imposed borders, participants were encouraged to think about their own memorable childhood experiences. Each contributor wrote down their initial recollections, then, with the help and questions of others, began to de- and re-construct these memory fragments in more detail. With each new round of writing, participants became more aware of the nuanced context that pieced these memories together. One major theme was, of course, the extent to which the political, economic, cultural, or religious setting of their lived childhood influenced the shape and mode of memory narration.

Many of those memories, perhaps not surprisingly, contained vivid associations of borders and divisions between the East and West as well as the language of Cold-War propaganda that penetrated children's daily lives in a myriad of ways. One participant, who had grown up in the 1950s United States, for example, remembered his family building a nuclear bomb shelter and his school making students practise 'duck and cover' drills, all of which caused him 'nightmares of nuclear Holocaust' ('The Nuclear Threat' n.d.). Another, who grew up in East Berlin in the 1970s and lived very close to the border wall that divided the city, recalled knowing that she needed to be extra careful not to play in the proximity of the wall where the border-patrol guards were stationed ('Divided Games' n.d.). In another example, the narrator recollected her family's first international trip in 1968 and how, on the way from Hungary to Czechoslovakia, they passed a number of tanks related to the recent Soviet invasion of Czechoslovakia: 'She remembers the silence in the car very clearly, the tanks in the rain, and the feeling she had: it was not fear, she could not comprehend what was going on. […] but it was dark and sad' ('Trabant' n.d.). These memories point to the various dimensions through which the Cold-War political propaganda and binary rhetoric asserted its presence in lived and internalised childhood experiences.

However, upon closer inspection, a substantial number of memories revealed children who questioned, expressed unconformity with, or resisted the Cold-War narratives to which they were constantly exposed, particularly those referring to the 'other side'. Common to many such memory stories is a focus on different kinds of physical objects. For instance, a workshop participant who grew up in the United States remembered the 'Doomsday Clock' poster and immediately associated it with the Cold War ('Doomsday Clock' n.d.). Another began his story with a memory of books by Russian writers, particularly Tolstoy and Dostoevsky, which he possessed and enjoyed reading as a teenager ('Love of Books' n.d.). A rotating globe and a cassette containing Sting's song 'Russians' came to mind for another participant who came of age in the 1980s United States ('Sting Cassette' n.d.). One woman, who grew up in a small industrial town in Kraków,

Poland, remembered her favorite activity: waiting for pen-pal letters from the opposite side of the 'Iron Curtain' ('A Letter from Florida' n.d.). Yet another participant from Poland recalled colourful items of clothing she saw coming from abroad and worn by a girl from 'the other side' ('Material Culture' n.d.). This spectrum enables us to grasp the variety of object types that appear prominently in the stories of the narrators. Specifically, it is through references to these objects that the memory solidified and developed in personal ways that contest the binary representations of 'the other' that were widespread in the public sphere.

The 'Other'

Throughout the stories, writers employ a certain mode of narration in relation to the objects that catalyse the story development. Their initial interaction with the objects usually included processing through sensory experience. For instance, the participant who enjoyed Russian novels readily commented: 'Something about the *tactile* nature of the books brought a sense of comfort, yet also a sense of disconcertment' (Love of Books n.d., emphasis in original). While looking at the pictures that came with the pen-pal letters from abroad, the Polish narrator of that story vividly recalled the excitement upon touching the pictures' surface: 'Pictures had such a *smooth texture* and they even *shone* gently. They were printed on Kodak paper, with the Kodak logo on the back side. The quality of the photos was stunning to her' ('Letter from Florida' n.d., emphasis in original). For others, the primary sensation associated with the objects was visual, whether looking at the 'Doomsday clock' poster ('Doomsday Clock' n.d.) or gazing in awe at the *colourful clothes* worn by children from the 'other side' ('Material Culture' n.d., emphasis in original). Hearing music was an especially powerful sensation for the participant from the US who recalled that 'The *melody* is set to a theme of Prokofiev, and that's when he really started to become curious' ('Sting Cassette' n.d., emphasis in original). Thus, we see that the memories began their trajectory with reflections on the physical and aesthetic aspects—touch, sight, and sound—of the object itself. The presence of the object in a given surrounding, coupled with some of its physical properties, introduces a certain idea of 'the other' and allows it to unfold.

As the narratives progress, the external properties and intended practical functions of the object give way to a different and more profound construction of meaning and purpose formed primarily through the particular context of interaction with the object. The encounters with the majority of these objects occurred in a space or setting that displayed or otherwise hinted at the division of the Cold-War worlds, such as the school classroom, family room with television or radio at home, or international summer camp. Nevertheless, participants recognised that engagement with the objects within the network of their social environment aroused feelings of interest, curiosity, and even admiration towards the 'other side'. They did not succumb to the then-common attitudes of hostility or silence towards those people and things on the opposite side of the border. The range of feelings that the participants describe strikes one as enormously rich and, as such, shows the possibilities of object-centred memory study as a method to research the impact of and response to the often unidirectional and politically saturated public narratives and discourse.

For instance, a childhood memory from a participant who grew up in Soviet Armenia but whose parents worked as medical doctors in Algeria revolved around what she called 'Catalogue of the Outside World'. She recalled being told that the presents her parents would bring each time upon their return were 'ordered through catalogues from France'. Whereas the narrator's first contact with these catalogues involved observing all the different articles and 'beautiful peoples' on their vividly coloured thin pages, they are the objects that become the 'mediator' (Wood 2009a, p. 160) of the more complex cognitive process that followed the initial sensory processing of the catalogue's intended function. She would make sure no one was around, then spent hours carefully studying each catalogue, 'secretly looking at the forbidden world'. Although she knew that the world the catalogue represented was 'forbidden' and she could not rationally explain her enchantment with the object—hence the clandestine consumption—these hours of content enjoyment and dissection made the represented 'other' look quite 'attractive' ('Catalogue of the Outside World' n.d.). Similarly, a memory story about a girlhood in Romania describes spending the day on the Black Sea beach and, after arriving home, 'flipping the pages of an illustrated children's book her cousin had brought from a trip to France' that reminded her of her time at the beach ('Naked at the Beach' n.d.). She and her friend could see 'dark-skinned children living in a tropical rainforest' in the photographs, but what struck the narrator while looking at them was the similarity between her experience and that of these children: both enjoyed summertime beach excursions while having no clothes on. After dwelling all day on this shared pleasure, she noted that the 'children from the illustrated book felt closer, like an unspoken presence in the room'. While the illustrated book had 'exotic' origins and clearly indicated a very different world, the narrator's interaction with it—a transaction between the object and the subject in a unique social setting (after a hot day spent at the beach)—was what produced the feelings of similarity with, followed by closeness to and even friendship with the children in the photographs.

In the home setting, the 'other' was sometimes as close as behind the button that led to the 'forbidden' TV channel. A workshop participant that spent her childhood years in East Germany remembered that, even though she was not supposed to watch the West German channel, she could not resist pressing the button that would take her to the other side full of possibilities: a colourful program of West German cartoons. In fact, she titled and formed the memory narrative around the presence and hidden function of that 'forbidden' button:

Back in the 1980s her family had a TV standing in their living room with several programme buttons. Two of them were marked with coloured dots—those were the two DDR programmes. Her parents told the kids that they were only allowed to watch those two, either the green one or the yellow button/programme. When the girl was at home alone after school one afternoon, she decided to switch to one of the other—forbidden—buttons to see what this was about. And there it was: colourful afternoon West German TV programme! She remembers being totally excited about watching a short cartoon that was shown between different broadcasts ('Mainzelmännchen'—little dwarfs that barely say more than 'Good evening' in a special way). At the same time she felt guilty because she did something that was explicitly forbidden. ('Forbidden Buttons' n.d.)

Other participants recalled situations wherein the objects that prompted contemplation were sent to them or brought to their attention by a representative of the 'other side'. Interaction with these objects initiated a cognitive process which, in turn, created enticing and alluring associations with the unknown. The narrator who grew up in a small Polish industrial town, for instance, wrote of taking part in pen-pal exchange with a campground-owning family in the United States. When she received her first letter from across the ocean in 1986, she did not know a word of English. However, the letter contained three colourful photographs of a family from Florida that showed them gathered together on a pier by the sea. The narrator remembered 'staring at them for hours trying to see every detail of a distant world', absorbing all the colours and facial expressions. To her, the photograph 'looked like a part of a show' ('A Letter From Florida' n.d.). Similar excitement and awe for 'the other side' was felt by another girl from Poland when she participated in an international summer camp and met a camper from Canada. She recalled that, at that time, the 'West' already looked like 'paradise', a feeling that was confirmed in this encounter. The narrator specifically remembered:

her clothes, so colourful, made of delicate fabric. She had two pairs of corduroy jeans, one violet, one pink. And also she was very active and athletic. She could do side straddle hops etc. Truly a princess for the kids from the Soviet bloc! ('Material Culture' n.d.)

These examples demonstrate well the variety of feelings associated with 'the other', which ranged from interest and enchantment to wonder and awe. They also show the objects acting as mediators, enabling the transactions that yielded these positive associations. In other words, we can understand the objects in these stories as 'technologies of memory' (Wood 2009a, p. 157) that create cognitive space wherein individuals create meaningful experiences that construct the story of their own childhoods. A closer look at the central narrational points further illuminates the cultivation of these counter-hegemonic visions.

When analysing the function of these objects, it is important to note that not all were everyday objects made particularly for children's consumption. On the contrary, most of the objects featured in these narratives were those intended to meet general consumer needs and preferences. Objects like shopping catalogues, music cassettes, and books targeted not only the young but also an older population. In fact, one could also argue that some objects, like shopping catalogues or novels, were aimed primarily at adult consumers. Moreover, one notices a distinction with regards to the objects' origins and distribution radius. One group of objects, like books or a globe, were normally found in everyday settings universally and might, then, be said to span or bridge the geopolitical divide. The second group of objects, including particular items of clothing, children's picture books, Kodak-produced photographs, or selected television programs, were produced for a certain region or country and, therefore, might deliberately utilise certain tropes of imagined division.

Regardless of the external function, distribution area, physical characteristics, or target audience of these objects, it is the moments of interaction with them in a given social environment that created what Elizabeth Wood calls the objects' higher, 'intrinsic' meaning (Wood 2009a). This intrinsic value, because it is ascribed through the individual's unique social context, varies from person to person, which means that the experiential transaction is always a different experience for each individual (ibid., p. 155). For instance, one participant remembers the 'Doomsday Clock' poster as an object that incited both fear and curiosity at the same time, but this can by no means act as an indicator of any other subject's experience of the poster; each person's contextualisation of the transactional setting would not correspond to that of any other. Nevertheless, the element that brings these memories together is the persistence of feelings ascribed to 'the other' and the continual significance of these feelings for the permanent place in the participants' memory repertoires. These are the qualities that, in any case, transcend the external properties of the objects and instead make them biographical or, to recall Heersmink's term, 'evocative' (2018, p. 1830). Indeed, the objects are not arbitrarily interwoven through these narratives but instead trigger distinctive emotional activity that serves as a constitutive substance of the memories themselves and the patterns through which they are laid out to form the stories about 'the others'.

The 'Self'

Learning about 'the other' through objects suggests another major thread that connects these experiences and memories—understanding and learning about 'the self'. Ideas of 'self' as remembered by the participants are characterised by feelings of curiosity, inquisitiveness, and grit. As such, they are important in the analysis of this interactive process. Participants consistently referred to their own desires as children to explore and push the boundaries imposed by the adult world while trying to imagine 'the other'. These were the main elements around which the constitution of 'the self' revolved. Instead of settling for the readily accessible concepts, they recalled actively questioning the uniform and predominantly negative representations of 'the other' in the context of the Cold War and attempting to actively and creatively visualise the lives of those who dwelled on the 'other side' of these real and/or imagined borders. Such recollections from stories discussed throughout this chapter show that the narrators, as a consequence of interacting with objects, construct themselves as people open to new concepts. They think of themselves as capable of seeking knowledge of and consistently and actively envisioning 'the other' in non-hegemonic ways.

The emergence of ideas about 'the self' through imagining 'the other' proceeds in the following way. Initially, children's eagerness to explore those unfamiliar places and people was aroused by their interaction with objects, but knowledge about those places and people was, for some reason, inaccessible or restricted. Some imaginings of 'the other' stayed in the abstract form, such as for those participants who wondered about 'distant lands', what communism and its 'belief system' were like, or if life was 'different' elsewhere. Others, who were able to meet or otherwise catch a glimpse of real people from 'the other side', either in person or through other kinds of objects (from printed pictures, television, or magazines), scrutinised these images which, in turn, became archived in their memories. Since narrators foregrounded these objects in their storytelling, one notices two types of dynamics at play in that regard: active physical contact with the objects through sensory input as well as the cognitive responses that the transaction inspired with regards to 'the other'.

Both produced a myriad of associations and feelings that, in turn, grounded each participant's sense of themselves within their respective environments.

While physical interaction implied an encounter via one of the physical senses (touch, hearing, smell, or sight), the subsequent cognitive processing was critical to the development of participants' own investigative attitude. This manifested both in mental visions of 'the other' as well as an active interest for further knowledge. Such is well illustrated by the narrator who described the motivating effect of Sting's song on a radio cassette: 'He was always curious as to why they were constantly given information that painted a bleak picture [but after listening to the song on the cassette...] He had *no choice* but to investigate' ('Sting Cassette' n.d., emphasis in original). Likewise, the memory story centred on books by Russian authors recalls them as both a source of information and the springboard for additional knowledge pursuit, all of which worked to establish these sentiments as integral to the narrator's own being: 'Their physical presence, the tactile experience of them always brought comfort and questions simultaneously. They served as surrogate teachers, friends, and travelled to places distant, exotic, and mysterious ('Love of Books' n.d.). This particular example exposes well the interdependent nature of relationship between 'self' and 'other', where the seeking of knowledge about 'the other' constitutes the basis for forming ideas of 'self' in adult storytelling.

Memories of self-formation through objects help us to understand children's positions within and across their respective societies, independently of Cold-War geopolitical identifiers. Indeed, narrators repeatedly identified curiosity as the key attribute that enabled them to challenge the scarcity of information and to act on their desire to know. This demonstrates the capacity of children to disturb their environments, even those characterised by a highly controlled influx of politically sensitive, adult-managed information. For example, although one participant from East Germany knew that her parents would not let her go to West Berlin to participate in the music quiz she learned about by secretly listening to a West German radio station, she still 'prepared an argument' for the conversation with them ('Secret Radio' n.d.). Similarly, the girl who watched the West German television program 'hidden' behind the 'forbidden' red button on the remote control in her East German living room decided to confront her parents about their unwillingness to let her access it. She remembers 'telling her mother that she had watched the cartoon and asked her why she wasn't allowed to watch something nice like that' ('Forbidden Button' n.d.). The objects in these contexts highlight not only the exigency of creating ideas about 'the self' through investigation of the unknown but also the ways in which that process sheds light onto larger social configurations in which children, evidently, were not supposed to partake.

Recognising these properties that abet the creation of ideas related to the 'self' through object-mediated activities is another crucial facet that establishes a clear linkage across these memories from various global settings. Even though the memories are told from the adult point of view, the ways in which participants describe their action against the adults' ideology vis-a-vis their engagement with objects is an important facet of memory stories. The value of these subjective accounts, in fact, points to children's role in troubling the dynamics of the adult and, specifically, the Cold War-partitioned world. Thus, such findings add to the scholarship that strives to reorient the problem of children's agency as an adult-imposed construct by focusing on its implications in children's immediate settings and acknowledging its ability to transgress adult-imposed boundaries (Gallagher 2019; Maza 2020).

These collections of adult-generated memories of childhood have shown the properties of objects as a 'technology of memory' (Wood 2009b, p. 121) that, in the narrators' storytellings, facilitate not only the development of relationships between themselves and adult-designated political 'others' but also realisations about how that quest forged their own ideas of 'self.' In such a setting, objects serve as nodal points in decolonising the history of lived 'Cold-War' childhoods from geopolitically imposed binaries and divisions. It would be too far-reaching to argue that such moments determined the very trajectory of professional and/or personal lives for these participants, but their own recollections highlight the essential role of objects in the construction of the geopolitically situated 'self' both in their memories of childhood and their identity writing in adulthood.

Conclusion: Troubling the Binary Cold-War Conditioned Narratives

The multilayered insights presented here open up new research frontiers for examining memory as a scientific instrument and a window into histories of childhood, particularly of those whose voices have been silenced or otherwise neglected due to the attention given to hegemonic geopolitical actors and global diplomatic and economic trajectories (Silova et al. 2017). Traditional approaches to childhood history frame growing up during the Cold War as an 'engineering project', designed and managed by the state leadership for the purposes of producing 'ideal' youngsters who will uphold the ideological principles of the nation. This chapter contests such top-down perspectives by acknowledging and validating personal histories that, through childhood memories, do not conform with such authoritarian narratives. Despite the everyday exposure to propaganda that drew clear lines between 'us' and 'them', the narrators of these memories attest to an increasing desire among children to know, understand, and even admire those on the 'other side'. Their voices speak loudly to the gap of historical knowledge that only human research participants can help us address. In such a context, this chapter calls a complication of the concept of real and imaginary borders as the framework which, until recently, has dominated the study of the Cold-War period.

Specifically, analysing objects as the anchors of memory stories reveals their role in prompting interrogations of the unidimensional image of 'the other' rooted in Cold-War rhetoric. Objects' interactive capacities allowed the vision of 'the other' to acquire much more creative, mystical, seductive, and even pleasurable qualities. Objects offered opportunities for bridging the knowledge gap—the limited information offered within the participants' social networks—and, in most cases, inspired further investigation about 'the other.' This, in turn, fuelled the construction of individuals' ideas of 'self' through the process of information-seeking initiated by sentiments of acquisitiveness and wonder.

These recollections affirm the potentials of adult-narrated childhood experiences as research data that re-establish personal accounts as valuable tools in destabilising collective, politically shaped, and adult-centred history-writing. It argues for the unquestionable importance of childhood as a remembered lived experience despite it being a rarely studied aspect of history itself. This chapter has shown that memories make a strong case for positioning subjective accounts as pillars for decolonising and re-configuring top-down historical accounts that revolve around East-West geopolitical categorisations. Academic research that facilitates such reflections in the form of memory workshops can also provide opportunities, spaces, and useful tools for personal introspection in the ever-present quest for knowledge and identity.

References

Aydarova, E., Z. Millei, N. Piattoeva, and I. Silova. (2016). 'Revisiting Pasts, Reimagining Futures: Memories of (Post) Socialist Childhood and Schooling'. *European Education*, 48(3), 159–69, https://doi.org/10.1080/1056 4934.2016.1223977

Bronfenbrenner, U., and J. C. Condry Jr. (1970). *Two Worlds of Childhood: US and USSR*. New York: Russell Sage Foundation

Gallagher, M. (2019). 'Rethinking Children's Agency: Power, Assemblages, Freedom and Materiality. *Global Studies of Childhood*, 9(3), 188–99, https://doi.org/10.1177/2043610619860993

Grieve, V. M. (2018). *Little Cold Warriors: American Childhood in the 1950s*. Oxford University Press, https://doi.org/10.1093/oso/9780190675684.001.0001

Hartman, A. (2008). *Education and the Cold War: The Battle for the American School*. New York: Palgrave Macmillan

Heersmink, R. (2018). 'The Narrative Self, Distributed Memory, and Evocative Objects'. *Philosophical Studies*, 175, 1829–849, https://doi.org/10.1007/s11098-017-0935-0

Holt, M. I. (2014). *Cold War Kids: Politics and Childhood in Postwar America, 1945–1960*. University Press of Kansas, https://doi.org/10.1353/book45088

Kirschenbaum, L. A. (2013). *Small Comrades: Revolutionizing Childhood in Soviet Russia, 1917–1932*. Routledge

Kordas, A. M. (2015). *The Politics of Childhood in Cold War America*. Routledge, https://doi.org/10.4324/9781315655208

Maza, S. (2020). 'The Kids Aren't All Right: Historians and the Problem of Childhood'. *American Historical Review*, 125(4), 1261–285, https://doi.org/10.1093/ahr/rhaa380

Mezzadra, S. and B. Neilson. (2013). *Border as Method, or, the Multiplication of Labor*. Duke University Press, https://doi.org/10.2307/j.ctv1131cvw

Ouma, C. E. (2020). *Childhood in Contemporary Diasporic African Literature*. Springer International Publishing, https://doi.org/10.1007/978-3-030-36256-0

Peacock, M. (2014). *Innocent Weapons: The Soviet and American Politics of Childhood in the Cold War*. UNC Press Books, https://doi.org/10.5149/northcarolina/9781469618579.001.0001

Raleigh, D. J. (2013). *Soviet Baby Boomers: An Oral History of Russia's Cold War Generation*. Oxford University Press

Rawnsley, G. D. (2016). *Cold-War Propaganda in the 1950s*. Springer, https://doi.org/10.1007/978-1-349-27082-8

Silova, I., Z. Millei, and N. Piattoeva. (2017) 'Interrupting the Coloniality of Knowledge and Being in Comparative Education: Post-Socialist and Post-Colonial Dialogues after the Cold War'. *Comparative Education Review*, 61(S1), S74–S102, https://doi.org/10.1086/690458

Silova, I., N. Piattoeva, and Z. Millei. (2018.) *Childhood and Schooling in (Post) Socialist Societies. Memories of Everyday Life*. London: Palgrave MacMillan, https://doi.org/10.1007/978-3-319-62791-5

Winkler, M. (2019). 'Children on Display: Children's History, Socialism, and Photography'. *Jahrbücher für Geschichte Osteuropas*. (H. 1), 3–10

Wood, E. (2009a). 'Saving Childhood in Everyday Objects'. *Childhood in the Past*, 2(1), 151–62, https://doi.org/10.1179/cip.2009.2.1.151

—— (2009b). 'The Matter and Meaning of Childhood through Objects', in *Technologies of Memory in the Arts*, ed. by L. Plate and A. Smelik. (pp. 120–131). Palgrave Macmillan, https://doi.org/10.1057/9780230239562_8

Snowflake[1]

Iveta Silova

Her most favorite New Year costume was made with the participation of all family members, which made it very special. The girl's mother, who worked as a nurse in the local hospital, brought home some medical gauze from work. It was then washed and heavily starched to create a ballerina-like tutu, which was a part of the snowflake look. The girl's grandmother sewed the costume, adding a sparkly silver garland from the New Year's tree—carefully attaching it to the edges of the tutu. But the most magical part was her father's construction of a snowflake crown! It was made of the silver lining from his cigarette boxes, carefully unfolded and straightened out, then glued onto the cardboard and cut and shaped into a delicate crown. The cigarette smell faintly emanated from the crown, but it did not bother the girl at all. It was a familiar smell associated with her father and it was comforting. It was as if her father was with the girl during all rehearsals and performances! The girl wore the costume with great joy and pride—she knew that nobody else would have exactly the same costume, although there would be many other snowflakes at the New Year's celebrations in the kindergarten.

---

1   This is a childhood memory produced as part of the Reconnect/Recollect project discussed in the introduction to this book.

Photographs of Iveta Silova dressed as a snowflake at her kindergarten New Year's party in Soviet Latvia, n.d. From Iveta Silova's family archive.

New Year's Frog[1]

Nelli Piattoeva

New Year celebrations in kindergartens and schools were common across the Soviet Union. The girl's frog costume consists of a newly purchased white-and-green dress, a pair of gloves and a hat sewed by her mother. The gloves and the hat were made from grandmother's green satin coat lining.

1 This is a childhood memory produced as part of the Reconnect/Recollect project discussed in the introduction to this book.

Photographs of Nelli Piattoeva dressed as a frog for a New Year's party, n.d. From Nelli Piattoeva's family archive.

13. Anarchive and Arts-Based Research:
Upcycling Rediscovered Memories and Materials

Raisa Foster

Humans living in postindustrial societies have slowly realised that the ecological crisis is a crisis of our culture. Therefore, to address the ecocrisis, we need to understand our place as humans in a radically new way. We cannot continue to elevate ourselves above the rest of nature and exploit other lives in pursuing just our own interests. Archiving is one example of the human tendency to conquer and control culture and knowledge. *Anarchiving* has been thus suggested as a counteract that welcomes transformation and reciprocal knowledge-creation in multiple complex relations between different times and spaces and between people and the more-than-human world. In this chapter, I ask how arts-based research can be understood as a practice of anarchiving that challenges the assumptions of novelty and originality in art and in life. By applying contemporary art's philosophy of (un)doing the existing unsustainable structures and values, it is possible to imagine more sustainable art-making processes and to adopt sustainable orientations towards life more generally. As example, in this chapter, I describe how I upcycled rediscovered materials in my art (drawings, videos, and sound artworks) instead of starting from mental (genius) ideas and raw (virgin) materials—an approach that allows for complex meanings to emerge in-between the materials and memories.

Floods in Australia, drought in Somalia, microplastic found in human blood—news stories worldwide are telling apocalyptic narratives of the ecocrisis. Humans living in postindustrial societies have slowly realised that the ecological crisis is a crisis of our culture (Plumwood 2005). Therefore, we must fundamentally rethink how we consume, build, and move around. It is evident that even if quick, sustainable solutions to the escalating environmental catastrophe are implemented, small changes are not enough. Innovations in recycling and green energy are more than welcome, but what is desperately needed is a transformation comparable to a spiritual awakening (Vadén 2016). We must critically reflect on and rearticulate our values and the concepts of human and reality. The illusion of the world in which things are hyper-separated and humans are in total control of reality and truth must be radically rethought.

Archiving is one example of the human tendency to conquer and control culture and knowledge (Derrida 1995; Trouillot 2015). Its selective practices ignore subjects that are, for example, racialised and indigenous (Ware 2017), disabled (Britton et al. 2006), and other-than-humans (Miller 2021). Archives are also based on the idea of time as linear and space as stable (Brothman 2001). In acknowledging the hegemonic power structures of archiving, some critical scholars and artists have introduced '*counter-archiving* as a method of interrogating what constitutes an archive and the selective practices that continuously erase particular subjects' (Springgay et al. 2020, p. 897, emphasis in original). 'Anarchiving' (Massumi 2016; Springgay et al. 2020) has thus been suggested as a counteract that welcomes transformation and reciprocal knowledge-creation in multiple and complex relations between different times and spaces and between people and the more-than-human world.

In this chapter, I ask how arts-based research can be understood as a practice of anarchiving that challenges specifically the assumptions of novelty and originality in art and in life. After introducing the concept of upcycling used in design and art, I will briefly outline the idea of anarchiving as a research-creation method (Springgay et al. 2020). I will then discuss my artistic process that started from childhood memories collected in the Reconnect/Recollect project. The artistic practice generated drawings, videos, and sound artworks in which the collected memory stories were combined with my personal experiences and transformed into poetic and metaphorical representations. I created the works by repurposing video footage and life drawings that already existed in my personal archives.

Upcycling in Art

The green shift in production means more emphasis is put on reusing something considered waste (Hole and Hole 2019). Things destined to be destroyed are transformed into something else for environmental purposes in the recycling process. Recycling materials saves landfill space (Tam 2008), and it also takes part in resource conservation by reusing discarded instead of new materials (Reijnders 2000). Transforming existing things into new products also means that far less energy and water are used in production than the process that starts from raw materials (Del Ponte et al. 2017). However, the traditional idea of recycling can be described as 'downcycling' if materials are transformed into something with less value than the original thing (Geyer 2016). 'Upcycling', by contrast, adds more value to the materials. Upcycling is thus a specific concept in design that describes a process of transforming waste materials into new products of higher value (Bridgens et al. 2018).

In the arts field, too, using recycled materials is a growing—but not a new—trend. For example, Pablo Picasso's collage work created from newsprints and other pieces of paper or Marcel Duchamp's and Robert Rauschenberg's repurposing of objects such as bicycle tires and street signs are some early examples of upcycling of materials for artistic purposes (Somerville 2017). Likewise, sustainable art composed from plastic bags, pieces of clothing, glass bottles, or other waste that would end up filling landfills or floating in rivers and oceans may delight with its creativity (Odoh et al. 2014). It must be noted, though, that upcycled art can also play a role in capitalist production as a form of 'aesthetic economy' (Böhme 2003) if the waste is transformed into an aesthetic form only to satisfy art buyers' desires for beauty and playfulness. In such cases, the central aim for upcycling in art may simply be profit-making.

However, contemporary art can be a powerful tool to criticise capitalist production or push audiences to reflect on postindustrial societies' modernist belief in continuous progress and consumerism (Foster 2019; Martusewicz et al. 2015; Mears 2018). For example, the meaning of installations and performance art must often be understood beyond monetary value, in the relations they create (Foster and Martusewicz 2019; Mears 2018).

Upcycling can also be reflected in how artistic practice can challenge the assumption of novelty and originality in arts. How can new artworks be created from ideas and materials that the artist already has instead of starting from scratch? Originally a dance practitioner, I have been troubled by the short life-cycle of stage performances in the freelance field of performing arts. A lot of effort and resources are put into making an artwork that only gets a few showings. My perhaps unconscious response was to form a habit of repurposing in new works not only props and costumes but also ideas, images, and movement sequences from my older works. This practice of 'recycling old materials' has been a way of continuing my artistic process instead of thinking of my artworks as end products, which should not be touched after their completion (see also Foster 2019). For example, in 2012, I created a stage work entitled 'Ketjureaktio' (Foster 2012) or 'Chain Reaction' in English. Then, in 2016, I transformed the choreography into a dance film 'Sounds of Grey' (Foster 2016). I also repurposed some of the leftover footage from the film in three of my video works (see 'Lupina' 2018). In these works (see Figure 13.1), I did not only recycle ideas and movements from my previous works but also props such as cardboard boxes, business cards, and feathers. The continuous artistic process generated not only new artworks as static products but as an ongoing and messy entanglement of expressions, relations, sensations, and layers of interpretations and meanings in constant flux.

Fig. 13.1 Raisa Foster, artworks made from upcycled material and mental resources: [top] 'Ketjureaktio', a stage performance, 2012; [middle] 'Sounds of Grey', a dance film, 2016; [bottom] 'Lupina', a video work, 2016. Photographs by Mikko Korkiakangas (2012) and Raisa Foster and Mika Peltomaa (2016).

In short, the idea of upcycling in arts can be understood from a very concrete point of view of repurposing materials in a way that adds value to them. For example, installations and sculptures in visual arts and props and costumes in performing arts can be made from discarded materials, or the upcycling can happen by simply framing an everyday object such as a porcelain urinal as an artwork, like Duchamp's 'Fountain' (1917). However, upcycling can also be a more conceptual practice of exploring what is meant by originality, creativity, and novelty in arts in order to move beyond the modern assumptions that materials and ideas, objects and subjects, are static and disconnected from each other.

Anarchiving

The word 'archive' has its origin in the Latin *archīa*. Also, in Greek, *archeîa* means 'public records' and *archeîon* 'town hall, public office'. In today's use of English, the noun 'archive' refers to a collection of records or historical documents of or about an institution, family, person, or nation. It also names the place where such records are kept. The verb 'archiving' refers to the action of storing documents, data, or things in a repository. It could be said that archives are based on the idea of time as linear: the archive consists of past events and historical objects and documents. The idea of space in archiving is stable: the archived things are stored in a particular physical or digital site to be kept intact. The archive, both a collection of data and a place, is thus assumed to be objective and static (Brothman 2001), similarly to the conservative idea of an artwork as a consumable product to be preserved in bubble wrap in museums. Still, as it is impossible to store all knowledge and each culture in archives, archives always represent partial truths (Trouillot 2015). The selective practices in archiving enforce power and control (Derrida 1995; Springgay et al. 2020): whose stories are worth keeping? Who decides how the culture is stored and how the collected data is used?

Unlike the idea of the archive as linear, stable, and static, the anarchive is understood as responsible, reciprocal, and in constant flux (Springgay et al. 2020). The anarchive is not a repository of the past but a springboard for the now and the future. It is not a thing but a process (Springgay et al. 2020). Furthermore, anarchiving is not about storing and searching for the 'truth' but asking about what new thoughts, emotions, and sensations it opens (Deleuze and Guattari 2004), similarly to the recycling and upcycling in art that reopens the process for new meanings, feelings, and experiences.

Brian Massumi (2016) describes the anarchive as 'a repertory of traces' which carry the potential to initiate something new. The idea of a trace suggests the existence of some documentation, an object, a memory story, or something else, from which the traces originate. So, the anarchive continues the idea of the archive but allows it to turn in new directions. Massumi (2016) stresses that an anarchive is not contained in an object as a documentation of the past, instead, it is 'a feed-forward mechanism' that lures for further meaning creation. In this way, it is just like a piece of contemporary art that, at first, may seem odd and meaningless but, later, may evoke multiple emotions and interpretations (Foster 2019). The anarchive is activated between the various archival forms it may take and the verbal and material expressions and interactions it further generates. Thus, anarchiving is a practice of creating collaborative encounters (Massumi 2016).

Anarchiving can be seen as countering hegemonic structures and colonial knowledge (Springgay et al. 2020). It brings forward voices from the margins and notions of the unknown. More importantly, the meanings in an anarchive arise in multiple relationalities of past and future, of here and there, and of people and the more-than-human world. Anarchiving recognises the value in the transformation of things, in instability, and in unknownness.

Arts-Based Research with Memory Stories

I started to work in the Reconnect/Recollect project in October 2020. At that point, many memory stories were already archived on the project website. My first task was to read through all the memories. I looked specifically at the memories related to the moments when children participated in and with the more-than-human world. I read stories about lives in the countryside, about harvesting, and about humans interacting with other-than-human animals. I was captivated by the memory vignettes expressing children's experiences of being curious and fascinated about all of the lives and deaths they encountered in the day to day.

The archived memories evoked my personal memories of childhood and from more recent moments in my life. I started to discuss the memories through academic writing but also by practicing art. The practices of artmaking and more traditional academic research informed each other in ways that could not be described as straightforward; it became impossible to draw a clear line between these activities. Presenting and discussing the memories, ideas, and artworks at conferences (see, e.g., ZIN et al. 2021) played a major part in developing my artistic practice and interpreting it. Drawing and working on video and sound editing, coupled with the collaborative reading of memories with a group of multidisciplinary researchers, helped me to further conceptualise, for example, the phenomenon of ecosocialisation (Keto and Foster 2021; Foster et al. 2022b), imagination and metaphor (Foster et al. 2022a), and the paradox of tragedy in art (Foster 2023). Also vice versa, various theories greatly influenced my artistic practice. See, for example, video artworks 'The Body' (Foster 2021a) and 'Tiny Creatures' (Foster 2021b) as well as the sound artworks '63 Windows' (Foster 2021c) and 'Which Came First, the Chicken or the Egg?' (Foster 2021d).

The starting point of my multidisciplinary art practice is the human's bodily relation to the world. We live in and engage with the world not just through our thinking minds but primarily as emotional and sensing bodies (Merleau-Ponty 2008). However, this is something that humans tend to forget (Keto and Foster 2021). The illusion of human separation from the rest of the living world causes ecological problems, which are, in fact, the problems of our culture (Plumwood 2005): modern humans have failed to adapt their culture to the planetary boundaries (Steffen et al. 2015). We live in the world as if we were 'pure' conscious beings without a body and without relation to our environment or other living beings (Varto 2008).

Arts-based research (Barone and Eisner 2011; Knowles and Cole 2008; Leavy 2015; 2019) shifts between intuitive and analytical ways of knowing (see also Kallio 2010). The sensory, emotional, and cognitive dimensions are inextricably intertwined in artistic, embodied ways of knowing. This kind of experiential knowledge is often multifaceted and thus difficult to discuss (Parviainen 1998). However, this should not be seen as a weakness in arts-based research because one of its central values is its ability to bring out momentary and partial knowledge and, at the same time, perhaps capture the essence of humanity and reality (Kallio 2010). The difficulty of verbalising an experience with clarity does not mean that the phenomenon did not exist or could not be studied. In contrast, the phenomenon must be studied—but through new methods such as art-based ones. Artistic inquiry can be used to address something that escapes verbal definitions. With arts-based research, it is also possible to reach a wider audience than traditional academic research because art touches the recipient emotionally and not just cognitively (Leavy 2015).

I presented my artistic research based on the Reconnect/Recollect memory archive in my solo exhibition entitled *More than Human* (Foster 2021) in June 2021 in Tampere, Finland. The exhibition consisted of charcoal, chalk, and ink drawings but also sound and video art. I explored memories that describe childhood experiences in different environments and interactions with other living beings. Through my artworks, I looked at how humans are in direct contact with the world precisely through their sensuous bodies. Through bodily perceptions, it is also possible to understand how the world is in us, as we carry sensations, emotions, and memories in our living bodies (Merleau-Ponty 2008; Parviainen 1998).

The collected memory stories were combined with my personal experiences and were transformed into poetic and metaphorical narratives in the video and sound artworks. The works were created from repurposing video footage that I already had in my personal archives. The drawings were also created by upcycling, continuing my previous drawings by editing, erasing, covering, and otherwise destabilising them. The sensuous body was, thus, not only the topic of my drawings but also the process of drawing itself was a strongly embodied experience.

Rediscovering Memories and Materials

The modern assumption of artmaking is that the artist first has an idea, then presents it in the form of art, as a painting, theatre or dance piece, musical composition, or some other medium (Foster 2019). From this perspective, the artist's job is to produce novel creations from their original—and often described as 'genius'—ideas (Montuori and Purser

1995). Similarly, in the context of the memory project, one may expect that the artist has illustrated the collected childhood memories as such. This understanding of art is seen in some audience responses, too. For example, the recipient of an artwork may try to figure out the artist's intention or the memory that inspired it. So, one looking at art may expect to find a singular, coherent story, message, or meaning in that work (Landau et al. 2006).

Contemporary art practice often challenges modern assumptions, such as rationalism, individualism, instrumentalism, consumerism, mechanism, the idea of continuous progress, and centric thinking (Foster 2019). It does so not just with its content but also through its form and methods. For example, a collectively created multidisciplinary art project can problematise the overpowering effects of rationalism and individualism and help us grow towards a more holistic or community-oriented worldview. When art is approached as an immaterial process rather than a material product, consumerism is questioned. Similarly, instrumentalism is challenged when focus is placed on the intrinsic value of art and the relationalities of things. The meaning of contemporary art lies in its capacity to invite practitioners and audiences into the unknown and to initiate multiple interpretations. It thereby undermines the idea of mechanical production and the belief in continuous progress. Contemporary artworks can help people value diversity and mutuality in both people and the natural environment, which awakens criticality towards anthropocentrism, androcentrism, and ethnocentrism (see Foster 2019).

In short, the potentiality of contemporary art education lies in the alternative models of thinking and the practice of undoing to build sustainable life orientation. To be clear, in contrast to the idea of 'sustainable development', which focuses only on 'greening' the continuous growth (see OECD 2011), 'sustainable life orientation' refers to the pursuit of life as an integral and meaningful part of the more-than-human world (Foster et al. 2019). Contemporary art practice, which helps to recognise the intertwinement and intrinsic value of all life forms, can accelerate the debate to resolve planetary crises and strengthen hope for the future (Foster et al. 2022c).

In the memory project, one of my artistic practices was drawing, which built on my previous life-drawing studies. Life drawing, the drawing of a human model, has been a pillar of general art education since the Renaissance (Skaarup 2017). The roots of this tradition stem from ideals of European culture in which the man is a measure of everything and specifically his body as a significant mediator of beauty, goodness, and truth (Sawday 2013). However, as a practice, life drawing can challenge such ways of seeing. In life drawing, one must forget the rational idea of a human figure and settle down to genuinely perceive the model as it is and to recognise the lights and shadows, space, rhythm, continuums, and contrasts. So, the practice requires close observations. One must draw what is seen through the eyes rather than what is known by the mind about a human figure. In that sense, life drawing can be taken fundamentally as a practice of the 'phenomenology of perception' (Merleau-Ponty 2008). It is not about copying a pre-existing—concrete or imagined—object but instead 'laying down of being' in the act of drawing itself (ibid., p. xxii).

When creating the drawings for the *More than Human* exhibition, I did not start with a clear idea, an 'imagined object', or a 'mental vision' but with materials that I found in my personal archives. I started to add other layers on top of these drawings, allowing multiple relations to emerge in the image. Trusting the embodied process, I engaged with these drawings intuitively rather than intellectually (Foster 2019; Kallio 2010). Each addition, deletion, line, and rubbing-out sought to bring back to life drawings that were once discarded. Moment by moment and stroke by stroke, I witnessed the 'miracle of related experiences' that emerged in my drawing (see also Merleau-Ponty 2008, xxiii). I made careful observations and selections but also embraced coincidences and improvisations (see also Kallio 2010) with the aim of doing and undoing an image that would breathe again and invite observers, too, to live with the work. The resulting image was a surprise for me. My original drawing, one that had been just a practice study of a human figure, was 'upcycled' into an artwork via this artistic process (Figure 13.2.).

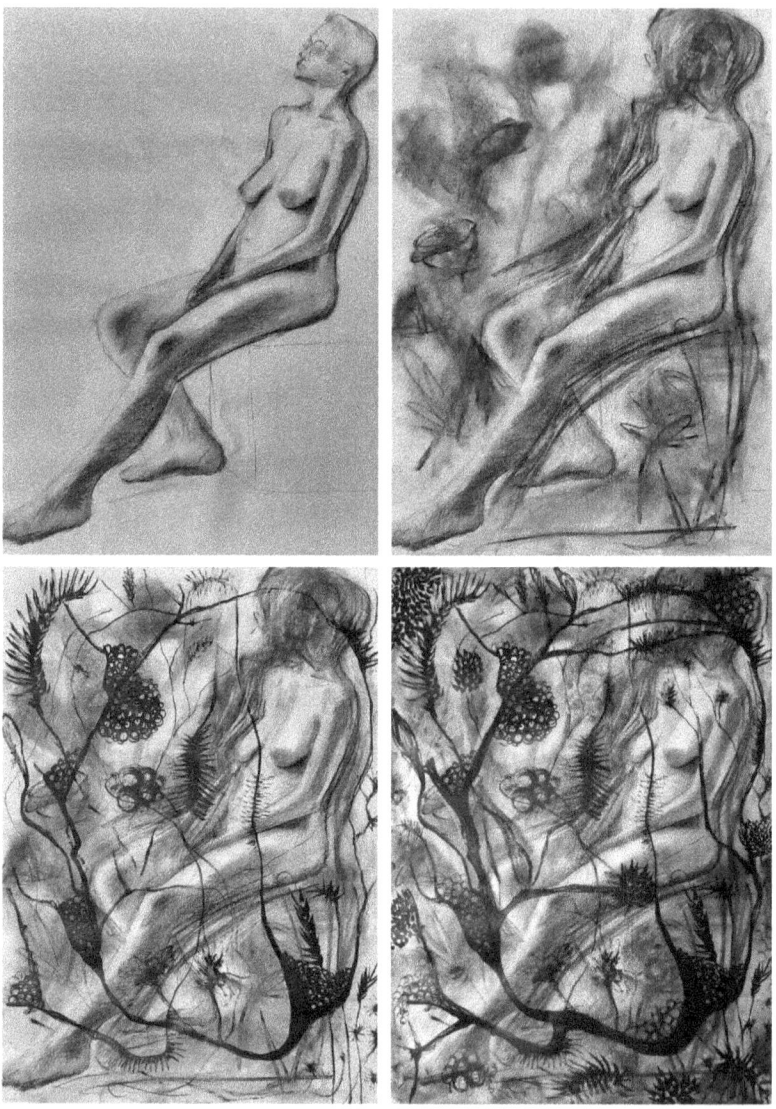

Fig. 13.2 Raisa Foster, untitled life-drawing study that was upcycled by adding layers and framing it as an artwork, 2021. Photograph by Raisa Foster, 2021.

All of the drawings I presented in the *More than Human* exhibition were created from pre-existing materials. The ideas, interpretations, and meanings of the artworks only came later. Therefore, it could be said that I did not produce the works but, instead, rediscovered them. After forgetting them, as one might do with memories, I found these drawings again and found something more in this creative process. Even though my drawings were not explicitly connected to the stories of the project or my own childhood memories, together with other works, they formed the overall experience of the exhibition, in which the memory stories' themes of body and sensibility, life and death, and the intertwining of humanity and the rest of life were communicated through different artistic means, reinforcing further relations and meanings in between each other.

The video works I presented in the exhibition were created similarly by upcycling old materials. For example, the video work, 'Tiny Creatures' (Foster 2021b), was created from the footage of two videos that I found on my computer. First, I read the memory 'Water Lilies' (n.d.), which tells the story of a child spending a lazy summer day by a pond (Foster et al. 2022b). The child is observing an orchestra of bugs, bees, and flies. She is fascinated by this miniature world, so tiny in size but so rich in sound and visual details.

Fig. 13.3 Raisa Foster, still from a video artwork 'Tiny Creatures', 2021.

While I was reading this memory story, I remembered being on holiday in Malta a couple of years ago. I was amazed by ants running across the concrete paving in front of an abandoned hotel complex. I found the video footage of these ants in my personal digital archive. Rewatching this, I then remembered another video that I had filmed on top of the

Oslo Opera House. The second film clip pictured tiny humans walking along a shore. I superimposed these two pieces of footage together with a narrative composed from the memory, and that is how the video art piece, 'Tiny Creatures' was born (see Figure 13.3). Again, it could be said that I discovered the work rather than produced it. Upcycled art was created in this process of rediscovering the video materials and recollecting my personal memories similar to the memory story. The memory archive was also turned into an anarchive by making new connections through this artistic engagement with memories and materials.

I did similar upcycling with my sound installation. The sound work 'Which Came First, the Chicken or the Egg?' (Foster 2021d) tells a memory-story of a child visiting a chicken farm that was operated by her father in Hungary (Foster et al. 2022b). When I read the child's memory of being afraid of stepping on the hundreds of tiny chicks on the barn floor, I remembered the hundreds of empty eggshells stored in my attic. I had used these eggs in a stage performance in 2006 and another in 2010, but I had not had any use for them for ten years afterwards. The child's memory of the chicken farm asked for these eggs to be recycled in this sound work. The sound art installation involved the eggs being scattered around a plinth to give the audience a similar feeling of risk that they, too, might step on the fragile chicks (Figure 13.4). Again, the memory archive was transformed into an anarchive: the memory and the eggs together work as traces that carry the potential to evoke new relations and meanings in between the installation and a person experiencing it.

Fig. 13.4 Raisa Foster, 'Which Came First, the Chicken or the Egg?', sound art installation, 2021. Artist's photograph.

Conclusion

For me, art is not 'just art' but a transformative action at its best. To address the ecocrisis, we need to understand our place as humans in a radically new way. We cannot continue to elevate ourselves above the rest of nature and exploit other lives in pursuing just our own interests. We need to understand that there are no humans without well-functioning ecosystems. However, adopting a sustainable life orientation does not have to mean scarcity and suffering. On the contrary, as we connect with others—human and more-than-human— we can find our lives enriched through and in these rediscovered, significant relationships.

I hope the examples of my arts-based research have shown that the idealisation of an artist's—or a human—task to produce novel and original works (of art) from 'pure' ideas or materials can and should be challenged. Furthermore, with contemporary art's philosophy of (un)doing the existing unsustainable structures and values, it is also possible to imagine more sustainable art-making processes. As example, in this chapter, I described how I have upcycled rediscovered materials in my art instead of starting from mental (genius) ideas and raw (virgin) materials, which allowed for complex meanings to emerge in-between the materials and memories.

We can look at the conservative idea of artistic production as an archive that aims to capture and preserve the artist's original and novel ideas. In relation to the childhood memory project, one may assume that the artist has aimed to illustrate the archived memory stories as such. However, in this project I have approached artmaking as a creation of new connections, an 'anarchiving' that aims to generate continuous relations between diverse memories and materials. I hope that this generative process initiated by the artistic engagement does not stop in my 'finished' artworks. As I and others revisit my drawings, videos, and sound works, they will function as a repertory of traces that keep stimulating new, unexpected responses and contribute to an ongoing anarchiving of childhood memories.

References

Barone, T., and Eisner, E. W. (2011). *Arts Based Research*. Sage, https://doi.org/10.4135/9781452230627

Bridgens, B., Powell, M., Farmer, G., Walsh, C., Reed, E., Royapoor, M., Gosling, P., Hall, J. and Heidrich, O. (2018). 'Creative Upcycling: Reconnecting People, Materials and Place through Making'. *Journal of Cleaner Production*, 189, 145–54, https://doi.org/10.1016/j.jclepro.2018.03.317

Britton, D. F., Floyd, B., and Murphy, P. A. (2006). 'Overcoming Another Obstacle: Archiving a Community's Disabled History'. *Radical History Review*, 2006 (94), 212–27, https://doi.org/10.1215/01636545-2006-94-212

Brothman, B. (2001, January 1). 'The Past that Archives Keep: Memory, History, and the Preservation of Archival Records'. *Archivaria*, 51, https://archivaria.ca/index.php/archivaria/article/view/12794

Böhme, G. (2003). 'Contribution to the Critique of the Aesthetic Economy'. *Thesis Eleven*, 73(1), 71–82, https://doi.org/10.1177/0725513603073001005

Deleuze, G., and Guattari, F. (2004). *A Thousand Plateaus: Capitalism and Schizophrenia*, trans. by B. Massumi. Continuum. (Original work published 1988)

Del Ponte, K., Madras Natarajan, B., Pakes Ahlman, A., Baker, A., Elliott, E., and Edil, T. B. (2017). 'Life-Cycle Benefits of Recycled Material in Highway Construction'. *Transportation Research Record*, 2628(1), 1–11, https://doi.org/10.3141/2628-01

Derrida, J. (1995). 'Archive Fever: A Freudian Impression'. *Diacritics*, 25(2), 9–63, https://doi.org/10.2307/465144

Foster, Raisa (2012). 'Ketjureaktio' [Video]. YouTube, uploaded by Raisa Foster, 18 April 2013, https://www.youtube.com/watch?v=SImOapepywY

—— (2016). 'Sounds of Grey' [Video]. YouTube, uploaded by Raisa Foster, 3 March 2018, https://www.youtube.com/watch?v=4Q4HmCghWjY

—— (2018). 'Lupina' [Video]. YouTube, uploaded by Raisa Foster, 16 May 2018, https://www.youtube.com/watch?v=3XTZAUk5EGU

—— (2019). 'Visual Art Campaigns', in *The Oxford Handbook of Methods for Public Scholarship*, ed. by P. Leavy. (pp. 383–418). Oxford University Press, https://doi.org/10.1093/oxfordhb/9780190274481.013.12

—— (2021a). 'Raisa Foster: The Body (a viewing copy)' [Video]. YouTube, uploaded by Raisa Foster, 12 April 2022, https://www.youtube.com/watch?v=RTC-jm9iCQs

—— (2021b). 'Raisa Foster: Tiny creatures (a viewing copy)' [Video]. YouTube, uploaded by Raisa Foster, 1 September 2022, https://www.youtube.com/watch?v=_2QXbHGT1eU

—— (2021c). '63 Windows' [Mp3 track], https://drive.google.com/file/d/1HGO2xTT920BgNIQulUdusV1PROp19-5P/view

—— (2021d). 'Which Came First, the Chicken or the Egg?' [Mp3 track], https://drive.google.com/file/d/1vyES4UZWuOd-auUyNjyFoHN6Fi-hM8jW/view

—— 'Raisa Foster: *More than Human*'. (2021, July). [Blogpost], Memories of Everyday Childhoods: De-colonial and De-Cold War Dialogues in Childhood and Schooling, https://coldwarchildhoods.org/blog/raisa-foster-more-than-human/

—— (2022). *Raisa Foster*. Artist portfolio, https://www.raisafoster.com/

—— (2023). 'The Living Dying Body: Arriving at the Awareness of All Life's Interdependencies through a Video Artwork'. *Research in Arts and Education*, 2023(1), 31–42, https://doi.org/10.54916/rae.126189

Foster, R. and Martusewicz, R. (2019). 'Introduction: Contemporary art as Critical, Revitalizing, and Imaginative Practice toward Sustainable Communities', in *Art, EcoJustice, and Education. Intersecting Theories and Practices*, ed. by R. Foster, J. Mäkelä and R. Martusewicz. (pp. 1–9). Routledge, https://doi.org/10.4324/9781315188447

Foster, R., Salonen, A. O. and Keto, S. (2019). 'Kestävyystietoinen elämänorientaatio pedagogisena päämääränä' [Sustainable Life Orientation as a Pedagogical Aim], in *Opetussuunnitelmatutkimus—ajan merkkejä ja siirtymiä*, ed. by T. Autio, L. Hakala, and T. Kujala. (pp. 121–43). Tampere University Press, https://trepo.tuni.fi/bitstream/handle/10024/118706/kestavyystietoinen_elamanorientaatio_pedagogisena_paamaarana.pdf

Foster, R., Törmä, T., Hokkanen, L., and ZIN, M. (2022a). '63 Windows: Generating Relationality Through Poetic and Metaphorical Engagement'. *Research in Arts and Education*, 2022(2), 56–67, https://doi.org/10.54916/rae.122974

Foster, R., ZIN, M., Keto, S. and Pulkki, J. (2022b). 'Recognising Ecosocialization in Childhood Memories'. *Educational Studies*, 58(4), 560–74, https://doi.org/10.1080/00131946.2022.2051031

Foster, R., Salonen, A. O. and Sutela, K. (2022c). 'Taidekasvatuksen ekososiaalinen kehys: Kohti kestävyystietoista elämänorientaatiota' [The Ecosocial Framework for Art Education: Towards Sustainable Life Orientation]. *Kasvatus*, 53(2), 118–29, https://doi.org/10.33348/kvt.115918

Geyer, R., Kuczenski, B., Zink, T., and Henderson, A. (2016). 'Common Misconceptions about Recycling'. *Journal of Industrial Ecology*, 20(5), 1010–017, https://doi.org/10.1111/jiec.12355

Hole, G., and Hole, A. S. (2019). 'Recycling as the Way to Greener Production: A Mini Review'. *Journal of Cleaner Production*, 212, 910–15, https://doi.org/10.1016/j.jclepro.2018.12.080

Kallio, M. (2010). 'Taideperustainen tutkimusparadigma taidekasvatuksen sosiokullttuurisia ulottuvuuksia rakentamassa' [Art-based Research

Paradigm Building the Socio-Cultural Dimensions of Art Education]. *Research in Arts and Education*, 2010(4), 15–25, https://doi.org/10.54916/rae.118716

Keto, S., and Foster, R. (2021). 'Ecosocialization—An Ecological Turn in the Process of Socialization'. *International Studies in Sociology of Education*, 30(1–2), 34–52, https://doi.org/10.1080/09620214.2020.1854826

Knowles, J. G., and Cole, A. L. (eds). (2008). *Handbook of the Arts in Qualitative Research: Perspectives, Methodologies, Examples, and Issues*. Sage publications

Landau, M. J., Greenberg, J., Solomon, S., Pyszczynski, T., and Martens, A. (2006). 'Windows into Nothingness: Terror Management, Meaninglessness, and Negative Reactions to Modern Art'. *Journal of Personality and Social Psychology*, 90(6), 879–92, https://doi.org/10.1037/0022-3514.90.6.879

Leavy, P. (2015). *Method Meets Art: Arts-Based Research Practice* (2nd edn.). Guilford

Martusewicz, R., Edmundson, J. and Lupinacci, J. (2015). *EcoJustice Education. Toward Diverse, Democratic, and Sustainable Communities* (2nd edn.). Routledge, https://doi.org/10.4324/9781315779492

Massumi, B. (2016). 'Working Principles', in *The Go-To How To Book of Anarchiving*, ed. by A. Murphie. (pp. 6–8). The SenseLab, http://senselab.ca/wp2/wp-content/uploads/2016/12/Go-To-How-To-Book-of-Anarchiving-Portrait-Digital-Distribution.pdf

Mears, E. (2018). 'Recycling as Creativity: An Environmental Approach to Twentieth-Century American Art'. *American Studies Journal*, 64(5), https://doi.org/10.18422/64-05

Merleau-Ponty, M. (2008). *Phenomenology of Perception*. Routledge Classics

Miller, S. E., Jernigan, C. M., Legan, A. W., Miller, C. H., Tumulty, J. P., Walton, A., and Sheehan, M. J. (2021). 'Animal Behaviour Missing from Data Archives'. *Trends in Ecology and Evolution*, 36(11), 960–63, https://doi.org/10.1016/j.tree.2021.07.008

Montuori, A., and Purser, R. E. (1995). 'Deconstructing the Lone Genius Myth: Toward a Contextual View of Creativity'. *Journal of Humanistic Psychology*, 35(3), 69–112, https://doi.org/10.1177/00221678950353005

Odoh, G. C., Odoh, N. S., and Anikpe, E. A. (2014). 'Waste and Found Objects as Potent Creative Resources a Review of the Art-Is-Everywhere Project'. *International Journal of Humanities and Social Sciences*, 3(6), 1–14

Parviainen, J. (1998). *Bodies Moving and Moved: A Phenomenological Analysis of the Dancing Subject and the Cognitive and Ethical Values of Dance Art*. Tampere University Press

Plumwood, V. (2005). *Environmental Culture: The Ecological Crisis of Reason*. Routledge

Reijnders, L. (2000). 'A Normative Strategy for Sustainable Resource Choice and Recycling'. *Resources, Conservation and Recycling*, 28(1–2), 121–33, https://doi.org/10.1016/S0921-3449(99)00037-3

Sawday, J. (2013). *The Body Emblazoned: Dissection and the Human Body in Renaissance Culture*. Routledge, https://doi.org/10.4324/9781315887753

Skaarup, B. O. (2017). 'Applied Science in the Renaissance Art Academy', in *Art, Technology and Nature: Renaissance to Postmodernity*, ed. by C.S. Paldam and J. Wamberg. (pp. 105–16). Routledge

Somerville, K. (2017). 'Trash to Treasure: The Art of Found Materials. *The Missouri Review*, 40(3), 49–67, https://doi.org/10.1353/mis.2017.0040

Springgay, S., Truman, A., and MacLean, S. (2020). 'Socially Engaged Art, Experimental Pedagogies, and Anarchiving as Research-Creation'. *Qualitative Inquiry*, 26(7), 897–907, https://doi.org/10.1177/1077800419884964

Steffen, W., Richardson, K., Rockström, J., Cornell, S. E., Fetzer, I., Bennett, E. M., Biggs, R., Carpenter, S. R., De Vries, W., De Wit, C. A., Folke, C., Gerten, D., Heinke, J., Mace, J. M., Persson, L. M., Ramanathan, V., and Sörlin, S. (2015). 'Planetary Boundaries: Guiding Human Development on a Changing Planet'. *Science*, 347(6223), https://doi.org/10.1177/0973408215600602a

Tam, V. W. (2008). 'Economic Comparison of Concrete Recycling: A Case Study Approach'. *Resources, Conservation and Recycling*, 52(5), 821–28, https://doi.org/10.1016/j.resconrec.2007.12.001

Trouillot, M. R. (2015). *Silencing the Past: Power and the Production of History*. Beacon Press

Vadén, T. (2016). 'Modernin yksilön harhat ja ympäristötaidekasvatus' [The Biases of the Modern Individual and Environmental Art Education], in *Taidekasvatus ympäristöhuolen aikakaudella—avauksia, suuntia, mahdollisuuksia*, ed. by A. Suominen. (pp. 134–42). Aalto ARTS Books

Varto, J. (2008). *The Art and Craft of Beauty*. Helsinki: University of Art and Design

Ware, S. M. (2017). 'All Power to All People? Black LGBTTI2QQ Activism, Remembrance, and Archiving in Toronto'. *TSQ: Transgender Studies Quarterly*, 4(2), 170–80, https://doi.org/10.1215/23289252-3814961

ZIN, M., Albarran, E. J., and Foster, R. (2021). *Tentacular Anarchive: Memories of Childhood through Scholarly, Pedagogical, and Artistic Engagements* [Online transmission of hub opening session]. 'Spinning the Sticky Threads of Childhood Memories: From Cold War to Anthropocene', https://events.tuni.fi/recollectreconnect2021/

The Tailor[1]

Thoma Sukhashvili

The art project 'The Tailor' tells the story of my mom, Maia Sukhasvilli, and the first flag of Georgia. The flag was gifted to my dad and was remodelled by my mom, first as a dress, then as a bag for carrying products. This demonstrates how a purely national symbol can become an item for daily use.

The Flag, 1990

Your dad brought the flag in 1990. It was a personal gift from Zviad Gamsakhurdia, who gave it to him before he became the president of Georgia. It was said that the burgundy symbolized Georgian blood and the black and white in the left corner represented war, pain, loss, and ethnic conflicts. However, our family were internationalists who were constantly visited by friends of different nationalities and religions—Ossetians, Russians, Chechens, Azeris, Ingushetians, Armenians, and so on—this flag brought nothing to us but ridicule from the nationalists.

---

1 This is a childhood memory produced as part of the Reconnect/Recollect project discussed in the introduction to this book.

Thoma Sukhashvili and Maia Sukhashvili, 'The Tailor', as displayed in the Finnish Labour Museum Werstas, n.d. Photograph by Zsuzsa Millei.

The Dress, 1993

I always used to sew my own clothes. I also worked at a factory for a while until I got married. When the war started, everything, including clothes, became harder to find. At that time, I had already had my first child and I was very thin, no longer in good shape. There were no jobs, so I was unemployed. While your dad was fighting in the Abkhazia War for several months, I had no choice but to sew a dress from the flag. I was constantly wondering and worrying about how others would perceive it. To be honest, I was afraid that people would tell me that I should not have sewed it and I would have felt ashamed.

Once I took you to the doctor while wearing the dress. It was a cold day and the doctor asked if I had anything else to wear. I said nothing, I did not know whether she recognized the flag cloth or whether she mocked me because the dress was not suitable for the cold weather. I could not even tell her that I did not have any other dresses, or that I sewed this one from the flag because I was afraid she would get angry with me. When your dad arrived and saw the dress, he did not say anything but I could tell that he was a little bit offended. However, he knew that our family did not have any other choice.

The Bag, 1996

Things got harder after I had my second child. He was born with two congenital diseases. However, we could not survive by staying home. I was forced to work outside the village, bringing and selling fruits and other products in Tbilisi. This was how I earned money for bread and medicine. As I did not have a big bag, I thought the dress could be turned into a bag as it was made out of durable cloth. I remodeled the flag/dress into a bag and went to 'Dezerter Bazaar', using it to carry home things.

14. Anarchive, Oral Histories, and Teaching Comparative Cold-War Childhoods across Geographies and Generations

Elena Jackson Albarrán

Childhood is a normalising phase of life. Each individual's subjective experience becomes the baseline for establishing a worldview and evaluating differences encountered in others. Yet scholars of childhood have demonstrated that formative years are often informed by political, cultural, and social trends. During the Cold War, citizen and identity formation at the hands of state and media influences was particularly strident. This chapter provides a practical application of childhood studies scholarship to undergraduate education in the context of a semester-long project assigned in an undergraduate history course at a Western university. Oral history projects that connect textbook narratives with the memories of living family and community members help to dismantle the East-West divide, generate empathy, and promote self-reflection of the students as agents of their own historical moment.

The year is 1962. Tensions between the United States of America and the Soviet Union have gradually grown tenser over the coming months, now at an all-time high since the Soviets placed missiles in Cuba, a communist country fresh from its own revolution. People were terrified all across America, wondering if they would be caught in nuclear warfare. Although what I have just relayed may sound like a reading from a history excerpt, I am honored to say that I know someone who was a part of the history of this time. (Student Reflection 2022)

This pedagogically oriented chapter showcases the experiences and opportunities of integrating the Cold-War childhood memories anarchive into two undergraduate courses taught to three different cohorts of students. The course 'Comparative Cold War Childhoods', taught to US students in a European study-abroad program, sought to make optimal use of the Reconnect/Recollect project and its multiple intellectual and creative activities. The course 'World History since 1945' was taught in a conventional US undergraduate setting to non-history majors fulfilling distribution requirements for a liberal-arts degree. To gain context, students in both courses studied the construction of ideological systems and institutions on both sides of the Iron Curtain, especially as they influenced children. These were augmented by guest testimonies of Cold-War childhoods that belied the propagandistic characterisation of the Other constructed in both East and West. They participated in the virtual exhibition opening of *Kaleidoscope* (2021), utilised the Cold-War Childhoods memories anarchive, read some of the texts published in *Childhood and Schooling in Post/Socialist Societies: Memories of Everyday Life* (Silova et al. 2018), and conducted their own oral histories of a family member or acquaintance who grew up in the Cold War, from which they extracted first-hand anecdotes, observations, and memories that aligned with the spirit of the memories anarchive. Students in the 'Cold War Childhoods' course engaged in a semester-long project, while students in the 'World History since 1945' course conducted a truncated version of the oral history assignment.

This chapter will also emphasise the generative capacity of this kind of intellectual model by showcasing its multiple products. I participated in one of the memory workshops (and contributed lightly to the anarchive), and through those relationships I was able to conceptualise the pedagogical goals of these courses as well as to make meaningful contacts. The student assignment, a capstone project of the courses, intends to achieve the following pedagogical objectives: deconstruct the Cold-War ideological binary, cultivate intergenerational empathy as well as intercultural curiosity and appreciation, deconstruct childhood as a social category, enhance awareness of historical legacies of personal and familial experiences and migrations, and introduce critical approaches to the political economy of childhood.

On Becoming a Cold-War Kid

'I know we are supposed to interview somebody who grew up during the Cold War, but I'm having a hard time finding somebody who was alive back then.' This casual student confession made after class cleaved a rift between us, one that I scrambled to seam back together by gently reminding her that I was alive 'back then'. Despite the expanded horizons promised by a liberal-arts education, generational uniformity on a residential college campus limits perceptions of the human condition. Furthermore, the narrow rubric of 'History' creates a false sense of distance from the people whose transformations of identities, nationalities, economic fortunes, and political affinities we approach through published narratives as belonging to the past. Teaching the Cold War through collective family biographies offers an opportunity to extend twentieth-century histories into the present. It affirms the power of historical scholarship through oral histories that reiterate documented observations of living through a particular moment. And it can bridge the generational gap. As with the history teacher who experimented with offering herself as a primary source for teaching her students about 9/11, drawing from family memories of the recent past provides 'evidence of humanity in this history' (Johnson 2021).

In fact, my own reconstructed memories of growing up at the end of the Cold War informed the creation of the 'Comparative Cold War Childhoods' course, prompted by participation in the Reconnect/Recollect memory workshop in October 2019. I had previously not considered my childhood, spent in rural northeastern United States, to have been marked by the Cold War, as no geopolitical forces were evident, nor did we undergo any forced migration or change in status. But participation in the workshop alongside a group of international peers made me see the interconnectedness of our fates and fortunes. I recalled watching the NBC Nightly News, which projected flashes from far-flung geographies into my 1980s living room, and marvelled that I could share both a room and a history with people who inhabited those places decades ago.

Clear snapshots from those days pieced together improbable scenes from my fragmented memory: I remembered Samantha Smith, a child ambassador to Russia in 1983, being pushed on a swing—by Gorbachev? She was my age at the time of her trip, and I was fixated on the details of her journey, but my adult memory had conflated her trip with other snippets of news from Russia that had filtered into my growing consciousness, allowing for slippage of fact. It was a passing story of public interest at the time, but, in retrospect, I can interpret the coverage of Smith's trip—and my childhood reception of it—as part of a publicity stunt for the warming of East/West relations that were already beginning to take place behind the scenes ('Growing Up on "This" Side' (n.d.)). Through such media outlets targeted to appeal to my demographic, I internalised the subtle messages about the potential dangers of engaging in diplomacy with Russia, affirming the dual-propaganda campaigns by the US and the USSR to control the narrative of Samantha's ambassadorship (Peacock 2019). Not until my participation in the workshop did I have the opportunity to interrogate my complicity in the Cold-War project as a recipient of propaganda.

As a historian of childhood, I am tuned in to the generational nuances of children's socialisation and the extent to which many of our core identities might actually be constructed (in part) by the state, especially in politically-charged contexts. On occasion, I have turned the lens of historical scrutiny inward to interrogate the Cold-War conditions in which my own childhood might have been forged by forces other than my nuclear family and my own will (Albarrán 2021). The lessons learned when we see ourselves as products of historical forces can be revelatory. I wanted to impart that self-awareness of our relationship to the past to students of history.

The Course: Comparative Cold War Childhoods

The course 'Comparative Cold War Childhoods' was designed as a mid-level undergraduate course in History for students at a liberal-arts university in the United States. It sought to bring together historical and interdisciplinary scholarship on the history of childhood at the service of Cold-War history epistemology. How might we see this global epoch that raised three generations in a different light if we included the politics and experiences of childhood in the official narrative?

The introductory unit of the course established the constructedness of childhood over time, including an overview of how idealised childhoods occupy official discourse, and divergent experiences are marked as transgressive and marginalised from popular view. The childhood-studies framework thus established, the course then focused on the ways that Cold-War politics and ideologies shaped childhoods in the First, Second, and Third Worlds. The course centred on the similarities and differences of children growing up on either side of the Iron Curtain divide. The chronology was split into three loosely defined generations: the Cold-War consensus generation (1940s–50s), the dissenting generation (1960s–70s), and the media generation (1980s). Course themes included explorations of propaganda, consumption and consumerism, peace, youth organisations, child diplomacy, material culture, popular culture, and ideological formation, with an effort to give as equal weight as possible to the ways media and political entities constructed these domains of childhood in both the East and the West. Students engaged with scholarship from historians of childhood, primary-source material in the form of media clips, visual propaganda, and commercial advertisements, and the invaluable anarchive of firsthand memories compiled in the database *Memories of Everyday Childhoods: De-Colonial and De-Cold War Dialogues on Childhood and Schooling* (additional assigned course readings include Bogic 2018; Dror 2016; Dubinsky 2012; Fattal 2018; Funder 2003; Fürst 2015; Ivaska 2015; Godeanu-Kenworthy 2020; Stearns 2017; Vavrus 2021).

The primary assignment for this semester-long course was the Oral History Project named 'Growing Up as a Cold War Kid'. This involved a series of tiered assignments, both individual and in groups, that culminated in a critical collective biography of three generations of Cold-War children. As a starting point, students initially conducted very short interviews with three people who would have been ten years old anywhere between 1946 and 1991. From this initial bank of informants, students would each select one that seemed to be the most promising for an in-depth interview, the content of which would be transcribed and then critically analysed in historical context. As students learned more content about the shape of geopolitical events, cultural contexts, and popular references, this growing knowledge base enriched the interview-and-analysis process. The assignment structure was as follows:

Stage 1: Cultural Zeitgeist Crowdsourcing

Working together as a class (using Google's Jamboard tool, a digital whiteboard that can be saved as a PDF and used later as a reference), students drew from the first few weeks of course readings and lectures to populate lists of keywords that defined each generation. They sorted keywords into the categories of Politics, Ideologies, Organisations, and Popular Culture, trying to generate references that were as specific as possible (brands of commodities, television shows, names of politicians, pieces of legislature, keystone events, for example). The platform also allowed students to import iconic images that characterised each generation.

Stage 2: First-Round Interviews

Students conducted three short interviews with informants identified from their family, community, religious congregation, or place of employment. The goal of this stage of interviews was to identify a subject who had enough specific memories or anecdotes from their childhood, and willingness to engage in the interview, to supply material for discussion and analysis in the context of the cultural politics of the Cold War. Ideal subjects were effusive, had many stories to tell (or demonstrated interest in indulging in childhood memories prompted by the line of questions posed by the student), or were inspired by the initial interview to talk to a friend or dig out a photo album to enhance the memory.

Prior to conducting these interviews, students read *Oral History* (2022), a brief guide published by the University of North Carolina Chapel Hill, which prepares students for the ethics, methods, and structure used by oral historians. As per these recommendations, students filled out a worksheet for each interview subject that included confirmation of oral agreement to participate in the project, identification of the generation that most aligned with their childhood, a list of questions asked, an evaluation of the interview subjects' responsiveness, and comments on the viability of the informant as a subject for the final project (informants had the right to remain anonymous, if they chose, and students could assign a pseudonym). Based on the worksheets, students submitted a rationale for their final selection.

Stage 3: Group Development of Final Interview Subjects and Themes

Once again as a class, taking into consideration the responses garnered by the first-round interviews, and drawing from the wealth of detail found in assigned readings and lecture materials, students developed a list of categories, themes, and sample interview questions that corresponded to each generation. These were not intended to be prescriptive but, rather, to create a bank of common experiences that characterised each respective generation in order to give the interview subject a starting point from which to share their memories. Sample interview questions might not resonate with some, while unleashing a torrent of memories from others. Some interview questions were: how did your school react to political events (assemblies, policies, codes, or curriculum)? What did you think/hear about the Black Panther party? Were you afraid of being drafted for Vietnam? What was the gender dynamic in your family? Did you drink milk? Was there any point at which you were afraid of radiation? Was there a moment when you or your parents started to distrust the government? How did you view 'the Other' (Russians, or some other Other)? Was religion a defining factor in your childhood, and what bearing did that have on your political beliefs?

Stage 4: Follow-Up Interview

Using the class-generated interview questions as a baseline, students followed up in a longer-form interview with their selected subject. These interviews were conducted in-person, over the phone, via online conferencing, or, in some cases, through a series of email or even text-message exchanges. Students submitted the transcript of the full interview, including questions asked, with editorial clarifications as needed. This oral history transcript served as the primary source material for the final written analysis. I submitted comments on the transcript indicating areas in the interview that lent themselves to analysis or that needed clarification in footnotes.

Stage 5: Written Oral History Draft

This draft included a preface of a brief biographical paragraph identifying the oral history subject (or pseudonym) and relevant information about their age, geography/nationality, social class (if stated), and the general conditions of their upbringing. Following this was the entire interview transcription, including questions asked, lightly edited for clarity where needed, in first-person narrative style, with complete sentences that retained the tone of the answers given. Students used footnotes to annotate, in their own words, when clarifications or fuller historical context were needed to explain the meaning of a reference. If they made a passing mention of a significant historical event, name, industry, organisation, or other item of interest without explaining it, this helped clarify things for the readers.

Following the bio and transcript, students conducted a two-to-three-page analysis of the oral history. This was a reflection on the underlying political, social, economic, or cultural tensions that affected this person's childhood, informed by our assigned readings and class discussions. They made specific references (citing their sources) and used their interview to demonstrate how the subject's childhood seemed either to be a product of the times described or to depart significantly from that usually assigned to their generation in the mainstream narrative. An important comparative aspect to this project was in finding a memory in the anarchive database that they could draw into conversation with their interview subject's childhood narrative—these could be similarities or differences, but the observation had to be developed around a common keyword or reference point.

In the analysis, they considered the questions: What seemed to be the values held by this generation, and how and where were they reinforced? How did Cold-War narratives, rhetoric, propaganda, or material circumstances inform this person's worldview? How does their experience, or their perception of their experience, compare with others of their generation? Compare with the *Memories of Everyday Childhoods* database to find contrasting experiences for your analysis. How do your experiences (international travels, reading firsthand accounts of other childhoods, learning more about the mutual propaganda machines constructed by the First- and Second-World powers, etc.) help you to understand this person's childhood in a broader historical context?

The project concluded with a bibliography of all works cited and sources referenced.

Stage 6: Peer Review

Students uploaded the complete draft (including bio, transcript, analysis, and bibliography) to a shared drive, and each was randomly assigned to conduct peer reviews of two other project drafts. Students read the transcript and analysis for clarity, but more importantly, they looked for opportunities to deepen the analysis. This was an opportunity for students to demonstrate what they had learned about the nuances of each Cold-War generation or, perhaps, the cultural differences that might distinguish one childhood from another. They could comment on similarities with their own interview subjects' stories (finding commonalities that reinforced certain arguments about identity formation as a generational process) or remark on unexpected differences (cautionary tales to avoid falling into causational arguments). Students reminded each other of the connections between these family histories and the national narratives we studied in class, enhancing the collective process of applying learned material to the project.

Stage 7: Cold-War Childhood Memories Class Database

Using the *Memories of Everyday Childhoods* anarchive as an inspiration, students identified passages in the original transcript that could be excerpted as Cold-War childhood memories, evocative of a historical moment without requiring further explanation or context to interpret them. The final product was a collective memory database that represented a cross-section of the class's relationship to Cold-War histories, whether through family heritage or an affective tie to a kinship network (a neighbour, employer, or other member of the student's community). These memory-stories were compiled anonymously in a shared drive, with only a list of keywords as titles or introductions. Following are a few examples:

Catholicism, Religion, Prayer, School, 60s, USA

I remember we would take time out of our class day to pray every day for the conversion of Russia's citizens to Christianity. Every day in class we would take time to do that.

Malaysia, USA, Propaganda

I saw that on tape delay at the US Embassy because a country on the equator does not air the ice hockey games. We went to the embassy and they had a big party to watch the game. In order to go to the Embassy you had to be invited. They had this program called USIS in which you could check out documentaries and films on US things and watch them. Part of the propaganda to promote US culture. This program was promoted by the American government and anyone could participate, not just US citizens. My dad would rent movies on a Friday night.

Hockey, Memory, Russia, Olympics, Ohio, USA

I played hockey that morning of the game that we beat the Russians (it was a night game), and we still had to win the gold against Finland. That one was a morning game at around 10 am and after we won, we ran out and played hockey that day. You'd sling your skates around your neck with the shoestrings tied and skates banging the whole way. I remember almost RUNNING the whole 10 minutes it took to get to the frozen lake to play hockey! ... The Soviets were always messing with the rules trying to tilt them and cheat or do something. And the big thing was that all our best athletes were pros, so they were playing for money. But the Russians didn't believe in any of that, ya know, the whole collective and nobody makes money, and so all of their best players would play for the national team. So, it was our college kids vs. the best players in the world! We definitely wanted to beat them bad and my friends and I talked about how stupid and unfair it was, so that's why we were so happy when they won.

Stage 8: Final Oral History Project

Students incorporated edits from my draft reviews, and the comments from the two peer reviews, to make any corrections and enhance their analysis of the interview according to the following suggestions:

Bio. Is the biographical preface descriptive enough to provide necessary background and context? Is the interviewee's age and generation clearly defined? Are other relevant characteristics presented (geographic location, urban/rural upbringing, socio-economic status or class, political or religious tendencies in the family, etc.?). Not all of these are relevant for each interview, but in some cases a description of characteristics not explicitly brought up in the interview help to contextualise comments or observations made.

Interview transcript. Is the transcript written clearly and does it accurately reflect the voice and tone of the interviewee's responses? Be sure to add in clarifications where needed. For example, if an important word or phrase is left out and you need to include it for clarity or to make the sentence work better grammatically, you can add words or phrases to the transcript [in brackets]. This signals to the reader that you, the editor, have added something for clarification. Do you need to define a person, place, or thing mentioned in passing so that the reader gets the reference? This could be a reference to a last name, or a political figure, or a local eatery, or a favorite toy, or a family member. Add a footnote and include your own explanation for the reader.

Analysis. Place this person's childhood, as described by them in their own words, in the context of the comparative Cold-War childhoods that we have been studying this semester. Is this person's experience typical of their generation, or do their stories and memories depart from the expected characterisations of how they grew up? Are there surprising similarities or differences from the experiences of their peers in the US? Or in the USSR/Eastern bloc? What are some of the broader political and social events, discourses, or themes that defined their generation on the national and global scale, and how can you see those playing out in their everyday experiences? In this section, I'm looking for lots of comparative work. To do that, bring in as many specific examples from class readings, film clips watched in class, propaganda posters, documentaries, socialist memories websites, etc. as you can find. Consult the syllabus and class notes to review the materials that we have covered. Review the insightful comments from the peer review in our shared drive. Cite specific page numbers when you have them.

Bibliography. Please include full bibliographical citations of all materials consulted, both assigned class readings and any external sources that you might have used.

Demographics and the Master Narrative

The student-body demographic for this class, including but not limited to their national and ethnic heritage, has implications for the conclusions we draw from the oral histories to create a collective biography. This midwestern, public university in the United States is a Predominantly White Institution (PWI), a feature that scholars have observed to be detrimental to pedagogies that introduce cultural diversity (Morales and Raible 2020).[1] Not surprisingly, a vast majority of students' interview subjects overwhelmingly bear out the demographic breakdown of university enrolments, representing white, rural, Judeo-Christian families in the Midwest. At first glance, the content of the interviews reveals uniform childhoods: private Catholic education, military service, Boy or Girl Scouts membership, 'Duck and Cover' drills in school, uninterrupted education, and economic stability consistently appear in individual stories across the

---

1   Fall 2021 enrollment data for Miami University identifies 76.6% of the student population as white, 4.9% Hispanic/Latino, 4.0% Black, 4.0% multi-racial, and 2.5% Asian. www.miamioh.edu/diversity-inclusion/data-reports/index.html.

three generations. Cold-War memories invariably honed in on the moments of prolific media coverage: the Cuban missile crisis, Vietnam War footage, Reagan's speech at the Berlin Wall, the fall of the Berlin Wall. Reading each other's oral histories, twenty-first-century students with personalised algorithmically curated media playlists marvelled at the common cultural references of their parents' and grandparents' entertainment programming: *Father Knows Best*, the *Rocky* franchise, and *Rocky and Bullwinkle* all received multiple unprompted mentions in the childhood reminiscences.

It might be tempting to paint the Cold-War generations in the West with a single brush, pointing to these cultural trends as evidence that state and media interests successfully constructed the childhoods that they idealised. Yet doing so would fall into the same trap as those who crafted the hegemonic Soviet childhood narrative: 'the predominant descriptions of the region often employed the framework of totalitarianism and discussed socialist countries in monolithic terms, highlighting the dichotomies between East and West' (Piattoeva et al. 2018, p. 3). Foregrounding childhood memories of the Soviet era have demonstrated both an appreciation for nuance and diversity across the socialist landscape and the power of the everyday in revealing that children are more than just 'passive receivers of societal norms' (Piattoeva et al. 2018, p. 4). Much as the post/socialist memory workers sought to dismantle the single story of Soviet childhoods, our stories help us to question the story the West has constructed about itself in diametric opposition to the Soviet childhood trope. A critical analysis of our informants' stories of growing up in the West unearths a wealth of details that reveal children as more than simply constructs of a national propaganda machine. Their stories reveal independent thinking and sentiments of dissent.

The apparent demographic uniformity might also suggest homogeneous worldviews, but a closer look at the interview subjects' intersected lives reveals a host of international experiences, diverse national or ethnic heritage, or affective ties to other cultural traditions. Informants traced their Cold-War memories to Israel and Palestine, Russia, Germany, and Malaysia. They married, lived next door to, served alongside, shared a dorm with, or befriended people from India, Croatia, the segregated South, Cubans, Jewish people,

Vietnam veterans and anti-war protestors alike. The diversity of individual stories belies the narratives of whiteness and American exceptionalism that prevail in this part of the country and that the students have internalised as part of their latent identity formation. Personal stories of hardship also challenged the perception of the student body as coming from affluent backgrounds or as beneficiaries of generational wealth. This assignment offered them a rare opportunity to interrogate the unstable constructs of whiteness and US national identity.

The quiet heterogeneity of our collective biography notwithstanding, students did note the surprisingly strong trends that marked each generation. For subjects who grew up in the 1940s–50s, their negative assessment of 'communism' and 'Russians' and supportive stance regarding US military operations in places like Korea and Vietnam were less likely to have undergone meaningful revision over time, suggesting the socialising power of the first wave of Cold-War educational propaganda. For those coming of age in the 1960s–70s, a political reawakening seemed to mark the generation, as they expressed sympathy with or involvement in Civil Rights activities and anti-war protests. And for those who grew up in the 1980s, the popular and material cultural references resounded in the form of conspicuous consumption (or aspirations to shop) in a world in which capitalism seemed poised to prevail over the version of socialism purveyed in movies and television. A discussion of these observed generational trends led us to draw two conclusions: first, the Cold-War publicity machines achieved a measure of success in constructing childhoods (or inciting generational pushback); and second, a more diverse student body (national, ethnic, racial, or religious) would yield a much more nuanced story about the construction and breakdown of the Cold-War consensus. Within our group, we had no representation of the Third World or the Global South, a striking omission for this era of world history, as scholars are working to put the majority of the world's population more meaningfully into the Cold-War narrative (Prashad 2007).

Another important conclusion drawn from this assignment was that, regardless of the ideological conformity observed at peak moments of geopolitical tensions, many interview subjects who confessed to prejudices, bias, or extreme political positions in their youth had since moderated their stance. The capacity for evolution in political thinking is not one of the official narratives of the Cold War—the reification of a diametrically opposed East vs. West and the intransigence of thinking on either side. But one student interviewed their mother—described as an intelligent, independent thinker who did not subscribe to a political position—and expressed surprise at her admission that, as a child, she had hated Russia and communism. The mother's self-awareness allowed her to acknowledge that she had fallen sway to a propagandistic media landscape, but her distance from that now provides anecdotal evidence that the totalitarian socialising aims of the state need not have a permanent grip on the ideological formation of its citizens.

The Value of Seeing Ourselves in History

Experimenting with oral history as a tool for teaching the Cold War has the obvious benefit of allowing students to see the legacy of historical processes, conflicts, propaganda machines, policies, and migrations in their own lives. But the framework of childhood adds another dimension to the pedagogical possibilities of such an approach. Here, I discuss the tacit conclusions that could be drawn from the surprising commonalities and divergences that these interviews yielded.

The Cold-War era provides a particularly suitable laboratory for examining childhood—the stark binary worldview set forth on the ideological plane disproportionately implicated children as subjects, objects, and agents (Levison et al. 2021). Images of children served as powerful propaganda fodder within the two spheres of influence, especially in the early years of the Cold War, inciting individuals to contribute to the consensus solicited by their respective state. By the 1960s, though, Cold-War dissenters mobilised images of children abandoned by society to critique the Cold-War narrative, leading to a breakdown of consensus (Peacock 2014, pp. 5–7). Testaments from the oral histories revealed undeniable evidence of ideological indoctrination, especially for the first Cold-War generation. Classrooms, youth organisations, and religious communities all served as laboratories for the politicisation of children, leaving indelible impressions about good and evil on young minds that withstood the ideological challenges posed by later generations. Students expressed surprise when interviewing family members of an older generation that some of the antiquated anti-Russian, anti-Communist vitriol still echoed in their twenty-first-century ruminations.

But a closer look at the ways that the memories departed from the expected patterns of generational identity formation reveals more about what a lens of childhood can tell us about conventional Cold-War wisdom. In the US, the narrative of Western affluence was constructed against the image of Eastern austerity. But several students' interview subjects relayed stories of childhoods in rural Kentucky, or Appalachian West Virginia as being completely disconnected from consumer capitalism, relying on a community-sustenance economy premised on collectivism and reciprocity. Even though such livelihoods modelled the socialist ideal much more than the capitalist one, the children growing up in those circumstances did not use such ideological frameworks to politicise their childhoods. Invention born of scarcity defined their 'normal' American childhood, out of the mainstream by any definition. Such childhoods, considered in the halo of post-Cold-War validation of a narrative in which capitalism vanquished communism, affirmed an American ethos of 'pulling oneself up by the bootstraps.'

On the other hand, as consumer culture accelerated in the latter half of the Cold-War, children expressed agency through their economic behaviour, quietly exerting powerful influence through actions that often fly under the radar of historians because of how children have historically been coded as dependents (Sosenski Correa 2012). Children's persistence and creativity in acquiring a desired object seems to be universal. Evidence of children's conspicuous consumption practices in the West, compared to the *kulturnost* ethos of consumption in the East, or the steady filtering of Western goods into places like Yugoslavia and late-socialist Poland that straddled the Iron Curtain, all reveal children's consumption as a normalising factor that elides the constructed cultural differences between communism and capitalism (Burrell 2011; Drakulić 1991).

The lens of childhood helps us to dismantle, or at least contextualise, Cold-War narratives. Ruling Cold-War officials continued to think of children unilaterally as products, proof, or assets in political machinations. Yet historians of childhood know that children as subjects, objects, and agents continue to respond to material and ideological forces in diverse ways. A look at Cold-War history subverts the power dynamic of the story—the causational forces, the socialising institutions, and the material conditions artificially created by state decisions fall to the background—and, through children, we see the nuances of history, the subjectivity of human actors, and the permeability of the Iron Curtain.

When asked to reflect on the exercise, students expressed appreciation for the opportunity to ground their own family histories in the context of the drier textbook narratives. One student remarked that, prior to the class, they felt no connection to history; after interviewing their grandfather who lived through the Cold War, they began to see themselves as a historical actor as well, living through a pandemic and controversial presidential election that would mark the pages of future history books.

Students gained empathy for historical subjects, having a better understanding of the contexts that led them to make unsavoury choices or hold untoward opinions. One grandmother conveyed a second-hand story of a friend who had served in the Vietnam War, and the emotional impact of that story held enough power to transmit feeling across generations and continents. Another student's mother travelled to Russia in the late-1980s as part of a People-to-People child-ambassador exchange, and the student was astonished to hear her mother describe the architecture of the Hermitage, the colour of the sky, and the flavours of the food of a country that usually only entered the American imaginary as the 'evil empire'. As her mother recounted her journey from decades past, she realised that nobody had ever asked her about how this exchange shaped her as a global citizen—not her parents, not her teachers, not her partner—until she had been prompted to reflect on her child ambassadorship in the context of Cold-War geopolitics. She was able to articulate her childhood experiences as part of a transformational moment on the eve of the dissolution of the Soviet Union, giving her the opportunity to historicise her own experiences.

For Western students, especially those in the United States, the Cold-War narrative has rarely been dismantled or questioned by previous generations of their families. It was accepted as fact. Learning to read personal testimonies comparatively, against the official history and alongside the anarchive memories of counterparts from across the Cold-War divide, allowed students to read their own family histories critically, and ultimately helped them to see themselves as both constituted by, but also free from being tethered to, the historical forces that inform their own lives.

Reflecting on history through the lens of their family member's youth made students consider themselves as historical actors living through a significant moment of their own. They noted that future historians—or their own children conducting oral history projects?—might look back at Brexit, the COVID-19 pandemic, or contested presidential elections as significant junctures in history's trajectory. 'There are so many stories in history that don't get told because people just don't ask,' reflected the student whose mother had been a child ambassador to Russia:

The fact that she went abroad when she was younger than me makes history feel so close, like my mom is only in her 40s but she went to the Soviet Union during a period of tension and change that ended up being crucial historically, and she didn't know that at the time.

References

Albarrán, E. J. (2021). '"So How's your Childhood Going?" A Historian of Childhood Confronts her own Archive, in *Children and Youth as Subjects, Objects, Agents: Innovative Approaches to Research Across Space and Time*, ed. by D. Levison, M. J. Maynes and F. Vavrus. (pp. 13–32). Palgrave MacMillan, https://doi.org/10.1007/978-3-030-63632-6_2

Bogic, A. (2018). 'Tito's Last Pioneers and the Politicisation of Schooling in Yugoslavia', in *Childhood and Schooling in Post/Socialist Societies: Memories of Everyday Life*, ed. by I. Silova, N. Piattoeva, and Z. Millei. (pp. 127–44). Palgrave MacMillan, https://doi.org/10.1007/978-3-319-62791-5_7

Burrell, K. (2011). 'The Enchantment of Western Things: Children's Material Encounters in Late Socialist Poland'. *Transactions of the Institute of British Geographers*, 36(1), 143–56, https://doi.org/10.1111/j.1475-5661.2010.00408.x

Drakulić, S. (1991). *How we Survived Communism and Even Laughed*. W.W. Norton

Dror, O. (2016). 'Love, Hatred, and Heroism: Socializing Children in North Vietnam during Wartime, 1965–75'. *The Journal of the History of Childhood and Youth*, 9(3), 424–49, https://doi.org/10.1353/hcy.2016.0054

Dubinsky, K. (2012). 'Children, Ideology, and Iconography: How Babies Rule the World'. *The Journal of the History of Childhood and Youth*, 5(1), 5–13, https://doi.org/10.1353/hcy.2012.0009

Fattal, I. (2018, January 4). 'Why Do Cartoon Villains Speak in Foreign Accents?'. *The Atlantic*

Funder, A. (2003). *Stasiland: Stories from Behind the Berlin Wall*. Harper Collins

Fürst, J. (2015). 'Swinging across the Iron Curtain and Moscow's Summer of Love: How Western Youth Culture went East', in (pp. 237–59). Palgrave MacMillan

Godeanu-Kenworthy, O. (2020, February 21). 'My Dictator: Growing Up in Ceausescu's Romania'. *Popula*, https://popula.com/2020/02/21/my-dictator-growing-up-in-ceausescus-romania/

'Growing Up on "This Side"'. (n.d.). *Memories of Everyday Childhoods: De-Colonial and De-Cold War Dialogues on Childhood and Schooling*, https://coldwarchildhoods.org/portfolio/growing-up-on-this-side/

Ivaska, A. (2015). 'Movement Youth in a Global Sixties Hub: The Everyday Lives of Transnational Activists in Postcolonial Dar es Salaam', in *Transnational Histories of Youth in the Twentieth Century*, ed. by R. I. Jobs and D. Pomfret. (pp. 188–210). Palgrave MacMillan, https://doi.org/10.1057/9781137469908_9

Johnson, J. (2021, September 9). 'The Professor as a Primary Source'. *Perspectives on History*, https://www.historians.org/research-and-publications/perspectives-on-history/september-2021/the-professor-as-a-primary-source-9/11-history-and-memory

'*Kaleidoscope: Children of the Cold War* Exhibition Opening' (2021, February 25). *Memories of Everyday Childhoods: De-Colonial and De-Cold War Dialogues on Childhood and Schooling*, https://coldwarchildhoods.org/exhibition-opening/

Levison, D., Maynes, M. J. and Vavrus, F. (2021). 'Introduction', in *Children and Youth as Subjects, Objects, Agents: Innovative Approaches to Research Across Space and Time*, ed. by D. Levison, M. J. Maynes and F. Vavrus. (pp. 1–9). Palgrave MacMillan, https://doi.org/10.1007/978-3-030-63632-6_2

Morales, A. R. and Raible, J. (2020). 'To Teach as We are Known: The "Heart and Soul" Labor of Teacher Educators of Colour Working in PWIs', in *Designing Culturally Competent Programming for PK-20 Classrooms*, ed. by K. Sprott, J. R. O'Connor, Jr., and C. Msengi. (pp. 79–97). IGI Global, https://doi.org/10.4018/978-1-7998-3652-0

Oral History. (2022). The Writing Centre, University of North Carolina at Chapel Hill, https://writingcentre.unc.edu/tips-and-tools/oral-history/

Peacock, M. (2014). *Innocent Weapons: The Soviet and American Politics of Childhood in the Cold War*. University of North Carolina Press, https://doi.org/10.5149/northcarolina/9781469618579.001.0001

—— (2019). 'Samantha Smith in the Land of the Bolsheviks: Peace and the Politics of Childhood in the Late Cold War'. *Diplomatic History*, 43(3), 418–44, https://doi.org/10.1093/dh/dhy092

Piattoeva, N., Silova, I. and Millei, Z. (2018). 'Remembering Childhoods, Rerwriting Post/Socialist Lives, in *Childhood and Schooling in Post/Socialist Societies*, ed. by I. Silova, N. Piattoeva, and Z. Millei. (pp. 1–18). Palgrave MacMillan, https://doi.org/10.1007/978-3-319-62791-5_1

Prashad, V. (2007). *The Darker Nations: A People's History of the Third World*. The New Press

Silova, I., Piattoeva, N. and Millei, Z. (2018). *Childhood and Schooling in (Post) Socialist Societies: Memories of Everyday Life*. New York: Palgrave Macmillan, https://doi.org/10.1007/978-3-319-62791-5

Sosenski Correa, S. (2012). 'El niño consumidor. Una construcción publicitaria de la prensa mexicana en la década de 1950', in *Ciudadanos inesperados: Espacios de formación de la ciudadanía ayer y hoy*, ed. by A. Acevedo Rodrigo and P. López Caballero. (pp. 191–222). El Colegio de México

Stearns, P. N. (2017). *Childhood in World History* (3rd edn.). Routledge, https://doi.org/10.4324/9781315561363

Pink Flamingo[1]

Iveta Silova

It was supposed to be a very ordinary spring morning in Stučka, a small town in Soviet Latvia named after Lenin's communist friend Petr Stučka. It was 1982. The statue of Stučka was towering on the town's main square, which was curiously located not in the center, but on the edge of the town by the river. In less than a decade, the town would be renamed Aizkraukle, after the 14th century Livonian Order castle, the ruins of which still remain there. And Petr Stučka would be gone.

The girl lived just a few blocks away from the square, in a 9-story 'high rise' apartment building by the riverside. Every morning she would get up and look outside the window—the river was usually gray and gloomy, but sometimes deep blue and playful. She could see the forests growing alongside the river, the concrete blocks fortifying the river dam and shores, and the hydroelectric station in the distance. The girl liked observing the subtle changes in the river—its colors and moods. Looking from the fifth floor down, the dominant colors were gray in the winter, with the sprinkling of white when it snowed. In the spring and summer, different shades of blue and green mixed together and brightened the morning color palette. Greeting the river was a morning ritual, marking the beginning of another day.

One spring morning, something entirely unexpected happened. As the girl looked outside the window to greet the river, the colors were all mixed up! Amidst the gray and blue and the budding green, there was a bright pink spot! What could it be? How confusing! The girl's mind was racing trying to figure it out. It took a few minutes. Flamingos! The girl could not believe her eyes. She knew they did not belong there. She saw flamingoes on TV before, watching

---

1 This is a childhood memory produced as part of the Reconnect/Recollect project discussed in the introduction to this book.

the 'Around the World' program, and she read about them in children's books, including her favorite Alice in Wonderland. But here? In her own town?! How could this be?

Excited, she called her parents and grandparents. She then ran to get her friends. Skipping breakfast, they rushed down to the river to greet the surprise visitors. Soon the entire town was buzzing with the news of the visiting flamingos. Children and adults were coming to greet them, take pictures, or simply stand quietly nearby observing the birds. And flamingos greeted people back, gracefully nodding their long necks. Visitors from another world.

It always remained a mystery—what were the flamingos doing there in a small Soviet town? How did they get to the girl's river? And why? And would they ever come back again? Staring outside the window every morning, the girl kept looking for new shades and colors to appear again.

15. Connecting Across Divides:
A Case Study in Public History of the (E-)Motion Comic 'Ghost Train—Memories of Ghost Trains and Ghost Stations in Former East and West-Berlin'

Sarah Fichtner and Anja Werner

In this chapter, we describe the process of—and reflect on our experiences with—creating the collaborative, international motion comic 'Ghost Train—Memories of Ghost Trains and Ghost Stations in Former East and West Berlin', which is based on memories that we shared in a Reconnect/Recollect project workshop. During this workshop, Sarah Fichtner shared her West Berliner childhood memory of accidentally riding an underground train through 'ghost stations' of East Berlin. In turn, Anja Werner recalled a scene from her East German childhood of when she actually heard such 'ghost trains' rumbling underneath an apartment in East Berlin. From the experience with our motion comic, we gather that motion comics, because they are pieces of art, can add additional layers to history work. They do so by working with and addressing emotions, thus becoming (e-) motion comics as they connect people through memories across divides, time, and space.

In collective-biography work, memories may connect persons, themes, and material things or objects. Objects referenced in memories connect people through their materialities, such as a bed that one person sleeps in and another one makes, or a train that one travels on and the other hears going by. It is almost as if, through these objects, one person becomes a participant in another's memory and, thus, earlier life. The memories complement one another, thus allowing remembering participants to come to terms with them by encountering another person's recollections of the same objects or events.

This effect is not limited to the two people sharing their memories but also transfers to those who are listening to the memories or watching the outcome in the form of a motion comic. Authors and audiences may enter into each other's experiences through tangible means, thanks to an 'absent presence' (Mazzei 2003, p. 27). They thus create connections even across divides, time, and space, deepening our understanding of situated perspectives through shared memories.

In working with shared memories, visual media—in contrast to texts—offer different representational possibilities and modes of impact: They directly draw us into the story, make interconnections tangible and give 'data'—in our case, memory—a face, a voice, and a feeling. Visual media thereby present an easily accessible form of knowledge transfer that is far from being unidirectional.

In this chapter, we describe the process of—and reflect on our experiences with—creating a collaborative, international motion comic 'Ghost Train—Memories of Ghost Trains and Ghost Stations in Former East and West Berlin' (Fichtner and Werner et al. 2020). In four subsections, which are devoted to the processes of connecting, transforming, collecting, and transferring, as well as a concluding section of reflecting, we address the following questions: How is a connection created through a remembered material thing, here, the train? How does your own story become the story of others when it is translated into pictures and different languages? What happens as it takes on a life of its own? What kind of reactions does this trigger in recipients from near and far and across generations? Last but not least, what potential does this experience offer us for educational memory work—a form of Public History—across and about divides, allowing viewers to grasp the absent presence of others in all our lives?

Connecting Through Remembered Things in Shared Memories: How it All Started

The motion comic 'Ghost Train—Memories of Ghost Trains and Ghost Stations in Former East and West Berlin' is based on childhood memories that we shared in September 2019 in Berlin during a workshop organised by the Reconnect/Recollect project.[1] Sarah Fichtner shared her West Berliner childhood memory of accidentally riding the underground train through 'ghost stations' of East Berlin when she was trying out a different and unknown way home from school. Here is a snippet of her memory story:

At Kurt Schumacher Platz in the West, the girl enters the U6 with her friends. For the first few stations she enjoys the ride. She feels independent and grown up. But her joyful and proud laughter stops abruptly when the train does not stop anymore. It passes through numerous, dimly lit, dark and empty 'ghost stations' that look like construction sights. Passing through those stations the train slows down. It does not stop. In the tunnel it regains speed. The girl panics. She realises that they are in the East: Even more disturbing: They are underneath the East. One of her friends starts to cry, wondering if they will ever get back to their parents. Is the train really taking them to their home destinations? Will they have to stay in the East? There are other passengers, but this does not prevent the children from feeling lost and alone.

When she had finished her story, a woman whom she had not known prior to this workshop, Anja Werner, recalled a scene from her East German childhood. Here is a snippet from Anja's memory story—with her family, she is visiting friends in East Berlin and finds herself alone in a room:

There's another one of those white Mohair rugs on the floor in front of the desk. She yawns. Why not lie down now?

As she's lying on the floor, she can suddenly hear a sort of rumble coming from below. Just a short rumble—and gone. Silence. She holds her breath, waits… there it is again. She doesn't know what that rumble is. Is she scared? No, just wondering. There it is again. And another. Always a brief interval of silence in between. The girl darts to her feet and runs to the living room. What's this rumbling noise? It's a short rumble, then it stops, and after a while there's another one. What is it?

---

1   The motion comic was realised thanks to the generous support of the Kone Foundation, Finland, which financed the Reconnect/Recollect project.

During the workshop, we juxtaposed our two memories, so that the audience learned simultaneously what the two girls inside and above the train felt and thought.

It was fascinating to experience how our two memories joined together, how we became part of each other's memory by telling them jointly from two situated perspectives, from two sides of the Berlin Wall, and focusing on the same 'thing': the underground train. This train in its Western materiality can be understood to symbolise mobility as well as adventure but, with it, also the fear of border crossing. The absent presence of the train(s) in the East simultaneously stands for structural immobility that is being confronted with the powerful imagination of children and, thus, is resolved in a soothing way. Anja remembers:

> I was very much surprised and delighted to hear Sarah's story. So, I got up to talk about my mirroring memory of when I actually heard such 'ghost trains' rumbling underneath an apartment in East Berlin. Having both stories side by side felt like finally seeing the complete picture, and that to me personally felt soothing in some ways. It was like truly re-uniting the country by uniting our memories and making sense of them as a whole.

Intuitively, we both knew that this had to be captured in the form of a joint story. It was equally clear that this story needed a livelier and more emotional medium than the plain text. So, the idea was born to make a motion comic—or an (e-)motion comic as we like to call it—as this medium helps us both to transport and to deal with different kinds of emotions, such as fear and joy paired with excitement and curiosity, while also evoking such feelings in the viewer. We will come back to this later.

Transforming Memories: An International, Collaborative, and Creative Adventure

Motion comics are digital, moving-picture stories with text and sound that can easily be shared on the internet (Smith 2015). They allow us to tell a story-in-motion through images but are less complicated and less expensive to make than a cartoon or animated film, as fewer images are needed to make them work. Motion comics, consequently, are an effective and practical way to turn a written story into an animated video.

To transform our childhood memories into a motion comic, we called upon the illustration duo Azam Aghalouie and Hassan Tavakoli, originally from Iran. Sarah knew them from an earlier project, the Encounters Media Workshop (Medienwerkstatt Encounters). Azam and Hassan arrived in Berlin in 2017 and have remained fascinated with the extraordinary history of the city ever since. They listened to our story and were captivated.

We had initially written our two stories as two individual texts using the third-person perspective, following the advice of Susanne Gannon, who introduced us to the method of collective biography during the Reconnect/Recollect workshop (see Davies and Gannon 2006). We observed the reactions of our fellow participants and carefully considered their requests that we provide more or different details of almost-forgotten aspects. The basic idea of the memory sharing during that workshop was to explore experiences of childhood in the context of the Cold War. How did children live through everyday life in a divided world? Which moments did they memorise as 'special'? In short, how did children make sense of growing up in the Cold War? How has this affected the adults into which the children grew?

The outcome was surprising. The memory sharing created a type of community across time and space that included not just those who told memories on their own or as a group, but also those who listened and watched. As the Reconnect/Recollect project and workshop organisers Silova, Piattoeva, and Millei observed already in 2018, 'we felt a very personal connection during storytelling—almost as if we were related', and like them, we too 'were curious to explore these connections further' (Silova et al. 2018, p. v).

Our initial thought was to see what happened if we joined an East- and a West-German perspective of a memory involving an object like the train. In the process, our shared memory took on a life of its own, creating something new as we went along. It also gained from the addition of perspectives from another cultural context thanks to the involvement of our Iranian friends. This transnational approach to German public history became an important aspect of our work as we embarked on a follow-up project.

In the following, let us explore our experiences in more detail, starting with a step-by-step look at the creative process behind 'Ghost

Train'. As a first step, we had to shorten both texts and merge them into one script with different chapters, applying a consistent narrative style. For instance, we chose to introduce both little girls with a similar phrase about the year in which they were born. In Anja's case:

The girl was born in February 1976 in a strange little country whose leaders once upon a time had decided to build a big wall around it so that no bad people could get in, or so they claimed. But the little girl already knew only too well: No one could get out, either. Her life was one of longing to see what lay beyond that wall. Was there anything at all?

And in Sarah's case:

She was born in April 1979 on what she perceived as an artificial island called West Berlin. She grew up in an apartment facing the train rails that connected 'her' island with the 'rest' of West Germany. Being surrounded by 'the East' and having people refer to places in the South as 'West Germany' definitely messed up her geographic sense of orientation.

We also had to smooth over or omit some details, such as references to the day of the week and time, in order to create a coherent narrative that was not openly self-contradictory.

Our motion comic raises questions about realism in artwork just as it touches on discourses about representations of the past that are central to historiography. This became obvious in the creative process. When we asked artists Azam and Hassan if they could transform this shared story into a motion comic, they read the text carefully and asked us to provide visual material, such as photographs of ourselves as children at the age we are in the story. This was necessary because our memories are based on actual events that can be located in time and space. Then again, as we will show below, the motion comic took on a life on its own—one that is, ultimately, fictional. We helped it on its way, perhaps, as we also took some liberties with the 'facts'.

To grasp a sense and a feeling of the 1980s in the divided Berlin, the artists asked us for visual references to specific elements that we mentioned in our story, such as a school backpack, a toy police car, the furniture in the East Berlin apartment, the mohair rug, the radio. We provided them with photographs, taken at around the time of our story, of the divided Berlin, the bus, and the underground as they looked back then. We found some relevant images among our personal photograph collections, including those shared with Azam and Hassan in preparation of the motion comic (see Figures 15.1, 15.2, and 15.3).

Fig. 15.1 Anja at age six, around the time the 'Ghost Trains' incident happened. Photograph by Klaus Becker, Naumburg (Saale), 1982.

358   (An)Archive: Childhood, Memory, and the Cold War

Fig. 15.2 Sarah at around age eight or nine. Photograph by Barbara Fichtner, Schwege, 1987.

Fig. 15.3 Sarah's school backpack. Photograph by Barbara Fichtner, Berlin, 1985.

We also researched representative images on the internet that reflected the shape and look of things in our memories or simply represented the time and place in question. Already at that point we found a few 'mistakes'. That is to say, we found examples of how our personal memories differed from the reality that others had captured in photographs. For instance, Anja remembered the Berlin Wall passing right through the Brandenburg Gate because that is how she perceived it at the age of six during a walk on the day of her memory. The research for the motion comic revealed that—seen from the East Berlin side—the Wall actually ran 'behind' the Brandenburg Gate. Eventually, we dropped the Brandenburg Gate from the visuals because it would have complicated the narrative structure. We did keep other critical points, though, such as the question of what the Berlin metro trains looked like in the 1980s. How much liberty could we take in depicting them? Moreover, Sarah and Anja disagreed over the title of the motion comic. While Sarah rode on only one train, Anja heard several. Should it be 'Ghost Train' or 'Ghost Trains'? We wondered if it was possible to alternate, since the motion comic could be found on the internet no matter which version is searched? Was there a way to reflect both of our perceptions of the number of trains?

Dealing with such discrepancies raised the question of how authentic the visuals needed to be. They needed to provide a sense of the different time and space, but would they have to be authentic replicas, historically 'correct'? Is it even possible to create authenticity in retrospect? After all, memories can be faulty or change over time, an idea that we felt should somehow be incorporated into the motion comic by including 'visual inaccuracies'. In the end, our goal was not so much to reconstruct past events as a form of oral history but to focus on how children made sense of such events and what they took from it into adulthood, which also included changing images and shifting perspectives.

Based on the visuals we provided, Azam and Hassan created their first drawings with pencil as thumbnails and transformed our story into forty-nine images that they showed to us to get feedback (see Figure 15.4). We realised at this point that some pictures needed more or different details, that our story was inaccurate in some aspects and needed to be adjusted, or that Azam and Hassan had a really interesting perspective on some scenes that we had not seen before.

The motion comic thus became a collaborative adventure. This was an important step in bringing the story to life, in turning two individual memories into a collaboratively created image of a specific time period in the past.

Fig. 15.4 Thumbnails: forty-nine images for the 'Ghost Train' story. Illustrations ©Azam Aghalouie und Hassan Tavakoli. Photograph by Sarah Fichtner, 2020.

At this point in our creative process, the Covid-19 pandemic started, and we did almost all our work together online. While we had not planned on collaborating through the internet, being suddenly forced to do so highlighted the potential of this particular medium for our project: our memories might not only cross divides but be available to audiences online. We would return to this idea when, after the release of the 'Ghost Train' motion comic, we started thinking about a follow-up project. But back to the creative process.

We decided to have two different colour schemes for the different narrators, and Azam and Hassan experimented with different shades to get the right mood. They then prepared the first actual sketches (Figure 15.5 and Figure 15.6).

Fig. 15.5 Sample illustration from Sarah's part of the story. © Azam Aghalouie und Hassan Tavakoli, 2020.

Fig. 15.6 Sample illustration from Anja's part of the story. © Azam Aghalouie und Hassan Tavakoli, 2020.

On the basis of these drawings, Azam and Hassan prepared a first video. Meanwhile, we recorded our stories in German and English. The original plan had been to meet and record it together in one session. But, because of the pandemic, we had to record the narration each on our own. It took some experimenting with our personal equipment until we had recordings that matched in quality and tone. As a finishing touch, we added some music.

The motion comic 'Ghost Train—Memories of Ghost Trains and Ghost Stations in Former East and West Berlin' was released on 9 November 2020, the anniversary of the fall of the Berlin Wall. It stands for encounters on multiple levels: memory meets memory, East meets West, two German stories meet the imaginative force of Iranian artists, illustration turns into motion picture. The ten-minute motion comic is available on YouTube in English and in German.[2]

Collecting Reactions: Shared Memories–Shared Analysis

After its online premiere in 2020 and after each public screening, we asked the audience to share with us anything that the motion comic might have triggered.[3] It was like 'spinning the sticky threads of childhood memories' even further ('Spinning the Sticky Threads of Childhood Memories' 2021). We had reactions from people from diverse generations and backgrounds that reached us via comments and personal messages on social media, through email, in direct oral feedback after screenings, and on conference message boards. Viewers' responses ranged from overall appreciation and observations of how the motion comic 'touched' them to the sharing of additional childhood memories related to ghost trains in Berlin and to the fall of the Berlin Wall. These memories connected with ours mainly on an emotional level, which is why we came to think of our motion comic as an (e-)motion comic. For example, one such contributor wrote,

> This is the heart-warming story of two children and their family and friends in East- and in West-Berlin before the Wall came down. It's timely, the Wall came down 31 years ago, today! Although I didn't live in Berlin during that time, this post-War period affected me greatly and now this cine-cartoon and its underlying story touches me deeply. Hope that all will enjoy watching it and think how we can learn from the past. ...

---

2   Sarah Fichtner, Anja Werner, Azam Aghalouie, Hassan Tavakoli (2020). 'Ghost Train—Memories of Ghost Trains and Ghost Stations in Former East and West Berlin'. YouTube, uploaded by Medienwerkstatt Encounters, 8–9 November 2020, English version: https://www.youtube.com/watch?v=CvoAOMDLszk German version: https://www.youtube.com/watch?v=6NaKHmVRac8

3   We would like to thank all the people who got in touch with us sharing their experiences, memories, and emotions as they watched this motion comic.

15. Connecting Across Divides

Viewers were reminded of their own childhood experiences of the Cold War; they said they were transported back in time. One person described it as follows:

> I remember the time I was an 8-year-old girl in San Diego consciously watching the news for the first time. I remember the excitement of watching people tearing down a wall, celebrating, crying, hugging each other. All that visible emotion and there was a strong sense of hope that came out of a place called Berlin. Little did I know, I have grown to call that place home for over a decade now. Another memory of the divide was when I was hospitalized a few years ago. One older woman in the bed next to me was from the former West and another older woman on the left of my bed was from the former East. That one week stay was memorable for the stories they told me; how their lives and relationships took very different turns, and the conversations between family members with me in the middle.

Another person wrote:

> I just watched your little piece of art and was immediately put back into my childhood. I can share every word of what you said about travelling through ghost stations. I did so many times as line 6 was my line into 'the world' (I lived near Tempelhof Airport then). So, thank you for this reminder of times long past (I just turned 60).

As mentioned before, the processing of memory also raised questions of authenticity. Right after the screening of the video at a conference, one person from the audience stood up and said:

> This triggered a lot of memories. I grew up in West Germany but spent a lot of time in East Germany. And—I know this is a very geeky detail, but as a child I was very fascinated by trains. So not only did I always want to ride the U6 and U8 when I was in West Berlin visiting my uncle, I also enjoyed listening to the rumble of the U6 and U8 when I was in East Berlin. And one even more geeky bit of information: The train in the film is a post-revolutionary version. At that time they had these handles that you could hardly move, they didn't have buttons, but that's maybe too much information... (laughing)

In-depth analyses of the symbolic meaning of underground trains were also among the feedback we received:

> I think for children, any means of transport is a symbol of adventure. So taking anything, a car, a train, an airplane, is a promise of something new, of something adventurous. And I think that especially subways and

airplanes amplify this much more, since they move either underneath the ground or above the ground. And feeling or knowing about a subway which is not existable for you or which brings you into a totally different world, it just emphasizes this difference and the possibility of entering a different world. So I think it's some kind of symbol or metaphor for those interconnected but strictly divided Berlins.

Another person shared the following insights with us:

It triggers the awareness that we are and were indeed connected through everyday experiences and major political processes despite our differences. It also promotes perspective-taking: an event (underground ride) is experienced in different ways by two children living in very different contexts. For both, however, the experience is disturbing in a human way. I therefore think that the project has also a high didactic value, e.g. for history or politics lessons. Thank you for sharing this wonderful work!

Yet another person revealed that she had been following the 'Ghost Train' story since its 'inception,' which led her to a remarkable analysis on the topic of movement and immobility that she published on a conference message board:

I was there when Anja and Sarah told their memories at the memory workshop back in 2019 and I was from the beginning drawn to them. I was mesmerized by the multiple layers of connectedness between the two stories. It never ceases to amaze me how hearing these entangled stories again and again brings up different feelings every time! As I saw the motion comic now, it became clear to me that there is also a story of movement/mobility vs. impossibility of movement/immobility. The 'ghosts' encountered by each girl are the ghosts of the 'other side' which can be both frightening and alluring at the same time. The ghost station is a symbol of immobility. It is static, caught in a state of permanence. For the observer, it is primarily a visual experience, a glimpse of the other side magnified by the presence of others sharing the same visions (i.e. the other girls on the train). What was originally an act of freedom (i.e. taking the unknown route home) became a state of feeling 'trapped' and a fear of being 'stuck' in the East. The ghost train, on the other hand, is a symbol of constant movement. In a rhythmic cadence, it embodies the cyclical movement between worlds, and reveals the mirage of mobility. It is primarily a sensory experience, a gut feeling, a sound leading to an imagination, amplified by the authoritative voice of the parents. What was originally a feeling of fear (i.e. hearing the rumble below and not knowing what it is) became an act of freedom, curiosity, and awe. I am drawn to reflect on what these movements mean in the different contexts, on what it means that movements may cut across times and spaces and go beyond physical and non-physical spaces, on how we may move while standing still and how we may not move while being fully mobile.

We were both touched and surprised by the thoughtful feedback of viewers that brought many new details to our attention and has the potential to inspire future investigations—for example, into trains as symbols of movement (or its absence) in this specific past. Most of all, we realised how emotional it can be to deal with the past when moving pictures are involved. Moreover, such emotions are not restricted to those who create the motion comic on the basis of personal memories; they also extend to those who watch it and relate to it through their own memories.

We did not get any feedback regarding a possibly disturbing or difficult emotion. We assume that the soothing message of our motion comic, which was to a significant degree inspired by the fact that we chose the perspective of innocent children, created a specific mood that touched viewers and evoked similar emotions in them. Memory work as an artistic process can, thus, produce almost therapeutic effects: it is not simply a means to deal with personal questions but a way of bringing about the realisation that we all might connect through our memories. A complex picture emerges of a creative process, historical research, and the uses and effects of public media that needs to be studied much more thoroughly in the future.

Transferring the Experience: Motion Comics as a Tool for Memory Work with Young People

When our motion comic was released and our memories started travelling around the world, provoking other people to share their reactions with us, Anja had the idea to use our experience as a tool for educational—and transcultural—memory work with young people. The basic underlying idea was to multiply and extend what we had learned in the process of creating and releasing our own motion comic. We wanted to engage young people as both producers and viewers of motion comics. Moreover, we wanted to include youths from families with migration experiences to open up paths to connect the various types of experience and thereby broaden our understanding of the history of the German division.

Our plan was to bring together the histories of the German division and of multicultural Germany by talking about border crossings within as well as to and from Germany during the Cold War and beyond. Together with the Marienborn Memorial to Divided Germany, which is a well-known former inner-German border crossing between Helmstedt in the West and Magdeburg in the East, we designed a project called 'MoCom: Motion Comics as Memory Work: A Project by and for Young People in West and East Germany with and without Migration Experience' (MoCom n.d.). It was financed by the federal program 'Youth Remembers/ Jugend erinnert', which is managed by the Federal Foundation for the Study of the Communist Dictatorship in Eastern Germany (a government-sponsored agency that focuses on critical public history about the German division). It was co-financed by the Foundation for Memorials of Saxony Anhalt, the federal state where the Marienborn Memorial is located.[4]

The project aimed to get young people interested in recent German history by drawing on and establishing links between different experiences with borders, dictatorships, and migration movements. Between the summer of 2021 and the end of 2023, we convened four groups of about three to six young people mainly between fifteen and twenty-five years of age from across Germany. With each group, we explored one of four different themes that address aspects of borders in a broad sense, namely: border crossings, escape and departure, shared (hi)stories, and arriving in a foreign country. We intertwined memories of the inner-German border with memories of border crossings, escape, and arrival in other contexts to create personal, transgenerational, transnational, and transcultural connections through shared memories.

Each group met regularly online to develop a concept and share their own memories as well as memories they collected in conversations with, among others, family members and friends. In addition to collecting memories in form of stories and interviews, participants collected objects, photos, pictures, songs, and sounds to be built into a written script for a collective motion comic. The scripts were developed conceptually and visually, together with professional artists, to create four motion comics of about ten minutes length in both English and German that could be easily shared online. The four motion comics are accessible on our project website and on YouTube. They are: 'Border Crossings', 'The Density of Freedom', 'Friendship Beyond Borders', and 'Wandering Roots'.

---

4   For more information on the 'MoCom' project, see https://mocom-memories.de/en/home/

Besides the online meetings, participants got together in two on-site workshops at the Marienborn memorial to experience the historic site in person. The first meeting was designed to help the group members to get to know each other, meet the artists, gather historical contexts, and exchange initial ideas about the project. The second workshop was a public premiere to present the motion comic to the German-speaking public. An online premiere shortly thereafter served to release the English-language version. Each motion comic was published with accompanying pedagogical material to be used in schools and other educational settings.

The 'Ghost Train' motion comic inspired us to initiate the 'MoCom' project and to get young people from diverse backgrounds involved in exploring their own and others' shared memories. By producing stimulating educational material for themselves and their peers, these young people became actively involved in public history—about and across divides.

Reflecting the Experience: In Lieu of a Conclusion

What exactly did we create with our 'Ghost Train' motion comic? It is not a documentation of history, but it certainly engages people in historical discourses. Academics are only beginning to assess the potential of motion comics for history education (Hashim and Idris 2016; Morton 2015). From the experience with our motion comic, we gather that motion comics, because they are pieces of art, can add additional layers to history work. They do so by working with and addressing emotions, thus becoming (e-)motion comics in the process of connecting people across divides, time, and space.

As a form of oral history, motion comics stress emotions in historical work by engaging the producers as well as the viewers with a theme from history by way of personal memories. The collage of different memories allows those who are involved to create a multi-layered vision of an historical instance as a shared group experience (in contrast to a personal experience) in a liberating, artistic fashion. In this process, the participating individuals add their personal perspectives to create something new that keeps growing as people continue to join the process by watching and commenting, thus establishing a dialogue across divides, time, and space.

As a piece of artwork—and of course, the lines are not clearly drawn between the historical and the artistic aspects; rather, they are blurred and sometimes hardly distinguishable—the motion comic addresses the senses. It evokes emotions that may have a soothing or even a healing effect. At least, this is our experience with this particular motion comic. The result is a multi-faceted dialogue that draws on aesthetic values as much as on memories of actual historical events.

For its ability to engage viewers emotionally, the (e-)motion comic as a concept deserves further application in public history education. It has the potential to draw people into historical reappraisals who might not do so otherwise. The medium of the (e-)motion comic offers a low threshold for bringing history to life, providing information, offering connecting points to unleash related personal memories, and, thus, nudging people to ask questions or simply to think about what is—or was—happening.

We would like to invite you, too, to share what came to your mind while watching our memory story. Were you reminded of a similar experience, of an emotion, a smell, a sound, a scene from your childhood? Are you irritated by 'inaccurate' details (as we suggested above, there are some; our memories are able to transform the past, and, after all, the motion comic is also a form of art)? Could such 'inaccuracies' have a productive effect on your memory work? Please share your reaction to the 'Ghost Train' motion comic and become part of the 'Cold War Childhoods' memory archive.[5]

References

Davies, B., and Gannon, S. (eds). (2006). *Doing Collective Biography: Investigating the Production of Subjectivity*. Open University Press

Fichtner, S., Werner, A., Aghalouie, A., Tavakoli, H. (2020). 'Ghost Train—Memories of Ghost Trains and Ghost Stations in Former East and West Berlin'. YouTube, uploaded by Medienwerkstatt Encounters, 8–9 November 2020, English version: https://www.youtube.com/watch?v=CvoAOMDLszk German version: https://www.youtube.com/watch?v=6NaKHmVRac8

Hashim, M. E. A. H. B., and Idris, M. Z. (2016). 'Theoretical Framework and Development Motion Comic Instrument as Teaching Method for History Subject'. *International Journal of Academic Research in Business and Social Sciences*, 6(11), 249–60, https://doi.org/10.6007/IJARBSS/v6-i11/2394

---

5 Please use this template, indicating that your comments are connected to the 'Ghost Train' motion comic: https://coldwarchildhoods.org/sharing-memories/

Mazzei, L. A. (2003). 'Inhabited Silences: In Pursuit of a Muffled Subtext'. *Qualitative Inquiry*, 9(3), 355–68, https://doi.org/10.1177/1077800403009003002

'MoCom—Motion Comics as Memory Work', https://mocom-memories.de/en/home/

Morton, D. (2015). 'The Unfortunates: Towards a History and Definition of the Motion Comic'. *Journal of Graphic Novels and Comics*, 6(4), 347–66, https://doi.org/10.1080/21504857.2015.1039142

'Spinning the Sticky Threads of Childhood Memories: From Cold War to Anthropocene'. (2021). Tampere University, https://events.tuni.fi/recollectreconnect2021/

Silova, I.; Piattoeva, N.; Millei, Z. (eds). (2018). *Childhood and Schooling in (Post) Socialist Societies: Memories of Everyday Life*. New York: Palgrave Macmillan, https://doi.org/10.1007/978-3-319-62791-5

Smith, C. (2015). 'Motion Comics: The Emergence of a Hybrid Medium'. *Writing Visual Culture*, 7, https://www.herts.ac.uk/__data/assets/pdf_file/0018/100791/wvc-dc7-smith.pdf

Traveling Stones[1]

Oshie Nishimura-Sahi

It was a summer Sunday. Taken by her grandpa, she went to Mt. Inunaki to spend a summer day by the river. She was observing the stones along the river, letting her little feet swim in the cold, soothing water. Every stone was tiny and round, and so smooth to the touch. She also liked the nice and cold weight when she took one in her hand. She decided to take a white, smooth, and charming stone with her for the memory of the day. Showing her favorite white stone to her grandpa, she told him that she wished to bring it home. But he answered her with an apologetic smile:

> Unfortunately, we can't take her home. Do you know why she was smoothed like this? Since she was born in a mountain somewhere, she has been rolling in rivers and probably even seas while rubbing her sharp edges. And now she found a nice place to have a rest. So please don't disturb her enjoying her journey. Let her just be here where she belongs at this moment.

'Boring', she thought, but finally she returned the charming stone to the riverside. Where will she go now?

---

1   This is a childhood memory produced as part of the Reconnect/Recollect project discussed in the introduction to this book.

16. Re-membering Ceremonies:
Childhood Memories of Our Relationships with Plants

Jieyu Jiang, Esther Pretti, Keti Tsotniashvili, Dilraba Anayatova, Ann Nielsen, and Iveta Silova

---

Drawing on collective biography, memory work, and diffractive analysis, this chapter examines childhood memories of our entanglements with plants. By approaching research as a ceremony, our goal is to reanimate the relationships we have shared with plants and places, illuminating multiple intra-actions and weaving different worlds together. Our collective ceremony of re-membering brings into focus how plants called us forward, evoked our gratitude and reciprocity, shared knowledge, and offered comfort, companionship, love, belongingness, and understanding throughout life. The process of our collective re-membering and writing has turned into a series of ceremonial gatherings and practices, bringing forth vivid memories, poetic expressions, and creative drawings. As humans, we have often (re)acted to plants' generous gifts in meaningful gestures and communications that have co-created and made visible our deeply felt inter-species love and care.

Deep in the summer garden
She overheard farewell whisperings
Grandfather's words in the air lingering
Bumbieris tree listening, bowing in solace
She stood there silently, witnessing
Re-membering ceremonies, ceremonies re-membering

In May, she bathes in lavender
Baskets of blooms, aromatic flowers fill the air
'It's the *Lilacs*', she confirms
May Baskets brimming with childhood excitement
Seasons changing, seasons celebrating
Re-membering ceremonies, ceremonies re-membering

She marvels, fiery red *Cambará* flowers
Tiny bouquets, revealed in the early hours
She spreads the flowers, cradling the departed bird
While crafting her good-byes, a ceremony occurred
Grandma's yard, a sacred space she holds in her heart
Re-membering ceremonies, ceremonies re-membering

In spring, she searched for *Gai/biksītes* dressed in yellow
Danced with tiny fairies in a sunny meadow
The fairies' magic is revealed in time
Spells cast in tea, with golden signs
Warming, soothing, healing
Re-membering ceremonies, ceremonies re-membering

含羞草 was shy, so was the girl
Covered with its leaves, like the shell covering the pearl
The grass was gone after teaching her braveness
But those dashes of green forever twirl
The energy from the grass was never fading
Re-membering ceremonies, ceremonies re-membering

Хосма coloring her eyebrows a deep green
Illuminating her femininity in her teenage moods
Connections, built in between
Sunshine in summertime brightening their spirits
The liquid woad a modern eye shadowing
Re-membering ceremonies, ceremonies re-membering

Sitting on the ვაშლის tree branches, climbing
She swayed with the branches, wind blowing
By generously giving its fruits
The ვაშლის tree set itself free
Harvesting the autumn ვაშლის tree
Re-membering ceremonies, ceremonies re-membering

Fig. 16.1 Authors' drawings and invocation: a ceremony of re-membering our relationships with plants. Jiang, Pretti, Tsotniashvili, Anayatova, Nielsen, Silova, 2023.

Weaving together our childhood memories across space and time, this poem is our collective invocation that marks a ceremony of re-membering our relationships with plants (Figure 16.1). Both personal and shared, it is a belated message of gratitude to our plant companions—flowers, shrubs, herbs, and trees—for inviting us into more-than-human relationships decades ago. It is also a humble gesture of reciprocity to honour and rekindle these special relationships despite modern pressure and expectation to distance ourselves from the living world. Our intention is to reconnect with our plant companions through childhood memories, rebuilding 'the connections and relationships that are us, our world, our existence' (Wilson 2008, p. 137), and in this process, remind ourselves and our readers that 'the world could well be otherwise' (Kimmerer 2013, p. 189)—more connected, interdependent, and reciprocal.

In the anthropocentric age where life is dominated by institutions of modernity, whether socialist or capitalist, the beat of 'progress' undermines our capacity to pause and notice the infinite ways of being in the animate world. At the same time, hierarchical binaries that dominate western culture—nature/culture, female/male, matter/mind—hyper-separate humans from the ecological communities we inhabit, while relegating the non-human 'other' to oppositional subordination (Plumwood 2009). As children, we speak with plants and animals as if they are our kin. But as we grow older, we are quickly retrained to abandon and forget these relationships. As Robin Wall Kimmerer (2013) explains, when we tell children that 'the tree is not a *who*, but an *it*, we make that maple an object; we put a barrier between us, absolving ourselves of moral responsibility and opening the door to exploitation' (p. 57, emphasis in original). And yet, even as 'the language of animacy teeters on extinction', Kimmerer (2013) reminds us that 'the animacy of the world is something we already know' (p. 57), even if we may be forgetting some of its grammar. It is always already part of us, quietly kept in our memories, carried in our bodies.

In this chapter, we invoke our plant companions from childhood and beyond, zooming out of the Cold-War era and bringing into focus multi-species relationships with a longer history and future than the Cold War. On both sides of the Iron Curtain, our plant companions taught us to stay present in the moment, paying attention to 'here' and 'now' rather than worrying about the past and the future. *Cambará*, an inexpensive ornamental bush commonly known as 'lantana', bloomed by a grandmother's yard wall in a working-class home in urban Brazil, embracing and enchanting little girls. 含羞草 (pronounced as *Han Xiu Cao* in Chinese and identified as *mimosa pudica* in Latin) grew by the school gates in southern China and was known for its special ability to close leaves like a book, 'with a shy look' ('含羞' or Han Xiu), if anyone touched it. An apple orchard in Georgia was fondly re-membered as ვაშლის ბაღი (pronounced as *vashlis baghi* in Georgian) for bringing families together for the ceremonial act of apple harvesting. A *bumbieris* ('pear' in English) tree stood tall in a grandmother's garden and a delicate primrose, or *gaiļbiksīte* in Latvian grew in the meadow by the river, next to the tall apartment buildings and sometimes on the edge of the forest across Latvia. Хосма (or 'woad' in English), a native to the steppe of Central Asia, was known for its indigo ink used for crafts, beauty, and medicine in Uighur culture. And lilacs were popular in the United States among little girls for their distinct floral scent emanating from precious 'scratch-n-sniff' Barbie stickers and May Basket arrangements.

By inviting our childhood plant companions into co-presence, we enter this research as 'a ceremony that brings relationships together' (Wilson 2008, p. 8). Turning to our childhood memories, we can hear again the quiet echo of trees whispering in our grandparents' gardens, breeze in the scent of lilacs in May baskets and Barbie 'scratch-n-sniff' stickers, feel the sensation of a cold dye from a ceremonial plant on our eyebrows, and sense the love and care emanating from the delicate flowers growing by the of side of the road or in the hidden corner of a garden. And then we start to re-member things we did not know we have forgotten. In this chapter, we pick up the scattered threads and fractured glimpses of our fading childhood memories and weave them together in ritual practices to reconnect with our plant companions as kin in a more-than-human world. By coming together to share our childhood memories, the relationships between us and our plant companions—as well as the connections between our different 'selves' across time and space, and among each of us across different contexts and cultures— become clearer and clearer, closer and closer.

Memory Research as Ceremony

> When we share our memories
> We celebrate them as ceremonies
> Drawn from our bodies
> Re-membering

Sharing the wisdom of indigenous elders, Kimmerer (2013) says that 'ceremonies are the way we "remember to remember"' (p. 5). Whether activated through official ceremonies or everyday ritual practices, memory plays a vital role not only in sharing knowledge and experience across space and time but also in connecting human beings to both their pasts and their futures, as well as to other human and more-than-human beings. Thus, in this research, we approach working with memory from a broader ecological and Indigenous perspective, as ecomemory, where the process of re-membering links human and nonhuman beings and their entangled histories into 'an extended multispecies frame of remembrance' (Kennedy 2017, p. 268). From this perspective, memory—and the process of re-membering—becomes a form of connection and solidarity between humans and non-humans that enables us to re-member and re-make worlds together.

As we prepared the shared spaces and ways for 'remembering to remember', it seemed only fitting to approach our memory research as a ceremony itself. Wilson (2008) writes that approaching 'research as ceremony' helps to raise our consciousness, bring relationships together, and bridge spaces between humans and nature. In this process, not only the 'doing' of research is a ceremony, but our writing, too, acquires ceremonial effects—from gathering together to share our memories to inviting our plant companions to join us in re-membering our mutual relationships, to making space for multispecies awareness and 'arts of noticing' (Tsing 2015), to expressing gratitude for our more-than-human entanglements, to reconnecting and learning from and with our plant-kin, to creating a manuscript that can be read (and felt) as a ceremony.

Inspired by the evocative methods of collective memory work (Haug et al. 1987), collective biography (Davies and Gannon 2006, 2012; Pretti et al. 2022; Silova et al. 2018), and diffractive analysis (Barad 2007; Davies and Gannon 2012; Mazzei 2014), we start with the assumption that other ways of relating and knowing are possible, but they require that we 'revitalize the arts of noticing' in our research and practice (Tsing 2015, p. 37). Noticing brings the awareness of the existence of multispecies worlds and realities that we all inhabit, helping us recognise the deep and entangled histories of multispecies being and becoming, while moving us away from a binary hierarchy of othering and opposition against other species (Bozalek and Fullzgar 2022; Van Dooren et al. 2016). According to Van Dooren et al. (2016), such a multispecies approach enables research to get immersed in the 'multitudes of lively agents that bring one another into being through entangled relations that include, but always also exceed, dynamics of predator and prey, parasite and host, researcher and researched, symbiotic partner, or indifferent neighbor' (p. 3).

In an effort to further attune to the arts of noticing and the acts of re-membering these multispecies common worlds we inhabit(ed) (Common Worlds Research Collective 2020), we rely on the 'sensibility of all our embodied faculties' (Taguchi 2012, p. 272) to engage with memories that dwell in our minds and bodies, as well as material objects and natural landscapes. Our collective process of re-membering entails several processes of engagement: (i) re-membering our relationships with plants and sharing our memory stories with each other; (ii) carefully listening, reading, and re-reading each other's memory stories to bring more details into focus; (iii) noticing the interferences and threads running through each other's memory stories; and (iv) weaving the different memories together by reading memory stories through one another. Instead of reflecting on our experiences, we engaged in a diffractive analysis of memory stories (Barad 2007) by attentively reading memories through one another, recognising differences and similarities, while paying attention to our entangled relationships with other species. In the process of reading and re-reading each other's memories diffractively, we recognised the deep interconnectedness of our childhood memory stories that transpired across four different continents and six countries.

Across different contexts and time periods, our plant companions often invited us into ceremonial acts and rituals during our different life transitions, our teaching and learning processes, and our personal and collective growth. Kimmerer (2013) explains that 'ceremonies large and small have the power to focus attention to a way of living awake in the world. The visible becomes invisible' (p. 36). Our childhood ceremonies with plants were simple acts that helped us focus our attention on the (sometimes) invisible multiplicity of life in the world. Through the processes of collective memory work—what we call here, the ceremonies of re-membering—we have become aware of how the barriers between us and plants began to disappear, revealing the coexistence of deeply entangled multispecies worlds, which we have always already belonged to. In our intra-active research process, we thus became writers and readers of/with the memory stories (Haraway 2016). In the sections below we share our childhood memory stories, highlighting through our ceremonies of re-membering how we communicated, learned, and bonded with our plant companions and the land we shared. We illustrate how plants have inspired us to express gratitude and practice reciprocity, taught us to communicate with a more-than-human world, shared lessons beyond binaries and categories, and helped us reconnect with the multiple worlds we have inhabited in our lifetimes.

Ceremonies of Gratitude and Reciprocity

When we recall our memories
Our hearts fill with appreciation
With gratitude for old friends
Thankful for otherworldly connections

Ceremonies can be performed both as single acts, and as well as a broader way of being in the world—a gratitude-based way of living—that focuses human attention on an ethical relationality in/with other species (Kimmerer 2013). Gestures of appreciation and gratitude for the land are ceremonial acts that occur through 'ritual(s) of respect: the translation of reverence and intention into action' (ibid., p. 35). Additionally, Moore and Miller (2018) detail how gratitude connects us to the earth and strengthens human relationship to the natural world. Thus, the expression of gratitude between humans and non-humans can be a form of ceremonial practice that builds and strengthens connection, and establishes a relationship of care and reciprocity, while recognising mutual interdependence (Kimmerer 2013; Moore and Miller 2018).

The ceremonies we witnessed and participated in as children enmeshed us in plantworlds, attuning us to the characters, doings, and movements of plants. They helped us recognise invisible qualities of plants by channelling our attention to the many possibilities of intra-acting with each of them (Barad 2007). In our childhood memories, ceremonial acts of gratitude for the land and for plants were abundant, human and non-human beings showed appreciation and reverence towards one another in gentle ceremonial intra-actions that connected them through very deep bonds. In the company of our elders, both human and vegetal, we observed and experimented with our arts of noticing, performing our own playful ceremonies, plucking flowers to make wishes, extracting tint to wear as ceremonial makeup, listening to the sounds of morning greetings and afternoon goodbyes. These plants entered our worlds and invited us to enter theirs by our mutual openness in reciprocal more-than-human relationships.

Kimmerer (2013) explains that attentive engagement in/with plant worlds is accessible through remembering. As adults immersed in modernity, we may have forgotten how to communicate and engage in ceremonial acts with plants, but the ability to attune to other worlds, including plant worlds, is available to us as we re-member past encounters (Pretti et al. 2022). Thus, re-membering our childhood ceremonies, such as memories of accepting an apple tree's invitation to climb it or of talking to a shy plant, is a path to re-member how to engage with plants as kin and, moreover, to be re-minded that an attuned, gratitude-based existence is not something to be learned (or re-learned) but something to re-member.

Ceremonial expressions of gratitude were abundant in our memories. In one recollection, a girl showed delicate awareness and care for her grandfather's ვაშლის ბაღი (apple orchard) in rural Georgia by joining her family in the yearly apple-picking season, and attentively accepting an apple tree's invitation to climb it and gently relieve the trees of their heavy fruits:

It is apple picking season, everyone is trying to make it to the village for the weekend to help grandparents with harvesting. The girl is the youngest, and she starts climbing the tree with her bucket and picking the apples. The trees are about 8–10 meters high. She knows that she can reach the branches that others cannot. She feels it is risky to go on higher and thinner branches, especially when the wind is shaking the branches on which she stands or holds on. To reach the apples, she pulls down a branch with one hand and picks the apples with the other. As the branch gets free from the fruit and she lets it go, the branch jumps higher and the girl feels that she is liberating the branches from the heavyweight. She gets more enthusiastic to reach the thinner branches that might be broken if they cannot hold the fruit weight. She also enjoys taking breaks by sitting on the convenient branch and eating apples. Although she gets tired and feels pain in her feet, she wants to relieve the trees from the burden and moves from one branch to another and then to another tree.

In this memory the girl re-members her agility and familiarity with apple trees, gently using her body to reach the fruits and relieve the trees' branches, preventing them from breaking. She is happy to join in the ritual of apple picking, she is gentle and careful, enjoying the trees' company and fruits while working with her human and more-than-human family.

Examples of such connection and care emerged in other memories as well. In a quiet backyard in Brazil, another girl regularly visited grandma's *Cambará* plant to admire and confide in her vegetal friend, exchanging awe and tenderness with the delicate flowers. In another memory, across the world, a young girl in China used only her heart to speak to a shy plant in order to avoid disturbing such a sensitive being. These simple acts of tenderness and respect were all constituted of ritual visits and ceremonial gestures of appreciation and care for those plants.

While sharing memories and following the many sprouts that emerged from plant ceremonies, we noticed that once we practised our gestures of gratitude towards the land and the plants, we were immediately recognised and reciprocated by the plant world. 'The land knows you, even when you are lost', Kimmerer (2013) explains. Similarly, Moore and Miller (2018) affirm that 'as soon as you give thanks to something it gives thanks back' (p. 5). As expected, the girl in the apple orchard receives the tree's recognition and gratitude in return. The girl re-members how the trees' branches jumped with relief when their apples were harvested, and how she was delicately held by the tree even when climbing the thinner branches:

The girl has been climbing on the trees for as long as she re-members herself, she can sense how much pressure she can put on and distribute on the branches so that they don't break, and she trusts that the branches will also hold her.

Similarly, in Kazakhstan, a girl's grandmother showed respect for the Хосма [woad] plant by seeding it every spring and picking only a small amount of leaves in the summer. By respecting the plant's life cycle and nurturing its growth and regeneration, the girl's family and Хосма developed a ritual of care and affection. In reciprocity for the generous contribution to its regeneration, Хосма helped the girls in the family transition from childhood to adulthood through the ritual of painting the eyebrows and eyelids. In this intergenerational interspecies relationship of mutual care, Хосма mediated an important transition in the lives of all women in the family and in the village:

Хосма *is my grandmother's favorite plant. She seeds it every spring in small quantities, and in summer, the grandmother is ready to use. My cousin goes and harvests a handful of leaves after. I squeeze woad's leaves with the help of my hands. Here we go. There is a dark green liquid that is put on brows. I was eight or ten when I knew I wanted to have dark and beautiful eyebrows. Another important thing was putting the liquid on the eyelids as a modern eye shadow. Nevertheless, only older girls can do it, so we, as eight-ten-year-olds, were jealous of our older girls putting them on. We wanted to be older, and we wanted to be beautiful like them. I remember my cousin or aunt or mom painting my eyebrows. This event was fascinating to all of us—sitting in the circle, talking about different things, laughing was an integral part of painting woad liquid on our faces.*

These multispecies exchanges of care, trust, gratitude, and reciprocity strengthened the bonds between the plants and humans, revealing wisdoms that can be accessed and created by the entanglements between humans, non-humans, landscapes, ceremonies, and memories (Basso 1996; Moore and Miller 2018).

Ceremonies of Communicating with Plants

When we recall our memories
Nature communicates to us
Each season invites us to participate
In weaving our bodies together

Our childhood memories of entanglements with plant worlds tell about our attunement to the rhythms, cycles, and doings of more-than-human others. Some of our plant companions blended into landscapes, going mostly unnoticed, while others grew seasonally, appearing at certain times of the year, letting us know of changes about to come. Taking cues and listening to how and when plants grew, reproduced, and withered, we learned the language of plants, and learned how to communicate back with them through words, actions, emotions, touch, and thoughts. In these reciprocal cycles of communication, we were 'linked in a co-evolutionary cycle' (Kimmerer 2013, p. 124), wherein humans and plants benefitted from our spoken and unspoken communications. Plants communicated with us by their growth, their strength in holding us, their comfort in moments of grief and sadness, and their assistance in life's transitions. They were part of our own ceremonies and invited us into their rituals and cycles, being constant companions across our memories. While ceremonies and rituals are typically studied through the lens of human culture, they are also part of non-human worlds. We noted that the ceremonies and rituals across our memories communicated local traditions and shared knowledge as a 'crystallization of the collective wisdom' (Zheng 2018, p. 817). An example can be seen in the memory of the girl who used *Cambará* flowers in a funeral ceremony for her deceased bird. The memory communicated how the girl went to her plant friend to find strength, peace, and joy in a time of sorrow.

In our memories, we often became part of plant ceremonies and rituals already underway. The cyclical arrival of warmer weather, blossoms, and plants bearing fruit were direct communications from the plant world that it was time for seasonal ceremonies and local rituals such as apple picking or eye shadowing. In these instances, ceremonies and rituals 'married the mundane to the sacred' (Kimmerer 2013, p. 37), mediating the intersection of plant and human rituals. For example, the arrival of the spring season communicated the arrival of the May Day celebration where children gathered flowers in May basket arrangements to hang on neighbours' doors. In this memory, May baskets marked a seasonal ritual shared within the local community.

After they talked about a May Pole and the May Day Celebration at school, the girl came home from school and made May Baskets for her neighbor. Her mom gave her some chocolate candies to put inside and she went outside to pick some flowers from the front yard. She didn't really have many flowers in her front yard so she wandered around the houses close to hers and found some flowers from a neighbor's yard. They were little lavender flowers, the kind that smelled just like the Barbie stickers she loved. The basket was loaded with flowers and chocolates and smelled of a sweet spring. She was ready for delivery when the sun was beginning to set; the spring weather was warming up and the low sun cast a golden hue to everything as it neared time to deliver the May basket.

In this memory, ordinary flowers found in yards and gardens were transformed into ceremonial symbols of love and friendship, which were shared with neighbours and friends during our ceremonies. Kimmerer (2013) describes how gardens (and flowers) reflect both spiritual and material matterings, the May-Day flowers symbolised the relationality of being 'loving and being loved in return' (Kimmerer 2013, p. 123).

In another memory, a girl learned to communicate directly with plants by secretly observing her grandfather's farewell to his plant companions in the garden before an unexpected surgery. In this memory, the girl remembers her grandfather's vulnerability when he was communicating with the plants:

The girl spent most of her summers in the family summer garden, which was located close to the small town where they lived in an apartment building. But one day something unusual happened. The girl was surprised and curious to see her Grandfather alone in the garden. She kept very quiet and pretended not to notice him, digging a hole way deeper than she intended and hoping that she would hear snippets of the conversation between her Grandfather and the plants. The wind was blowing quietly through the garden and it felt very warm on her skin. The wind carried only some words to the girl, but she knew that her Grandfather was saying goodbye to the garden—apple trees, pear trees, the currant bushes, the peas weaving on the fence around the yard. He paused for a long time next to the bumbieris (pear) tree, which was bowing low, her branches full of fruit and close to breaking from the heavyweight she had to carry. The tree seemed to bow even lower after the conversation with the Grandfather. It was a day before her grandfather went to a hospital for a surgery, leaving the small town in the countryside to go to the capital city.

The girl was fascinated by how the grandfather took time to speak with each plant, 'gently touching the leaves of the berry bushes and the bark on the trunks of the fruit trees, she suddenly realised the significance of the upcoming surgery and the significance of the garden in his life, and her life too'. In this memory, it is not only the vulnerable connection between the grandfather and the plants that is striking but also the connection that was created between the girl and her grandfather through the plants. The narrator of this memory later noted, 'It was special that he shared this moment with me. [We] both knew that we were in each other's presence at that moment, but neither one spoke about it at that time or afterwards'. The grandfather allowed the girl to witness his conversation with plants so that she could see how they were important members of the family. As he communicated his goodbyes, the grandfather modelled for the young girl his knowledge that 'each place was inspirited, was home to others before we arrived and long after we left' (ibid., p. 34). Communicating with plants through whispered prayers and good-byes was ritual in itself (Siragusa et al. 2020) and, as the young girl witnessed, she learned that she too could trust her plant companions in the gardens. Grandfather's goodbye ceremony reminds us how plants are natural listeners and can help us in the transition between worlds. In this sense, our plant ceremonies served as a channel for us to better understand how we were connected to our worlds, our families (both living and ancestral), our cultures, and our lands.

Ceremonies of Teaching and Learning

When we recall our memories
We celebrate the wisdom of nature's teachers
Humbled by ancient pedagogies
We learn to live together, live in love

Kimmerer (2013) tells a story about Skywoman leaving plants behind as our teachers. Across our memories, we commonly see plants as teachers, noting how their teachings are distinct from regular lessons at school. In mainstream Western school pedagogies, we learn about plants in a scientific way, reducing plants to their classifications and biological qualities (Kimmerer 2013). Fundamentally, modern schools inculcate and discipline us to learn one hegemonic way of relating to plants, that of scientific knowledge-making, relegating plants to a place of separation, 'othering'—framed as exploitable objects to be grown, used, and destroyed by humans (Haraway 2016)—rather than companions or 'teachers', able to link us in and through learning processes as a 'connective tissue' between different worlds (Warner 2007, p. 17, see also Silova 2020). Along with the 'knowledge' about plants, our learning at school was limited to 'scientific descriptions' and pictures of pressed specimens in textbooks and labs. In this process, we lost opportunities of building intimate connections with plants, experiencing emotions together, gently touching each other's vivid lives, as well as learning from each other through warm and comfortable connections (Kimmerer 2013). From the scientific learning process to the scientific knowledge per se, modern schools give full expression to human arrogance and human-centric ontology (Silova et al. 2020; Stengers 2012), while closing the doors to other worlds.

In our childhood memories, however, we re-member a different kind of pedagogy by learning with and from the plants (not only about them), transforming and expanding learning from solely mental and cognitive processes to our bodily, emotional, and spiritual learning. The relational learning between the girls and the plants reveals 'the matter that matters' (Barad 2007, p. 210) in each moment uncovering possibilities to notice, learn, and re-member through movements, fragrances, pigmentation, taste, and our physical and emotional connection with the plant world. Our childhood memories with plants suggest that teaching happens in every ceremonial moment when beings express mutual aspiration and initiate reciprocal understanding of each other, regardless of categories of beings, educational settings, and the hierarchies of knowledge. In other words, plants could be our teachers, teaching and inspiring us in a more ceremonial way, about how to connect and live sympoietically in more-than-human worlds. In one memory, for example, the girl communicated with 含羞草 (the *Mimosa pudica*) about the sensitivity, cowardice, and bashfulness in her personality, while the flower provided the girl with courage and bonded understanding. At that ceremonial moment, the plant taught her to be brave and confident in acknowledging and accepting the true but different self when being with others:

Every time after school when she walked along the rows of 含羞草 *(mimosa pudica), she would stop and look at them quietly. She did not talk to or touch them, but only squatted down, looked at them, observed them, and said 'hi' in her heart to them. She thought that even talking loudly would make them close their leaves. 'I don't want to bother them. They prefer to hide themselves because they are too shy.' She said to herself, 'it is not a big deal, see, the plants are sensitive, too, and there are specific sensitive plants. It is the same for people like me. I am not strange. It is okay to be shy.' She thought with hope and thrill, and suddenly she felt the energy of the plant, because they were not plants anymore—they were similar kinds of beings with similar characteristics. They are her close friends, even though they never had conversations out loud. Every time she quietly walked past them, they seemed to be talking to her: 'Be strong and be yourself—we are all quiet and it is okay to act like that in school.*

As we noticed similar ceremonial moments of learning from plants in our childhood memories, we began weaving our memory stories together. We regard our childhood memories and interactions with plants as ceremonial teaching and learning experiences for three reasons, each of which highlights an aspect of difference from mainstream pedagogies. First, the processes of teaching and learning in our memories with plants were not linear or progressive, unlike those typically found in schools. Rather, the girls' memories describe the so-called teaching and learning experiences that happened in our connections and communications with the respective plant companions naturally, iteratively, and periodically. In other words, there was neither an established route and procedure for successfully achieving pedagogical aims, nor prescribed scientific steps and schedule to realise the illusion of making educational progress.

We re-membered and experienced diverse types of relationships with plants, which were filled with emotion, love, and sincerity, and which emerged again and again in our lives. For example, in the family garden where the girl spent most of her time during the summer, she learned about different types of garden work, meeting different berry bushes, and learning to make friends with the garden plants through multiple communications and visits. More importantly, at a deeper level, when she saw her grandfather stopping and saying goodbye to the bushes and trees, and when those plants responded to her grandfather and comforted his fear of separation by offering their quiet company, the garden plants became her teachers in facing life's difficult moments. These 'teacher-student' relationships were built upon the girl's periodical and iterative intra-actions with plants in the garden over several summers. Those subtle moments of communication transformed into emotional ceremonies, during which plants and bushes taught the girl about the reluctance of farewells, the comfort of companionship, and the mood of optimism when facing bumps in life.

Another important distinction is the relatively equal positions of teachers and learners. In the girls' memories, we were in contact with the plants who could be regarded as teachers, in the capacity as children with our simplicity, kindness, and careful attempt. From the girls' perspectives, although we were born and grew up in the group of human beings, there was no prejudice and arrogance in a sense of knowing and interacting with other species, including plants. From a learners' view, the botanic 'teachers' for us were not as unapproachable as the teachers in formal classrooms. Plants were unable to talk, but they taught through generous companionship, comfort, and patience. For instance, in the memory of harvesting apples, the girl felt the branches of the tree supporting her, bouncing and playing together, and generously sharing the fruit. In another memory of a teenage girl, the squeezed leaves of the woad plant produced a dark green liquid, which then transformed into a natural eyebrow dye, teaching her the feeling of beauty, the wish of growing up, and the joy of practising in the ceremony together with her peers. In our childhood memories of teaching and learning, the plants and us were equally different, and the bonding between us was woven based on an equal relationship of knowing each other. In this sense, the regular mode of teacher-centred or student-centred learning was challenged and changed. Instead, the relationships of interdependence and reciprocity constituted ceremonies where every being—human and more-than-human—was included and warmly affected.

Furthermore, the content of our teaching and learning with plants was different compared to modern schools which define knowledge in narrow, fragmented, and programmed ways. The girls' memories talk about learning as a ceremony filled with love, relief, displays of natural emotions, and unique bondings. For example, the cyclical elapse of time was taught by the plants in May, and so it was re-membered by the girl in a beautiful and ceremonial way for life. By preparing her May basket, the purple lilacs and their 'sweet spring' fragrance helped the girl experience and re-member the May-Day celebration, her lovely friendship, and the passing of time in a sensory as well as natural way. What the lilacs shared with the girl was the cyclical nature of time, the ritual of enjoying friendship, and celebrating holidays and seasons in the lapsing time.

Finally, the unique teaching and learning experiences with plants were always intimate encounters that favoured exploring multiple worlds and building connections and relationships with more-than-human beings. An example happened in a memory with the *Cambará* bush, when the girl is being called by the flowers. She attends to the call, touches the flowers, picking only a few and arranging them in her hair, while visiting the private and quiet place under the bush again and again. These experiences formed a special bond between the girl and *Cambará*, in childhood and beyond. *Cambará* was not a regular or common bush anymore but a dedicated companion that helped the girl to understand and experience connections with different beings.

Ceremonies of Reconnecting with the More-than-Human World

> When we share our memories, we intertwine
> In rhizomatic relationships, silent connections
> The fibers link ritually between multiple worlds
> Maintaining connections through devout affections

Every connection we made with plants and every ceremony of re-membering took us back in time and in space, opening up possibilities to explore our connections to plants, to places, and to our (multiple) selves. Attachment to and rootedness in place is reinforced in memory work (Lewicka 2013), which can be seen in the girls' memories as they re-membered past and current houses, villages, cities, and, in most of them, their countries. Moreover, relationships with plants created an emotional belonging to a particular place, 'anchoring emotions of attachment, feelings of belonging, willingness to stay close, and a wish to come back when away' (Lewicka 2013, p. 66). Working with memories of close relationships with plants, we are able to restore intimate attachments to the plants and reconnect our ties to the land.

In talking about home and land, Kimmerer (2013) describes how plants, or memories about plants, have the ability to re-connect us with our 'home'. She writes that plants are 'integral to reweaving the connection between land and people. A place becomes a home when it sustains you when it feeds you in the body as well as spirit. To recreate a home, the plants must also return' (p. 259). In one example of our memories, the *gaiļbiksīte* (primrose) flower comes back into the girl's life again and again across many years, reminding the girl of knowledge she had forgotten and rekindling their relationship:

There was a small yellow flower, which would appear in a girl's life in most expected and unexpected times. It bloomed in late spring, usually in May and early June, when the days were becoming longer and warmer in Latvia, and the sun would not set until way after the girl's bed time. The flower would appear in the meadow by the river, next to the apartment building where the girl lived, and sometimes on the edge of the forest nearby. It was a delicate light green stem crowned by a cluster of small yellow flowers, which had a soft sweet fragrance. To the little girl, who was about 5 or 6 years old at that time, they looked like fairy princesses, so small you could hardly notice the beautiful yellow and green lace on their dresses. When the girl grew a little older, around 10–11 years old, the fairy princesses showed up at school. In a botany lesson, she saw them in her textbook. She learned that the flower was called Primula Veris in Latin. Several years later, when the girl was 15 or 16 years old, she was at home, drinking herbal tea on one late winter day. She had a cold and her mom made a special tea from a mixture of several different herbs. The tea was soothing and sweet. The girl recognised a special fragrance of the yellow fairy princesses as she drank it. The smell took her into the yellow fields by the edge of the forest that day. The sun was high in the sky and it made her warm. Many years passed by. The girl did not think about the yellow princesses for a long time. But one day she went to an exhibition in a capital city, far away from her home. It was in a building of the former biology department of the university, which was converted to a museum. She entered one of the rooms, which had glass cabinets on each wall. Behind the glass were lots and lots of dry flowers and grasses. Each one had a tag with a Latin name and a scientific description. Little princesses were there, too. 'Primula Veris', the tag said.

Connection with home and land is one of the vital aspects of childhood memories, and thus, present in all of our memories. At Oma's garden in Latvia, where grandfather said goodbye to the plants, by the *Cambará* bush in another grandmother's garden in Brazil, and in the Kazakhstan village where the woad was seeded every spring, the girls developed deep emotional and physical connections to the plants and the land through meaningful ceremonies, and they were relived those decades later, with the help of memories. According to Kohn (2013), 'there is something about our everyday engagements with other kinds of creatures that can open new kinds of possibilities for relating and understanding' (p. 7, see also Haraway 2008). These deep connections and communications with plants rooted in familiar land were ceremonial entries into multi-species relationships in girls' stories. These common worlding ceremonies strengthened a deep intimate relationship with plants and places, making it possible for the girls to re-member important knowledges, connections, and possibilities of relating to non-human beings (Pretti et al. 2022). For example, a place is 'comforting and comfortable' in the grandfather's goodbye memory. Similarly, a little girl finds comfort in the presence of the *Cambará* bush, which became a 'private sacred place of communion with loss, and a place to connect with her own feelings and with the plants in grandma's yard':

The girl was about five years old, and she spent a lot of time at her grandmother's house. Her family lived on the same street as Grandma, and very early in the mornings, the girl's grandmother would go out to the yard to water her garden and tend to the plants. The girl always followed Grandma. The girl wandered into the darker colder area of the yard by the wall and found a flat spot where there was a Cambará bush. The tiny multi-coloured bouquet-like flowers enchanted the girl, and the bouquets were so full that the girl could pick several flowers without her aunt noticing much damage to the plant. The girl started to visit her Cambará bush alone when her cousins were not around, and delicately touched the flowers before picking them to play love me, love me not, or arrange them in her hair as she explored the garden with grandma before the day began. Grandma didn't mind, instead, she looked over from time to time, in between talking to her own favorite plants. Soon after, when the girl's bird died, she wanted to bury it next to the Cambará bush. Her older brother got a small cardboard box, and they filled the box with Cambará flowers around the green parakeet's body. It gave the girl some comfort that the flowers that she knew and loved would keep her bird company, and it also gave her comfort to know that she could visit the Cambará bush later, and be with them both.

These multispecies ceremonial acts in our memories blur the western unidirectional lines of agency, profoundly re-minding us of our already ongoing connections with our more-than-human companions. The girls were growing in kinship with the land, bonding deeply with their non-human friends and teachers, with no categorisations or hierarchies between them in girls' memories. Wynter's (1984) concept of We/I as 'natural beings' mirrors this dynamic in re-membering the girls' intra-actions with plants by showing how the boundary-maintaining system becomes subversively blurred and reconfigured through memory. Re-membering and re-connecting with plants thus reconfigures our relationships to the land—the places we inhabited in the past, and the places where we live now.

In Lieu of Conclusion: Re-membering Ceremonies, Reconnecting Across Worlds

Memories dwell in most common, but often unexpected, places. They root in our physical bodies, material objects, and natural environments. They intersect personal histories, social orders, and geological landscapes. They encompass cognitive processes and affective dimensions. And most definitely, they do not exclusively belong to the human domain (Pretti et al. 2022). Therefore, it is not only the single dimension or aspect of reality that exists in re-membering, but the fuzzy, marginalised, and fluid details across the boundaries among multiple worlds are also embedded in our memories. Memories build bridges between worlds and species by connecting us with each other. In a reiterative, cyclical, and community-oriented process, working with memories invites more memories from various worlds: 'You hear one memory, you tell one' (see introductory chapter by Mnemo ZIN).

In the process of our collective-biography research, we have noticed that the memory research itself has ceremonial effects, unexpectedly forming a ritual of collectively coming together to share memory stories and connecting memories and relationships across time and space. Whether meeting physically or virtually, our research gatherings involved elements commonly present in more formal rituals and ceremonies: from sharing space and taking turns to share memory stories, to purposefully seeking links to the past and creating a communal experience where everyone participates not only intellectually but also intensely emotionally. While our childhood memories were shared, heard, and written in our gatherings again and again, we felt that this research process and writing was 'the climax of the ceremony' for 'it all comes together and all those connections are made' (Wilson 2008, p. 122). At this climax of the research, we wove together our scattered memories from distant childhoods, strengthening the connections with each other—memories, plants, and us—and transforming them into a spiritual and creative composition.

Our ceremonial re-membering of the relationships with plants awoke our attentiveness, enabling us to experience how the 'arts of noticing' extended our ways of being and knowing to the multispecies world, reminding us about the frames of our daily lives and that the 'making worlds is not limited to humans' (Tsing 2015, p. 22). In the collective process of re-membering, we helped each other to delve into the physical, sensorial, and emotional layers of our memories, which opened up the space to re-connect with the more-than-human worlds and to notice what had gone unnoticed in our daily lives in the anthropocene. Therefore, through our ceremonial research we re-membered not only the stories of our relationships with the plants, but we also retrieved and revived our noticing abilities from our childhood that had been fading throughout our life course shaped by the concept of modernity and mainstream western pedagogy. We re-membered the textures, smells, and colours through our bodily and sensory memories; we re-membered dazzlingly intimate emotional relationships with the plants that enabled us to become vulnerable and feel reciprocal trust, love, care, and gratitude; we re-membered experiencing the healing power of plants. Memories of such intimate relationships with plants created space for us to explore, experience, and re-learn ways of being and knowing without fear, helping us to once again 'come into coexistence with others' (Malone and Fullagar 2022, p. 116).

While re-learning the ability to engage in a collective re-membering ceremony with the multispecies world, we were also reminded that ours was never a unidirectional relationship with plants. It was always a reciprocal ceremony accomplished by the connected and collective 'us'. We would like to close with the poetic expression of love and gratitude to our plant companions:

> Re-membering with gratitude and reciprocity
> Rekindled care through ceremonial memory
> Mutually communicating with plants

Hearing the wind and flowers chant
Plantcestors as our life teachers
Learning from all nature's creatures
Reconnecting with more-than-humans
We cross the worlds through ceremonies

References

Barad, K. (2007). *Meeting the Universe Halfway: Quantum Physics and the Entanglement of Matter and Meaning.* Duke University Press, https://doi.org/10.2307/j.ctv12101zq

Basso, K. H. (1996). Wisdom Sits in Places: Landscape and Language among the Western Apache. University of New Mexico Press

Bozalek, V. and Fullagar, S. (2022). 'Noticing', in *A Glossary for Doing Postqualitative, New Materialist and Critical Posthumanist Research across Disciplines*, ed. by K. Murris. (pp. 94–95). Routledge, https://doi.org/10.4324/9781003041153

Common Worlds Research Collective. (2020). *Learning to Become with the World: Education for Future Survival.* Paper commissioned for the UNESCO Futures of Education report, https://unesdoc.unesco.org/ark:/48223/pf0000374032

Davies, B., and Gannon, S. (eds). (2006). *Doing Collective Biography: Investigating the Production of Subjectivity.* Open University Press

—— (2012). 'Collective Biography and the Entangled Enlivening of Being'. *International Review of Qualitative Research*, 5(4), 357–76, https://doi.org/10.1525/irqr.2012.5.4.357

Haraway, D. (2008). *When Species Meet.* University of Minnesota Press.

—— (2016). *Manifestly Haraway.* University of Minnesota Press, https://doi.org/10.5749/minnesota/9780816650477.001.0001

Haug, F.; Andresen, S.; Bünz-Elfferding, A.; Hauser, C.; Lang, U.; Laudan, M.; Lüdermann, M.; and Meir, U. (1987). *Female Sexualization: A Collective Work of Memory*, trans. by E. Carter. Verso

Kennedy, R. (2017). 'Multidirectional Eco-memory in an Era of Extinction: Colonial Whaling and Indigenous Dispossession in Kim Scott's *That Deadman Dance*', in *The Routledge Companion to the Environmental Humanities*, ed. by U. K. Heise, J. Christensen, and M. Niemann (pp. 268–77). Routledge, https://doi.org/10.4324/9781315766355

Kimmerer, R. (2013). *Braiding Sweetgrass: Indigenous Wisdom, Scientific Knowledge and the Teachings of Plants.* Milkweed editions

Kohn, E. (2013). *How Forests Think.* University of California Press, https://doi.org/10.1525/california/9780520276109.001.0001

Lewicka, M. (2013). 'In Search of Roots: Memory as Enabler of Place Attachment', in *Place Attachment: Advances in Theory, Methods and Applications*, ed. by L.C. Manzon and P. Devine-Wright. (pp. 49–60). Routledge

Malone, K. and Fullagar, S. (2022). 'Sensorial', in *A Glossary for Doing Postqualitative, New Materialist and Critical Posthumanist Research across Disciplines*, ed. by K. Murris. (pp. 116–17). Routledge, https://doi.org/10.4324/9781003041153-58

Mazzei, L. A. (2014). 'Beyond an Easy Sense: A Diffractive Analysis'. *Qualitative Inquiry*, 20(6), 742–46, https://doi.org/10.1177/1077800414530257

Mooer, K. P. and Miller, T. F. (2018). 'Gratitude as Ceremony: A Practical Guide to Decolonisation'. *Journal of Sustainability Education*, 18

Plumwood V. (2009). 'Nature in the Active Voice'. *Australian Humanities Review*, (46), 113–29, https://doi.org/10.22459/ahr.46.2009.10

Pretti, E. L.; Jiang, J.; Nielsen, A.; Goebel, J.; and Silova, I. (2022). 'Memories of a Girl Between Worlds: Speculative Common Worldings. *Journal of Childhood Studies*, 47(1), 14–28, https://doi.org/10.18357/jcs202219957

Silova, I., Piattoeva, N., and Millei, Z. (eds). (2018). *Childhood and Schooling in Post/Socialist Societies: Memories of Everyday Life*. Palgrave Macmillan, https://doi.org/10.1007/978-3-319-62791-5

Silova, I. (2020). 'Anticipating Other Worlds, Animating Our Selves: An Invitation to Comparative Education'. *ECNU Review of Education*, 3(1), 138–59, https://doi.org/10.1177/2096531120904246

Silova, I.; Rappleye, J.; and You, Y. (2020). 'Beyond the Western Horizon in Educational Research: Toward a Deeper Dialogue about our Interdependent Futures'. *ECNU Review of Education*, 3(1), 3–19, https://doi.org/10.1177/2096531120905195

Siragusa, L.; Westman, C. N.; and Moritz, S. C. (2020). 'Shared Breath: Human and Nonhuman Copresence through Ritualized Words and Beyond'. *Current Anthropology*, 61(4), 471–94, https://doi.org/10.1086/710139

Stengers, I. (2012). 'Reclaiming Animism'. *E-flux Journal*, (36), https://www.e-flux.com/journal/36/61245/reclaiming-animism/

Taguchi, H. L. (2012). 'A Diffractive and Deleuzian Approach to Analysing Interview Data'. *Feminist Theory*, 13(3), 265–81, https://doi.org/10.1177/1464700112456001

Tsing, A. L. (2015). *The Mushroom at the End of the World*. Princeton University Press, https://doi.org/10.1515/9781400873548

Van Dooren, T.; Kirksey, E.; and Münster, U. (2016). 'Multispecies Studies: Cultivating Arts of Attentiveness'. *Environmental Humanities*, 8(1), 1–23, https://doi.org/10.1215/22011919-3527695

Warner, M. (2007). *Fantastical Metamorphoses, Other Worlds: Ways of Telling the Self*. Oxford University Press

Wynter, S. (1984). 'The Ceremony Must be Found: After Humanism'. *Boundary*, 2, 19–70

Wilson, S. (2008). *Research is Ceremony: Indigenous Research Methods*. Fernwood Publishing

Zheng, D. (2018). 'Study on Red Yao Wedding Ceremony under the Perspective of Communication Ceremony' [Conference Presentation] 4th International Conference on Education and Training, Management and Humanities Science

List of Figures and Other Illustrations

Fig. I.1	Sára Gink, *BETŰVÁSÁR—ISBN 963 18 1254 5*. Mixed media, 160×190 cm. Photo by Zsuzsa Millei of installation at the 'Whale of a Bad Time' exhibition, Budapest 2020.	p. 13
Fig. I.2	Sára Gink, *BETŰVÁSÁR—ISBN 963 18 1254 5*. Mixed media, 160×190 cm. Photo by Zsuzsa Millei of installation at the 'Whale of a Bad Time' exhibition, Budapest 2020.	p. 13
Fig. I.3	Sára Gink, *BETŰVÁSÁR—ISBN 963 18 1254 5*. Mixed media, 160×190 cm. Photo by Zsuzsa Millei of installation at the 'Whale of a Bad Time' exhibition, Budapest 2020.	p. 14
Fig. 3.1	Hanna Trampert, *Was uns verbindet*, 2019, 80×60 cm.	p. 81
Fig. 3.2	Hanna Trampert, *Travel in Space and Time*, 2019, 100×100 cm.	p. 82
Fig. 3.3	Hanna Trampert, *End of the Day*, 2019, 50×100 cm.	p. 83
Fig. 3.4	Hanna Trampert, *Together*, 2019, 70×90 cm.	p. 83
Fig. 3.5	Hanna Trampert, *Memory 1*, 2020, 100×100 cm.	p. 84
Fig. 3.6	Hanna Trampert, *Memory 2*, 2020, 100×100 cm.	p. 85
Fig. 3.7	Hanna Trampert, *The Girl with the Balloon 1*, 2020, 70×90 cm.	p. 86
Fig. 3.8	Hanna Trampert, *The Girl by the Sea*, 2020, 70×90 cm.	p. 87
Fig. 3.9	Hanna Trampert, *The Girl with the Balloon 2*, 2020, 70×90 cm.	p. 88
Fig. 3.10	Hanna Trampert, *Friends 3*, 2021, 50×60 cm.	p. 89
Fig. 3.11	Hanna Trampert, *Self-Portrait*, 2021, 50×60 cm.	p. 90

Between Chapters 5–6:

'Smuggling Jewelry', a memory-story video by Tatyana Kleyn. p. 135

Photograph of Tatyana with her family in her birth city of Riga in the Soviet Union, 1977. From Tatyana Kleyn's family archive. p. 137

Photograph of Tatyana, her aunt Doris, and Charley the Great Dane. Riga, 1977. From Tatyana Kleyn's family archive. p. 137

Between Chapters 6–7:

Photograph of the author and her father in a military uniform, n.d. From Khanum Gevorgyan's family archive. p. 160

Fig. 7.1	Photograph of Claudia, Diana, Fabiana, me, and two unrecognised friends at my place, Buenos Aires, circa 1978. From Nano Belvedere's personal archive.	p. 175
Fig. 7.2	Inés Dussel, untitled drawing of a sailboat, 1975.	p. 176
Fig. 7.3	Inés Dussel, untitled drawing of a house with a gabled roof, 1975.	p. 178
Fig. 7.4	Photograph of a Catholic friend's celebration of communion, Buenos Aires, 1975. Author's family archive.	p. 180
Fig. 7.5	Inés Dussel, *Apple = Two Faces*, drawing, 1977.	p. 183
Fig. 7.6	Photograph of the author's fifth-grade class in Primary school, Buenos Aires, 1976. Author's family archive.	p. 186

Between Chapters 10–11:

Photograph of Tatyana (back row, fifth from the left) with her gymnastics team in Tiananmen Square. Beijing, China, 1989. From Tatyana Kleyn's family archive. p. 256

Between Chapters 12–13:

Photographs of Iveta Silova dressed as a snowflake at her kindergarten New Year's party in Soviet Latvia, n.d. From Iveta Silova's family archive. p. 304

Photographs of Nelli Piattoeva dressed as a frog for a New Year's party, n.d. From Nelli Piattoeva's family archive. p. 306

List of Figures and Other Illustrations 397

Fig. 13.1	Raisa Foster, artworks made from upcycled material and mental resources: [top] 'Ketjureaktio', a stage performance, 2012; [middle] 'Sounds of Grey', a dance film, 2016; [bottom] 'Lupina', a video work, 2016. Photographs by Mikko Korkiakangas (2012) and Raisa Foster and Mika Peltomaa (2016).	p. 311
Fig. 13.2	Raisa Foster, untitled life-drawing study that was upcycled by adding layers and framing it as an artwork, 2021. Photograph by Raisa Foster, 2021.	p. 318
Fig. 13.3	Raisa Foster, still from a video artwork 'Tiny Creatures', 2021.	p. 319
Fig. 13.4	Raisa Foster, 'Which Came First, the Chicken or the Egg?', sound art installation, 2021. Artist's photograph.	p. 320

Between Chapters 13–14:

Thoma Sukhashvili and Maia Sukhashvili, 'The Tailor', as displayed in the Finnish Labour Museum Werstas, n.d. Photograph by Zsuzsa Millei.	p. 327

Fig. 15.1	Anja at age six, around the time the 'Ghost Trains' incident happened. Photograph by Klaus Becker, Naumburg (Saale), 1982.	p. 357
Fig. 15.2	Sarah at around age eight or nine. Photograph by Barbara Fichtner, Schwege, 1987.	p. 358
Fig. 15.3	Sarah's school backpack. Photograph by Barbara Fichtner, Berlin, 1985.	p. 358
Fig. 15.4	Thumbnails: forty-nine images for the 'Ghost Train' story. Illustrations ©Azam Aghalouie und Hassan Tavakoli. Photograph by Sarah Fichtner, 2020.	p. 360
Fig. 15.5	Sample illustration from Sarah's part of the story. © Azam Aghalouie und Hassan Tavakoli, 2020.	p. 361
Fig. 15.6	Sample illustration from Anja's part of the story. © Azam Aghalouie und Hassan Tavakoli, 2020.	p. 361
Fig. 16.1	Authors' drawings and invocation: a ceremony of re-membering our relationships with plants. Jiang, Pretti, Tsotniashvili, Anayatova, Nielsen, Silova, 2023.	p. 372

About the Contributors

Dilraba Anayatova is a PhD student in the Educational Policy and Evaluation program at Mary Lou Fulton Teachers College, Arizona State University. Born and raised in rural Kazakhstan, she enjoyed her grandmother's big garden with various flowers, fruits, and vegetables, especially sitting there with female family members and putting medicinal woad ink on their eyebrows. Dilraba is interested in rural education and the interaction of environmental education in and outside classrooms with human and non-human teachers. ORCID ID: 0000-0002-4714-6715

Elena Jackson Albarrán is a Cold-War kid who grew up in the West, and as a historian of childhood, has begun to see her own life as part of a historical era, informed by the structures, policies, news cycles, and cultural values of the time. Through her work with the collective-biography project, she has found ways to bring Cold-War history to life through oral history projects with her undergraduate college students at Miami University, Ohio, United States. She is author of *Seen and Heard in Mexico: Children and Revolutionary Cultural Nationalism* (Nebraska 2015), among other articles and chapters. She teaches Comparative Cold War Childhoods and World History since 1945, when she is not teaching Latin American Studies courses. Her latest book *Good Neighbor Empires: Children and Cultural Capital in the Americas* is forthcoming from Brill. ORCID ID: 0000-0002-8321-6661

Nadine Bernhard was born in the late GDR and spent the first nine years of her childhood in this system. She also experienced the fall of the Berlin Wall and the transformation process and its impact on her everyday life, her family and friends, which strongly influenced her identity. She was fortunate to meet the editors of this book in Berlin and to participate in the Reconnect/Recollect project. Nadine works as

Professor for Higher Education in the Context of Digital Transformation and Diversity at the Technische Universität Berlin and her research interests are thus mainly in the evolution of postsecondary education, inequality studies in education, and internationalisation. However, the Reconnect/Recollect project touched her academically and personally so much that she decided to also study (post-)socialist childhood memories more intensively. ORCID ID: 0000-0001-5062-3685

Erica Burman grew up in Liverpool, UK, and so had a different Cold-War childhood from most of the other contributors to this volume, albeit obviously still subject to its dynamics in ways she attempts to explore in this chapter. Erica is author of *Child as Method: Othering, Interiority, and Materialism* (Routledge, 2024), *Developments: Child, Image, Nation* (Routledge, 2020, 2nd edition), *Fanon, Education, Action: Child as Method* (Routledge, 2019), *Deconstructing Developmental Psychology* (Routledge, 3rd edition, 2017, 4th in preparation). Erica's research has focused on critical developmental and educational psychology, feminist and postcolonial theory, childhood studies, and on critical mental health practice (particularly around gender and cultural issues). Her recent work addresses the connections between emotions, mental health and (social as well as individual) change, in particular as anchored by representations of, and appeals to, childhood. She sees debates about children and childhood as central to current theories and practices around decolonisation, as indicated by her current work on 'Child as method', in which the Reconnect/Recollect project has played an important role. ORCID ID: 0000-0002-2504-5120

José Cossa was born and raised in Maputo, Mozambique. A Global African scholar, poet, and educator who has learned the value of memories as a means to connect what seems to have passed with what is currently occurring and what seems to still need to materialise. He embraces the understanding that in African cosmologies the future is already here since the past, present, and future are interlinked, juxtaposed, and not mutually exclusive. Therefore children, youth, the elderly, the unborn, and the living dead are part of this complex interlinked, juxtaposed, and not mutually exclusive reality. Their memories and our memories of them matter and must be kept alive. ORCID ID: 0000-0002-9586-4287

Inés Dussel grew up in Cold-War Argentina and her early experiences with political involvement and military and paramilitary repression marked her life. She was active in human rights struggles during the post dictatorship, and co-produced teaching materials and teacher education courses that took memory politics as a central public and pedagogical issue. She moved up and down the American continent quite a few times. She currently works at the Department of Educational Research at CINVESTAV, Mexico City, where she has some wonderful colleagues and students. She thinks of herself as a public intellectual interested in the pasts and futures of schooling and cultures, which she sees as institutions or forces for the commons. The history of education has been a persistent focus of her work, and from 2022 to 2025 she is the president of the International Standing Conference for the History of Education (ISCHE). ORCID ID: 0000-0003-3983-3985

Kathleen Falkenberg grew up in the former German Democratic Republic, a country that no longer exists. Witnessing the transformation years after the fall of the Berlin Wall and the manifold challenges this brought to family and friends she developed an ever-growing interest in (post)socialist identities, presents and pasts. As a researcher in Comparative and International Education at Humboldt-Universität zu Berlin she learned about Reconnect/Recollect project, which turned out to be a transformative encounter both personally and academically. In her research, Kathleen, furthermore, explores different conditions of growing-up and learning, including assessment in school from a justice-theory perspective or marketization effects in early childhood education. ORCID ID: 0000-0002-3170-7098

Sarah Fichtner grew up on what she perceived as an artificial island called West Berlin. She is a social anthropologist and education researcher, interested in the process of 'doing school' and what it takes to shape the school of the future, whether in Germany or Sub-Saharan Africa, where she spent quite some time. She has also been working on childhoods in the context of flight and migration. As the project coordinator of the activist 'encounter' network and inspired by her Mnemo ZIN colleagues, Sarah Fichtner became interested in collective and artistic biography and memory work as a means for transcultural learning.

Raisa Foster is a multidisciplinary artist and researcher living and working in Tampere, Finland. She holds the title of associate professor in social pedagogy at the University of Eastern Finland and dance pedagogy at the University of the Arts Helsinki. She investigates current social and ecological issues through dance, drawing, video art, and writing. The starting point of her artistic and philosophical research is human's bodily relationship with the world. ORCID ID: 0000-0003-2661-6041

Susanne Gannon grew up in Australia during Cold-War times, influenced by western perspectives and popular culture imports from the USA. As a teacher and a researcher, much of her work has involved trying to unpick taken-for-granted ways of thinking and being in the world, including childhood experiences. Collective biography has become an important and versatile methodology for pursuing this work in the company of others. Her books drawing on collective biography are *Doing Collective Biography* (co-edited with Bronwyn Davies, Open University Press, 2006), *Pedagogical Encounters* (co-edited with Bronwyn Davies, Peter Lang, 2009), and *Becoming Girl: Collective Biography and the Production of Girlhood* (co-edited with Marnina Gonick, 2014, The Women's Press). ORCID ID: 0000-0003-2182-3615

Katarzyna Gawlicz grew up in socialist Poland, moving back and forth between a small village and a large city. As a teenager, she spent one summer at a pioneer camp in the former Soviet Union, which was for her an illuminating experience of political socialization (whose meaning she grasped only later). Currently, she works as an associate professor of education at the University of Lower Silesia, Poland. In her teaching and research, she has focused on power relations and democracy in early childhood education, children's rights, transformative learning through action research, and, recently, on relations between childhood and nation, and education in times of climate crisis. ORCID ID: 0000-0003-1668-5393

Khanum Gevorgyan is a representative of the 'independence generation' in Armenia, coming from a rural village, where the memories of the Armenian genocide, Soviet Armenia, and post-Soviet hardships not only impacted the lives of the adults but also her own childhood. She grew up trying to figure out what her role is among great historical happenings in the region. Wars of all sorts—dolma wars, cultural wars, territory wars—led her to understand the critical nature of memories. Despite the various emotional tantrums that her memories brought, she finally made peace with her memories and first unlocked a memory a few months ago, which is saved in the pages of this book. ORCID ID: 0009-0001-5388-0377

Jieyu Jiang's research focuses on exploring multiple ways of conceptualizing the notion of a teacher, teacher qualities and subjectivities in human and more-than-human worlds and educational policy borrowing and traveling in international background. In her childhood, unlike other outgoing children her age, she was shy to communicate with her classmates. Passing by the mimosa pudica on her way to and from school every day, she always stopped to talk to them in her own bashful way. ORCID ID: 0000-0002-1734-4091

Irena Kašparová is a Czech social anthropologist, who enjoys freedom coming out of her discipline, as well as out of her liminal life experiences. A daughter of a protestant priest, she spent her childhood in Sudeten, the border zones of socialist Czechoslovakia, where the family was exiled to live; and her teens in Middlesbrough, Britain, where the family migrated after the change of regime. Having the experience of internal political refugee as well as that of an Easterner in the West, politics and power had a profound impact upon her awareness of the self and became an intrinsic part of her identity. Currently, Irena heads the Social Anthropology department at Masaryk University Brno, Czech Republic and enjoys study of childhood, education and qualitative research methodology. ORCID ID: 0000-0002-1148-9417

Tatyana Kleyn was born in the Soviet Union (currently Latvia) and migrated to the US as a political refugee at a young age. Her family was resettled in Columbus, Ohio by HIAS, a Jewish American nonprofit organization. She spent the second half of her childhood in Poughkeepsie, New York. Tatyana's experiences as an immigrant and language learner paved the way for her to become Professor of Bilingual Education and TESOL (Teaching English to Speakers of Other Languages) at The City College of New York. She is Principal Investigator of the CUNY-Initiative on Immigration and Education (CUNY-IIE). For more information, visit: TatyanaKleyn.com. ORCID ID: 0000-0002-2128-6429

Pia Koivunen grew up in Northern Finland and became fascinated by history as a child. She works as senior lecturer in European and World History at the University of Turku and holds the title of associate professor in Russian history. She is specialised in Soviet political and cultural history, her research interests including cultural Cold-War, memory politics, the history of experience, cultural diplomacy, mega-events, museums, children, and youth. Currently, she leads a research project 'Mission Finland. Cold-War cultural diplomacy at the crossroads of East and West', funded by the Research Council of Finland. Her recent publications include a monograph *Performing Peace and Friendship. The World Youth Festival and Soviet Cultural Diplomacy* (De Gruyter, 2023). For information on the 'Mission Finland' project, visit: https://missionfinland.utu.fi/en/project/. ORCID ID: 0000-0001-6142-1595

Zsuzsa Millei was born in Hungary. After migrating to Australia in 2000, she enrolled in a PhD program. Her thesis focused on the history and politics of early childhood education and care in Western Australia. She had to be persuaded that there might be value in a study between the Australian system and the socialist Hungarian one, which she undertook later. She is still somewhat puzzled—although much less after the Reconnect/Recollect project—when researchers express enthusiasm for research on socialist childhoods. Perhaps it is due to her upbringing in a socialist country characterised by its explicit official politics (standing in line). At the same time, perhaps growing up in this context is what ignited her interest in researching children, childhood, and politics. She is also Mnemo ZIN with Nelli Piattoeva and Iveta Silova, good friends and comrades in research, art, and having fun. ORCID ID: 0000-0003-4681-6024

Olga Mun is a doctoral researcher at the Department of Education, University of Oxford. She researches epistemic injustice in global science and ways to build more inclusive and just research cultures. One of her recent publications focuses on non-Western ways of knowing such as South Korean philosophy of *jeong* (kindness) in relation to nature, humans, and higher education. You can watch her TEDx talk on decoloniality in Central Asian science at https://www.youtube.com/watch?v=-YwxUO47YYE. Olga is a zinester, her latest research project focuses on the epistemic repair in international higher education by engaging with the knowledges from the Global South in rethinking the themes of sustainability.

Ann Nielsen has been an educator for over 20 years having worked as a classroom teacher, master teacher, school administrator and in the last ten years has broadened her interests to the lived experiences of teachers globally. Her research interests include the lived experiences and subjectivities of teachers and teacher leaders, education for sustainable futures, memory work, visual and post qualitative methodologies. Ann grew up in the midwest region of the United States where she celebrated the spring flowers on May Days.

Oshie Nishimura-Sahi grew up in a rural area in Southern Osaka, Japan. Living with her grandparents who ran a small fruit farm on a hill, she spent her childhood with pear trees, cattle, bugs, a Shinto shrine, and Jizo stone statues. Stories told by her grandparents about a more-than-human world are also an essential part of her childhood memory. Those fragments of childhood memory gave rise to her interest in studying educational practices in terms of non-human actors which are capable of changing the world. She is currently studying transnational policy movements, drawing upon Actor-Network Theory (ANT), for her doctorate. She is a doctoral researcher in the Faculty of Education and Culture at Tampere University, Finland. ORCID ID: 0000-0001-7842-0409

Petar Odak was born in the last years of Yugoslavia, witnessing its violent dissolution firsthand, and spending his formative years in the seemingly never-ending post/socialist transition to something worse. His recently defended PhD project (in Gender Studies at Central European University in Vienna and at the Institute for Cultural Inquiry, Utrecht University) revolves around different emanations of the ghosts of socialist pasts within the post/socialist affective capitalism. Therefore, the essay in this volume comes as a result of a very needed personal, political, and professional self-reflection. Currently, he is a Visiting Teaching Fellow at Humanities and Practicing Arts Programs at Al-Quds Bard College in Jerusalem, Palestine.

Jennifer Patico is Professor and Chair of Anthropology at Georgia State University in Atlanta. A sociocultural anthropologist, she has conducted ethnographic research in both Russia and the United States, with a focus on themes of consumption, class and selfhood in both contexts. Her career in anthropology—and her participation in the Cold War Childhoods memory project—were inspired by her participation in the youth musical production *Peace Child* in her hometown of Columbia, Maryland and ultimately in Tashkent, Uzbekistan, where she collaborated with U.S. and Soviet teens during the last days of the Cold War. She is the author of *Consumption and Social Change in a Post-Soviet Middle Class* (Stanford University Press 2008) and *The Trouble with Snack Time: Children's Food and the Politics of Parenting* (New York University Press 2020). ORCID ID: 0000-0003-2932-8707

Nelli Piattoeva was born and raised in the Westernmost part of the USSR and continued her education across the border in Finland where she currently lives and researches different aspects of post-Soviet educational transformations including digitalization, national assessments, and nationalism. Studying childhood memories and lived experiences of (post)socialism, she seeks to understand how state policies are enacted—absorbed, resisted or ignored—by adults and children on the ground. She also feels a strong need for more research on childhood, including children's relational agency, in educational sociology and policy studies that tend to predominantly focus on policies and adults' experiences thereof. She has found great inspiration and comfort in engaging with artistic methods and collective biography through collaboration with and friendship of Zsuzsa Millei and Iveta Silova as the Mnemo ZIN collective. ORCID ID: 0000-0003-0963-1901

Ivana Polić is a 1990s child, born and raised in Croatia after its secession from socialist Yugoslav federation. For her, participation in the collective-biography project provided a unique opportunity to re-examine her own idea of self via childhood memories. The peculiar position of her own family history from socialist Yugoslavia as well as memories of growing up in war-torn Croatia provided a unique opportunity to 1) deconstruct childhood experiences against the binary Cold-War framework and 2) position them within the broader context of connections to other participants' memories of growing up across the globe. She is currently a lecturer at University of California San Diego and the University of San Diego, with research interests related to the history of children and childhood in (post)socialism.

Esther Pretti is a postdoctoral researcher at the School of Sustainability and the Walton Sustainability Teacher's Academies at Arizona State University. Her work is concerned with the relationships between humans and non-human beings, especially in urban areas, where she relies on posthuman and Indigenous scholarship to examine the hierarchies of knowledge and being that are often overlooked in environmental and sustainability education. From a very young age she found comfort and companionship amongst tropical plants in Brazil, being met with beauty, refuge, and solace by a Cambará bush in her grandmother's yard. ORCID ID: 0000-0003-3930-8021

Josefine Raasch is a social anthropologist. Growing-up in East-Berlin, she was a proud member of the socialist children and youth organizations. Later, working as a physiotherapist, she experienced the fall of the wall with confusion and questions. Another thirteen years later, she started studying European ethnology and education, followed by a PhD in Science and Technology Studies in Melbourne, Australia. The world was a different place after the wall fell, and even more so after experiencing Australia; so, Josefine has found her passion for investigating and translating logics. This passion found fertile grounds in postcolonial discourses on knowledge production. She then worked eight years in different positions in academia before she became a Senior Learning Designer at Germany's leading business school. This school is located in the former state council of the German Democratic Republic and Josefine felt the irony every time she walked through the halls. Now, she works as an Agile Coach. ORCID ID: 0009-0005-4701-6637

Rahim Rahimov joined the Cold-War childhood collective memories and biography project as a political analyst. His involvement in that project eventually led him to become a researcher of one of the greatest Azerbaijani-Turkish intellectuals, Ahmet bey Agaoglu, and his legacy. Indeed, that project inspired him to childhood memory studies, which represent to him a new perspective to look into the world that has shaped us. Rahim was born in Soviet Azerbaijan, USSR but grew up in both Soviet and post-soviet independent Azerbaijan. Perhaps, as a child of the transition period, his desire to contemplate the logic of a (dis-)connection between these two worlds underlies his interest in the memory studies. His latest publication is *Between Russia and Islam* (Lynne Rienner Publishers, London, 2023). ORCID ID: 0000-0002-1127-1020

Beatrice Scutaru was born and lived for the first six years of her life in socialist Romania. After the violent change of regime, Beatrice witnessed the country's transformation and its impact on her family, friends and everyday life. At the same time, certain things didn't really seem to change. These experiences nourished an ever-growing interest in researching and reflecting on both changes and continuities between socialism and post-socialism. This, combined with her interest in childhood and growing up in Europe after 1945, led to her interest in the Reconnect/Recollect project. This turned out to be a transformative encounter, both personally and professionally. Within this project, Beatrice was not only inspired and challenged to engage with and think of new ways of producing and analyzing sources, but she also discovered and built a strong, diverse, and supportive transnational community. ORCID ID: 0000-0002-3760-0937

Iveta Silova grew up in Latvia during the late Soviet period. She spent a lot of time outside, playing in her family's summer garden, wandering along the river on the edge of her hometown, and exploring nearby meadows and forests. During this time, she learned to speak with trees and make friends with yellow fairies. Iveta now works as a Professor and Associate Dean of Global Engagement at Mary Lou Fulton Teachers College at Arizona State University. Her research examines the intersections of postsocialist, postcolonial, and decolonial perspectives in envisioning education beyond the Western horizon. She is particularly interested in childhood memories, ecofeminism, and environmental sustainability. She enjoys being a part of the Mnemo ZIN collective with Zsuzsa and Nelli. ORCID ID: 0000-0002-8897-8016

Thoma Sukhashvili was born in 1991 in a small town of South Ossetia, a breakaway territory of Georgia, and resided there until the 2008 war. Presently, he is an artist and researcher based in Tbilisi. Thoma earned a Master's in Applied Psychology from the Georgian Institute of Public Affairs (GIPA), focusing his research on nationalism, ethnic conflicts, and generational traumas. For the past eight years, he served as a photojournalist, but he has transitioned to working in the field of human rights in Central Asia.

Lucian Țion travelled the whole wide world before deciding to return to his native Romania, which he had left four years after the 1989 revolution. His journeys were not fruitless: he got his BA at Middlebury College in the U.S., his MA at the University of Amsterdam, and finally his PhD at the National University of Singapore. He couldn't decide whether to follow an artistic or an academic career, and therefore he chose to do both. He is currently assistant professor at the University of Amsterdam and Babeș Bolyai University of Cluj. He usually publishes on Chinese and Romanian cinemas—but also on postsocialist Romanian nationalism—in journals such as *Quarterly Review of Film and Video*, *Comparative Literature Studies*, and *Senses of Cinema*. ORCID ID: 0000-0003-2434-7298

Madina Tlostanova grew up in the North Caucasus in the 1970s–1980s. In her fluid identification, she combines indigenous Circassian and Uzbek origins linked to the darker colonial spaces and histories of the Soviet empire. Having spent three decades in the belly of the beast (Moscow) she finally moved to Sweden in 2015 to make one of her previous hobbies, feminist and gender studies, into a 'profession'. She is a decolonial feminist thinker and writer, professor of postcolonial feminisms at the Department of Thematic Studies at Linköping University, Sweden. She focuses on decolonial thought, postsocialist human condition, artivism, feminisms of the Global South, critical future studies. Her most recent books include *What Does it Mean to be Post-Soviet? Decolonial Art from the Ruins of the Soviet Empire* (Duke University Press 2018), *A New Political Imagination: Making the Case* (co-authored with Tony Fry, Routledge 2020), *Decoloniality of Knowledge, Being and Sensing* (Almaty, Kazakhstan: Center of Contemporary Culture Tselinny 2020), and *Narratives of Unsettlement: Being Out-of-Joint as a Generative Human Condition* (Routledge 2023). ORCID ID: 0000-0002-0727-2098

Hanna Trampert is an artist and art therapy consultant. Born in 1963 on the Baltic Sea in Poland, she has lived in Germany since 1985. Hanna is a member of the Federal Association of Visual Artists, Bundesverband Bildender Künstler (BBK), having published pictures in the book

German-Polish Bridgebuilding at Municipal Level ([n.p.]: Kliomedia, 2012). For the last twenty years, she has participated in numerous solo and group exhibitions, including the 'International Artists Encounter'. In her paintings, she focuses on human beings and their experiences. She is fascinated by memories and by the experiences that show themselves in people's facial expressions, and she find space on canvas or paper to register those. In her work, influential family stories become works of art.

Keti Tsotniashvili was born in Georgia during the time of Perestroika (Restructuring) and her childhood was shaped by the uncertainties and joys of navigating the turbulent 1990s of post-Soviet time and space. In her childhood, she enjoyed climbing and interacting with tall apple trees, learning from and with them while visiting her grandparents in the village and engaging in the family's ceremonial act of apple harvesting. Keti recently obtained her PhD in Educational Policy and Evaluation from Arizona State University. Her dissertation research explores transformation of academic identities in post-Soviet Georgia. Her research interests also include decolonial theories and postsocialist transformations, academic cultures, higher education systems and policy, childhood memories, and environmental sustainability. ORCID ID: 0000-0003-4354-8183

Nadia Tsulukidze was born in Georgia. After finishing Music College, she lived and studied dance in Germany. Coming back to Georgia in 2004 as a freelance artist, she collaborated with visual artists and co-founded a multimedia performance group 'Khinkali Juice'. In 2010, she finished Master of Theater Studies at DasArts in Amsterdam with the documentary theatre piece *Ready for Love or Seven Fragments of Identity*. In 2013, she created another documentary performance *Me and Stalin* in collaboration with the Kaaitheater Brussels, Frascati Amsterdam, BIT Theatergarasijen, and Schlachthaus Theater Bern. Nadia explores the body as the result of constant negotiation between social construction and personal choice. She defines this process as performative, as it employs performing the self in relation to the 'other'. She sees 'the self' as a narration, constructed of personal memories. 'The self' is the author and the object of the narration at the same time. Nadia's work is framed by this perspective and directed towards the exploration of her own 'self' in a specific framework.

Stefanie Weiss was born in Nürnberg, Germany to a German father and Mexican mother. After moving over the Atlantic several times during the first six years of her life, her family settled in Mexico where she currently lives. She is an actress and for many years directed a professional acting school, has a Master degree in Educational Research Sciences, a Bachelor of Psychology, and a Bachelor of Acting. She has been acting for the last twenty-four years, but her other passions are research and teaching. Currently, she also directs the project 'Open Space Theater for Domestic Workers' where, for the first two years, she worked according to the methodologies of the construction of collective memories and the construction of collective biographies. She has translated thirteen German plays into Spanish, seven of which have been published, as a way of contributing to the dissemination and enjoyment of German drama in Mexico. ORCID ID: 0009-0002-8374-5560

Anja Werner grew up in small-town East Germany during the Cold War, where she was prepared to live in a world that today no longer exists. She, therefore, became a writer and historian. She is currently affiliated with the University of Erfurt in Germany. In her research and teaching she focuses, among other things, on digital memory work in transcultural contexts with a special interest in educational exchanges among Black and/or Deaf people from the West and the Global South. Together with Sarah Fichtner, she initiated a motion comic project about memories of the German division at the Marienborn Memorial to Divided Germany (https://mocom-memories.de/en/home/). In her ongoing book project, she examines two deaf missionaries, African American Andrew Foster and his German wife Berta Zuther-Foster, who, between 1957 and 2009, opened more than thirty schools and churches for the deaf in thirteen African countries.

Mnemo ZIN is a composite name for Zsuzsa Millei, Iveta Silova, and Nelli Piattoeva who grew up on the Eastern side of the Iron Curtain—Zsuzsa in Hungary, Iveta in Latvia, and Nelli in Karelia. Our paths first crossed ten years ago through an informal exchange of childhood memories and quickly evolved into close collaboration using collective-biography research. Our collective name acknowledges the interdependent nature of our work against the individualist, hierarchical, and competitive culture of modern academia. It is inspired by the stories from Greek mythology, especially *Mnemosyne*—the goddess of memory, daughter of Gaia, and the mother of the nine Muses.

Index

agency (children's agency) 7, 60, 244, 251, 261, 277, 299, 344
alternative memorialization 288–290
anarchive 5, 8–12, 14–16, 21, 23, 95, 167, 169, 171, 307–308, 312–313, 320–321, 330, 333, 336, 338, 346
Anthropocene 12, 22, 391
archive 5–6, 8–12, 14–16, 37, 39, 53, 59, 167, 169, 188, 198–199, 220, 240, 242, 252, 259–261, 264–269, 272–273, 277–278, 285, 308–309, 312–313, 315, 317, 319–321, 368
Argentina 20, 167, 169–170, 173–174, 185, 187, 266
Armenia 125, 156–158, 161–165, 266, 293
art 5, 7, 9, 12, 15–17, 23, 107, 122–123, 130, 188, 215, 289, 307–310, 313–318, 320–321, 326, 351, 356, 363, 367–368
arts-based research 307–308, 313–315, 321
arts of noticing 22, 375–376, 378, 391
aspiration 152, 237, 249, 251, 342, 384
attunement 377–378, 380
Australia 266, 308
Azerbaijan 162, 266, 283

Berlin Wall 14, 36, 52, 341, 354, 359, 362
body 8, 11–12, 14–16, 57, 77, 135, 138, 146, 170, 193, 196, 199, 212, 214–215, 217, 219–220, 222, 225–227, 231, 236–246, 248–253, 257–258, 288, 314–315, 317, 319, 340, 342, 373, 375–376, 379–380, 388–390
borders 11, 14, 30, 49, 79–80, 90, 92, 94–95, 97, 106, 110, 125, 135, 138, 168, 193–194, 196, 198, 202–203, 224, 227, 250, 253, 283–291, 293, 297, 300, 354, 365–366

boundaries 52, 80, 139, 152–153, 169, 195, 230–231, 259, 277, 287–288, 297, 299, 314, 390
Brazil 170, 266, 374, 379, 388

capitalism 6–7, 9, 17, 21, 31, 35, 61, 94–95, 102, 108, 120, 139–140, 142–143, 153, 196, 213–214, 230, 262, 266, 269, 273, 309–310, 342, 344, 373
Caucasus 125, 127, 129–130
Ceaușescu, Nikolae 70, 118, 246–247
ceremony 124, 181, 371, 373–379, 381–387, 389–391
childhood 5–7, 9–12, 14, 16–20, 23, 27, 32, 44–45, 48, 51–52, 60, 66, 70, 79–81, 86, 90, 94–97, 99–100, 103–105, 109–112, 119–127, 129, 134, 139–140, 143–144, 153, 156, 158, 161–163, 165, 167, 169, 172, 175, 186–188, 191, 193–194, 196–199, 216–217, 219, 227, 229, 241, 245, 251, 253, 259–265, 268–270, 275–277, 285–291, 293–294, 299–301, 308, 314–316, 319, 321, 329–339, 341, 343–345, 351, 353, 355, 362–363, 368, 371, 373–374, 376–378, 380, 384–388, 390–391
childhood memories 5–7, 9–12, 14, 16–18, 23, 27, 44–45, 48, 60, 79–81, 121, 143–144, 156, 161, 167, 187, 193–194, 196–199, 216–217, 219, 229, 259–261, 263–264, 277, 285, 287, 289, 293, 300, 308, 316, 319, 321, 330, 334, 338, 341, 351, 353, 355, 362, 371, 373–374, 376–378, 380, 384–386, 388, 390
China 106, 255–256, 374, 379
Cold War 5–12, 14, 16, 18–19, 21–23, 27–28, 32, 45, 52–53, 58, 60–61, 70, 72, 79, 93–96, 99, 104–105, 107–112, 139, 142–144, 151, 153, 167, 170, 193–194, 198–199, 219, 229, 237–238, 240–241,

251, 253, 260–262, 266, 285–291, 293, 297–300, 329–334, 337–339, 341–346, 355, 363, 366, 368, 373
collective biography 5, 9, 11, 56, 60, 170, 174, 198, 237–240, 251–252, 265, 288, 334, 340, 342, 351, 355, 371, 375, 390
collective memory work 7, 264–265, 277, 288, 375, 377
Comăneci, Nadia 241, 246–248, 252
commodities 139–140, 143–144, 146, 149, 151–153, 218, 269, 334
competition 17, 238, 242, 249, 267
compliance 37, 71, 99, 244, 258
consumerism 20, 31–32, 35, 139–141, 145, 147, 152–153, 164, 216, 296, 310, 316, 333, 344
contemporary art 307, 310, 313, 316, 321
Crimea 149
Czechoslovakia 19, 216, 266, 291

desire 18, 21, 23, 29, 36, 45, 105, 109, 142–143, 153, 237–238, 241–242, 245, 247, 250, 253, 264, 298, 300, 344
drawing 175, 177, 182, 184, 314–315, 317

Easter 126–127
East/West 11, 100, 110, 139, 152–153, 191, 251, 261, 286, 289, 291, 330, 332, 341, 343, 351–353, 362
elite sport 16, 19, 237–238, 241–242, 249–253
(e-)motion comics 351–354, 356–357, 359, 362, 365–368
England 93, 102–103
environmental crisis 153, 307–308, 321
escapism 119, 251, 272
ethnodrama 19, 193–194, 198–200

feminisms 101, 235
Finland 16, 48, 51–54, 58–63, 65, 68–69, 143, 266, 281, 315, 338, 353

gender 18–19, 96, 101, 104, 164–165, 198–199, 216, 227, 241, 265–266, 271, 276, 335
generations 21–23, 33, 97, 106, 119–120, 122, 148, 161, 173, 180, 186, 193, 198, 333–337, 339–346, 352, 362

Georgia 126, 266, 326, 374, 378
German Democratic Republic (GDR) 21, 36, 44–45, 82, 121, 191, 202, 237, 242, 259–260, 262, 264, 266–268, 271, 274–276, 294, 298, 363, 366
ghost trains 351–353, 355, 359–360, 362, 364, 367–368
Gorbachev, Mikhail 16, 51, 53–54, 58–73, 332
gratitude 22, 371, 373, 375, 377–380, 391

H.I.J.O.S. 169, 173–174, 186–188
historical research 19, 51, 54, 365
Hungary 107, 161, 217, 224, 237, 242, 249, 291, 320

injury 222, 237, 242, 250–251
intergenerational relationships 7, 21–22, 331, 380
internal emigration 119
intimacy 21, 139, 143, 149, 153–154, 170, 193, 216, 229, 240, 244, 253, 384, 387, 389, 391
Israel/Palestine 112, 341

Jewish identities 96–109, 111–112, 341

Kazakhstan 266, 380, 388

Latvia 217, 349, 374, 388
leisure time 142, 144, 246, 248, 262–263
lost generation 119–120, 122

materiality 8, 12, 15–16, 109, 121, 139, 141–144, 146–147, 151–154, 172, 198, 220, 237–238, 287, 290, 313, 316, 333, 337, 342, 345, 351–352, 354, 376, 382, 390
memories 5–12, 14–23, 27–41, 43–46, 48–49, 51–60, 62–74, 78–82, 84–85, 90, 93, 95, 104–111, 119, 121, 126, 132, 135, 139, 142–152, 156, 158–165, 167–175, 177, 179, 186–188, 191, 193–194, 196–200, 213, 215–221, 223–225, 228–231, 235, 237–242, 244–248, 250, 252–253, 259–278, 285–301, 307–309, 313–317, 319–321, 329–338, 340–341, 344, 346, 351–356, 359–360, 362–368, 370–371, 373–391

memory stories 5–6, 8, 11, 14–15, 23, 36, 60, 64, 69, 71–74, 95, 111, 143–144, 199, 217, 220, 229, 237–239, 241, 252, 259–262, 264–267, 270, 273, 275–277, 289–291, 299–300, 309, 313, 315, 319, 321, 376–377, 385, 390
memory work 5, 7, 11, 17–19, 104, 109–110, 144, 172–173, 238, 240, 259, 264–265, 277, 288, 352, 365–366, 368, 371, 375, 377, 387
menarche 16, 19, 21, 213–230
menstruation 213, 215, 228–229. *See* menarche
Mexico 11, 289
military dictatorship 20
minimal self 122
Mozambique 78
multiculturalism 365

New Year 132, 157–159, 163–165, 303, 305
non-human teachers 22, 48–49, 187, 373, 375–378, 380–381, 389–390, 392
North Caucasus 125

objects 8, 10, 14–15, 18, 20–21, 32, 36, 41, 48, 69, 84, 109, 140, 143, 146, 148, 162, 213–214, 217–221, 229–230, 247, 268, 285–287, 289–300, 309, 312–313, 317, 343–345, 351–352, 355, 366, 373, 376, 383, 390
oral history 53, 329–330, 336, 343, 346, 359, 367
other worlds 121, 250, 378, 384

pedagogy. *See* teaching/pedagogy
pioneer 7, 117, 131, 149–150
Plants 22–23, 371, 373, 376–391
Poland 32, 79–80, 87, 97, 145, 191, 202, 216–217, 266, 292, 295, 344
postsocialism 7, 9, 21, 28–29, 31–32, 35, 45, 60, 94–95, 97, 109, 111, 139, 141–144, 146–147, 153, 161, 168, 247, 259–261, 277, 289, 341
public history 355, 366–368

race 33, 95–96, 100, 102, 104, 119, 146, 188, 308, 340, 342

reciprocity 8, 22–23, 344, 371, 373, 377, 380, 386, 391
Reconnect/Recollect 5, 11, 32, 48, 60, 79–81, 86, 89–90, 186, 191, 194, 219–220, 229, 259–260, 264–265, 277, 285–286, 289, 308, 313, 315, 330–331, 351, 353, 355
redoubling 119
repressive regimes 106, 168, 170, 173, 197, 236
resistance 19, 109, 197, 261, 270
risk 55–56, 97, 172, 195, 197, 214, 225, 237, 240, 242, 245, 247–248, 251–253, 263–264, 320
Romania 53, 70, 145–147, 216, 237, 242, 246, 266, 269, 293

Schadenfreude 42
secrecy/secrets 6–7, 16, 19–20, 45, 121, 140, 148, 157, 168–171, 173, 176, 181–182, 193–201, 212–214, 216–217, 219, 221, 223–224, 227–228, 230–231, 269–270, 293, 298
self (self/other) 10, 21, 29, 31, 37, 39–40, 44, 55–58, 60, 99, 102–103, 111, 117, 121–122, 139, 141, 144, 146, 153–154, 168, 170, 187–188, 195–196, 216, 228, 231, 239, 250, 252, 259, 278, 285, 287, 290, 297–300, 329, 332, 343, 356, 374, 384, 387
situated perspectives 217, 352, 354
socialism 6–7, 9, 18–22, 28–29, 31–32, 35, 45, 52, 56, 60, 80, 94–95, 97, 101–103, 106, 108–109, 111, 121, 125, 139–144, 146–147, 152–153, 161, 168, 194, 196–198, 201, 204, 213, 216–217, 219, 225, 229–231, 241, 247, 259–263, 265–266, 268, 276–277, 288–289, 330, 340–342, 344, 373
soft power 16, 19, 237, 241
Soviet Union 7, 22, 51–52, 60–63, 68–70, 79, 95, 97, 105–108, 111–112, 125, 127–128, 131–132, 135–136, 140–141, 144, 156–159, 161–164, 216, 235, 266, 281, 283, 285, 305, 329, 332, 338, 340–341, 343, 345–346

sports 16, 52, 237–242, 244–252, 255, 263, 267
stereotypes 18, 31, 102, 241, 259, 277
subjectivities 16–17, 22, 29, 54–55, 94, 96, 109, 226, 237, 345
summer 125, 130, 149, 157, 175, 203, 245–249, 252, 281, 283, 293, 295, 319, 349, 366, 370, 380, 382, 385
summer camp 149, 246–248, 293, 295
sustainability 23, 164, 307–309, 316, 321

teaching/pedagogy 5, 20–22, 111, 156, 170, 235, 288, 330–331, 343, 367, 376, 383–387, 391
tension 194, 200, 258, 346
testimony 35, 173, 286
training 19, 73, 168, 237–239, 241–242, 245–252

trauma (traumatic events) 27–29, 36, 38–41, 43–45, 96, 167, 172–174, 186–188

Uniform childhood 264
unsupervised times 18–19, 259, 261–270, 272–277
upcycling 16, 23, 307–310, 312–313, 315, 317, 319–321

Video art 123, 174, 309–310, 314–315, 319–320, 354, 363

Youth organisations, movements 7, 52, 100–101, 103, 241, 262, 333, 343, 366
Yugoslavia 28–29, 33, 39, 44–45, 224–225, 266, 344

Zionism 99–103, 105, 108, 110, 112

About the Team

Alessandra Tosi was the managing editor for this book.

Jennifer Moriarty proof-read and indexed the manuscript. Anja Prichard styled the text.

Jeevanjot Kaur Nagpal designed the cover. The cover was produced in InDesign using the Fontin font.

Jeremy Bowman typeset the book in InDesign and produced the EPUB edition. The text font is Tex Gyre Pagella and the heading font is Californian FB.

Cameron Craig produced the PDF and HTML editions. The conversion is performed with open source software freely available on our GitHub page at https://github.com/OpenBookPublishers.

This book need not end here...

Share

All our books — including the one you have just read — are free to access online so that students, researchers and members of the public who can't afford a printed edition will have access to the same ideas. This title will be accessed online by hundreds of readers each month across the globe: why not share the link so that someone you know is one of them?

This book and additional content is available at: https://doi.org/10.11647/OBP.0383

Donate

Open Book Publishers is an award-winning, scholar-led, not-for-profit press making knowledge freely available one book at a time. We don't charge authors to publish with us: instead, our work is supported by our library members and by donations from people who believe that research shouldn't be locked behind paywalls.

Why not join them in freeing knowledge by supporting us: https://www.openbookpublishers.com/support-us

Follow @OpenBookPublish

Read more at the Open Book Publishers BLOG

You may also be interested in:

The Form of Ideology and the Ideology of Forms
Cold War, Decolonization and Third World Print Cultures

Francesca Orsini (editor)

https://doi.org/10.11647/OBP.0254

ANZUS and the Early Cold War
Strategy and Diplomacy between Australia, New Zealand and the United States, 1945–1956

Andrew Kelly

https://doi.org/10.11647/OBP.0141

Second Chance
My Life in Things

Ruth Rosengarten

https://doi.org/10.11647/OBP.0285

Play in a Covid Frame
Everyday Pandemic Creativity in a Time of Isolation

Anna Beresin, Julia Bishop (editors)

https://doi.org/10.11647/OBP.0326

www.ingramcontent.com/pod-product-compliance
Lightning Source LLC
Chambersburg PA
CBHW040746020526
44116CB00036B/2961